CRUISING FOR TROUBLE

CRUISING FOR TROUBLE

Cruise Ships as Soft Targets for Pirates, Terrorists, and Common Criminals

Cdr. Mark Gaouette

FOREWORD BY KENDALL CARVER

 PRAEGER

AN IMPRINT OF ABC-CLIO, LLC
Santa Barbara, California • Denver, Colorado • Oxford, England

Library of Congress Cataloging-in-Publication Data

Gaouette, Mark.
  Cruising for trouble : cruise ships as soft targets for pirates, terrorists, and
common criminals / Mark Gaouette ; foreword by Kendall Carver.
    p. cm.
  Includes bibliographical references and index.
  ISBN 978-0-313-38234-5 (hard copy : alk. paper) — ISBN 978-0-313-38235-2 (ebook)
1. Cruise ships.   2. Piracy.   3. Maritime terrorism.   4. Hijacking of ships.
5. Cruise ships—Accidents.   I. Title.
  G550.G36   2010
  364.16'4—dc22   2009050857

ISBN: 978-0-313-38234-5
EISBN: 978-0-313-38235-2

14 13 12 11 10   1 2 3 4 5

This book is also available on the World Wide Web as an eBook.
Visit www.abc-clio.com for details.

Praeger
An Imprint of ABC-CLIO, LLC

ABC-CLIO, LLC
130 Cremona Drive, P.O. Box 1911
Santa Barbara, California 93116-1911

This book is printed on acid-free paper (∞)
Manufactured in the United States of America

For Mona, Jean-Louis,
and my father

CONTENTS

FOREWORD

Around January 1, 2006, four victims of crimes on cruise ships, among them this writer, got together to form International Cruise Victims Association (ICV). Within the relatively short time that this group has been in existence, many other victims and friends from around the world have joined our efforts. The organization has grown to several hundred members and friends located in 16 countries. ICV is a group that comprises victims who survived and family members of victims who did not survive crimes on cruise ships.

Our purpose from the start was to initiate efforts to reform the cruise line industry and to force it to better protect passengers and crew members in the future. Each board member who volunteers his or her time brings a unique skill and background to ICV. More than a year ago, the author of this book and I began to discuss the threat of piracy and terrorism against cruise ships. The author brought to ICV a unique talent, since he had served as head of security for two major cruise lines. During his tenure as head of security, he gained firsthand experience with the crucial issues that needed to be addressed, especially since one of his ships was actually attacked by a band of pirates.

When we formed ICV and started this journey, we could never have anticipated the path that we would take to achieve these goals. We were up against an industry that spent approximately $6 million just in 2008 on lobbying, with the goal of avoiding any type of regulations that would protect not only the passengers and crew members but also the ships themselves from acts of terrorism. What have we learned in our journey over the past three years? Some of the important items include these: cruise ships do not have legal responsibility for investigating crimes that may occur during a cruise. Cruise ships do not have legal responsibility for medical care provided to passengers during any cruise. Cruise ships do not have legal responsibility for any excursions that they may sell to their passengers, even though they earn a substantial commission from these excursions.

The cruise ships do not investigate crimes but only voluntarily report them to law enforcement agencies. These agencies say they do not have the resources to follow up on the crimes that are reported; in effect, crimes that occur on cruise ships are not professionally investigated or followed up on by those in a position to enforce the law. As a result, criminals and those who commit crimes on cruise ships know that they will probably not be prosecuted, let alone convicted. From court documents obtained by the *Los Angeles Times* and published on January 20, 2007, it has been determined that the number of sexual crimes committed aboard the ships of the Royal Caribbean Cruise Line between 2003 and 2005 was significantly higher than reported by the cruise line industry in congressional hearings. A detailed analysis of these court records by Dr. Ross Klein, an expert in this area, indicates that the actual sexual crime rates are 50 percent greater for passengers on cruise ships than in the average American city. It is also worth noting that 80 percent of all crimes involve crew members. There are many reasons why these statistics are so high, but the most important is the lack of law enforcement authority on any of these ships.

In view of concerns about terrorism, additional independent security is necessary to protect passengers and crewmembers. In the October 16, 2006, issue of the *Insurance Journal*, an article entitled "Maritime Terrorism Risk Extends to Cruise Ships and Ferry Boats" indicated that cruise ships and ferry boats need additional protection against terrorist attacks that could kill and injure many passengers and cause serious financial losses. This conclusion was based on a new RAND Corporation report. Since the cruise lines have failed to take the necessary steps to protect the passengers on their ships, it appears that the only alternative is for legislatures to require improved accountability. In the United States, this is starting to happen.

I, along with other ICV members, was called upon to testify at three congressional hearings in the House of Representatives during 2006 and twice in 2007. In addition, we testified at a hearing in the U.S. Senate in 2008. In the first hearing, in March 2006, instead of just telling our tragic stories as victims, we presented a 10-point program based upon the experiences of our many members that we believed would improve safety. One of the main points was the requirement that cruise ships provide independent security both for the safety of the passengers and for protection against terrorist attacks. This was the same approach that the airlines took when they added sky marshals after 9/11.

We have learned that studies by the RAND Corporation indicate that cruise ships are indeed a major target for terrorist attack like the one that occurred in September 2001. In the Senate hearing, chaired by Senator John Kerry (D-MA), at which I appeared in June 2008, I devoted eight pages of testimony to the issue of terrorism. At that time, it seemed as if terrorism was not on the minds of the Senate panel, who were more concerned about actual crimes committed on these ships. In my testimony, one of my main points was the importance of requiring that ships offer independent security both to protect passengers and to guard against any type of attack. In the spring of 2008, legislation was introduced in California by State Senator Joe Simitian (D) to add independent marshals on cruise ships. This was an effort to protect cruise ship passengers against crimes, protect the cruise ship against terrorists, and monitor the cruise ship for pollution. Because of a massive effort by the Cruise Line Association, the bill did not make it out of the final committee in the California legislature.

In conjunction with efforts by the ICV, Representative Doris Matsui (D-CA), in the U.S. House of Representatives, and Senator Kerry, in the U.S. Senate, introduced, on March 12, 2009, major legislation to improve safety on cruise ships. Entitled the Cruise Vessel Security and Safety Act of 2009, the legislation would provide for transparency in reporting crimes, improved crime scene response, improved security training procedures and better enforcement of safety and environmental standards, as well as other measures to protect cruise ships from terrorism. "What we have found through hearings is truly alarming," says Congresswoman Matsui.[1] "There is little to no regulation of the cruise industry and far too many crimes go unprosecuted each year. When a goliath like the cruise ship industry will not act in the best interest of the customers who are entrusting it with their personal well-being, then Congress has a responsibility to step in and shed some sunlight on the problem." Senator Kerry added, "Passenger safety should be the top priority for the cruise line industry, and it's clear that they have work to do."[2]

Since 1999, when the cruise lines adopted a "zero tolerance" policy concerning crimes, the number of reported sexual assaults has increased, and it appears that reporting of incidents continues to increase. We hope that the cruise line industry will accept the proposed changes to increase passenger safety; however, history has clearly shown that it will probably do everything possible to avoid this new legislation. With independent sky marshals on airlines, it is only logical to give the same protection to passengers on cruise ships.

The timing of this book and the discussion of the many issues related to the protection of cruise ships could not come at a more appropriate time. The author was one of the first security planners who has had firsthand experience in dealing with an actual attack by pirates on a cruise ship. His experience has taken on even more importance in the past year as more and more pirates continue to attack cargo and cruise ships. Because of his expertise, he was added to the board of directors of ICV in 2009. His concern about terrorism resulted in the addition to the Cruise Vessel Security and Safety Act of 2009 of a requirement that all cruise ships have on board equipment that would help repel pirates by emitting intense sound waves. Because the author has actually dealt with the problem of piracy, he has a unique perspective on how to protect cruise ships and how to alert the public to this new danger and best prevent similar attacks in the future.

Kendall Carver, President
International Cruise Victims Association (ICV)
August 2009

ABBREVIATIONS

ABOT	A1 Basra Oil Terminal
AMOC	Air and Marine Operations Center
A-Pass	Automated Personnel Assisted Security Screening
ASI	Air Security International
ASIO	Australian Security and Intelligence Organization
ASIS	American Society of Industrial Security
ATA	Anti-Terrorism Assistance (Program)
ATC	American Technology Corporation
ATHOC	Athens (Olympic) Organizing Committee
ATSA	Aviation Transportation Security Act
C4I	Command, Control, Communications, and Computers
CAMOC	Caribbean Air and Marine Operations Center
CBDR	Constant Bearing and Decreasing Range
CBP	Customs and Border Protection
CDSH	California Department of Safety and Health
CIA	Central Intelligence Agency
CIP	Carrier Initiative Program
CLIA	Cruise Line International Association
CNO	Chief of Naval Operations
COLREGS	Collision Regulations
CSI	Container Security Initiative
C-TPAT	Customs Trade Partners Against Terrorism
DHS	Department of Homeland Security
DOJ	Department of Justice
DSS	Diplomatic Security Service
DWT	Dead Weight Tons
ELN	National Liberation Army

FARC	Revolutionary Armed Forces of Colombia
FBI	Federal Bureau of Investigation
FEMA	Federal Emergency Management Agency
GAO	General Accounting Office
GICW	Gulf Intracoastal Waterway
GMDSS	Global Maritime Distress and Safety System
GPS	Global Positioning Systems
GRT	Gross Registered Tons
HAMAS	Islamic Resistance Movement
HDRU	Hazardous Devices Response Unit
HIV	High-Interest Vessel
HRT	Hostage Rescue Team
ICAO	International Civil Aviation Organization
ICCL	International Council of Cruise Lines
ICV	International Cruise Victims Association
IDF	Israeli Defense Force
IMO	International Maritime Organization
ISM	International Safety Management
ISPS	International Ship and Port Security (Code)
ISSC	International Ship Security Certificate
JI	Jemaah Islamiah
KAAOT	Khor Al Amaya Offshore Oil Terminal
LEGAT	Legal Attaché
LNG	Liquid Natural Gas
LPG	Liquid Petroleum Gas
LRAD	Long-Range Acoustic Device
LTTE	Liberation Tigers of Tamil Eelam
MILF	Moro Islamic Liberation Front
MARSEC	Maritime Security (Level)
MOTR	Maritime Operational Threat Response
MSC	Maritime Safety Committee
MSST	Maritime Safety and Security Team
MTCR	Missile Technology Control Regime
MTSA	Maritime Transportation Security Act
MVB	Moveable Vehicle Barrier
NCIS	Naval Criminal Investigative Service
NORAD	North American Aerospace Defense Command
NTA	National Threat Assessment
NTSB	National Transportation Safety Board
NVCG	National Volunteer Coast Guard (aka Somali pirates)
OAS	Organization of American States
OECD	Organization for Economic Cooperation and Development
OFAC	Office of Foreign Assets Control

OPSEC	Operations Security
OSAC	Overseas Security Advisory Council
PAWSS	Ports and Waterways Safety System
PFLP	Popular Front for the Liberation of Palestine
PFLP-GC	Popular Front for the Liberation of Palestine—General Command
PIJ	Palestinian Islamic Jihad
PKK	Kurdistan Workers' Party
PLF	Palestine Liberation Front
PLO	Palestine Liberation Organization
QE2	*Queen Elizabeth 2*
QM2	*Queen Mary 2*
RCCL	Royal Caribbean Cruise Lines
RHIB	Rigid Hull Inflatable Boat
RPAV	Remotely Piloted Aerial Vehicle
RPG	Rocket-Propelled Grenade
RSO	Regional Security Officer
SAC	Special-Agent-in Charge
SISCO	Security Identification Systems Corporation
SL	Sendero Luminoso (aka Shining Path)
SOLAS	Safety of Lives at Sea
SSMS	Security and Safety Management System
SWAT	Special Weapons and Tactics
TRIA	Terrorism Risk Insurance Act
UAV	Unmanned Aerial Vehicles
UNIFIL	UN Interim Force in Lebanon
USAID	U.S. Agency for International Development
USCG	U.S. Coast Guard
VBIED	Vehicle-Borne Improvised Explosive Device
VTS	Vessel Traffic Service
WBIED	Water-Borne Improvised Explosive Device
WMD	Weapons of Mass Destruction
WTO	World Trade Organization

one

MODERN CRUISE SHIPS: THEIR PREDATORS, THEIR VULNERABILITIES, AND THEIR VICTIMS

On November 5, 2005, the *Seabourn Spirit*, a Carnival Cruise ship under Princess Cruises management carrying 151 passengers and 161 crew from Alexandria, Egypt, to Mombasa, Kenya, came under attack from pirates off the coast of Somalia. Thanks to the swift, brave, and intelligent actions of the crew, which included the deployment of a "secret weapon" widely touted in the world media as a "sonic cannon," the attack was repelled with no loss of life and only minor damage to the ship from grenade and automatic rifle fire. The hitherto "secret weapon" was a prototype acoustic hailing device that had been installed on the ship by order of the author while he was serving as the director of security for Princess Cruises. Although the dramatically successful repulse of the Somali pirates by the *Seabourn Spirit* using innovative technology was widely reported and cheered by the world media, in the following months a large number of less dramatic cruise-related incidents with distinctly less happy outcomes went scarcely noticed in the media. These events, which occurred in rapid succession and in combination with mysterious passenger disappearances and sexual assaults, seemed to mark a disturbing trend in cruise ship travel in the years immediately following the terrorist attacks of September 11, 2001.

On September 12, 2001, 16 cruise ship passengers were tragically killed during a "flight-seeing" tour to the Yucatán coast.[1] On April 17, 2005, a cruise ship was struck and damaged by a large rogue wave.[2] On March 22, 2006, 12 American cruise ship passengers were killed in a tour bus accident while on a cruise ship excursion in South America. The bus carrying the cruise ship tourists plunged 300 feet down a mountainside in northern Chile.[3] The following day, March 23, 2006, off the coast of Montego Bay, Jamaica, a cruise ship fire killed one passenger and injured dozens more when a cigarette ignited flammable balcony material, setting the side of the cruise ship ablaze.[4] On July 18, 2006, the officer of a large cruise ship committed a serious seamanship error while piloting his ship, causing it to roll severely, toppling and traumatizing the passengers, and sending some of them to the hospital.[5] On April 6, 2007, a cruise ship sank after striking a charted reef in the Mediterranean, resulting in the drowning deaths of two passengers.[6] On November 23, 2007, a small cruise vessel sank in frigid waters in the Antarctic after hitting an iceberg, leaving the survivors to endure the elements in small life rafts until a rescue ship arrived.[7] Over this same period of months, a number of mysterious disappearances and deaths of cruise ship passengers, detailed in chapter 3, received more media play.

In all these unhappy cases, the cruise lines closed ranks and tried, generally successfully, to suppress and deflect media attention that could hurt their bottom line. On March 16, 2006, Bob Dickinson, then the CEO of Carnival Cruise Lines, the largest cruise line in the world, dismissed the disappearance of George Allen Smith IV from a competitor's ship in the Mediterranean as "a non-event."[8] A man's life was lost at sea under mysterious circumstances while he was vacationing on a cruise ship. Such a flippant characterization of the death of a cruise ship passenger seems to exemplify the cruise industry's stonewalling reflex, its downplay-everything response to the reality of the safety and security risks that cruise passengers face and the frequency and severity of the security incidents that they suffer.

After learning about Dickinson's remarks, George Smith's parents and sister wrote a letter to Carnival's board of directors demanding a public apology and his immediate termination. "These statements are despicable," wrote George and Maureen Smith and their daughter, Bree. "[Dickinson's] view that George's murder is a 'non-event' is definitely not shared by George's family and friends. . . . George's murder is not 'entertainment' to those of us that miss him and mourn his loss every day." The Smiths pointed out that the FBI and Congress have spent millions of dollars investigating the matter and cruise ship safety in general "so that similar 'non-events' do not happen to other cruise-ship passengers." Dickinson issued a statement saying he regretted causing pain to the family of the 26-year-old Connecticut man. "My comments were within a larger discussion on cruise industry issues and were not meant to minimize the tragedy of George Smith's disappearance," he later said.[9]

A "non-event" in the context of "a larger discussion on cruise industry issues"? Mr. Dickinson surely knew better than most that 24 so-called non-events occurred in a recent three-year period and that most of them occurred on his fleet of cruise ships. His cavalier attitude toward his passengers' safety was all the more reprehensible considering that his ample salary was paid by passengers who scrimp for years to pay for their cruise vacations. Some, like George Allen Smith IV, end up paying with their lives.

Although cruise ships account for less than 4 percent of all commercial maritime tonnage, their cargo is rather special, being composed of human beings. Fifteen million passengers go on pleasure cruises on each year in several hundred cruise ships that ply worldwide routes. Cruise ships have been steadily ramping up in size and passenger capacity and have become floating skyscrapers housing as many as 7,000 passengers. The newest behemoths have 16 passenger decks and carry four times as many passengers as the *Queen Elizabeth 2.*

Modern cruise ships—laden with passengers and booty and virtually undefended—make tempting prizes for pirates and terrorists and are easy marks for criminals and sexual predators. The taking of a cruise ship by pirates or terrorists—or an ad hoc combination of the two—has the potential for a titanic catastrophe on the scale of 9/11. The scourges of piracy and terrorism, both financed by international criminal groups, are increasingly intertwined: piracy on the high seas is becoming a key tactic of terrorist groups, while many of today's pirates are maritime terrorists with an ideological bent and a broad political agenda. Yet, the cruise industry's security programs to protect their passengers at sea and in port are pitifully inadequate to meet the rising threats.

After September 11, 2001, the U.S. government and the international community rallied to enact security measures to protect aviation and maritime travel. The United States passed the Aviation Transportation Security Act, in 2001, and the Maritime Transportation Security Act (MTSA), in 2002. The International Ship and Port Security (ISPS) Code was adopted by international agreement in 2002 and implemented in 2004. One would expect that, in view of such security regulations, the maritime industry would by now have standardized measures in place to protect equally all forms of commercial shipping and the ports they make harbor in.

In reality, however, even with the new ISPS Code, security standards and practices vary from cruise line to cruise line, from port to port, and from country to country. There are vast differences with regard to the use of the latest security technology, the recruitment and training of security personnel, and the approaches taken to risk management. While the ISPS Code and MTSA help to mitigate or reduce the threats posed by pirates, terrorists, drug smugglers, or the opportunist stowaway, they are not absolute guarantees of the security of any ship on the high seas. They also do not provide a safety umbrella outside the immediate port area. This is where the real dangers for the ships await.

As if these threats were not enough, passengers still face inherent risks while aboard cruise ships. Cruise ships today bear little resemblance to the Love Boat of TV fame. Far larger than even the great luxury liners of yesteryear, cruise ships today are competing for the title of the largest, the biggest, and the grandest cruise ship in the world. As cruise ships grow larger and more complex, there seem to be inadequate safety and security measures to go along with the increases in size and the shipboard features of these giant ships. Such measures are logically needed to protect passengers from the crimes, including sexual assaults that are sure to follow as passenger loads increase. Unchecked drug and alcohol abuses on these ships by both passengers and crew have led to needless death and injury. It is only logical to assume that such problems will come along with such growth. Risk on a cruise ship, however, is not an advertised feature on any travel brochure.

YOUR CRUISE VACATION: ALL RISK INCLUDED

Taking a cruise vacation on one of today's modern cruise ships can be a truly enjoyable and rewarding experience. Cruising has settled into a very affordable vacation for the average person or family. When such costly amenities such as food, entertainment, recreation, and sightseeing are factored in, cruising becomes a very attractive and exciting alternative to traditional land vacations and destinations. Whereas in decades past cruising was reserved for the well-to-do and served as a major form of transportation for those wishing to cross expansive oceans, today's cruise ships set sail to exotic ports of call for the sheer pleasure of the vacation experience. Suitcases are unpacked once, and passengers enjoy round-the-clock entertainment, meals, beverages, swimming pools, spas, restaurants, buffets, discos, movies, and casinos, all for one inclusive price. The cruise industry is acutely aware that there is a huge untapped market of potential cruise customers in the United States; only 16 percent of the U.S. population has ever taken a cruise.[10] When industry leaders ask themselves what will entice first-time customers to book cruise vacations, they arrive at this answer: bigger ships, more exotic destinations, greater variety in shipboard activities, tremendous food, and surprising affordability—all under the implicit assurance of carefree fun in perfect safety.

The cruise lines today provide a ready-made vacation experience for every class of passenger. Different cruise lines market to different customer profiles: the party crowd, families with small children, the sedate retiree set, off-beat naturalists. There is a cruise ship destination for almost every vacation group and price range. Cruise ships of unimaginable scale ply the waters up and down the coasts of the United States and to foreign ports of call. Cruise ships generally have set itineraries between their embarkation and debarkation ports. After taking on passengers in the ship's home port in the United States, Europe, or the Mediterranean, they set out to sea and make scheduled port calls to disembark passengers for a day of sightseeing, shopping, and adventure.

Some cruise lines still make standard crossings of the Atlantic or the Pacific. Other lines have their fleets in Alaska in the spring and summer and then send them to the Caribbean in the winter months. Still other cruise lines offer exotic itineraries that include sailing off the coasts of Asia, Africa, the Mediterranean, and the Middle East. Cruises can be as short as three days or a month or longer in duration. When cruise ships are not plying the high seas, they do the North American milk runs along the western coastline, the Mexican Riviera, and the eastern seaboard.

But the cruise lines' skillfully marketed image as providers of worry-free pleasure cruises runs aground on the reef of cruel statistics. In direct proportion to the colossal dimensions of its ships and passenger volume, the cruise line industry experiences a higher frequency of security incidents and is more vulnerable to security threats than any other form of transportation or vacation platform. True, cruise ships are heavily regulated and inspected by multiple layers of U.S. governmental and international oversight to ensure their compliance with external security measures and internal safety, sanitation, and environmental standards. But cruise passengers are ill served when they are lured into believing they are on a floating fortress of fun, safe from the dangers and tensions left behind on land.

The truth is that there have always been inherent risks to this form of travel and that they have been getting worse. You and your family are more likely today to be the victims of sexual assault on a cruise ship than on dry land. And that's just the beginning. The cruise passenger faces multifarious risks: from professional criminals and con artists; from stowaways, from pirates, and from terrorists; from fellow passengers under the influence; from inept, unstable, or mutinous crew members; from accidents; from communicable disease; from the unavailability of adequate emergency services; and from sexual predators and criminals of opportunity among the passengers and crew. Each of these risks may be conveniently divided into those that the cruise passenger faces on the ship and on those that he or she faces on shore at ports of call. Vacationers are unlikely to encounter many of these threats, such as pirates, while at traditional land vacation destinations such as Las Vegas or Disneyland, unless you count the wax figures at the Pirates of the Caribbean attraction.

Onshore tourist venues, sightseeing attractions, and recreational activities actually pose greater risks to cruise passengers than do shipboard environments. Cruise ships routinely disembark as many as 3,000 American tourists at one time in the ports of foreign countries. Many of these U.S. citizens have never before traveled or set foot outside the United States. Once ashore, they may endeavor to see and experience all they can in the 8 to 10 hours that the cruise ship has allowed for that particular day in port. Few day-trippers pause to reflect on the risks that they face in foreign ports of call. Security officers in foreign ports, such as coast guard and police, are generally not at the same level of training and readiness as passengers are accustomed to expect in their U.S. counterparts.

When cruise ships call on a foreign port, their hosts generally do the best they can to provide robust security, at least up to the front gate of the port. These countries know that cruise ships bring large sums of tourist revenue. Countries such as Egypt and Jamaica depend on tourism to sustain their economies. They redirect scarce police resources to the ports when the cruise ships call in an effort to provide enhanced security. But, when passengers venture off the beaten path or book excursions under the mistaken assumption that the operators adhere to security and safety standards approved by the cruise lines and comparable to those to which they would be subject in the United States, there is the potential for real tragedy. The risks of injury or even death are significant for the unprepared adventurer who, lacking in proper skill and instruction, is lured into risky outdoor activities such as scuba diving or paragliding. Sightseeing conveyances such as private planes or helicopters have claimed the lives of many cruise ship passengers who mistakenly believed that the craft were inspected and regulated by the cruise lines because the flights were endorsed and sold by the cruise ship line as part of tour packages. Likewise, unwary cruise ship passengers ashore can fall victim to scams, crime, and criminal or terrorist violence because they assume that the ship's security umbrella covers these exotic locales and extends over their onshore activities. In some countries, moreover, local law enforcement and medical resources have limited capabilities for responding to crimes and accidents.

Safely back on ship, cruise passengers are nonetheless far from home free. Serious risks still abound, of different types and on more frightening scales. Conduct that would get someone arrested on a plane or in a hotel routinely occurs on cruise ships without criminal or civil legal repercussions. This legal passivity on the part of cruise lines results from the desire to avoid adverse publicity and from their security officers' lack of formal authority to act as law enforcers. Because the professionalism of the security staff is questionable, it is not all that unusual to look at today's headlines and read about passengers falling off cruise ships or disappearing into thin air or suffering some other mishap. There is no Office of the Inspector General for the cruise industry that oversees the professionalism of its security forces. Nor is there any legal requirement that the cruise lines prevent, investigate, or—until recently—even report crime that occurs on cruise ships.

The cruise ship passenger's ticket says that if passengers conduct themselves inappropriately, they are subject to removal from the ship at the next port of call. But this option is so rarely used that it is not much of a deterrent to bad behavior. Instead, the ships depend on their private security officers and their general crew, untrained and unauthorized in security matters, to police the thousands upon thousands of passengers on the ship. Beyond screening passengers for contraband when boarding the ship and providing them cruise cards and safes to use on board, the cruise lines offer little in the way of crime prevention.

Yet, cruise ships are ad hoc communities composed of a floating cross-section of society, encompassing the full human spectrum of the good, the bad, and the ugly. The bigger any community becomes, the greater the likelihood that it will include some specimens of extreme badness. And, in the programmed saturnalia of a pleasure cruise, the opportunities for being bad multiply, and even the good and not-so-bad are likely to succumb to uncustomary bad behavior.

That leaves the cruise lines free to decide what security on their ships should look like and how they should react to breaches. Is this a big concern? It is if you are the victim of a crime. When accidents and crimes occur on and off these ships at a frequency known only to the cruise lines and are allowed to go virtually unchecked by any authority other than that imposed by the cruise lines themselves, then a cruise undertaken in search of rest and relaxation can, for many, end up in tragedy. Real progress can be made only when real efforts are made to counter and prevent these incidents from occurring, rather than sweeping them under the carpet to avoid at all costs unwelcome headlines. This is an activity on which the cruise lines spend a great deal of time; bad publicity, after all, can sink a cruise ship quicker than any iceberg.

Many internal and external security issues are, strictly speaking, beyond the cruise lines' ability and legal authority to control. But these limitations do not excuse the cruise lines from their obligation to warn their passengers about the specific risks they face as guests aboard the ship or as day-trippers ashore. The issuance of the all-purpose cruise card to serve as room key, charge card, and security pass to get on and off the ship and the mandatory lifeboat muster at the beginning of each cruise are not sufficient to discharge the cruise lines' responsibility for the security of their passengers. But cruise lines are, for commercial reasons, extremely reluctant to play up risks or to alter routines even though to do so would plainly enhance their passengers' safety, as when cruise lines ignore an increase in crime, a terrorist threat, a health risk, or political instability that makes it advisable to cancel or reschedule stops at certain foreign ports of call.

The cruise lines reflexively find that it is less cost-efficient to address security and safety issues preemptively than it is to deal with disgruntled passengers and aggrieved relatives after security and safety incidents have occurred, using a mix of low-profile litigation, out-of-court cash settlements, blanket denial, and even character assassination and intimidation. Some aggrieved passengers may suspect collusion among corporate executives. But such practices and priorities are just the industry's natural modus operandi within the existing legislative and regulatory frameworks. Security at all levels is, in fact, a besetting concern and an open topic in the cruise line industry.

Cruise line security experts meet regularly in various forums to debate security legislation as it affects their industry, to share best practices, and to discuss innovative approaches to safety and security on their ships and in the ports they visit. They also share the presumption that the commercial interests of their industry dictate and restrict what can be done, even as cruise ships have become increasingly dangerous despite changes in the international maritime security model put in place after September 11, 2001. Only since the emergence of a vociferous movement in Congress and among the public calling for the overhaul the legislative and regulatory framework within which the cruise industry operates its security programs has the possibility arisen for remedying the industry's security shortcomings. However, more needs to be done.

Modern cruise ships are floating communities, and it would be naïve to think that all the elements of society, both good and bad, are not represented on them at any given moment. Passengers are under the mistaken assumption that criminal laws are not enforceable on the high seas. Security and safety incidents have always occurred on cruise ships, but until now they have not received the kind of negative publicity that the cruise lines fear. The general public can choose whether to travel on cruise ships, and the paying passenger has a right to expect that certain measures will be taken to protect his or her security and safety. The alarming truth, however, is that criminal incidents, safety accidents, and unacceptable crew and passenger behavior will likely increase as more and more passengers are crowded onto these ships. It is only logical to assume that, as cruise ships grow ever larger and multiply in number and as ports become more and more crowded, these incidents will increase proportionately.

CONGRESS LISTENS TO THE CRUISE SHIP VICTIMS

Cruise ships, because of their design, their high profile, and their popularity, are beginning to suffer from their own growing pains. Ships are becoming increasingly larger and are carrying ever greater numbers of passengers. Internal safety and security incidents that are far removed from the terrorist or pirate threat are beginning to dominate discussions of maritime security. How the cruise lines are reacting to these security concerns is now an issue of great interest to the U.S. Congress and to public watch dogs groups concerned with Congress's lack of regulatory oversight. The International Cruise Victims Association (ICV), an organization dedicated to reform in the cruise industry, put it this way: "The cruise industry has historically remained focused on how to keep their ships moving. Following numerous high-profile incident reports, the ICV considers that current onboard cruise line security management appears to lack adequate passenger and crew safety training, especially in response to reports of incidents."[11]

The Subcommittee on National Security, Emerging Threats, and International Relations began looking into cruise line safety in 2005, spurred on by the *Seabourn Spirit* attack and by the strange disappearance, in July 2005, of a 26-year-old honeymooner from a Royal Caribbean vessel that was cruising in the Mediterranean. This was not the first time that Congress had beat the drum for reform in this industry, which many observers, including some in Congress, consider loosely regulated. In the most recent round of congressional hearings, Christopher Shays, at that time a Republican congressman from Connecticut, pushed for bipartisan legislation to improve disclosure requirements related to crimes on cruise ships in order to increase the transparency of the industry. In a later statement, he stated that passengers have a right to know the safety records of the vessels they board.[12] Congressman Shays accurately summed up the problems facing the cruise industry in his opening statements before the subcommittee, on December 13, 2005:

> Just two days ago, Coast Guard officials began conducting search operations in the waters north of the Bahamas because a cruise ship passenger was reported missing. In early November, modern day pirates fired mortars at a cruise ship off the coast of Somalia. These are two recent additions to a growing manifest of unexplained disappearances, unsolved crimes and brazen acts of lawlessness on the high seas. According to industry experts, a wide range of criminal activities, including drug smuggling, sexual assaults, piracy and terrorism, threaten the security of maritime travel and trade. Today we begin an examination of the complex web of laws, treaties, regulations and commercial practices meant to protect lives and property in an increasingly dangerous world. Ocean travel puts passengers and crews in distant and isolated environments and subjects them to unique risks and vulnerabilities. Like small cities, cruise ships experience crimes—from the petty to the profoundly tragic. City dwellers know the risks of urban life, and no one falls off a city never to be heard from again. Cruise passengers can be blinded to the very real perils of the sea by ship operators unwilling to interrupt the party for security warnings. And after an incident occurs, a thorough investigation can be profoundly difficult when the crime scene literally floats away, on schedule, to its next port of call.[13]

To paraphrase Congressman Shays, city dwellers know what urban risks they face when they leave their homes. This is in sharp contrast to the situation of a cruise passenger, who, while at sea, may experience criminal activity that is both unreported (to law enforcement authority) and unprofessionally investigated. And, because passengers have few legal rights under international maritime law and little recourse against the cruise lines, they appear to be at greater risk for cruise ship crime than would be expected.

In March 2007, just days before Congress was to hold another round of hearings on cruise ship security practices and procedures, the Cruise Line International Association (CLIA), an industry advocate for the cruise lines, along with the FBI, accepted a set of security provisions requiring the cruise lines to report crimes at sea.[14] The cruise lines agreed to this voluntarily because, as they told the FBI at the time (in 2007), they had adopted a policy of "zero tolerance" for shipboard crimes in 1999. The FBI was surprised to learn of this so-called policy and admitted that it (the FBI) lacked the fundamental resources to investigate crimes at sea.[15]

Nevertheless, the cruise industry continued its policy of zero tolerance hoping to appease the seagoing public even as the FBI's record of prosecution for *any* crime aboard ship continued to be negligible. This convenient arrangement continued until legislation was introduced in Congress by Senator John Kerry (D-MA) and Representative Doris Matsui (D-CA) in 2009. The bill, entitled the Cruise Vessel Security and Safety Act of 2009, requires sweeping changes in the way criminal activity is reported and investigated on cruise ships in U.S. waters.

Although other reforms are being promoted by various organizations and are under consideration by various legislative bodies and agencies, including the U.S. Congress, for many victims they offer too little too late. The requirement to report crimes expeditiously does not remedy the need for better prevention and investigation capabilities on ships. The cruise ship victims who testified before Congress certainly felt this way. Susan DiPiero, whose son Daniel disappeared from Royal Caribbean's *Mariner of the Seas* in May 2006 under mysterious circumstances, spoke for all when she said: "Until it is more profitable to make ships safe than to settle law suits, then I don't believe the necessary changes will come at the hands of the cruise lines."[16]

Many lawmakers at the hearings agreed. Representative Matsui, who participated in the hearings because one of her constituents was the victim of an alleged rape on a Royal Caribbean ship, told cruise line officials: "A common theme of this panel is that you still don't get it."[17] The chair of the Subcommittee on Coast Guard and Maritime Transportation, Congressman Elijah Cummings (D-MD), hit the nail on the head when he stated: "Cruise ships should improve their security and safety measures and overall responsiveness because it's good for their bottom line. It's good business for business to be the best that it can be."[18]

OLD AND NEW PREDATORS: PIRATES AND TERRORISTS

Thanks to advances in maritime engineering and vast improvements in satellite communications and navigational systems, modern cruise ships are practically immune from sea conditions that have caused vessels to founder in the past. However, new threats have emerged that threaten the safety of cruise line travel. Many of the early tragedies aboard cruise ships were linked to some monumental accident caused by human error or by acts of war. Some of the more famous examples from the past century include the sinking of the SS *Titanic* passenger liner, which sank in 1912 after striking an iceberg; the sinking of the passenger liner *Lusitania,* in 1915, by German torpedoes; and the sinking of the passenger ship *Andrea Doria,* in 1956, after it collided with another passenger liner.

But the main causes of cruise ship tragedies have shifted course in the past 50 years from accidents and acts of war to acts of terrorism and piracy. The record now includes the seizure of the cruise ship *Santa Maria,* in 1960, by armed Portuguese nationalists; the sinking of the Greek passenger ship *Sanya* by terrorists from the Palestine Liberation Organization (PLO), in 1973; the hijacking of the cruise ship *Achille Lauro,* in 1985, by armed PLO terrorists; the hijacking, in 1996, of the passenger ferry *Avrasya*; the destruction by terrorists of the passenger ferry *Superferry 14* in 2004; the attack on the cruise ship *Seabourn Spirit* by pirates, in 2005; and, in 2008 and 2009, pirate attacks on the cruise ships *MV Nautica* and *MSC Melody.*

These and other maritime incidents are part of a larger discussion on maritime security that aims to keep the world's economy flowing by keeping the sea lanes open and the seaports free of weapons of mass destruction. While these threats are being dealt with by maritime governments, the risks to cruise ships now also includes the threat from mines, combat scuba divers, unmanned aerial vehicles, and other deadly terrorist efforts to destroy shipping. More alarming to the discussion of cruise ship security are the motives of today's terrorist groups.

Today's terrorist groups that are already active in maritime terrorism have little interest in negotiating terms for their captured comrades. Their goal in attacking maritime targets has turned from hostage taking, as in the *Achille Lauro* hijacking, to the complete destruction of the ship and all aboard. Their suicidal tactics have rendered some of the traditional maritime security precautions obsolete. The stark reality made clear by recent history is that the jihadists do not seek autonomy, independence, revolution, control of the reins of government, or political reform. They have much broader aims, achievable only through perpetual war. The jihadist's enterprise aims at incitement. A jihad is more than a military doctrine; it is about conversion and personal salvation.[19]

While the face of terrorism has changed over the years, the scourge of piracy on the high seas has essentially remained intact and appears to be increasing to alarming levels in certain areas of the world. The pirate attack on the cruise ship *Seabourn Spirit* off the coast of Somalia in November 2005 was a brazen attempt by well-organized Mogadishu pirates to exploit a yet-untapped source of revenue. While some maritime experts have suggested that the attack, complete with automatic weapons and rocket-propelled grenades, may have been a terrorist attack, the openness of the ship, which was armed with only fire hoses and a long-range acoustic device (LRAD), demonstrated the vulnerability of ships operating in regions known for pirate activity. The economic repercussions to the cruise industry had the ship been overrun by the pirates cannot be overstated. The cruise lines, for obvious reasons, were quick to move on and to downplay the incident and its significance.

Cruise ships are still desirable targets for international terrorist groups and are likely to remain at the top of al-Qaeda's and other terrorist organizations' wish lists. All evidence suggests that the maritime domain is still at risk from al-Qaeda, as well as from a number of other terrorist groups that realize that the world's oceans are convenient not only for moving arms and illicit and illegal cargo but also for launching attacks in complete anonymity. In that respect, the terrorists share a tactic with the pirates; their attacks, launched in deep-ocean obscurity, use "mother ships" from which bands of criminals prey on unsuspecting ships that pass too close to their area of operations.

Cruise ships, unlike other passenger vessels such as ferries, are considered by many in the cruise line security field as "hard targets" for a number of reasons. Those who say that terrorists would not be interested in attacking them or that pirates do not want to seize them should look at the record of terrorist plots and successful maritime attacks already carried out by al-Qaeda, the Abu Sayyaf Group, Jamaah Islamiya, Hamas, Hezbollah, and the Liberation Tigers of Tamil Eelam, as well as by Somali pirates, to see what these groups are capable of in the maritime domain. However, the term "hard target" with regard to cruise ships seems outdated in today's discussion of maritime security, especially as it applies to the supposed difficulty of attacking them.

Modern pirates and terrorists groups have shown a willingness to conduct preoperational vetting of their attack plans and have demonstrated their ability to attack cruise ships. Because of these facts, the cruise lines are acutely aware of the damage a pirate or terrorist attack would inflict on their industry. One deadly incident could cause passenger bookings to plummet, such as happened to the aviation industry after 9/11. They understand that, surpassing all the other catastrophes that might befall their industry, terrorist or pirate attacks would grab instant international headlines and instill fear and undermine confidence in prospective passengers. Because of the large numbers of passengers carried by cruise ships and what they represent, cruise ships may be at the top of the target list of these maritime predators.

YOUR CRUISE SHIP: LOOKS CAN BE DECEIVING

Perhaps you are new to cruising and are reading this book while on a cruise vacation and wondering, "What threats? What risks? Am I not as safe as in my own hometown on this modern ocean liner?" If you are on a cruise ship or have ever taken a cruise, you may believe that, because you board the ship in a U.S. port and wade past metal detectors and X-ray machines just like those at the airport, your security once aboard the ship is virtually guaranteed. Once aboard, you are issued your own personal cruise card, which you have been told protects your identity, your valuables, and even the safety of your family. And certainly you are immune while on this modern ship from the perils of sea travel such as collisions, fires, and rogue waves, not to mention changing sea conditions that can make a walk across your stateroom or a swim in the ship's pool a terrifying prospect. Surely this cruise line has prepared every port of call you are about to visit in accordance with "American standards."

Your belief that your fellow cruise passengers are all upstanding citizens who have saved their money as long as you have to take this vacation reassures you about your family's safety; you assume that none of these passengers are sexual predators or prone to violence if served an overabundance of alcohol. Your children are as safe as if in your own backyard and will certainly not have the opportunity to indulge in underage drinking or risk being injured by risky horseplay while on the ship. And most certainly the friendly crew members who serve you—most from countries you have never heard of—are ready to protect you in an emergency, and, of course, all speak English. The cruise line certainly has had crew members screened by the U.S. government before they began working for the cruise line; surely the medical personnel on the ship to whom you may need to turn to in a health emergency are competent medical doctors with established practices and reputations.

Finally, if you are injured, harmed, or the victim of a crime, you expect that the criminal act will be professionally investigated by competent investigators with real law enforcement authority available to seize and collect evidence, interview witnesses, and call for specialized investigative assistance. And, of course, you believe that there are numerous avenues by which to pursue your grievance in U.S. courts or in international venues in accordance with clear jurisdictional boundaries that will readily resolve your claim.

You would be shocked to learn that all these perceptions are false.

The public's beliefs about shipboard security perceptions are a force multiplier for cruise ships and can even work to the cruise lines' advantage. Like any other form of security countermeasure, what is *not* advertised becomes an advantage. Keeping the cruise lines' security plans and precautions out of the public discussion is crucial and is often enough to keep the pirates and terrorists guessing about the security strengths and weaknesses of ships. There are many security force multipliers on which cruise lines depend. Anything that would weaken cruise lines' posture or offer an advantage to criminals, pirates, or terrorists, is not discussed here. However, there are some security experts who are willing to go to great lengths to reveal all sorts of security vulnerabilities in just about every industry. They do this not for malicious purposes but to provoke a response from the government and especially from the private sector. While to many observers it may seem like the sky is falling, their aim is to wake up those with responsibility for security and to take the bull by the horns and to inform the public about the potential for risk.

As an example, an article appeared in the December 2007 issue of *Professional Pilot*. The author, Marvin Cetron, is president of Forecasting International. His study for the Pentagon, "Terror 2000," written in 1994, contained an accurate prediction of the attack on the Pentagon in September 2001. Back then, his predictions were not given much credence. Today, however, he writes in earnest about the possibility of "worst-case scenarios." His article "Ten Terrorist Plots Waiting to Happen" appears to have taken the guesswork out of the terrorists' job; it included target feasibility studies, success probabilities, and required resources; offered a destruction analysis; and predicted the overall impact of the described attacks on the world. In essence, it provided a one-stop shopping list of terrorist targets. In a caveat at the beginning of the article, the author offered the following apology: "I no longer worry about giving the bad guys ideas. They are smart and dedicated, and they will think of any attack we can, and probably others as well. That is why I am writing this article. It is not enough to have the experts watching potential targets; we need to get as many eyeballs on them as possible. It is important for ordinary citizens to know where the dangers lie."

The threats being discussed today with regard to maritime security and specifically cruise ships are nothing new; they were debated in various forums before September 11, 2001, and have been analyzed since that date. From the terrorist hijacking of the cruise ship *Achille Lauro,* in 1985, to the pirate attack on the *Seabourn Spirit,* in 2005, cruise ships have been and remain targets of great value to both pirates and terrorists. It is important to understand these threats and how they relate not just to cruise ships but to the entire maritime industry.

Cruising for Trouble exposes the acute vulnerability of cruise ships and their passengers, both on the high seas and in domestic and foreign ports of call. The number of piracy and criminal incidents has shot up in 2008 and 2009 as the world economy deteriorated, but there has been no proportional increase or enhancement in onboard security personnel, external tactical units, preventive screening, or coordinated response planning in the face of the growing threat of acts of piracy, internal and external terrorist attacks, and common criminality. Cruise passengers sauntering up the gangway of a cruise ship for a carefree holiday are oblivious to the very real security dangers they face. This book sounds a clarion call to the scores of millions of actual and potential cruise passengers and their advocates and urges them to compel the cruise industry, the national and transnational security agencies, the maritime regulators, and legislators to strengthen and reform the cruise industry's security programs before catastrophe strikes. This book details the many security defects and vulnerabilities of cruise ships, identifies remedies, and makes the case for the urgent implementation of these protections.

These claims are based on my personal experience in the cruise line industry and with the U.S. military and government. This experience has allowed me to judge the progress or lack thereof in acting to counter the threats that cruise ships now face. I have been involved in planning for ships' internal security and in countering external threats from pirates and terrorists. I was responsible for the security of a large international cruise ship company. I traveled around the globe preparing cruise ship destinations for the arrival of some of the largest cruise ships in the world. The efforts of the particular cruise company I worked for were extraordinary with regard to security and countered the traditional views of what cruise line safety and maritime security should look like. At the core of this effort was a belief that there was always more that the cruise line could be doing to protect the passengers and crew and to secure the safety of the ship and the ports of call to which they sailed. My goal in undertaking this study has been to render objective judgments, but in many cases that objectivity has led to irrefutable conclusions about where cruise line safety and maritime security are headed.

In recent years, most of the efforts to reform cruise line security, particularly with regard to passenger safety, have come after a maritime disaster or as a result of a public outcry following a needless cruise ship tragedy that involved loss of life or physical injury. Few of the reforms in the industry have been initiated by the cruise lines themselves. In my years with the cruise lines, I saw new and innovative security concepts being implemented on a grand scale and with the support and endorsement of top management. However, this experience was probably the exception, rather than the rule. It is perhaps disappointing to the prospective cruise ship customer that, in the cruise lines' attempts to expand their industry by providing bigger and more impressive ships, they have, until recently, ignored one of the primary concerns of today's travelers—their safety.

two

CRUISE SHIPS IN THE CROSSHAIRS: PIRATES AND TERRORISTS

Piracy is defined as the seizing of a ship to loot and plunder by organized and armed criminal gangs on the high seas. It is, after a terrorist attack, perhaps the most significant and dangerous security threat a cruise ship faces out on the open ocean. It is also, coincidently, the easiest to mitigate. First, the cruise lines can simply avoid areas where pirates operate. Unfortunately, when pirates control the strategic choke points of the world's oceans, the strategy of avoidance begins to impact on the cruise lines' schedules and itineraries. Usually, at some point in the cruising season, cruise vessels must cross these troubled waters as the cruise lines move their fleets from ocean to ocean.

Although cruise ships infrequently traverse the troubled waters off the coast of Somalia, where as of this writing there have been at least three notable pirate attacks against cruise ships, they still must pass close to the pirate areas near the Straits of Malacca and in the South China Sea, as well as other areas less known for pirate attacks, such as the southern Caribbean and even the inland rivers of South America. Fortunately, aside from the attacks on the *Seabourn Spirit,* the *MSC Melody* and the *Oceania Nautica,* no attacks have been attempted against the larger cruise lines such as Crystal, Radisson, Seven Seas, Princess, Silverseas, and Royal Caribbean, whose ships sail through some of these trouble zones to make calls on such ports as Hong Kong; Alexandria, Egypt; and the Suez Canal. Piracy is big business in and around all these areas, with attacks occurring with military-like precision.

Maritime pirates are nothing new. In certain respects, piracy is really the oldest form of maritime terrorism. Until recent times, it made sense to commit acts of piracy against maritime shipping. Cargo ships and treasure ships presumably had something of value that the pirates wanted to plunder. The goal of the pirate was monetary gain through criminal means. Those goals are the same today; however, the new twist on piracy is to hold entire crews hostage for the monetary value the pirates can leverage from their flag states or owners. The terrorist, on the other hand, aims to inflict damage on maritime targets not for any direct monetary gain but for the sheer political or economic benefit that may come about because of the act. Regardless of the motivation behind piracy or terrorism, cruise ships cannot necessarily employ the same defenses against the two different threats. Pirates normally carry out their raids using greater numbers of personnel than do terrorists, whose tactics so far have included attacks carried out by no more than a few suicidal jihadists using a small boat. Even before the implementation of the International Ship and Port Security (ISPS) Code, there was little expectation that these strict maritime security measures would do anything to rid the world of the menace of piracy.[1] The reasons are obvious. The operating procedures of the pirates call for armed attacks on the high seas or in open waters, away from the security procedures and fortifications offered by ports. The stalwart defenses called for in the ISPS Code that protects ships and deters terrorist acts in port serve only to prevent security incidents being launched from land. The ISPS Code were really aimed at preventing terrorist actions, curbing the flow of stowaways, and standardizing the maritime security practices in ports throughout the world. Apart from the part of the Code that requires duress signals and automated tracking devices, there is little in them that is aimed at preventing acts of piracy at sea, and even these measures are reactive. This means that they are implemented after an incident or attack has occurred. Once the ships pull in their gangways, they are essentially on their own and must depend on whatever defenses and plans they have prepared to handle incidents while at sea. Countermeasures against pirates were and still are the responsibility of the individual ship owners; in the absence of such measures, the cooperation of the international maritime community is sought. Vigilance, however, is still the best defense against maritime marauders.

For centuries, slow-moving merchant vessels and cargo ships were targets for heavily armed bands of pirates. Even with today's advances in technology, military presence, and international agreements that cover the world's oceans, piracy remains a serious threat. The threat is evident to ships that must pass through or near vital shipping lanes, such as the Red Sea and its approaches to the Suez Canal and the Straits of Malacca. The statistics are paralyzing. In 2004, 325 attacks on merchant ships, tugs, barges, and yachts were reported; about 30 seafarers were killed, 86 kidnapped, 148 taken hostage, and 59 injured. While these figures are staggering, some maritime analysts believe that these figures do not capture the true depth of the problem; if the suspected number of unreported attacks is added, these figures would increase by 25 to 30 percent.[2]

Unfortunately, since 2004 the frequency of piracy attacks has remained unchanged or increased, especially with regard to crews taken hostage. In the first six months of 2009, for example, piracy attacks around the world more than doubled from the year before; 240 attacks were reported during the first six months of that year, compared with 114 the same period in 2008. The rise in overall numbers is almost entirely a result of increasing Somali pirate activity in the Gulf of Aden and off the east coast of Somalia, with 86 and 44 incidents, respectively, reported in these locations.[3] This swath of ocean is where many Americans first became aware of the piracy menace when the cargo ship *Maersk Alabama* was hijacked in April 2009 by Somali pirates and the ship's captain was taken hostage in an epic sea drama that played out on the cable news networks and ended with the deaths of three pirates at the hands of U.S. Navy SEAL sharpshooters. This was not the end of pirate attacks on the *Maersk Alabama,* however. Another group of Somali pirates in small, high-speed skiffs attempted to retake the vessel in a similar attack in mid-November 2009. The ship was about 600 miles off the northeast coast of Somalia as it headed for the Kenyan port of Mombassa when again, armed pirates came within 300 yards of the ship. This time, they were met by crew members who turned the newly acquired Long-Range Acoustic Device (LRAD) on them.[4]

Piracy is just as prevalent elsewhere in the world, and just as violent. Worldwide, the International Maritime Bureau (IMB) reports that in the first six months of 2009 alone, a total of 78 vessels were boarded worldwide, 75 vessels were fired upon, and 31 vessels were hijacked; some 561 crew members were taken hostage, 19 were injured, 7 were kidnapped, 6 were killed, and 8 are missing. The attackers were heavily armed with guns and knives in the majority of incidents. Violence against crew members continues to increase. The waters off Nigeria in particular continue to be a high-risk area. The majority of attacks are against vessels that support the oil industry. As was the case for piracy attacks off the east coast of Africa, attacks in Southeast Asia and the Far East increased by 100 percent between the first quarter of 2008 and the corresponding quarter of 2009, from 10 to 21. There was a difference, however, in the types of pirate attacks being carried out in Southeast and East Asia; the attacks in 2008 were against vessels at anchor, whereas those in 2009 targeted vessels at sea.[5] Given these statistics, the International Maritime Bureau has indicated that it is likely that piracy and robbery in Southeast and East Asia will increase; the Bureau has urged shipmasters to remain alert and to be aware of the risks while at sea and in the ports visited during their voyage.

There is some good news, however, to report in the Straits of Malacca, where recent statistics indicate a noticeable reduction the frequency of pirate attacks. The continued efforts of Indonesian authorities should be noted for their effectiveness in decreasing the number of incidents of piracy and armed robbery in their waters. Only two incidents have been recorded for the Malacca Straits in 2009.

As we have seen from the statistics, off the east coast of Africa, particularly near the coast of Somalia, piracy has continued to the point of becoming an international maritime crisis. Emboldened attacks on cruise ships, private yachts, merchant vessels, and even international aid ships have sent governments scrambling for a response. The first pirate attack on a luxury cruise ship occurred in this part of the Indian Ocean, with a dramatic outcome.

THE PIRATE ATTACK ON THE *SEABOURN SPIRIT*

In early November 2005, a few months after leaving Princess Cruises as their director of security, I was notified by a colleague that the *Seabourn Spirit*, a small cruise ship operated by Seabourn Yachts under the management of Princess Cruises, had been attacked off the coast of Somalia. The attack apparently was carried out not by an Islamic terrorist or other extremist group but by pirates. The report indicated that no one was killed or seriously injured after the ship was hit by rocket-propelled grenades and fire from automatic weapons launched by pirates in an apparent attempt to board the ship. The incident was covered extensively by the news media because it was the first time a cruise ship had been attacked and because the cruise ship apparently carried a "secret weapon" used to repel the attackers. The secret weapon was called a sonic cannon and was actually a Long-Range Acoustic Device, or LRAD for short. The pirates had fled after being subjected to the LRAD's piercing tone (the LRAD is discussed in greater detail in chapter 4). This nonlethal technology was part of the Princess Cruise security model implemented fleet-wide earlier that year. Princess had made it a top priority to counter waterside attacks, and LRADs were part of its strategy for achieving this. The effort seemed to have paid off in a big way when pirates attacked the *Seabourn Spirit* and the LRAD was used defensively to repel them.

The *Seabourn Spirit* was one of three small cruise ships operated by Seabourn Yachts, a subsidiary of Cunard Cruise Line. Known for its luxurious accommodations and pampering crew, the ship can carry 208 passengers and 164 crew. In early November 2005, the *Spirit* was making its way down the East African coast after leaving Alexandria, Egypt. The ship had just received the LRAD, a new piece of security equipment from Princes Cruises headquarters. Despite warnings by the International Maritime Organization (IMO) regarding pirate attacks in this region, the *Seabourn Spirit* had been steaming between 80 and 100 miles off the east coast of Somalia, a location notorious for pirate attacks on private boats and merchant vessels. At the time, it was recommended that ships transiting this area stay 100 miles from land; although the ship later reported that it was at this distance, other sources, including the senior security officer on board the *Spirit,* reported that the ship was closer than 80 miles off the coast and perhaps even as close as 60 nautical miles from shore.[6]

A little before 6:00 A.M. on November 5, the ship's chief officer spotted what appeared to be a small fishing boat approaching quickly from behind the ship's stern. Michael Groves, the ship's security officer, was a British policeman employed on contract by Seabourn Yachts while on a sabbatical from the police department. He was immediately called to the bridge. The ships' officers quickly realized their precarious situation when another small boat appeared on the opposite side of the ship and the crew members in that small boat brandished automatic weapons. The men in that boat suddenly began firing at the ship with AK-47s, and Groves could see them preparing to launch a rocket-propelled grenade (RPG). As he began hearing the bullets pinging off the ship's hull, the ship's captain, Sven Erik Pedersen, screamed over the ship's announcing system that everyone should "stay inside, we're under attack."[7]

The captain then ordered the passengers to get down inside the ship as he tried to reassure them of their safety. Most of the passengers were instructed to take refuge in the ship's dining room, while many others were awakened in their staterooms by gunfire and were afraid to move. As the captain increased the ship's speed to try to outrun the attackers, Groves grabbed a fire hose near the bridge, charged it with highly pressurized water, and turned it on the pirates. The hose had little effect on the attackers; the pirates had probably been subjected to this kind of ship's defense before. As the battle began to rage, the fire hoses were no match for the machine guns that were now firing indiscriminately at the ship. The crew continued in its efforts to reassure the frightened passengers amid the sounds of gunfire emanating from outside.

"I heard what sounded like a crack from outside the ship at 5.50 A.M.," said Norman Fisher, a lawyer from the north of London, recalling the incident later in an interview. "I looked out the window and saw a small boat with about five people in it, about 20 yards away. Two of them had rifles, and one had some kind of rocket launcher and were preparing to fire [it] at the ship."[8] Then, according to witnesses, there was a loud noise, not like a detonation but more like a crash, like the sound of metal being ripped apart, as one RPG exploded against the hull and pierced the ship's hull into a passenger cabin. A frightened couple was huddling inside the room when the remnants of the rocket-propelled grenade landed only feet from them. Although shaken, they were unhurt, although their cabin was very badly damaged by the force of the RPG ripping through the room.

The International Maritime Organization does not endorse the use of weapons on merchant vessels, let alone endorse the arming of cruise ships. Thus, the *Spirit* found itself at least 80 miles off the coast of a hostile shore in a desperate situation and with little to defend itself. The hope of rescue from a friendly coast guard or navy after the attack commenced early in the morning was remote. The ship was now under full military attack with nothing to use to answer the RPGs and automatic rifle fire. That is when Security Officer Groves realized that the only hope for defending the ship lay in the LRAD.

Despite his continuing efforts to spray the attackers with highly pressured water, Groves concluded that the fire hoses were not going to repel the attack and that he had to use the Long-Range Acoustic Device mounted on the stern of the ship. Aside from the high-pressure fire hoses, which are no defense against automatic weapons, the LRAD was truly the ship's only real defense against the pirates. When the other pirate boat moved in closer to the ship and aimed another rocket launcher, Groves ran across the deck toward the LRAD at the stern amid the indiscriminate rifle fire and dove to the ground just as another rocket went off just inches over his head. Groves felt an excruciating pain in his ears. In apparent shock, he lay frozen on the deck until Som Bahadur Gurung, the master of arms, appeared out of nowhere and dragged him back across the deck and out of fire from the AK-47s.[9]

Gurung, a former British Army Gurkha, was one of two ship security personnel trained in the use of the LRAD. He activated the LRAD, turned the volume up (on the warning tone), pointed the device at the pirate's boat, and watched the pirates' faces grimace with pain as the LRAD's deafening sound pierced their boat. The sound had an instantaneous effect on their actions. It immediately disrupted the attack, and the pirates could be seen holding their hands over their ears in confusion while trying to locate the source of the excruciating sound. After spotting Security Officer Groves and Master at Arms Gurung on the fantail with the oddly shaped disc pointed at them, the pirates opened fire again with their automatic weapons.

In an instant, Gurung was knocked unconscious after being hit by a piece of shrapnel that dislodged from the LRAD after it was hit by a stray bullet. Incredibly, even after being hit, the LRAD, was not disabled; instead, it kept emitting the shrieking sound.[10] Groves resumed the operator's position on the LRAD and continued to torment the attackers with high piercing tones while dodging bursts of automatic gunfire. After fighting a losing battle with the LRAD and the ever-increasing speed of the ship, the attackers fled after spending 30 minutes trying to disable the ship.

The USS Gonzales (DDG 66), a U.S. Navy ship on patrol in the Red Sea, was one of the first U.S. warships on the scene to render assistance to the Seabourn Spirit the following day. The Gonzales deployed its explosive ordnance team to remove what was thought to be the unexploded RPG lodged in the Spirit's hull. The Navy technicians determined that the object in question was actually the remains of a rocket motor and not the warhead from the RPG, which had detonated on impact against the ship's hull.[11]

The commanding officer of the USS *Gonzales* forwarded the following report to the U.S. Commander, Fifth Fleet, in Bahrain after meeting with the cruise ship's captain:

> In evading the pirates, the Captain of the ship did everything that he was supposed to. He mustered the passengers and crew internal to the ship with the exception of security personnel. . . . The security team also did well. Under fire, they charged fire hoses to keep the pirates from boarding, they assisted passengers to get them inside the skin of the ship, and they deployed the LRAD. The Security Officer was

The remnants of one of the rocket-propelled grenades (RPGs) that struck the cruise ship *Seabourn Spirit* is shown lodged in its hull after an attack by pirates near the coast of Somalia on November 5, 2005. Personnel assigned to the U.S. Navy Explosive Ordnance Disposal Mobile Unit Eight (EODMU-8) boarded the *Seabourn Spirit* the following day while the ship was at sea to remove the RPG; they determined that the object in question was actually the remains of a rocket motor and not the warhead from the RPG, which had detonated on impact. (U.S. Navy photo by Engineman 1st Class Kelly Franz)

particularly enthusiastic about the performance of LRAD, and in his opinion it saved the day. He had his man focus the LRAD in the alarm mode, at max volume, directly at one of the pirate's small boats when it was about ten meters from the ship. The pirates actually covered their ears and began shooting at the LRAD. The one person injured in the attack was the LRAD operator, who received fragments in his head and wrist when a bullet passed through the LRAD. Despite the bullet hole, the LRAD kept working and the pirates turned outbound and abandoned their effort.[12]

The *Seabourn Spirit* recovered quickly. It was repaired and returned to service. The cruise company and the industry as a whole were eager to move on from this incident. The majority of the crew and passengers survived the ordeal more or less without injury. The only injured crew member, Som Gurung, the Nepalese Gurkha who had operated the LRAD while under fire and was hit by a bullet fragment during the attack, received no special medical benefit to cover his injuries from Carnival Cruise Lines, the parent company of Seabourn Yachts.[13] Michael Groves, the British policeman and ship security officer in charge of defending the ship, later suffered permanent hearing loss as a result of the RPG explosion and initiated a lawsuit against Seabourn Yachts and Carnival Corporation, its parent company, to recover earnings lost as a result of his injuries.[14]

In 2006, at a ceremony at Buckingham Palace, Michael Groves received the Queen's Gallantry Medal for heroism. Som Gurung, the Nepalese Gurkha, received the Queen's Commendation for Bravery. But the two security personnel who risked their lives to save the ship and all aboard were eventually released from the cruise line and lost their jobs for unspecified reasons. I was disappointed to learn of Michael Groves troubles after his heroism aboard the *Spirit*. I corresponded with him in early 2009 to see how he was recovering. His life is still in disarray due to his hearing loss, and he is unable to speak about his ordeal because of his pending litigation. (In November 2009, a full four years after the incident, Carnival Corp. has since settled out of court with Michael Groves.) It was hard to believe that the two crew members who reacted bravely under fire and risked their own lives to save the ship and the lives of those on board were treated in such an arbitrary manner by the cruise line. Unquestionably, their brave response and their use of the LRAD prevented a cruise industry disaster and probably averted an international incident of even greater proportions.

On a more positive note, I was happy that the LRAD had paid off where it counted most. The media had publicized the cruise industry's "new secret weapon" in the fight against pirates. I guessed incorrectly at the time that, having seen the potential for the LRAD and its value, other cruise lines would be lining up to order LRADs for their ships en masse. I was surprised to learn that, despite the attack and the success of the LRAD in defending the *Seabourn Spirit*, other cruise lines

In 2006, at a ceremony at Buckingham Palace, the hero of the *Seabourn Spirit,* Michael Groves (center) received the Queen's Gallantry Medal for heroism. Som Gurung (right), the Nepalese Gurkha, received the Queens Commendation for Bravery. The two security personnel who risked their lives to save the ship and all aboard were eventually released from the cruise line for unspecified reasons. (Photo courtesy of Michael Groves)

were still not interested in putting them on their ships.[15] After two more pirate attacks on cruise ships in pirate-infested waters off east Somalia and the approach to the Red Sea, the cruise lines are beginning to have second thoughts about acoustic hailing and warning devices. However, the Cruise Vessel Security and Safety Act of 2009 (discussed in chapter 6) will eventually require this technology on all cruise vessels calling on U.S. ports, primarily to help the ships enforce their restricted zones. Whether LRADs or similar devices will be enough to stem pirate attacks on cruise ships is questionable. LRAD technology was developed to provide a means for vessels to communicate with and hail other vessels entering into or encroaching on its restricted zone. With the increase in pirate attacks, the debate over the use of LRADs and other nonlethal protective measures has shifted to a debate about arming merchant vessels with guns.

PIRATES AND THE QUESTION OF GUNS ON CRUISE SHIPS

Following the attack on the *Seabourn Spirit,* numerous articles and blogs were written about the incident and the ship's response. Many outside the maritime industry questioned the safety of ships on the high seas. They asked why the cruise ship did not "fire back." Most casual observers were angry over the audaciousness of the attack by maritime criminals and were surprised to learn that cruise ships had nothing more than fire hoses (and the LRAD in the case of Seabourn ships) to protect them. Many were shocked to learn that not only cruise ships but all ships at sea do not have weapons aboard to protect themselves in these situations. Shotguns were once a featured attraction on cruise ships; they were used by passengers to skeet shoot off the fantail. However, that practice ceased years ago, not so much because of maritime terrorism or the debate about weapons on ships but because of lawsuits brought by passengers who had been accidentally shot by fellow passengers in a manner similar to the accidental shooting of a fellow hunter by former vice president Dick Cheney.

The IMO and the entire maritime community have always opposed arming vessels on the water for several reasons. To begin with, having guns on cruise ships or other vessels does not make sense for the same reason it does not make sense to arm pilots on jet aircraft. If you provide the guns on the airplane or ship, then they are available to terrorists, pirates, or anyone else bent on harming the vessel. All they have to do is figure out a way to get onto the ship; perhaps by buying a ticket? From that point, it is just a matter of getting access to the weapons, and there are any number of ways to accomplish this. There are also questions of training and liability on the part of the ship's crew and owner. But another reason is that if private craft and merchant vessels engage in running gun battles on the world's oceans, the risk of losing control of the sea lanes for all maritime traffic quickly escalates. Guns on cruise ships lead to bigger guns on pirate ships, so the argument goes.

Cruise lines are reluctant to talk about their specific security plans, fearing that the information could help terrorists, pirates, and others. In March 2004, Kenneth Bissonnette, a staff manager for surveillance and security at Carnival Cruise Lines, told the Associated Press that security personnel for the world's largest cruise line did not carry firearms but that they had other defenses, such as pepper spray. He said the company's security staff recruited heavily among Gurkhas, the elite Nepalese soldiers renowned for their fearlessness. When asked to confirm this, Tim Gallagher, a spokesman for company's parent, Carnival Corporation, declined to comment on the specific security procedures of the cruise line.[16] William Callahan, president and maritime security consultant of Unitel, said that cruise lines are reluctant to have armed guards on board because that might hurt their image with some passengers.[17]

The issue of arming merchant vessels aroused serious interest in the United States when, in April 2009, the *Maersk Alabama* was attacked by pirates who boarded the ship and took the captain hostage. The ship was carrying humanitarian aid to the war-torn country of Somalia when the hijacking incident took place. A dramatic end to the hostage taking came when three of four pirates were killed by U.S. Navy SEAL sharpshooters positioned on the USS *Bainbridge* as the pirates attempted to take the captain to shore on an *Alabama* lifeboat. A fourth pirate was taken prisoner by the U.S. Navy and returned to the United States, where he is expected to face charges of committing piracy on the high seas.[18]

The issue of guns on cruise ships surfaced again in late April 2009, a few weeks after the attack on the *Alabama,* when the cruise ship the *MSC Melody* was suddenly attacked. The rash of piracy attacks off the east coast of Somalia has now included at least three cruise ships. The cruise ship *Oceania Nautica* was attacked in December 2008 by pirates in the same swath of ocean in which the *Seabourn Spirit* had been assaulted by pirates two years earlier.[19] In these attacks, the same "mother ship" tactics appear to have been used by the pirates. While these stories have dominated the maritime security discussion about piracy, a greater debate developed after the attack on the third ship, the cruise ship *Melody*, about the use of handguns to repel the attack.

The Italian cruise ship, operated by MSC Cruises, was on a 22-day cruise from Durban, South Africa, to Genoa, Italy, and was headed to the Jordanian port of Aqaba. The *MSC Melody* was repositioning to the Mediterranean for the spring and summer cruising season and was steaming through the hostile waters off the coast of Somalia when it came under attack in much the same fashion as the *Spirit.* The *Melody* was not equipped with the LRAD sonic cannon. Instead, the Israeli security guards on board fired at the pirates with handguns reportedly stored in the captain's safe for just such emergencies. The sudden pirate attack and the unconventional response caught everyone off guard—the pirates, the crew, and the passengers.

"The attack felt like a war," said one passenger. It lasted for 30 minutes and resembled a running gun battle between the small pirate dinghy and the fast-moving cruise ship. "The pirates would have boarded had some passengers not fought them off with deck chairs being thrown overboard as they were clambering up the side but then security started the gunfire and, of course, pirates from their boat were letting us have it as well," said one passenger in an e-mail to her mother.[20]

While the handguns of the security crew were no match for the automatic weapons used by the pirates; the unexpected armed response by the crew and the increasing speed of the ship were enough to give the pirates no option but to retreat. A spokesman for MSC Cruises said that none of the 1,000 passengers and 500 crew were hurt in the gun battle.[21] Typically, the cruise line played down reports that the security staff on the ship had had to shoot it out with the pirates. But it was hard to get around the firsthand reports being circulated in various blogs and in personal e-mail that made their way into the mainstream media.

The high-seas gunfight is believed to be the first exchange of fire between a passenger vessel and pirate attackers since the start of the current wave of piracy off the Horn of Africa. As discussed previously, the placement of guns or any other weapons on board cruise ships is frowned upon by the international maritime community. The use of small arms (pistols or handguns) by the *Melody*'s crew was the captain's decision and was instantly praised by the owners of the cruise line but criticized by others in the maritime industry. The cruise line defended the greater good of doing all that is possible to save the ship and to avoid having the passengers taken hostage by the heavily armed pirates. It praised the captain for acting swiftly and decisively. But Andrew Mwangura, of the Mombasa-based East African Seafarers Assistance Program, said of the incident, "They should have used other means to shake off the pirates, like a loud acoustic device," referring to the LRAD.[22]

The use of guns during the *Melody* cruise ship attack and, in general, the presence of guns on nonmilitary ships has sparked a greater, long-running debate over whether to arm merchant crews as a means to protect themselves in the face of the pirate onslaught off the coast of Somalia. I was shocked to learn that any cruise ships would be transiting the pirate-infested waters and that the captain of the *Melody* had broken out guns allegedly locked in his safe. Yet, it is important to understand that this transit of the *Melody* through the pirate waters was part of a re-positioning cruise, for this puts the problem for the cruise lines in perspective. The problem is the same for the merchant vessels. There is simply no other (inexpensive) option for getting ships into the Mediterranean (or into the Indian Ocean) other than through the approaches to the Red Sea and the Suez Canal. Schedules, after all, must be kept.

Years earlier, in a conversation in the Princess boardroom with Peter Ratcliffe, who was then CEO of Princess, I predicted that the day would come when cruise ships would be overtaken by the means that we were then employing to protect them. I hinted that arming the security crews with guns might be the only way to protect the ship in instances where the sea lanes had become openly hostile. I soon learned that this view was extremely unpopular with senior Princess management, including Peter Ratcliffe. Despite the extraordinary security measures we were taking at the time to protect our fleet of cruise ships from attack, my suggestion was, perhaps, an idea that was ahead of its time.

As noted earlier, cruise lines have a choice whether to negate this type of threat by exercising risk management and simply avoiding the pirate-infested areas until the problem is brought under control by the international community. In the case of the Somalia pirates, this seems unlikely to happen any time soon. While cruises to the Middle East through the Suez Canal and into the Mediterranean are very popular, they are not essential sea routes that the cruise industry depends on in the way that other merchant shipping does. There are, fortunately, still plenty of ports of call and itineraries that the cruise lines can substitute until the problem off the east coast of Africa subsides. Shutting down any cruise itinerary for security or safety reasons creates doubt in the seagoing public's mind about their safety while at sea. The increased media attention that the pirate activity has created is something that the cruise lines wish would simply go away.[23]

The debate over the arming of merchant crews, however, will not go away anytime soon. Pierfrancesco Vago, chief of MSC Cruises, conceded the need for an industry-wide debate on the deployment of firearms aboard cruise ships after the failed pirate attack on the *MSC Melody*. Vago said that the controversial issue of deploying firearms on passenger ships, which some believe will only lead to an escalation of pirate violence, must be debated. While he would not be drawn into a discussion of the merits of company policy on the issue, the cruise line chief did reflect on the prospect of having 1,000 cruise ship passengers taken hostage. "That would have been a disaster," he said later. "But we need to sit down and discuss this [arming crews] internally, and we need to discuss it as an industry."[24]

The debate will likely center on several issues. Ship owners do not want crews to be armed because few merchant sailors have the requisite firearms training and because pirates who are financed by their ransom payments will always be able to buy larger weapons than ship owners, which will ultimately lead to an escalating maritime arms race. The international community worries that the escalating pirate activity will cause it to lose control of the sea lanes. Unfortunately, this is already occurring. There is also the fact that many international ISPS ports do not allow weapons of any kind to be introduced aboard ships. Given all these concerns, the possibility that ship owners will actually arm their crews seems remote.

Finally, another debate is already raging over the increased liability that will be faced by ship owners that do arm their crews. Issues such as whether the crews are properly trained in the use of weaponry, what the appropriate rules of engagement are, and ship owners' potential liability if the weapons are used against a hostile force will have to be discussed. Where will the boundaries be drawn? Will the guns be drawn by the security crews when stowaways are discovered, when criminals commit crimes, or to confront unruly passengers? These are volatile issues that will have to be confronted.

Most cruise ship passengers and the general public are outraged that the merchant companies and the cruise ships in particular are not firing back at the pirates, so public opinion appears to be with the ship owners. For now, the debate is centered on the piracy issue and liability. A sailor on the *Maersk Alabama* has sued the owners of the ship for not providing the crew with the means to protect itself. The captain of the *Maersk Alabama* testified at a hearing convened by a subcommittee of the Senate Foreign Relations Committee held early in May 2009 to discuss the possibility of arming merchant crews. Captain Richard Phillips told senators that "In my opinion, arming the crew cannot and should not be viewed as the best or ultimate solution to the problem. At most, arming the crew should be only one component of a comprehensive plan and approach to combat piracy."[25] Captain Phillips went on to say: "As for armed security details put aboard vessels, I believe, that this idea could certainly be developed into an effective deterrent. My preference would be government protection forces. However, as long as they are adequately trained I would not be opposed to private security on board. Of course, I realize that very clear protocols would have to be established and followed. For example, as a captain, I am responsible for the vessel, cargo, and crew at all times. And I am not comfortable giving up command authority to others including the commander of a protection force."[26]

John Clancey, chairman of Maersk, the parent company of Maersk Line, believes that arming crews on merchant ships is not the solution to the piracy problem. At the hearing, he said, "I know Captain Phillips prefers an armed capability for the crew onboard and I respectfully understand his perspective. . . . Captain Phillips is in agreement with vessel operators, his labor union, and the IMO, which points out that firearms are useful only in the hands of those who are properly trained, who regularly practice in their use, and who are fully capable of using them as required. Our belief is that arming merchant sailors may result in the acquisition of ever more lethal weapons and tactics by the pirates, a race that merchant sailors cannot win."[27]

Perhaps because of the lawsuit brought against the ship owner by a crew member on the *Alabama* or because of the lack of clarity on the issue in the latest Senate hearings, Maersk has seen fit to consider using the LRAD technology to add to a sensible "layered defense" against the pirate threat. The attack on the *Maersk Alabama* was seen as a game changer with regard to arming ships' crews. The issue has bogged down over questions of liability and who should actually be armed: the crews themselves or special security teams employed by the ship owners. The arming of merchant vessel crews is a slippery slope that the whole maritime industry must immediately find concurrence with lest they run the risk of dividing the ship owners and their crews in the face of escalating violence. For cruise ships, however, which transit hostile pirate waters in spite of government warnings to the contrary, the risks to passengers and crew are too great for them to be left without even the simplest means to protect themselves.

THE PIRATE-TERRORIST CONNECTION

The increased pirate activity off the east coast of Africa has been a boon for maritime security. Because of the notoriety and the threat to maritime commerce, efforts to curb the pirate threat have the support of the international community, which has sent its navies to patrol the approaches to the strategic shipping corridor of the Suez Canal. But have such efforts done anything to stop the threat from international terrorist groups, and are there links between the pirates and terrorist groups? These questions have been increasingly asked as pirate attacks have occurred with military precision off the coast of Somalia. After the attack on the *Seabourn Spirit,* many observers asked if it was possible that terrorists, rather than pirates, had attacked the ship.

The attack on the *Seabourn Spirit* in November 2005 was described in the media as an act of piracy primarily because the ship was transiting a stretch of ocean notorious for pirate attacks. However, others were quick to suggest the possibility of a maritime terrorist attack. Some have speculated that the attack on the *Seabourn Spirit* was something more than a futile attempt to board a tourist-laden cruise ship. The tactics used resembled those used in a naval attack, albeit an unsophisticated one. Recent evidence suggests that the Somali pirates may have received military training on how to carry out attacks on seagoing ships from Russia, in an echo of the cold war between the West and the Soviet Union that dominated international relations in the second half of the 20th century.

Sergey Bliznyuk, a retired rear admiral of the Soviet navy, said, "There are many former military men among the Somalis who have perfected the tactics of sea combat. The majority of these 40- to 50-year-olds were trained in the former Soviet Union. I myself taught at one point at a school in Baku [Azerbaijan], where we had 70 to 80 Somalis a year studying." The former Soviet admiral went on to say that Soviet officers had trained naval personnel from the government of President Siad Barre, who ruled Somalia between 1969 and 1991 after staging a military coup and that the Soviet Union taught not only Somali natives but also people from Yemen, Ethiopia, and others African countries.[28]

While it is possible that Somalis and Yemenis and other nationals have received naval training in the former Soviet Union, the question still remains, why attack a cruise ship? Were the men who attacked the *Seabourn Spirit* pirates or terrorists bent on destroying the ship? The attackers used automatic weapons and rocket-propelled grenades, at least three of which were fired, followed by several unsuccessful attempts to board the ship. Perhaps the attackers' failure to take the ship resulted in part from the captain's action to increase speed and his use of evasive steering.[29] The attack on the *Seabourn Spirit* resembled more of a terror attack if one examines the location of the RPG strikes. Consider that these attackers were firing broadside at a huge ship. It was a little like trying to hit the side of a barn. At least one RPG crashed through the ship's bulkhead and landed in an outer cabin where a frightened couple was huddling for safety. Fortunately, the device detonated on the outside of the ship's hull.[30] By all other accounts, the

other RPGs missed the ship or were fired high toward the bridge superstructure, where an explosion presumably would have killed or injured passengers and
crew, including the captain. The pirates' intent was clear in this attack: they meant
to kill passengers. These facts support the idea that the attackers were in fact terrorists, rather than pirates.

In a pirate attack, the whole point is to gain access to the ship. These pirates, if
they were intent on boarding, would have had made better use of their ordnance
by firing at the ship's propulsion astern or even at the ship's rudder. Experts believe that cruise ship design enhances ship safety because they have high free-
boards (the distance from the waterline to the first open deck). Additionally, most
cruise ships have antipirate screens, which are steel grates welded to the hull
to prevent easy boarding from the below-deck mooring stations at the stern of
the ship. Thus, boarding a cruise ship, even with grappling hooks, may add a bit of
swashbuckling to the pirates' operation, but the grappling hooks and ropes would
have been quite easy for the ship's crew to dislodge. Despite these design features,
some observers doubt that the pirates could have been kept from boarding the
Seabourn Spirit. Pirates have shown adeptness in boarding just about every type
of ship, from supertankers and container ships to tugs and merchant vessels. Getting aboard a cruise ship would not present insurmountable problems. Again,
this supports the idea that the attackers were not pirates.

Another possibility is that the attack on the *Spirit*, if it was a pirate attack, could
have been just a case of mistaken identity. The pirate criminals had been very successful at attacking and seizing small yachts and pillaging private sailing sloops
in the region prior to the attack on the *Spirit*. They may have mistaken the *Seabourn
Spirit* for a very large private yacht. Officials in the United Kingdom said they had
"pretty solid evidence" from diplomatic sources in the region that a "fundamentalist militia" had been operating in Somalia that had the capability to track ship
movements and monitor communications between ships.[31] But all this might
mean simply is that, whoever these fundamentalist are, they probably have access
to a maritime radio that can pick up the so-called bridge-to-bridge ship radio channel, which is no more than a maritime CB.

Ships that pass at sea often (if there is actually someone on the bridge) communicate their intentions to each other in this fashion. So, this information might
be of interest to terrorist groups or pirates who have the capability to monitor
these communications. They may be able to pick up the names of ships on their
target lists as they approach. Ships using the bridge-to-bridge channel including
cruise ships should be aware of the fact that when they are hailing another ship
and identifying themselves by giving their own ship's name, pirates or terrorists
may be waiting just over the horizon. There is evidence to suggest that the pirates
are being helped by an international syndicate with a base in London. According

to European military intelligence agencies, "well-placed informers" are in constant contact with control centers in Somalia. The control centers give the pirates information about ships in the area, including their routes and cargos. In some cases, hijackers even had details on the layout of ships, their ports of call, and the nationalities of those on board.[32] Such information networks are consistent with the needs of groups taking advantage of the sophisticate technology available in the modern era—but does that link them to international terrorism?

It appears that al-Qaeda does have links to Islamic extremist groups operating in Somalia, but, thus far, piracy and al-Qaeda's brand of terrorism have remained largely separate. That does not mean that the risks to shipping have decreased. A senior al-Qaeda member, Sa'id Ali Jabir Al-Khathim al-Shihri, has instructed his Somali allies to "increase your strikes against the crusaders at sea and in Djibouti."[33] The pirates and the terrorists appear to be linked through Islam, and theirs is a relationship purely of convenience. The two forces cooperate on arms smuggling, and the pirates are reportedly helping al-Shabaab, a group based in East Africa that United States says is a terrorist group with close ties to al-Qaeda, develop maritime capabilities. The entire Somali coastline is now under control of the Islamists. Andrew Mwangura, the head of the East African Seafarers' Assistance Program, has said that a link exists between the two groups. "According to our information, the money they make from piracy and ransoms goes to support al-Shabaab activities onshore."[34]

With regard to the attack on the *Seabourn Spirit,* it is doubtful that the pirates, if they were operating as pirates and not as terrorists, did not know exactly who and what they were attacking. The attack on the *Seabourn Spirit* may have been just a poorly planned and poorly executed attack by the same band of pirates that had been operating in the region for at least 12 months before the attack.

THE SOMALI PIRATES

The attack on the *Seabourn Spirit* must be put into the context of what was happening off the coast of Somalia in the months leading up to the brazen attack in November 2005. This examination may serve to explain the attack and to help us ascertain whether it signaled a new era of threats to cruise ships from terrorists or pirates and how cruise lines should prepare themselves. Piracy in the waters off the coast of Somalia is not a new phenomenon, and the attack on the *Spirit* did not happen in a vacuum. It was preceded by a series of attacks, each more brazen than the one before. And it appears that the attack on the *Spirit* has indeed set the standard for pirate attacks on cruise ships.

In December 2004, more than a year before the *Spirit* came under fire, the tactics that were used in the attack on it were already being used by a gang of pirates operating in the area. French and German naval vessels had been able to foil an attack on the cruise yacht *Lili Marleen* in the Gulf of Aden. Pirates had opened fire on the *Lili Marleen*, which had been transiting from Port Said in Egypt to the port of Salalah in Oman. The *Lili Marleen* was a small vessel, certainly not a cruise ship, and carried only 23 passengers, just the size vessel that would make a tempting target to pirates.[35]

The tempo of pirate attacks increased between March and November 2005, with a record 23 attacks during that period.[36] In July, in an attack that resembled the later *Spirit* incident, about 10 pirates in two small motor launches armed with rocket-propelled grenade launchers and automatic weapons opened fire and attempted to board the *Jolly Marrone,* an Italian cargo box ship about 100 miles (160 kilometers) off the coast of Somalia, almost exactly where the *Spirit* attack would take place. The ship escaped, and the crew was not injured, but the attack prompted the Italian government to dispatch Italian warships to protect their merchant vessels off the Somali coast.[37]

Something approaching an international incident occurred in July when the *Semlow,* a vessel chartered by the United Nations World Food Program, was hijacked and the crew taken as hostages. After a month of being held captive, negotiators thought they had secured the release of the vessel and the crew for an undisclosed ransom. The Somali pirates reneged on the deal however, and in a defiant act, turned around and found good cause for the ship by using it to hijack another cargo ship in September. The *Semlow* was used to board and capture the cement carrier *Ibnu Batuta* near the port of El Maan, Somalia.

The attack on the *Ibnu Batuta* followed a failed attempt by World Food Program officials to persuade the pirates on the *Semlow* to unload its cargo of food aid at El Maan. Finally, after a standoff that lasted nearly 100 days, the *Semlow* and its crew were released intact. The vessel's shipment of food, bound for the starving, war-torn population of Somalia, was also returned (despite rumors to the contrary). The crew of eight Kenyans, a Tanzanian engineer, and a Sri Lankan master were released unharmed.[38]

Somali sources that follow what is happening in their country say that that Somali warlords and businesses are using piracy to finance their enterprises and to generate money to recruit more fighters into their private armies. The piracy is focused on drugs, weapons, and human smuggling across the Gulf of Aden back into Somalia and, along with the trading of khat, a mild narcotic similar to coca leaves that is exported from Kenya to Somalia, is believed to be financing illegal fishing, logging, and mining ventures. Although pirates are not involved in the businesses themselves, they share in the ransom money paid to the warlords and businessmen. The Somali pirates receive protection from the warlords, and the businessmen negotiate ransoms on behalf of the pirates. The ransoms can be quite high. Recently, in June 2007, pirates hijacked the Danish ship *Danica White*; in August, its release was negotiated through an intermediary security firm for a $1.5 million ransom.[39]

According to a source with the Mombasa-based Seafarers Assistance Program, there were 29 incidents in Somalia in 2007, compared to only 8 in the same period in 2006 year. Of these attacks, 15 involved international, oceangoing vessels. During the attacks, 172 crew members were taken hostage.[40] The dominant Somali pirate groups include the National Volunteer Coast Guard (NVCG), based in Kismayu; a group in Puntland; and another in the town of Markeh. The most sophisticated of the pirate groups, Somali Marines (aka Somali Coast Guard), are believed to have carried out more than 80 percent of the attacks, since they have the capacity to operate in deep-sea areas, where they conduct their attacks from a mother ship.[41]

The U.S. Navy has been increasingly active in rescuing seized merchant ships, as have the naval forces of Germany, Italy, Britain, and the Netherlands. In November 2007, intervention by the U.S. Navy helped win the release of the *Ching*

Suspected pirates keep their hands in the air as directed by sailors aboard the guided-missile cruiser USS *Vella Gulf* (CG 72) in February 2009. Heavily armed pirates in small motor whaleboats such as these have been launching their attacks on merchant vessels and cruise ships from "mother ships" staged farther out to sea. Ships traversing the strategic corridor in the Gulf of Aden and its approach to the Red Sea and Suez Canal were at increased risk from pirates in 2008 and 2009. (U.S. Navy photo by Mass Communications Specialist 2nd Class Jason R. Zalasky)

Fong Hwa 168, a Taiwanese vessel that had been hijacked and held for six months. That same month, a helicopter from the USS *James E. Williams* helped the North Korean crew of the *Dai Dong Han* overpower Somali pirates who had seized their ship.[42]

It is perhaps a mistaken assumption that pirates are interested only in plunder—that is, robbing the ship and passengers of valuables before retreating back to their mother ships. There are a host of other options that are available to the pirates once the ship is seized. The vessel can be hijacked and resold on the black market, and the passengers can be held for ransom to increase profits. While maritime security experts and the cruise lines point out that cruise ships do not make attractive targets for terrorists because of their design and the problem of controlling a large number of persons, pirates may not attack cruise ships for a number of other, more obvious reasons. For one thing, cruise ships do not have attractive resale values, whereas pirates do a brisk business in seizing other vessels, especially mega-yachts, and then reselling them. Additionally, cruise ships do not carry cargos that are highly prized by pirates for their resale value on the black market. There are other deterrents, as well, that make pirate attacks on cruise ships a dangerous proposition for the pirates. Cruise ships are certainly much faster than slow-moving tanker or container ships, and they typically have well-trained crews, including security department commanded by former policeman or Royal Navy officers. Another deterrent is the distress signals required on all ships, including passenger cruise liners, by the ISPS. These duress signals, when activated, instantly alert cruise ship shore staff to the existence of an emergency.[43]

No terrorist organization has claimed responsibility for the attack on the *Seabourn Spirit.* If it was a terrorist attack, maybe the jihadists did not boast about it because it failed so miserably. In the absence of cheering crowds on al-Jazeera, the Arabic-language television station, we must ponder not who attacked the *Spirit* but why. The attack certainly was not a suicide attack like the assault on the USS *Cole* five years earlier. Perhaps the pirates or terrorists were testing the ship's response capability in preparation for some greater operation.

The attack on the *Spirit* occurred in al-Qaeda's backyard, in the area where the USS *Cole* had been bombed and the *MV Limburg* had been rammed by a small motorboat laden with explosives. But it is hard to imagine operational planning taking on the characteristics of a full-blown naval attack. However, farther away, in another pirate-ridden trouble spot near the Straits of Malacca, an area used by more than a quarter of the world's maritime trade, another incident has left maritime security officials puzzled.

After pirates boarded the *Dewi Madrim* in the Straits of Malacca, instead of plundering and pillaging the crew and cargo they proceeded to ask questions about steering the ship. After piloting the ship for an hour, they left, as quickly as they had come, reboarded their fast boats, and departed, without further incident or harm to the crew. The ship's captain, who was held below decks during the raid, was impressed by the pirates' handling of the ship. "I realized that they were completely familiar with all the equipment. Someone was expertly steering the vessel, reading the radar very well. I remember thinking: 'My God, he can handle the ship better than I can.' I'd thought pirates were just a bunch of petty robbers who jumped onto a ship, robbed the crew, and then disappeared. But these pirates were totally beyond my imagination. They were professionals."[44]

This attack was different from the two attacks that preceded the seizure of the *Dewi Madrim.* In those assaults, which occurred in April 2003, the pirates attacked two chemical tankers, the *Suhailaand* and the *Oriental Salvia,* with automatic weapons.[45] Just as the September 11 attackers learned to fly but not land an aircraft in preparation for the attacks on the Twin Towers and the Pentagon, the pirates in the *Dewi Madrim* attack were perhaps preparing for a future sea assault.

PIRATES AND TERRORISTS IN SOUTHEAST ASIA

Southeast Asia, a popular destination for the world's cruise ships, is not without its share of risks. Unfortunately, maritime terrorism is no stranger to this part of the world. Although cruise ships have not been targeted by pirates or terrorist groups, because of the volatility of the region cruise ships risk being caught up in transnational terrorism and regional acts of piracy. The Straits of Malacca and its strategic importance to global shipping are well known; in addition, cruise ships use this route as they shift from Asian itineraries to destinations in the Indian Ocean, Africa, the Middle East, and beyond. To generalize from the types of attack scenarios already uncovered, cruise ships risk getting caught up in terrorist plots to attack ports or naval warships or being the target of marauding pirates who routinely operate in these waters.

Nationalistic terrorist groups such as the Abu Sayyaf Group, which has strong ties to al-Qaeda, have already attacked a passenger ferry in the Philippines in what is currently the world's worst terrorist attack on a maritime vessel in terms of human lives lost. Terrorist organizations such as al-Qaeda are suspected of having a maritime capability through its legitimate shipping fleet.

One terrorist group, the Liberation Tigers of Tamil Eelam (LTTE), controls a freight forwarding business and up to a dozen cargo ships. The ships fly the common flags of convenience, like those of Panama, Honduras, or Liberia. Like al-Qaeda's alleged fleet of ships, most of the time the LTTE fleets are engaged in transporting legitimate cargo manifests such as timber, tea, rice, cement, and fertilizer. The fleet of ships, however, has also been reported to have carried weapons and ammunition for other terrorist groups, such as Harkat-ul-Mujahideen of

Pakistan, which is a member of the al-Qaeda-linked International Islamic Front. The ships have also carried war equipment to the Tamil Tigers in Sri Lanka.[46]

Other threats in the Asian region, however, include one of the oldest forms of maritime terrorism, piracy. It has been demonstrated that Indonesian pirates have the capability to attack very large ships in the Straits of Malacca, and, although they have never targeted cruise ships, they have gone after ships of comparable size. The large number of pirate attacks in the region, a number of which have involved the hijacking of high-profile vessels, has led antiterrorist strategists to worry that terrorists could use copycat methods to takeover a vessel for more sinister reasons. In a visit to Malaysia in 2005, Vice Admiral Terry Cross of the U.S. Coast Guard said that the ease with which pirate attacks were taking place in the Malaccan Straits could "alert terrorists to the opportunities for seizing oil tankers" and that "these could be used as floating bombs."[47] When the 1,289-ton MT Tri Samudra, a chemical tanker that was carrying a full cargo of inflammable petrochemical products, was hijacked by pirates in the Malacca Straits, the regional manager of the International Maritime Bureau was quoted as saying: "This is exactly the type of tanker that terrorists would likely use to attack a shore-based port or other facility."[48]

The Malaccan Straits are a narrow parcel of ocean that separates Indonesia and trading partners in the Indian Ocean such as India from the oil supply line flowing out of the Persian Gulf. Vessels bound from the Indian Ocean with their precious cargos of oil must use this "shortcut" to reach the Pacific trade routes. Carrying a third of the world's trade and half of its oil supplies, these vessels make security in the Straits a matter of grave concern to the stakeholders of Singapore, Malaysia, and Indonesia, the three countries that form its boundaries.

It is estimated that around 4.5 percent of the more than 63,000 ships that traverse the Straits of Malacca each year consists of passenger ships. Cruise ships have increasingly called on Asian Pacific ports, which are popular cruise destinations and markets. The cruising industry in the region has overcome the impacts of the slump caused by events such as 9/11, SARS, and the devastating tsunami in December 2004. The industry's growth has created a need for new cruise ship infrastructure. Singapore has announced plans to build a US$1 billion cruise center featuring a hotel, a convention center, and casino facilities. Other Asian ports, such as Shanghai and Hong Kong, are building new cruise facilities, as well.[49]

There has always been a debate over the possibility that the Straits might be blocked by a sunken vessel that would obstruct navigation. The narrowest point of the marked channel in the Malacca Straits is at One Fathom Bank, where the width is 0.6 nautical miles. Even if a ship were sunk at this point, which itself is not necessarily an easy task to accomplish, it would not block the Straits. Ships could continue to use the waterway by simply navigating around the sunken vessel. But this might not be possible if more than one vessel were sunk at the same time. The Malacca Straits would be closed to shipping traffic, forcing the vessels, particularly those on international voyages, to reroute around the Lombok and Sunda Straits. This would cause severe delays to shipping, as these alternate routes are longer (transiting the Straits takes at least a day). Shipping costs would increase, and world trade would be affected. The impact on the region's economies could be severe if the closure lasted more than a few days.

In an article in Singapore's major broadsheet newspaper, *The Straits Times,* on March 27, 2004, an expert on maritime security is quoted as saying that "[i]f terrorists want to mount a maritime strike here [Southeast Asia], sinking a ship in the Malacca Straits is the likely attack of choice." He went on to say that "It would enable them to wreak economic havoc worldwide by blocking the sea lane, and is also the easiest way to attack."[50] It is perhaps here that the strange case of the *Dewi Madrim,* mentioned earlier, comes into focus. Just as the 9/11 pilots needed to know how to fly the hijacked jets *precisely* into the World Trade Center as a prerequisite for their operational success, so too would the capability of the pirates (or terrorists) to pilot the ship to One Fathom Bank, where another hijacked ship would be waiting to be rammed and sunk, be critical.

There is good news to report, however. Pirate attacks have tapered off somewhat since 2005 in the Malacca Straits. Despite this decline, the International Maritime Bureau still issues warnings to commercial ships to remain cautious. The Straits suffered only 10 pirate attacks between January and September 2005, compared to 25 in the same period the previous year. Although there were fewer attacks, there appeared to be an escalation in the violence involved in the incidents, as well as an increasingly brazen nature to the attacks. From March 2005 on, there was a resurgence in the number of violent incidents involving kidnappings for ransom.[51]

Remarkably, cruise and passenger ships have been spared such violent attacks, which have been concentrated on tankers, tugs, and barges. Less encouraging is the news that the drop in pirate attacks during the period from 2004 into early 2005 is believed to be a result of the aftermath of the tsunami that occurred in December 2004. It has been suggested that pirates were just as severely affected by the disaster as the rest of the population and that their activities were curtailed by the heavy presence of relief vessels in the Straits.[52]

Although there are no recorded incidents of piracy or terrorist attacks on cruise ships and pleasure crafts in this region, the Malacca Straits in particular maintains a reputation as being unsafe. Any significant incident involving a cruise ship such as a pirate attack like the one against the *Seabourn Spirit* would effectively shut down this region, at least for passenger ships, until a security plan could be put into effect. Although a maritime security plan is being implemented on a limited scale by maritime governments, such efforts have not effectively stopped the pirates; it has only slowed them down a little.

TERROR ON *SUPERFERRY 14*

Attacks on passenger ferries instead of cruise ships offer enormous potential for both pirates and terrorists but have not been undertaken to any extent, with one very notable but little-publicized exception. The attack on the *MV Superferry 14* in the Philippines by the Abu Sayyaf Group in February 2004 is considered the worst terrorist attack on a maritime vessel. However, outside the Philippines, it generated far less media attention for the Abu Sayyaf Group than the September 11 attacks or the Madrid and London train bombings did for al-Qaeda, which claimed responsibility for these attacks. This disparity is in part a result of the initial denial by the Philippines government that the terror attack was anything more than a shipboard fire.

In fact, just after midnight, a bomb exploded on board the *Superferry 14* passenger ferry, which had left Manila Bay two hours earlier. The resulting fire caused the ship to capsize, and more than 100 people either were killed in the ensuing fire or drowned when the ferry capsized. The attack was unsophisticated but deadly in its results and demonstrates just how vulnerable ferries can be, not just in the Philippines but in all parts of the world.

The young man had purchased a ticket on *Superferry 14* in Manila on February 26, using an assumed name, a name that would have instantly led officials to take him into custody if it had been run through a terrorist database. There was no such capability in the Philippines in 2004. Armulfo Alvarado, according to Philippine officials, was the name of a deceased Abu Sayyaf terrorist group member. The imposter, whose real name was Redondo Cain Dellosa, purchased a ticket in the cheapest section of the ferry and placed a sealed cardboard box, which allegedly contained a television set, on a seat in the lower decks. It was common for passengers to board with bags and boxes after shopping sprees in Manila, so the sight of a young Filipino man carrying a television raised no suspicions. Certainly, the box was not x-rayed, for no such screening procedures exist on these intercoastal ferries. In reality, the box contained just over 3.5 kilograms of TNT.[53]

Dellosa, the Abu Sayyaf terrorist, slipped off the ship before it departed, and, shortly after 11:00 P.M., while the ferry was off the Philippine island of Corregidor, an explosion ripped through *Supperferry14*'s lower deck and ignited a fire that engulfed the ferry. In addition to those killed as a result of the fire and the ensuing panic, many others who remain unaccounted for in the tragedy are presumed dead. Dellosa was captured several weeks later. He confessed to placing

The burnt hull of *Superferry 14* lies on its starboard side as rescuers search for 180 missing passengers northwest of Manila on February 29, 2004. The ship was sunk using a small amount of TNT smuggled aboard the ferry by an operative of the Abu Sayyaf Group in the Philippines in the worst maritime terrorist attack ever recorded. More than 110 persons were killed. (AP photo/ Aaron Favila)

the bomb in a place where its explosion would cause the most panic. Although he said that the bomb was detonated by a timing device, this has not been definitively proved.

The Abu Sayyaf Group is an Islamic terrorist group using terror tactics in an attempt to achieve an independent Muslim republic in the southern Philippines. It is believed that Abu Sayyaf is connected to al-Qaeda. The group was formed in the early 1980s with support from Osama bin Laden's brother-in-law, Mohammed Jamal Khalifa. The group has gone through many transformations since the death of its leader, Abdurajak Janjalani, in 1998, and has dropped many of its religious goals in favor of kidnapping for profit through ransom. It has been paid millions of dollars by various foreign governments whose citizens have been kidnapped in the Philippines. In 2001, Abu Sayyaf kidnapped 3 Americans and 17 Filipino nationals. During a rescue effort, two Americans and one Filipino were killed.[54]

Abu Sayyaf may have returned to its Islamic roots with the attack on *Superferry 14* in a bid to achieve dominance over the traditional regional terrorist groups in the region, including the Moro Islamic Liberation Front (MILF), a much larger Filipino separatist group seeking an independent state on the Philippine island of Mindanao. The other groups include the well-known Jemaah Islamiah (JI), notorious for the Bali Sheraton hotel bombing in October 2002 that killed 200 people. JI has yet to attack maritime targets but is suspected of having training camps on the southern Philippine island of Mindanao. The fact that neither JI nor MILF has as yet attacked maritime targets does not diminish their force as terrorist organizations in the region. As in the Caribbean, the absence of spectacular terrorist attacks in the Straits of Malacca or in other regions of Asia does not translate into zero risks for the cruise lines. However, there is one region where the acknowledged risks to the cruise lines seem understated. It is in this region that some of the most violent and evolving terrorist tactics have put maritime security forces to the test on a recurring basis over the past three decades. It is also a popular cruise ship destination.

ISRAEL AND THE MARITIME SECURITY THREAT

Israel is arguably the most security-conscious nation in the world. It has seen multiple attempts to breach its maritime borders and infrastructure and has withstood more attacks on its people, borders, and sovereignty than any other nation in modern times. Israel's response has been reactive in nature in view of the changing terrorist tactics and the measures necessary to repel the threats to its security. While the threat has remained constant, the tactics have evolved over time as terrorists have naturally migrated to attempts to exploit Israel's maritime borders.

The tactics used against Israel by its enemies have been adopted by other terrorist groups. Taking a page from history, for example, the terrorists who attacked the city of Mumbai, India, in 2008 used tactics perfected during the height of terrorist sieges on Israeli cities. The wave of maritime assaults on merchant shipping off the coast of Somalia by pirates involve the "mother ship" tactics first used to conduct raids on Israeli towns in the 1970s. Any discussion of maritime security and cruise ship security therefore would not be complete without an examination of the history of maritime attacks directed against the State of Israel by various factions of the Palestinian liberation movement, which include the Palestine Liberation Organization (PLO), the Palestine Liberation Front (PLF), the Palestinian Islamic Jihad (PIJ), and other well-known terrorist organizations that dominate the region, such as Hamas and Hezbollah. These groups, in addition to the newly arrived al-Qaeda, have all defined their common enemy as the democratic State of Israel and have professed their intent to destroy it. Attacks have included sea-launched raids on Israeli cities, attacks against shipping, and threats to Israeli cruise ships. The changing tactics have also included the first use of antiship cruise missiles by a terrorist group.

One of the methods used by Israel's opponents has been the use of maritime terror tactics launched from the sea and directed at both maritime and land-based targets in Israel. To be successful in carrying out maritime terrorist attacks, terrorist groups need to have considerable knowledge of and sophisticated training in maritime skills, extensive resources, and adequate funding. All of the groups listed have proved themselves capable of carrying out maritime attacks not only against Israel but also against other Western military and civilian maritime targets.

Since the first maritime terror incident in Israel, in 1953, more than 80 maritime plots have either been foiled or conducted against Israel. These plots carried the potential for the murder of innocent civilians, security forces, naval personnel, and foreign tourists. Attacks have ranged from small raids on Israeli towns and cities launched from the sea, to deliberate suicide attacks on vessels, to plots to blow up cruise ships in foreign ports.[55] It is little wonder, then, that no other nation has more experience than the State of Israel in facing the challenge of maritime terrorism and in confronting issues pertaining to maritime security on a constant and reoccurring basis. As the global jihad movement has closed in around Israel, the number of incidents has increased, making a study of the history of these events useful as we try to put into perspective current threats to cruise ships, the maritime and transportation sector, and even the hotel industry.

We begin in the early 1970s. Large concentrations of Palestinians were relocated and settled in the southern regions of Lebanon as a result of their expulsion from Jordan by King Hussein. The Palestinians were undermining the stability of Jordan and using it to launch attacks against Israel, leading to Israeli reprisals against Jordan, so Hussein expelled the PLO and many Palestinians to protect his throne. It was here that the Palestinian liberation movements had begun to gain power after the creation of the State of Israel in 1948. The Palestinians immediately started to develop strategies for attacking Israel; their goal was to destroy it and to establish the State of Palestine in its place. Israel's northern borders were relatively weak and undefended in 1970. The PLO did not see a need to develop maritime capabilities during this period because it could mount cross-border land attacks on Israel from Lebanon without having to circumvent or penetrate Israeli defenses. However, also during this time, the leader of the Popular Front for the Liberation of Palestine (PLFP), Dr. George Habash, saw the need to isolate Israel from the outside and proposed a new strategy to cripple Israel.[56] He noted that Israel was "an island"; he therefore saw a need to block all access by air and by sea.

In March 1973, the PLFP succeeded in sinking the chartered Greek passenger ship *Sanya* while it was in harbor at Beirut, Lebanon. The ship was supposed to sail for Haifa, Israel, with 250 American tourists on board, but a limpet mine attached to its hull exploded prematurely, before the ship had sailed. The

Palestinian Fatah party and the terrorist group Black September claimed responsibility, admitting that the ship was supposed to have been blown up when it
made port in Haifa.[57] Although the *Sanya* sank in Beirut harbor, no deaths resulted from this early act of maritime terrorism. The attack on the *Sanya* preceded
the events, later that year, of the October War, also known popularly as the Yom
Kippur War.

In October 1973, Egyptian and Syrian forces launched a surprise attack on Israel in the Golan Heights, the Sinai Peninsula, and Suez. Israel's mobilization and
its ability to repel the invaders in the face of overwhelming odds proved how effective the Israeli military could be. The failure of the Egyptian and Syrian forces
to defeat Israel pushed Egyptian leader Anwar Sadat to adopt a diplomatic approach and to seek peaceful coexistence with Israel. With the hope of destroying
Israel and recapturing lost land fading, Palestinians were encouraged to take more
extreme actions.[58] While on the diplomatic front the Camp David talks between Egypt and Israel took place, the actions of the PLO became more violent.

The PLO concentrated on efforts to conduct cross-border raids from southern Lebanon into Israel in order to kill or capture Israelis who could be used as
bargaining chips with the Israeli government for the release of captured PLO
fighters. In response, the northern border defenses were strengthened by the Israeli Defense Force (IDF), forcing the PLO to find another way into Israel. The
result was the first attack on Israel conducted from the sea, in June 1974. Three
Palestinian terrorists sailed in a small boat from southern Lebanon and landed
on the beach in Naharia, in northern Israel. The terrorists seized four Israeli hostages from an apartment building whom they subsequently killed before being
killed themselves in a gun battle with Israeli security forces.[59] Eight other civilians were wounded in the attack.

As a result of this incident, the Israelis recognized the significant vulnerability
of their maritime flank, and they immediately increased security measures, setting up permanent naval patrols, radar stations, and coastal lookouts. They also
introduced for the first time maritime security zones in the northern coastal area
and prohibited boating, civilian shipping, and even swimming in coastal waters.
These measures seemed to stem the threat of maritime guerrilla attacks launched
from southern Lebanon. Although terrorists continue to try to use this approach
to this day, the last successful attack was carried out in 1979 by the Palestine
Liberation Front (PLF), which landed several terrorists in Naharia in a rubber
boat; the terrorists murdered an Israeli father and his four-year-old daughter before being killed by Israeli police in a gun battle. Abu Abbas, the terrorist leader of
the PLF who would later mastermind the hijacking of the *Achille Lauro* in 1985,
said that the Naharia raid and murder were in protest against the Egyptian-Israeli
Camp David peace accords.

The PLO was still convinced of the potential for maritime terror attacks against Israel but needed to find a way around the Israeli maritime security measures centered on the northern border areas. They turned to a tactic that employed a so-called mother ship, a large, oceangoing vessel, to transport the terrorist fighters out to sea from ports in southern Lebanon; the terrorists would then come in from the west in small boats or rafts in Israel's blind spot (i.e., maritime borders) and attack Israel's larger metropolitan cities. This technique is currently used by the Somali pirates along the eastern coast of Africa; as we have described, it was used to attack the cruise ship *Seabourn Spirit* in November 2005 and in most other pirate attacks in the region.

Using the mother ship tactic, the PLO launched an attack on Tel Aviv on March 5, 1975, Eight terrorists were transported by ship from Lebanon; they were transferred to small boats and then preceded toward the beach in Tel Aviv. The terrorists immediately raided the Savoy Hotel and barricaded themselves inside along with 13 hostages while demanding the release of Palestinian prisoners being held in Israel. As the standoff continued, an Israeli commando unit was called in and attacked the terrorists early the next morning. A fierce gun battle erupted that resulted in the deaths of three soldiers and eight hostages. However, the commandos killed seven of the eight terrorists and captured one.[60] The plan for this attack was later used in the attack on several Mumbai hotels in November 2008.

The Tel Aviv attack was planned by the PLO to disrupt an upcoming visit by Dr. Henry Kissinger, then the U.S. Secretary of State, who was attempting to jumpstart peace negotiations between Israel and Egypt. The terror plot was designed to kill both Jews and non-Jews and was intended to raise the stature of Yasser Arafat, the leader of the PLO, in the eyes of his supporters on the eve of the peace talks. Propaganda prepared by Arafat's Fatah Party was to suggest that the attacks were launched from Fatah cells inside Israel to discredit the peace process. Details of the PLO plot became known, however, when the mother ship was captured by the Israeli Navy as it attempted to flee to Cyprus.

The use of mother ships to land terrorists on Israeli soil instilled fear in the Israeli population, which now felt that no place in their homeland was safe from the terrorists. Additionally, as a result of the attacks on the Savoy Hotel in Tel Aviv, Israel's hotel industry suffered greatly as bookings, primarily by foreign tourists, dropping off sharply. Once again, Israel had to develop defensive countermeasures to prevent future attacks led by terrorists who had reached Israeli land from the sea.

The Israeli high command was quick to realize the country's vulnerability to maritime attacks launched from the deep-sea regions of the Mediterranean and, as a result, increased naval patrols along the Mediterranean coasts of Lebanon and Israel. Israel also established coastal observation points similar to those that already existed on the northern border all along Israel's coastline, as well as beach reconnaissance to spot potential invaders. More important, it used IDF aircraft to patrol the eastern Mediterranean for suspicious vessels. These patrols eventually prevented several attacks before the terrorists could reach Israeli waters; for example, a terrorist speedboat headed toward Tel Aviv was intercepted by the Israeli Navy in September 1976.[61]

In March 1979, the Israeli Navy succeeded in capturing the PLO mother ships *Ginan* and *Stephanie*. But by far the worst mother ship attack occurred the preceding March, when 11 terrorists landed in Maagan Michael Beach, north of Tel Aviv, from two small boats launched from a mother ship. Once on the beach, they immediately killed an American photographer and six other people they encountered before seizing two buses. In the process, they took 70 Israeli hostages, mostly women and children. The resulting massacre, which became known as the Coastal Road attack, eventually killed 37 Israelis and wounded more than 70. It was one of the deadliest attacks to date on Israeli soil.[62]

The terrorists packed the hostages onto one of the hijacked buses and attempted to drive into Tel Aviv but were blocked by police. The terrorists exploded a hand grenade inside the bus, causing it to catch fire. The resulting gun battle killed nine of the terrorists, while two were captured. But, because the plot had originally included 13 terrorists, 2 of whom had drowned on stormy seas during the voyage from the mother ship to the shore, Israeli security officials became alerted to the possibility that two of the terrorists from the Coastal Road attack had escaped.[63] They called for a curfew in the area between Tel Aviv and Netanya, the first since 1968, to help them locate the missing terrorists. The curfew was suspended the following day when the total number of terrorists involved was determined. The attack is significant because of the tactics used and the indiscriminate killing that took place and the fact that the raid was led by Dalal al-Maghrabi, a Palestinian woman whom PLO leader Yasser Arafat later praised.[64]

The Coastal Road attack prompted Israel to launch offensive strikes inside Lebanon in 1978 to knock out PLO strongholds. But, despite its overwhelming power, the IDF was unable to effectively neutralize the Palestinian terror networks. The United Nations eventually stepped in to restore the peace in Lebanon and established the UN Interim Force in Lebanon (UNIFIL). The Israeli incursions into southern Lebanon were, however, able to drive the terrorists out of the immediate border areas, which motivated the PLO to return to finding maritime avenues to attack Israel. This time, they focused on the unguarded regions of the Red Sea and the Israeli port of Eilat.

In September 1978, Fatah planned to ram a 600-ton freighter into the pumping stations of the Eilat-Askhelon pipeline and also to destroy its oil tanks by firing Katyuska rockets into the port. The freighter was loaded with six tons of high explosives. The attack was planned to coincide with Rosh Hashanah (the Jewish New Year), when the beaches would be crowded with tourists. The keel of the vessel was rigged to detonate when it touched the sandy bottom of the beach. The vessel *Agius Demitrius* was outfitted in Lebanon and quickly came under surveillance by the Israeli Navy. It was intercepted after transiting the Suez Canal while sailing under a Cypriot flag. After capturing the ship's crew, the Israeli Navy sunk it in the Gulf of Suez.[65]

The decade of the 1980s and 1990s brought more maritime attacks against Israel launched from sea. The decade also saw some of the most violent action in the Middle East, especially in Lebanon because of the chaos of the Lebanese civil war that erupted in the late 1970s. Several new and innovative attempts were made to attack Israel, including an effort to invade the Israeli homeland from the sea by using jet skis and a drive to seize Israeli vessels on the high seas and hold their crews for hostage or murder. The 1980s also saw the first suicide attack on an Israeli naval vessel.

On April 25, 1988, a member of Ahmad Jibril's Popular Front for the Liberation of Palestine—General Command (PFLP-GC) sailed an explosive-laden boat near an Israeli coastal defense vessel and detonated it. The suicide bomber was killed, but there were only minor injuries on the Israeli vessel.[66] The PFLP-GC had split from the PFLP in 1968, claiming that it wanted to focus more on fighting and less on politics. It also opposed Arafat's PLO. Today, it is still led by Ahmad Jibril, a former captain in the Syrian Army. With close ties to both Syria and Iran, it carried out attacks in Europe and the Middle East during the 1970s and 1980s and is known for launching cross-border terrorist attacks into Israel using unusual methods, including hot-air balloons and motorized hang gliders. The suicide attack became a staple of the PFLP-GC, which carried numerous such attacks on Israeli naval vessels through the 1990s.

Israel endured the assaults on its sovereignty from terrorists and still has one of the most proactive maritime security defenses in the world. The number of assaults peaked in the late 1970s and continued into the 1980s, when suicide maritime attacks were introduced. The 1980s were marked particularly by one single maritime terrorist event that included the targeted killing of an elderly Jewish American man in a wheelchair on the deck of a cruise ship—the hijacking of the *Achille Lauro* in October 1985.

The hijacking of the *Achille Lauro* is notorious in the annals of terrorism and is relevant in every maritime security discussion. Apart from the hijacking of the Portuguese passenger ship *Santa Maria* in 1960 by Portuguese nationalists, the attack on the *Achille Lauro* represented the first hijacking of a modern cruise ship by terrorists and resulted in the execution of an American passenger. The incident is generally used both to dramatize the vulnerability of cruise ships to hijacking and to suggest that a similar event could not necessarily be repeated today.

THE HIJACKING OF THE CRUISE SHIP *ACHILLE LAURO*

Because of the security measures put in place by the ISPS Code and by the Maritime Transportation Security Act, the biggest problem terrorists would face today in planning to hijack a cruise ship would be finding a way to introduce a cache of weapons onto the ship that they could use in the hijacking attempt. This obstacle did not present any difficulties to the *Achille Lauro* hijackers. They essentially walked on board the ship with their weapons. There are, however, stark differences between today's cruise ship security practices and those in place in 1985. The *Achille Lauro* is relevant to today's discussion of maritime security mainly as a point of comparison for today's security measures. The details of the hijacking provide glimpses of the difficulties in overtaking a cruise liner by force and then controlling large numbers of hostages while attempting to negotiate terms, but we certainly do not suggest that such an attack could not occur today.

There is one distinct difference between the *Achille Lauro* hijacking (and the model for cruise ship security as it existed before September 11) and terrorism today that must remain in focus. While the objective of the *Achille Lauro* hijackers is still steeped in controversy, one thing is now clear—today's terrorists would not plan to just hijack the ship. Like the Palestinian terrorists who hijacked airliners in the 1980s, the *Achille Lauro* hijackers wanted to seize the vessel and take hostages for use in eventual prisoner exchanges. Today's terrorist groups are no longer interested in such motives. They would be content with nothing less than the death of the passengers and crew and the total destruction of the ship.[67] For that reason, a modern, updated security response is required.

The hijacking of the *Achille Lauro* represents the only cruise ship death at the hands of terrorists. Because the object of the hijacking was a cruise ship, the hijacking aroused new fears; cruise ships were something that the public did not usually associate with terrorism. The *Achille Lauro* hijacking had a symbolic as well as a substantive impact on the world and aroused serious concerns as to whether additional, similar attacks on cruise ships would take place.[68]

In the mid-1980s, international terrorism was rampant all over the world but especially in the Mediterranean region. The bombing of the U.S. Marine barracks in Beirut, Lebanon, in 1983, was perhaps the most shocking example of terrorism to hit the United States. In fact, in 1983 there were more than 500 incidents of terrorism, 200 of which were directed against Americans. Other events that year included the bombing of Harrods in London, the bombing at Orly Airport in Paris, the destruction of a Gulf-Air flight in the United Arab Emirates, and the Rangoon bombing of South Korean officials—not to mention a brutal attack on a West Jerusalem shopping mall.[69]

In 1985, the year that the *Achille Lauro* was hijacked, international terrorism reached a peak. On June 14, two Lebanese Shiite gunmen hijacked a TWA jetliner on an Athens-to-Rome flight with 104 Americans aboard and forced it to fly to Beirut. A U.S. Navy diver, Robert Dean Stethem, was killed by the terrorists. On June 19, a bomb exploded at Frankfurt's international airport that killed 3 and injured 42. The Arab Revolutionary Organization, which some experts believed to be part of the Palestinian group led by Abu Nidal, claimed responsibility.

On July 1, terrorists bombed a building that housed the offices of TWA and British Airways in Madrid, Spain. One person was killed and 27 were wounded. On August 8, a car bomb exploded at the U.S. Rhein-Main Air Base, near Frankfurt, killing 2 Americans and wounding 20 Americans and Germans. The attack was attributed to Direct Action and the Red Army Faction. On September 3, in Athens, Greece, two grenades were thrown into the lobby of a Greek hotel and wounded 18 British tourists. A telephone caller told a Greek newspaper that, unless an unidentified Palestinian was released, the Black September guerrilla group "would fill Athens with bombs."[70]

Cruise liners, or cruise ships, as they were then already known, had come into their own by the mid-1980s. While some of today's better-known cruise ship brands did not exist at the time of the *Achille Lauro* hijacking, the industry realized that it had a stake in the outcome of that event. There were dozens of independent cruise ship companies offering Mediterranean cruises to the public, and the Chandris Company was one such company that offered low-cost cruises throughout the region. By the time of the hijacking, the *Achille Lauro* itself was already a very old ship. An attempt to add it to the dying transatlantic crossing route in 1959 ended with its being sold, in 1964, to Lauro Lines, which renamed it the *Achille Lauro,* after the company's owner.

In 1972, the passenger liner became a full-time cruise ship, but in the late 1970s it was impounded because of the company's financial troubles. It finally came back to life when Lauro Lines, as part of an agreement with Chandris Lines, began to offer Mediterranean cruises.[71] On October 3, 1985, some 750 passengers boarded the cruise ship for a 12-day cruise, calling at ports such as Naples, Italy; Alexandria, Egypt; Port Said, Egypt; Ashdod, Israel; Limassol, Cyprus; and Rhodes, Greece.

Leon and Marilyn Klinghoffer planned to celebrate their 38th wedding anniversary when they booked the cruise vacation along with several of their neighbors from Long Branch, New Jersey. Leon Klinghoffer, a 69-year-old retired merchant, had suffered two strokes that had confined him to a wheelchair. His wife, Marilyn, was 58 years old and had been recently diagnosed with cancer and given a year to live. These life realities had prompted the couple to book the cruise to spend as much time together as possible on one last vacation. Their cruise on the *Achille Lauro* began during an ominous time in the Mediterranean. Two days before the cruise, Israel had launched a long-range air strike against PLO headquarters in Tunis, Tunisia, killing more than 73 people and wounding about 100 others. Israel's strike was believed to be in retaliation for an attack by PLO terrorists in Larnaca, Cyprus, that had killed three Israelis. However, Israel claimed that the attack was part of a larger war on terror.[72]

The four hijackers on board the ship were quickly noticed by the other passengers and the crew, not because people thought they were possible terrorists but because they kept to themselves and did not display the friendly behavior normally associated with embarking on a cruise vacation. Some passengers tried to interact with the four young men, who claimed they were from Argentina. When one female passenger tried to strike up a conversation in Spanish, the hijackers seemed not to understand anything she said. In fact, the four hijackers had boarded the ship with forged passports from Norway, Argentina, and Portugal.

Boarding a cruise ship was not the rigorous process that it is today. If nothing else, the *Achille Lauro* hijacking demonstrated how easy it was for terrorists to penetrate whatever security measures were then in place. All that one had to do to buy a ticket was to present some form of identification. There was no cross-check of identities against the purchaser's passport or any effort to determine the validity of the passport presented. In fact, it was later discovered that one hijacker had simply glued his photo into his forged passport. There were other deficiencies in shipboard security that helped the hijackers carry out their plot, as well.

Cruise line officials acknowledged at the time that security precautions at the ports and aboard cruise ships lagged far behind those used at airports. At the time of the hijacking, there were no security regulations in the maritime industry that corresponded to those issued by the Federal Aviation Administration after the spate of airline hijackings in the 1960s and 1970s. According to one official, security measures on shipping lines consisted basically of limiting access to the ship to passengers with tickets and guests who registered when they went on board. Also, there was no screening of luggage as there is today. Unlike at airports, no x-ray or metal detection equipment was in use at ports or on the ships.[73] Several passengers later claimed there was no security screening on the ship when they boarded. But the lax security would hardly have mattered to the terrorists. They had planned their operation in detail for at least 10 months before they seized the ship, which refuted the idea, pushed by some observers, that the hijacking was in retaliation for the attack on Tunis.

According to documents that were uncovered after the incident, the goal of the terrorists was an attack on the Israeli port of Ashdod. One of the terrorists,

Masar Kadia, aka Petros Floros, aka Abdel Rahim Khaled, took at least two cruises on the *Achille Lauro* to conduct preoperational planning. Posing as a Greek shipping magnate under the name Petros Floros and accompanied on at least one of these trips by Magied al Molqi, the man who would lead the hijacking, he conducted these scouting trips to, among other things, survey the layout of the ship, assess security measures, note meal times and the normal activities of passengers and crew, and evaluate the relative competence and aggressiveness of specific crew members and the likely response of the ship's captain and crew.

On September 28, accomplices smuggled four Kalashnikov (AK-47) automatic rifles, eight hand grenades, and nine detonators abroad the Tunis-to-Genoa ferry, the *Habib*. These were then carried aboard the *Achille Lauro* by the four hijackers in their uninspected baggage on October 3, 1985, the same day the Klinghoffers boarded the ship.[74]

Although Israeli Intelligence had warned the intelligence services of Italy and several other friendly governments more than six months before the hijacking that terrorist groups were training to hijack a ship, Israeli Intelligence could not identify a target or a specific terrorist organization.[75] Before, during, and after the hijacking, the identity and affiliation of the hijackers was always in question. The hijackers later claimed to be part of the PLF, but, because the PLF was a generic term that covered three different and conflicting factions, their affiliation was never clearly established during the negotiations that ended the incident.

It was important to know the hijackers' identities because they could be expected to react quite differently to an attack by rescuers depending on whether or not they were supporters of Yasser Arafat's Palestine Liberation Organization (PLO). Two of the PLF factions were opposed to Arafat and were trying to get rid of him, whereas the third faction, led by Mohammed Abbas (alias Abu Abbas), remained loyal to Arafat. Abbas's group, which actually seized the *Achille Lauro*, had conducted seven major actions in the period 1978–1983, all of which involved attempts to take hostages and all but one of which involved attempts to infiltrate Israel. U.S. intelligence agencies guessed that the hijackers were probably opposed to the PLO and that the hijackers were probably making their way to Ashdod when something happened on board the ship that caused them to seize command.[76]

On day five of the cruise, when the ship docked in Alexandria, Egypt, most passengers disembarked and proceeded overland to tour the pyramids. They were scheduled to reboard the ship a day later when the ship arrived in Port Said, at the mouth of the Suez Canal. The next scheduled port after Port Said was Ashdod, the alleged target. The large number of passengers that disembarked in Alexandria left only 97 passengers of varying nationalities and more than 350 crew members, mostly Italian and Portuguese, on board. Whether the hijackers were

really discovered cleaning their weapons in their cabin by a steward, as is popularly believed, is still a matter of conjecture.

Whatever their motives for acting when they did, the terrorists stormed the
ship's dining room and fired their automatic weapons. They immediately demanded to speak to the ship's captain, Gerardo de Rosa. They threatened to kill
the passengers if the captain did not do what they told him. Incredibly, the crew
was allowed to return to running the ship after the captain agreed that he and his
crew would cooperate. The terrorists, meanwhile, held all the passengers in the
ship's dining room.

One passenger, however, a 53-year-old Austrian woman, was able to escape
the initial hostage taking by the terrorists in the dining room and hid in the
bathroom of an unoccupied cabin. Amazingly, she was found there, still hiding,
15 hours after the hijacking ended.[77] The hijackers used the ship's radio to demand that Israel release PLF prisoners it was holding. Then the ship simply disappeared into the Mediterranean. The hijackers were able to disable the ship's
transponder.

While out to sea, the hijackers asked the hostages if there were any Jews in the
group. Two elderly Austrians raised their hands and were immediately roughed
up and beaten by the terrorists. Seeing this, the Klinghoffers remained silent.
Later the hijackers divided the group and herded the 2 Jewish Austrians and the
15 Americans, including the Klinghoffers, onto an open deck and surrounded
them with gasoline and hand grenades. They told the captain that if a rescue attempt was made they would instantly kill the group.[78]

Because Leon Klinghoffer was confined to a wheelchair, the hijackers had
trouble moving him and his wheelchair up the steep deck ladders. Some of the
passengers later said that the terrorists were annoyed by Mr. Klinghoffer's slurred
speech and his slow acknowledgement of their demands. Whatever the reasons,
they took him, over protests from Marilyn Klinghoffer, to the ship's fantail. It was
the last time Marilyn Klinghoffer saw her husband alive. According to eyewitness
accounts by the crew, the oldest hijacker shot Leon Klinghoffer in the forehead
and then in the chest at point-blank range. Two crew members were then ordered
to dump his body, still in his wheelchair, over the side of the ship.[79]

After the ship was denied permission to make port in Syria by the Syrian government, the ship returned to Egypt. The hijacking ended soon after that. With
the ship anchored off Port Said, on October 9, Egyptian negotiators persuaded
the hijackers to leave the ship. They were promised free passage if, the negotiators said, no one on the ship had been harmed. Captain de Rosa spoke to the
negotiators and assured them that no one had been harmed even though he had
seen the blood-splattered shoes and pants of the hijackers after they had killed
Leon Klinghoffer. With that, the hijackers departed the ship under the custody

of the Egyptians, touching off an international standoff that involved the U.S. government, the Italian Prime Minister, the Egyptians, and Yasser Arafat over the fate of the hijackers.[80] Amazingly, after the departure of hijackers, the cruise ship company and the captain wanted to continue the cruise, as if nothing had happened. The ship, however, remained in Egyptian custody while the Egyptians proceeded with their investigation of the incident.

All of the hijackers were eventually captured. The alleged leader and mastermind of the hijacking was the pro-Arafat Abu Abbas. Arafat later tried to distance himself from Abbas. Years later, in 2003, Abu Abbas himself was captured by U.S. forces in Iraq at a PLF training base where he had fled and was attempting to live in anonymity. He once told reporters that the *Achille Lauro* hijacking was a mistake that led to other mistakes. He died in U.S. captivity in Iraq in March 2004, apparently of natural causes.[81]

Leon Klinghoffer's body later washed ashore in Syria. It was returned to the United States, and he was buried near his hometown in New Jersey. His family filed a $1.5 billion lawsuit against the PLO in a U.S. District Court. Although the case was never brought to trial because the federal district judge declared that the PLO was not a sovereign state, Yasser Arafat eventually settled with the daughters of Leon and Marilyn Klinghoffer for an undisclosed amount.[82]

Shortly after the *Achille Lauro* hijacking, another terrorist attack occurred in the Mediterranean. On November 23, in Athens, an Egyptian airliner was hijacked while flying from Athens to Cairo and forced to land in Malta. Five passengers were shot by the hijackers, two of them fatally, including one American. In Cairo, Egyptian police later stormed the plane, and 58 more people were killed. The hijackers said they were members of a group called Egypt's Revolution, but Abu Nidal's Arab Revolutionary Command and the Organization of Egypt's Revolutionaries also issued statements taking responsibility.[83]

The *Achille Lauro* itself never outgrew its reputation as a cursed ship. The infamous ship came to a tragic end when it caught fire on November 30, 1994, off the coast of Somalia in the Indian Ocean. Three passengers died in the blaze, while 1,900 others were transferred onto a rescue ship. The *Achille Lauro* eventually sank three days later, on December 2, exactly 47 years to the day after its maiden voyage. That left only the legacy of the *Achille Lauro* hijacking to debate.

While there was speculation that the hijacking of the ship itself was unplanned, the terrorists' aim, at least after the ship was seized, was to capture hostages. The hijacking made clear the difficulties of controlling large numbers of passengers with a limited number of terrorists, but, as demonstrated by the September 11 hijackers, even that obstacle did not stop terrorists determined to carry out their plot. The September 11 hijackers were not seeking to hold the passengers as bargaining chips in a negotiation; after the terrorists locked themselves in the

Photo of the Italian cruise ship *Achille Lauro* sailing for home after its weeklong ordeal at the hands of PLO hijackers in the Mediterranean in 1985. One wheelchair-bound American passenger, Leon Klinghoffer, was shot to death by the hijackers, and his body was dumped overboard. Security measures on cruise ships were strengthened by the IMO after the incident. (AP photo)

cockpits of the planes, the passengers were not a factor. A ship's environment is infinitely more complicated than that of an airplane, however.

For a mere four hijackers to seize and hold a multideck cruise ship, full of passageways and hidden service conduits, with close to 100 passengers and 350 crew members proves how daring the hijackers were—or how unprepared they were for such an operation. More remarkable was that they let the 350 crew members go on with their duties, which revealed an obvious flaw in the hijackers' plan. Any one of the crew members could have led a revolt, but the captain had given his word that his crew would cooperate, and he was doing what he thought best for all the souls on board his ship. Also, the success of the Austrian passenger in evading capture illustrates the problems the terrorists faced in controlling their hostages. It may also explain why the hijackers waited until after the ship had unloaded more than 600 passengers for a sightseeing tour to seize the ship. Finally, because the ship "disappeared" on several occasions on the high seas because its transponder was disabled, the press could not cover the unfolding drama the way it had covered the earlier TWA hijacking in Beirut. The so-called CNN effect did not serve the PLO's cause in the case of the *Achille Lauro* hijacking. The CNN effect is defined as "the impact of worldwide television news broadcasts on government decision-making in crises and wars. The ubiquity and timeliness of broadcasts by the Cable News Network (CNN) and other television news services can influence, for good or ill, the assessment of the intentions and capabilities of one potential or actual belligerent by another."[84]

The hijacking, like the airline hijackings of the mid-1980s, revealed the vulnerability of modern transport to terrorism. After the hijacking, the IMO used the *Achille Lauro* incident to model security provisions for cruise ships in a forerunner of the ISPS Code unveiled in 2004. Probably the greatest lesson that should be learned from the *Achille Lauro* hijacking is that, although the lapses in security that led to the hijacking have been addressed through such measures as the ISPS Code, new vulnerabilities have emerged. The terrorists' goals have evolved from mere hostage taking operations to suicide attacks whose goal is the complete destruction of the target and the deaths of as many people as possible. These are harsh realities for cruise ship security planners. Like the kamikaze attacks of World War II, such tactics are hard to defend against.

The cruise industry has become complacent because no hijacking like that of the *Achille Lauro* has occurred in the ensuing decades. However, as the Rand Corporation succinctly said at the time of the incident, "To view the seizing of the [*Achille Lauro*] cruise liner as an 'isolated incident unlikely to recur' would not only be wishful thinking, but also potentially dangerous thinking if it prevents the maritime community from becoming more attentive to the threat of terrorism."[85] Two decades later, something much worse than a simple hijacking was planned for a whole fleet of cruise ships. Remarkably, it is one of the least-known stories of cruise ship terrorism.

THE TERRORIST PLOT TO ATTACK ISRAELI CRUISE SHIPS

In early August 2005, in the coastal resort town of Antalya, Turkey, an explosion ripped through the night, spewing a fabricated improvised explosive device and what remained of Lu'ai Sakra's kitchen into the streets. Sakra was arrested several days later trying to flee Turkey and was charged with belonging to an illegal organization. As Sakra left the courthouse in Istanbul, he shouted: "I was planning an attack in open seas. Allah akbar, Allah akbar" (Arabic for "God is great").[86] Loa'i Mohammad Haj Bakr al-Saqa, otherwise known as Lu'ai Sakra, was a dedicated al-Qaeda terrorist who had taken it upon himself to wage a jihad against the United States and Israel. His plan to attack Israeli cruise ships in a Turkish port was less than 48 hours from implementation and would have been the deadliest attack on passenger cruise ships had it been carried out. It was uncovered purely by accident.

Al-Qaeda operative Lu'ai Sakra is arrested in Turkey. He confessed to planning to load high explosives on speed boats and crash them into Israeli cruise ships docked in Turkish ports. The attack was planned for August 5, 2005. Sakra was also one of the planners of the British Consulate bombing in Istanbul in November 2003. The explosives used in that attack, which killed 18 people and injured hundreds, were meant for Israeli cruise ships but were diverted to Istanbul when the cruise ships canceled their Turkish port call due to bad weather. (AP photo)

Excluding passenger ferries and river cruise boats, which have been attacked with deadly frequency by terrorists and nationalists in Egypt, Greece, Turkey, and the Philippines, if someone were to tell you that the only terrorist attack against a cruise ship was the case of the *Achille Lauro* in 1985, the person would be technically correct. However, this does not take into account that other cruise ships have been targeted for terrorist operations and criminal plots. In 1961, the Portuguese passenger liner *Santa Maria* was hijacked off the coast of Brazil by Portuguese nationalists.[87] The nationalists, led by a prominent political foe of Portugal's premier, Antonio de Oliverio Salazar, were among the ship's 600 passengers and took command of the ship after a gun battle in which one police officer was killed and several wounded. The United States was able to negotiate an end to the weeklong crisis after which more than 560 hostages were eventually released unharmed.

In 1972, a terrorist plot to hijack an Italian passenger ship sailing between Cyprus and Israel was foiled, and, in 1973, an American citizen was convicted of attempting to extort $250,000 from Princess Cruises by threatening to blow up one of its cruise ships at sea.[88] As previously discussed, also in 1973, the PFLP placed a mine on the passenger ship *Sanya*, a Greek charter ship carrying 250 U.S. tourists to Israel. The mine exploded prematurely, and the ship sank in Beirut harbor. Fortunately, there were no casualties.

Only with the capture of the al-Qaeda mastermind who had engineered the successful attacks on the USS *Cole* and the *MV Limburg* did we learn about other plots to attack cruise ships such as the *Queen Mary 2*. From the terrorist's point of view, the measure of his success is how much death and destruction he can cause. In the absence of terrorist attacks like those seen in Israel on a recurring basis, the West can measure its successes only by the number of attacks that have been prevented. Interestingly, in the case of Lu'ai Sakra, in a testament to his determination, the Syrian-born al-Qaeda-inspired operative came close to bombing Israeli cruise ships—not once but twice—and failed. As is now known, this same terrorist had planned to attack an Israeli cruise ship two years earlier but diverted those bombs to Istanbul, where they were used in the deadly bombing of the British Consulate in November 2003.

During the trial of the suspects in the 2003 Istanbul bombing, the accused terrorists admitted that their original target was an Israeli cruise ship in the Mediterranean. The terror group had loaded a truck with 30 bags of ammonium nitrate-fuel slurry (known as ANFO) and 10 five-kilogram boxes of explosives connected to a detonator that was to be controlled by a suicide driver.[89] In November 2003, the suicide bomber was sent to the Mediterranean port of Antalya, Turkey, where he waited for eight days for an Israeli cruise ship to dock. When the cruise ship failed to call at the port of Antalya due to bad weather, the suicide bomber returned to Istanbul, where he attacked the British Consulate, killing 18 people, including the British Consul General. One hundred others were severely wounded.[90] Five days prior to this event, two trucks carrying bombs slammed into the Bet Israel and Neve Shalom synagogues in Istanbul and exploded. The explosions devastated the synagogues and killed 27 people, most of them Turkish Muslims, and injured more than 300 others. Six Jews were among the dead. Turkish authorities said the same groups were behind all three attacks.[91] Had Sakra's original plan to blow up the five Israeli cruise ships in 2005, which were carrying more than 5,000 Israeli tourists been successful, the consequences would have been devastating.

Shortly after the explosion at Sakra's safe house in Antalya, in 2005, one cruise ship carrying more than 1,600 Israeli passengers toward Turkey was immediately diverted to Cyprus because of unspecified security concerns reported by the Israeli security services. Several days earlier, the Israeli government had ordered four other Israeli cruise ships carrying more than 3,500 people to Turkish ports to change course for Cyprus, citing a specific security threat in Turkey.[92] On August 6, Lu'ai Sakra was arrested, and the plot to attack cruise ships began to unravel. What is alarming is that neither Western intelligence nor any of its security services had detected the potentially deadly plots prior to Sakra's arrest.

Were Sakra's plans to attack cruise ships in Antalya a serious threat or the delusions of a frustrated terrorist who had 16 devoted friends? His subsequent interrogations have revealed startling revelations that allegedly link Sakra to the CIA, Osama bin Laden, Abu Musab al-Zarqawi, and Turkish and Syrian intelligence agencies. It is rumored that the confessed terrorist had advance knowledge of the 9/11 attacks, as well as the London and Madrid bombings. From all indications, one point is clear: not only was Lu'ai Sakra intent on killing Israelis and Americans on cruise ships, but he was willing to die in the process. According to the Turkish authorities who captured him, he may be one of the five most important members of al-Qaeda. Just who was Lu'ai Sakra, and how did he come within 48 hours of attacking cruise ships with 5,000 tourists on board?

Lu'ai Sakra at the time of his arrest was 32 years old. He was a Syrian national, born Loa'i Mohammad Haj Bakr al-Saqa. Lu'ai Sakra also used aliases: Lian bin Mohammed Saka, Abu Mohammed al-Suri, Abu Haya al-Suri, and Ala al-Din. Born in Aleppo, in Syria's north, Sakra was the son of successful factory owner. Sakra forsook a "rich life" for the struggles of radical Islam. Shortly before September 11, 2001, Sakra lived in a southern German town under the name of Louia Sakka, and he still has family in the Black Forest region. Sakra applied for asylum in Germany, but his application was rejected.[93] This prompted him to take his family out of Germany and to refocus his life on his terrorist ambitions.

On July 24, 2001, Sakra apparently went underground. His family flew from Germany to Damascus, Syria. On September 10, 2001—one day before the attacks in the United States—Sakra allegedly told the Syrian secret service that al-Qaeda planned attacks on America that would occur in the near future. Sakra gave vague details of "Operation Holy Tuesday," in which planes would be used as weapons and towers as targets.[94] The Syrians passed this information to the CIA immediately after September 11. The CIA was skeptical at first but soon started to look for Sakra.[95] For the Mossad (the Israeli intelligence agency) and the CIA, Lu'ai Sakra became one of the most wanted men in the world. German authorities, meanwhile, came to realize that they had possibly let a top member of al-Qaeda who had lived in the Black Forest area slip through their hands.

It is unclear when Sakra crossed paths with Abu Musab al-Zarqawi, al-Qaeda's leader in Iraq, but a Jordanian court convicted both men in absentia for plotting to attack an Amman hotel, as well as border crossings and Christian tourist sites in Jordan, during the celebration of the millennium. Zarqawi opposed the presence of U.S. and Western military forces in the Islamic world, as well as the West's support for and the existence of Israel. By 2003, Turkish prosecutors say, Sakra was planning the bombings of two synagogues, the British Consulate, and a British bank in Istanbul over two days in November that year. Although the attacks were originally aimed at Israeli cruise ships, Turkish authorities said that Sakra "proposed" the attacks, with specific approval from both Zarqawi and Osama bin Laden. Testimony in the mass trial of more than 70 Turks charged in the case indicated that Sakra provided all the funds for the attacks and allegedly cheered when they were carried out.[96]

Sakra arrived in Fallujah, Iraq, in March 2004 and helped fight against the U.S. Marines in their first attempt to take the city, in April of that year. He became one of Zarqawi's lieutenants and helped attack Abu Ghraib prison, where among the inmates were some of the Istanbul bombers. After the second U.S. Marine attack on Fallujah was successful, in November 2004, al-Qaeda allegedly convened a war council, where Sakra again proposed attacking Israeli cruise ships in Turkey, not only because there would be large numbers of Israeli citizens to murder but because he believed that U.S. soldiers from Iraq used the ships to go on "R&R."[97]

After faking his death in Fallujah and having plastic surgery to alter his face, Sakra returned to Turkey. According to Sakra's interrogation transcript, his mission to attack the Israeli cruise ships was financed by Taliban chief Mullah Omar, who allegedly gave him $50,000.[98] Once in Antalya, Sakra quickly prepared for his attack. Using the money given to him by Mullah Omar, he surveyed neighborhoods in Antalya, looking for an apartment with a good view of the harbor. He prepaid the rent on a villa close to the water and with a view of the harbor. He also bought a 27-foot yacht, the *Tufan,* which he kept at the marina near his apartment.

The yacht was equipped with diving equipment and a submersible water scooter that had the capability to run for 45 minutes at depths of up to 75 feet. Conducting his preoperational planning, he spent many days chatting with Israeli tourists about the cruise ships that called on the Turkish coastal town. Not wanting to suffer another failure like the one he had had in 2003 because of the unpredictability of the cruise ships' schedules, he learned the precise arrival times and routes of the cruise ships he planned to attack. Sakra spent the remainder of his time building a bomb. Allegedly, Sakra had learned bomb making in Iraq. He needed a pressurized cooker to distill hydrogen to increase its potency. A local metal worker in town who provided him with the cooker thought he might be producing drugs.[99]

Sakra had intended to finish assembling the bomb on his boat two days before the attack, but he was in the process of assembling the last stages of his bomb in his kitchen when something happened. His apartment held 200 pounds of aluminum powder, 1,000 pounds of hydrogen, and 13 pounds of C-4 plastic explosives. How the fire started is unclear, but it ended in a small explosion that set fire to the apartment. Fearing discovery, Sakra and another accomplice immediately hurried from the scene and took a taxi to Diyarbakir, Turkey, and booked a domestic flight to Istanbul. Sakra got as far as the police check at the airport, where he surrendered to police officers who found his ID suspicious. "I'm the one you're looking for," he allegedly told the police.[100]

As Sakra was brought into the courthouse in Istanbul, he told reporters that he had been prepared to attack NATO warships in the area if he had been unable to locate the Israeli passenger ships. "I have no regrets," Sakra shouted to journalists from a window after he was led into the courthouse. "I was going to attack Israeli ships. If they come, my friends will attack them. . . . I had prepared a ton of explosives."[101]

It is alarming to those charged with the security of cruise ships and to the maritime industry in general that Sakra was apprehended because of a bomb-making accident that he himself caused. As the maritime industry quickly braced for a new wave of terrorism directed against cruise ships, a shiver went through the maritime underwriting industry in London, which debated immediately raising the insurance rates for cruise ships.[102]

Although Western intelligence knew who Sakra was, it believed that he had died in Iraq a year earlier. Taking into account his failure in November 2003, it is unclear where Sakra actually found his inspiration to attack cruise ships and why he was so fixated on them. He may have been taking his lead from Abdul al-Rahim al-Nashiri, al-Qaeda's so-called admiral, who had been captured two years earlier and charged with masterminding the attacks on the USS *Cole* and the *MV Limburg*. Those attacks propelled al-Nashiri to instant fame and status within al-Qaeda. Lu'ai Sakra was perhaps trying to emulate the brilliant terrorist attacks on maritime shipping as a way to improve his own standing in al-Qaeda. Whatever Sakra's motivation, al-Qaeda clearly has come to appreciate maritime terrorist operations. Al-Nashiri, its most famous maritime terrorist, had carried out a successful maritime offensive in the Middle East before he too was captured.

MARITIME TERROR IN THE MIDDLE EAST

A year before the attacks on New York and Washington, D.C., in September 2001, 17 American sailors were killed when a small boat loaded with explosives detonated against the side of the USS *Cole* on October 12, 2000. From the very beginning, the FBI suspected that the attack was the work of Osama bin Laden and al-Qaeda.

I served for a time on annual reserve training with the Naval Criminal Investigative Service (NCIS) at Fifth Fleet Headquarters in Bahrain a couple of weeks after the attack on the USS *Cole*. Upon arrival at the NCIS Middle East Field Office in Bahrain, I was briefed on the investigation of the attack on the USS *Cole* and on what was known or, more precisely, unknown. Though it appeared that the investigation would be a lengthy one, as it turned out the lead FBI agent lasted only a month at the U.S. embassy in Yemen before being asked to leave by the U.S. ambassador. Underlying political wrangling behind the scenes was overshadowing a much more serious threat to U.S. personnel.

There was no question that a strained relationship between the FBI and the Department of State had developed over the FBI's conduct and mission in Yemen after the terrorist attack. This was a result of the dissention between then U.S. ambassador, Barbara Bodine, and the lead FBI agent, John O'Neil. The FBI was called to investigate the deadliest terrorist attack on a maritime target in U.S. history. Although the FBI had investigated the Khobar Towers bombing in Saudi Arabia in 1996, it had never deal with the challenges of investigating a maritime terrorist act under these circumstances and threat conditions. The FBI wanted the means to protect its personnel while conducting the investigation of the *Cole* bombing.

The U.S. ambassador and the special agent sent by the FBI to lead the investigation clashed constantly over protocol issues and spent crucial time at the beginning of the investigation debating such issues as whether FBI agents could carry weapons in Yemen. The ambassador thought that openly armed FBI agents running around Yemen would damage U.S.-Yemeni relations. A compromise was later worked out that allowed some of the FBI agents to act as bodyguards for the other FBI personnel assigned to the investigation.[103] Backing up the gun-carrying FBI agents were the diplomatic security special agents, called in from the United States and from U.S. embassies around the world.

Years later, in 2002, after serving at the U.S. embassies in Moscow and Beirut, I was chosen to fill a gap as the regional security officer (RSO) at the U.S. embassy in Sana'a, Yemen. I arrived at the embassy in Sana'a in mid-2002, shortly after the FBI had vacated its spaces and returned home at the end of its investigative effort into the USS *Cole* bombing. On the basis of what I learned later, I believe that I was perhaps lucky not to be at the embassy when the FBI was there. Its officials really had a difficult job and were not welcome at the embassy.

In the summer of 2002, to add to my concerns as the RSO at the U.S. embassy in Yemen, our country-team meetings had surfaced reports of al-Qaeda's interest in attacking other maritime targets in the Gulf of Aden. This was perhaps a reflection of the intelligence community's tendency to be overly cautious, considering what had happened in the port of Aden two years previous. There was a feeling that any terrorist threat, no matter what its level of credibility, was "put out there," just in case something actually happened in the future. If a terrorist attack occurred that was remotely linked to the previous intelligence reports, the intelligence community could say, "We told you so."

The attack on the USS *Cole*, like the later September 11 attacks, caught the intelligence community completely off guard. Although no one knew it at the time and while no target was mentioned, these maritime threats reports actually referred to the attack that would eventually take place against the *MV Limburg* several months later, in October 2002, in the Gulf of Aden. But few in the embassy in Yemen paid attention to the maritime intelligence being reported. There were more pressing threats to the embassy itself. Al-Qaeda was apparently threatening a possible suicide attack on our embassy building.[104]

Soon after I arrived in Sana'a, an explosion occurred in an al-Qaeda safe house in an apartment building near the embassy. I was called, along with the other security representatives at the embassy, including an NCIS special agent, to investigate the bomb scene. Two al-Qaeda terrorists had been killed while tinkering with an antitank rocket when the shape-charge of the bomb went off, setting fire to the unfinished apartment. Their badly burned bodies had been removed from the safe house by the time we arrived, and we were given an opportunity to conduct the post-blast investigation.

A large amount of TNT and plastic explosives was found in the safe house, along with AK-47s and armor-piercing rounds as well as the antitank rockets. There was only one target in all of Yemen at the time against which these weapons and ammunition could be used with any effectiveness; that target was the American embassy's armored vehicles.

A small group from the embassy, including myself, was invited by the Yemeni government to view the cache of explosive and weapons found in the safe house. The almost 300 pounds of explosives had been smuggled into Sana'a in crates with false tops filled with pomegranate fruit. As I surveyed the crates of explosives that filled the small Yemeni police office, our group from the U.S. embassy was told that they represented only half of the explosives used to cripple the USS *Cole*. The antitank rockets found in the safe house had implications for the *Cole* bombing, as well, because their shape-charges had been used in that attack to penetrate the ship's hull. Staring at this small arsenal of munitions and relying on my own knowledge of the *Cole* investigation, I reflected on the maritime implications of that operation, which had taken place two years earlier.

In 1998, the Yemeni-born Abdul al-Rahim al-Nashiri joined al-Qaeda. He was quickly tasked by Osama bin Laden with exploring the idea of attacking oil tankers off the coast of Yemen. But, as the difficulties of such an operation became apparent to the terrorist, his focus shifted to the U.S. naval warships, which took a little more than four hours to refuel in the port of Aden. In 1999, al-Nashiri began to put together an attack plan against a U.S. warship in port for a refueling stop. Relying on their intelligence about an upcoming refueling stop by the U.S. Navy warship USS *The Sullivans*, al-Nashiri and his accomplices hastily loaded a small boat acquired from Saudi Arabia with explosives.

On January 3, 2000, al-Nashiri and his team brought the boat to the harbor after receiving word of the arrival of the USS *The Sullivans*. Shortly after the launch, the boat sank in shallow water because of the large amount of explosives on board. The unsuspecting USS *The Sullivans* had come and gone from the port of Aden without incident, not knowing how close it had come to being attacked by al-Qaeda. What al-Nashiri had learned, however, in the failed attempt on the U.S. warship was that a rehearsal is an essential part of the successful outcome of any terrorist operation.[105]

Over the summer of 2000, al-Nashiri and his team salvaged the boat in Aden's harbor. With the lessons learned from their previous attempt, they refitted the small boat and resupplied it with fresh explosives. A new safe house that over-looked the port of Aden was acquired. Remarkably, the operation was still a complete secret from Western intelligence. Through al-Nashiri's own intelligence network in the port of Aden, he received word that the USS *Cole* would be arriving for a fuel stop in October.

On October 12, 2000, al-Nashiri transported the boat from the safe house to the harbor on a trailer and launched it into the water. Shortly after 11:00 A.M., the two suicide terrorists on board the boat waved and smiled at the sailors on the decks of the USS *Cole* as they approached the ship. The sailors believed that the small boat was part of the refueling services provided by the port and even waved back to the two terrorists. The resulting explosion struck amidships near where the ship's galley was located. Many sailors were lining up for the midday meal when the explosion ripped through the ship. The 500 pounds of TNT and C-4 funneled through a shape-charge tore a 40-foot hole in the ship's single hull at the water line on the port side. The explosion killed 17 sailors and injured dozens more. Swift damage control efforts by the crew saved the ship from foundering in the 1,800-foot-deep water.[106]

Because of the success of the USS *Cole* attack, al-Nashiri was instantly promoted within al-Qaeda and followed his success with a similar attack on the French oil tanker *Limburg* on October 6, 2002. Like the hijacking of the *Achille Lauro* 15 years earlier, which became a wake-up call for the cruise ship industry, the attack on the USS *Cole* was a wake-up call for the Navy as it considered the possibility of maritime terrorism directed against warships. Al-Nashiri's plans to attack other U.S. warships in the Strait of Gibraltar in the Mediterranean were frustrated by the U.S. Navy's hardening of its force-protection measures.

Port-side view showing the damage sustained by the *Arleigh Burke* class destroyer USS *Cole* DDG 67 on October 12, 2000, after a terrorist bomb exploded during a refueling stop in the port of Aden, Yemen. Seventeen U.S. sailors were killed in the attack. Abdul al-Rahim al-Nashiri, al-Qaeda's "prince of the sea," was later found to have planned the suicide bombing after failing to attack the USS *The Sullivans* in the port of Aden months earlier. (Official Department of Defense photo)

These measures may have inadvertently placed cruise ships higher up on the terrorists' target list. Because Navy ships were now utilizing stricter defensive measures against terrorist acts, al-Nashiri was forced to concentrate his efforts on "soft targets" such as cruise ships and other merchant shipping. Shortly before his capture by U.S. forces, in November 2002, al-Nashiri intended to use divers and swimmer delivery vehicles (SDVs) to attack ships and offshore installations. His plan called for al-Qaeda operatives to either plant explosives on the hull of a merchant ship that would be steered as a floating bomb or to use the SDVs, loaded with sealed explosives, to function as an "underwater suicide bomber."[107]

Al-Nashiri was captured by the United States in November 2002, shortly after the attack on the *MV Limburg*. He has been held at Guantanamo Naval Base as an enemy combatant since 2006. Late in June 2008, the Pentagon finally announced charges against him for his role in the USS *Cole* attack. Al-Nashiri was one of several captured al-Qaeda terrorists allegedly "waterboarded" by the CIA in its attempt to obtain the details of past and future plots against the West. The Bush administration maintained that waterboarding was legal when the CIA used it on al-Nashiri and also on top al-Qaeda detainee Khalid Sheikh Mohammed in 2002 and 2003.[108]

The Pentagon stated at its June 2008 press conference that al-Nashiri was the chief planner of the suicide boat attacks against the USS *Cole* and the *MV Limburg.* The Pentagon also announced that it planned to press for the death penalty for him if he was convicted. President Barack Obama, however, announced, early in 2009, that he had dropped plans to prosecute the alleged al-Qaeda terrorist for the moment and that he was seeking a further review of the case, the possible legal impact of the waterboarding, and al-Nashiri's status as an enemy combatant. What effects, if any, this will have on future al-Qaeda operatives who plan to act out their terrorist plots in the maritime domain remains to be seen.

While the capture of al-Nashiri was a significant blow to the maritime terror campaign of al-Qaeda, it by no means stopped the group's efforts to attack maritime targets, especially U.S. warships. However, while al-Qaeda's next attack, against the USS *Firebolt*'s motor launch, resulted in the deaths of U.S. personnel, the group's capability to strike with decisiveness at major targets like the *Cole* seemed to have been affected by the loss of its maritime terrorist planner. Its operations resembled the low-level maritime attacks on Israeli patrol boats by the PLO.

The USS *Firebolt* (PC-10) is a 170-foot, Cyclone-class patrol craft. On April 24, 2004, the ship was operating in the U.S. Fifth Fleet Area of Operations in the Northern Arabian Gulf under the operational control of Commander Task 55 in support of Operation Iraqi Freedom. The USS *Firebolt* operated with a crew from the USS *Thunderbolt* (PC-12), which enabled the *Firebolt* to operate year round in the Arabian Gulf using crews rotated from the United States. Its mission was to maintain a security zone of 4,000 yards (two nautical miles) around the Khor Al Amaya Offshore Oil Terminal (KAAOT). It did this by launching a rigid-hull inflatable boat (RHIB) with a three-man crew that was tasked with intercepting small "dhows," or fishing boats, that had strayed into the security zone. The security boats were to accomplish this by maneuvering and by using hand gestures or loud speakers to divert the dhows and fishing boats approaching the oil platforms. Occasionally, the RHIBs would maneuver alongside a dhow and display picture charts that depicted the security zone they were enforcing.

At 5:30 P.M., the *Firebolt*'s RHIB began its patrol with three personnel from the ship and an additional four-man boarding team from the U.S. Coast Guard's Law Enforcement Detachment. A half hour later, a suspicious dhow well inside the security zone made an abrupt maneuver toward the RHIB and, when it was within a short distance of the navy boat, exploded in an obvious suicide attack. The blast instantly killed three members of the RHIB's crew, including Nathan Bruckenthal, the first U.S. Coast Guard personnel killed in action since the

Vietnam War. The four other crew members were seriously injured. Sixteen minutes later, two more boats exploded near the A1 Basra Oil Terminal (ABOT),
causing analysts to believe that the vessel attack at Khor A1 Amaya was part of a
larger simultaneous and coordinated terrorist attack on Iraq's offshore infrastructure by al-Qaeda.[109]

According to a joint Reuters and Associated Press report, the attacks were attributed to al-Qaeda after a statement signed by al Qaeda-operative Abu Musab
al-Zarqawi, who appeared on the Muntada al-Ansar Islamist Web site. He said,
"We give you good tidings . . . your brothers with their boats target[ing] oil tankers. Let the whole world hear this: We have brought you a people who love death
just as you love life . . . and there will be many more attacks and operations, God
willing."[110]

Since the attack, the U.S. Navy has enforced a two-tier security zone surround-
ing both the KAAOT and ABOT facilities. Made up of an outer zone and an inner
exclusion zone, ships entering the outer warning zone—which extends 1.87 miles
from the terminals—must identify their name, destination, and the cargo of their
vessel. The right of free passage has been suspended within the inner zone, which
extends 1.25 miles from both terminals in all directions. No vessels are authorized
to enter the inner exclusion zone unless they are preapproved to use the offshore
oil facilities.[111]

In 2005, after the failed attempt to attack Israeli cruise ships in Turkey on August 5, al-Qaeda kept up its maritime offensive. On August 19, it fired Katyusha
rockets at two U.S. warships in Jordan's only port, Aqaba. The amphibious ships
USS *Ashland* and USS *Kearasarge,* assigned to the Navy's Fifth Fleet, had just
moored in Aqaba for a scheduled port call. The port of Aqaba sits at the closed end
of the long finger of water that makes up the Gulf of Aqaba. Just to the west is
Israel's port of Eilat.

A year earlier, as the *Star Princess* was about to a visit the port of Aqaba, I had
conducted a port inspection and had discussed with port officials their strug-
gling efforts to implement the ISPS Code. The port, although well protected with
an adequate fence, lacked rudimentary improvements to protect vehicle approaches to the piers. An obvious risk to the port's security was posed by the
steep cliffs overlooking the port, dotted with large warehouses that had security
implications for any ship in the harbor. Al-Qaeda evidently planned to use this
vulnerability to attack ships.

Now, at the direction of al-Qaeda leader Abu Musab al-Zarqawi, three members of a terrorist cell entered Jordan through the eastern desert using forged
Iraqi passports. They quickly made their operational headquarters by renting a
hilltop warehouse. There, they set up rocket launchers smuggled in from Iraq in
the gasoline tanks of a Mercedes truck. While the two U.S. Navy warships were in

port, the terrorist launched their Katyusha rockets, using a timing device. Two rockets overshot the warships, hitting a Jordanian military warehouse and killing a guard; a third rocket landed in Eilat, Israel, but did not cause any major damage.

Both U.S. naval amphibious ships left Aqaba shortly after the failed attack. Al-Zarqawi later claimed responsibility for the attack on the U.S. warships, saying the port was chosen because of the city's status as a center for tourism and because of the media attention a successful attack would have generated.[112] Three of the terrorist escaped to Iraq before the attack, and a fourth terrorist was later arrested.

For the time being, al-Qaeda's official maritime offensive was halted in the Middle East. Al-Qaeda has shown itself resilient and willing to wait in the shadows while it pieces together its trajectory of death and destruction. To believe that al-Qaeda, Hezbollah, Hamas, or any other Islamic fundamentalist group does not have the capability to strike at maritime targets in its own backyard is wishful thinking. But there are other areas of the world where the threat from these groups is just as prevalent. One of those regions is the most common port of call for cruise ships.

THE CARIBBEAN—WARNING OF THINGS TO COME

The Caribbean Sea is a vast tropical paradise interspersed with small lush islands. Less than 50 miles of ocean separate the closest Caribbean Islands from the tip of Florida. This maritime area is sometimes referred to as the United States' "third border." While there are two U.S. territories inside this domain (Puerto Rico and the U.S. Virgin Islands), the region is still vulnerable to security threats by terrorists and from drug and crime syndicates, as well as from illegal migration to the United States. Coast Guard Captain James Tunstall of the U.S. Coast Guard Sector Puerto Rico summed up it up this way: "It is easy to focus on the other borders of the United States because you hear more about them, but in the Caribbean, there is a 360 degree threat."[113]

The Caribbean, long a traditional cruise destination, remains the most popular spot for cruise ship vacationers, with 42.8 percent of respondents to an industry survey saying they were headed there in 2008.[114] So what are the implications for the security of both ships and passengers in the most popular cruise market? Latin America has often been called America's weak underbelly. There are both positive and negative aspects to how the threat of terrorism will interact with the growth of the cruise line industry in the region in the coming years.

The good news is that there has not been a significant act of maritime terrorism in this region, making it a relative safe haven for cruise ships. However, once the layers are pulled back, there exist in Latin America and in the Caribbean many significant social, political, and economic issues that threaten the expansion of the cruise ship business in the region. These issues present serious security threats that will influence maritime security. In short, the growing instability of the Caribbean and Latin American region will significantly impact the safety of cruise tourism if left unchecked. Unfortunately, many of these issues are beyond the capability of the cruise industry to influence.

One of the most disturbing trends is that Islamic terrorist groups are burgeoning in Central and South America and in the Caribbean. As their traditional power bases of Afghanistan and Iraq have become less hospitable, terrorist groups in the Western Hemisphere are becoming more evident and are active in the illicit drug trade, arms trafficking, money laundering, counterfeiting of U.S. currency, and the underground smuggling of people, arms, and cash across borders. Thus, with al-Qaeda on the run in other parts of the world, there is a growing risk that it will shift operations to Latin America, where the rule of law is corrupt and a growing Muslim population provides fertile grounds for recruitment.

These groups are already beginning to build critical infrastructure that may be used to launch transnational terrorist attacks. But that is only the beginning. There has long been a host of indigenous and domestic terrorist groups such as the leftist Revolutionary Armed Forces of Colombia (FARC);[115] the leftist National Liberation Army; and the communist Shining Path, aka Sendero Luminoso, in Peru. Despite government actions to curb their power bases and leadership, these groups continue to flourish. Considering their growth, along with the powerful Colombian drug cartels, the growing strife among the peasant populations, and the rampant crime and government corruption, it would be hard to find anything encouraging to say about the likelihood of the region's solving any of its problems in the near future.

The biggest challenge for the cruise ship industry as it faces these issues will be in mitigating the threats, not necessarily to their fleet of ships but to their passengers, by engaging in selective risk management. That said, when determining the vulnerabilities of a particular Caribbean or Latin American port of call, the cruise ship industry has always followed the guidance of the U.S. government (or the British and Canadian governments) with respect to travel warnings, which are not always promulgated for "nonterrorist" threats. Thus, in the absence of an official travel warning, the cruise lines consider passengers who go ashore as essentially on their own with regard to their own personal safety and security.

I served the U.S. State Department as a regional security officer in both Nicaragua and Bolivia. During the time I was in South America, I saw the effects of indigenous terrorism on the civilian population of Peru. The eventual decline of the Sendero Luminoso (Shining Path) followed the capture of its notorious leader, Abimael Guzman, known as Presidente Gonzalo. Shining Path was one of many groups around the world that grew out of the international communist movement of the 1960s. Its attempts to overthrow the democratic government of Peru launched a 30-year reign of terror. However, alarming evidence now suggests that Sendero Luminosa has re-emerged and has begun financing itself by producing illegal drugs, most of which are destined for U.S. markets. Today, SL continues both its drug-related operations and its paramilitary operations.[116]

Weak and corrupt governments in Latin America have led to social insecurity; distrust of the police, military, and security forces; an escalating crime rate; and the rise of Marxist-Andean terror groups. The bankrupt U.S. policy in the war on drugs helped lead to nationalist movements in the region and the first indigenous Indian president in Bolivia, who eventually became an ally of the government of the dictator Hugo Chavez in Venezuela.

Since the mid-1980s, U.S. security policy in the region has focused on the war on drugs, and there have been a number of military strategies for confronting that threat in the region. But those strategies have had a negligible effect on the production and sale of narcotics and have not stemmed the flow of illegal drugs into the United States. The limited effect of U.S. policies aimed at combating the illegal production of coca in the Andean nations has come at the cost of weakened democratic institutions, increased poverty, uncontrolled violence, and damage to the environment.[117]

More recently, the U.S.-led "war on terror" has threatened the hemisphere's agenda even further by causing the United States to view all the region's problems in terms of the terrorist threat to the United States and their effect on U.S. security. This has led to a further weakening of Latin American governments by encouraging them to divert scarce resources to combat the threat of terrorism. The diversion of resources from the war on drugs has led to an increase in drug trafficking, a public health crisis, and an increase in youth gangs and crime.[118]

In recent decades, Latin America has seen a dramatic growth in its Muslim population. The region has a diverse Muslim population of Arab descent, mostly from Lebanon, Syria, and Palestine. There is also a larger Christian population with roots in the same Levant countries and growing Muslim populations from Southeast Asia, particularly Pakistan, Afghanistan, and Indonesia, that has settled in Suriname, Guyana, Trinidad and Tobago, and throughout the Caribbean region. Because of intermarriage and conversion, Islam is one of the fastest-growing religions in Latin America.[119]

Al-Qaeda has demonstrated success in recruiting Muslim converts in Europe and in the United States, which is worried that the large population centers in Latin America may provide fertile ground for new recruits to al-Qaeda's cause. These Muslims have the ability to circumvent travel restrictions and blend easily into Western cities. The United States before 9/11 was concerned about the

tri-border area of Brazil, Argentina, and Paraguay, where the largest Muslim population is concentrated. This area has seen repeated activity by Hezbollah, particularly in Argentina, where in the 1990s a series of anti-Jewish bombings in
Buenos Aires was blamed on the terrorist group. Another alarming possibility is
that terror groups such as Hamas and Hezbollah might organize, along with drug
cartels, to move cash, arms, and people across porous borders.[120]

That Hezbollah is flourishing in the tri-border area of South America demonstrates the worrying worldwide reach of Islamist radicalism. The suspected
activities of these groups in this area range from counterfeiting U.S. currency to
drug smuggling, in what one Drug Enforcement official described as a "haven
for Islamic extremists."[121] According to the U.S. State Department, Hezbollah is
a multifaceted organization with a presence in every South American country.

In the mid-1990s, Hezbollah, operating out of the tri-border area, killed hundreds of people in a bombing campaign that included the Israeli embassy in Buenos Aires. Although Hezbollah denied responsibility for the attacks, there is
evidence that the attacks were personally masterminded by Imad Mugniyah,
who until his death, in Syria, in February 2008, was one of the FBI's top-10 most
wanted terrorists.[122] The FBI investigated the Buenos Aires bombings and found
that not only Hezbollah but also Iran were involved and that they were apparently seeking to retaliate for Argentina's ceasing to cooperate on nuclear research
and for Israel's assassination of former Hezbollah leader Sheikh Abbas al-
Musawi and his family in February 1992.[123]

Even before September 11, the tri-border area of South America apparently
had the U.S. government worried over increasing illegal activity by Iranian-
backed Hezbollah militia. Hezbollah has preyed on the frustrations of the 25,000
Arab residents, most of who came to South America from Lebanon after the 1948
Arab-Israeli war or after the 1985 Lebanese civil war. An investigation by NBC
News and Telemundo uncovered the details of a smuggling operations run by
Hezbollah that funnels large sums of money to militia leaders in the Middle East
and also helps further Hezbollah operations in South America.[124]

Since the events of the early 1990s, Hezbollah has increased its presence in
Latin America. For example, on the group's Web page, local Hezbollah militants
in Venezuela describe their fight against the United States as a "holy war" and
post photographs of would-be suicide terrorists with masks and bombs. Until recently, cruise ships made port in Isla Santa Margarita, off the coast of Venezuela.
Isla Margarita is a free-trade zone that is home to a sizable Arab Muslim (and Arab
Christian) community and is also cited as a potential terrorist base. Hezbollah
has also established Web sites in Chile, El Salvador, Argentina, and most other
Latin American countries.[125]

Because al-Qaeda was evicted from its operating base in Afghanistan, it has developed a closer relationship with Islamic extremist groups in Latin America. There is evidence to suggest that extremists linked to Hezbollah, Islamic Jihad, and al-Qaeda are now operating in Argentina, Ecuador, Honduras, Nicaragua, Paraguay, and Uruguay. There is even great concern over the threat that militant Islam might spread throughout Mexico. The growing Muslim community, which includes Muslim converts with Hispanic backgrounds, is starting to impact the illegal smuggling of immigrants along the major cities bordering the United States.[126]

More troubling is the strong indication that al-Qaeda, as well as other international terrorist groups, have made inroads in Trinidad and Tobago. Al-Qaeda's presence directly threatens U.S. interests in the Caribbean Basin and in Latin America. Because of their valuable energy reserves, their strategic location off the coast of Venezuela, and their growing Muslim population (which has in the past resorted to political violence), Trinidad and Tobago may offer a Muslim population, including Afro-Caribbean converts, that responds to al-Qaeda.

A fear of an al-Qaeda emergence in Trinidad and Tobago is fueled by the leadership of Yasin Abu Bakr, the founder of Trinidad and Tobago's Jamaat al-Muslimeen (Muslim Group). Abu Bakr attempted to establish the first Islamic nation-state in the Western Hemisphere. He is best known for leading more than 100 members of the Jamaat in storming the National Parliament and taking the prime minister and the cabinet hostage in 1990 during a dispute with the government over land ownership, poverty in the Afro-Trinidadian community, and general state corruption. The siege was marked by rioting and violence in the capital of Port of Spain that resulted in 23 deaths, scores of injuries, and heavy damages.

Although the coup failed, Bakr and his group are still active. The plot to attack planes at John F. Kennedy International Airport in New York has been linked to Jamaat al-Muslimeen. Early in June 2007, the Department of Justice announced that four individuals—two Guyanese nationals, one Trinidadian national, and one U.S. citizen of Guyanese origin—were being charged with conspiring to blow up fuel tanks and a fuel pipeline at the airport. One of those charged was Abdul Kadir, who is reportedly a business partner of Abu Bakr.[127]

The importance of maintaining political stability in Latin America in light of these disturbing trends cannot be understated. One concern relates to the strategic importance of the Panama Canal. In addition, the region is a major supplier of oil and gas to the United States. Just as significant is the fact that the Caribbean is the number one cruise ship destination in the world. Approximately 6.8 million out of nearly 10 million North American cruise passengers cruised within the Caribbean Basin in 2006. The region has many attractions, and anyone who has ever visited the lush tropical paradise can appreciate its beauty. But, as discussed earlier, the Caribbean is far from a safe haven against crime and security risks, an assertion seemingly confirmed by the U.S. government.

In June 2007, the U.S. Government Accounting Office (GAO) published the findings of its own investigation into the security aspects of Latin America ports. What the investigators found was alarming. They indicated that the implementation of the ISPS Code, in effect for more than three years at the time of the investigation, was not proceeding smoothly in the Caribbean. The GAO noted that the implementation of the ISPS Code in the region was especially important to the United States because of its proximity and because of the implications for criminal activity, including illicit narcotics trafficking, illegal migration, and corruption; for economic policy related to the high poverty rate; and for the substantial numbers of U.S. tourists and cruise ships that visit the region.

The GAO report focused on the general threats to port security. Terrorist threat scenarios considered most likely to be implemented in Latin American ports include suicide attacks carried out using an explosive-laden boat or a vehicle that is rammed into a vessel or facility and standoff attacks involving rockets, mortars, or rocket-propelled grenades. The GAO also cited a risk of armed assaults on vessels and infrastructure. The GAO evaluated other concerns for security in the region in addition to these attack scenarios. These included corruption and organized gang activities. According to various U.S. agencies that were interviewed for the study, corruption and its threat to the rule of law are serious concerns in the region. Some nations have identified organized gang activity within their port infrastructure. Additionally, the creation and sale of fraudulent documentation used to finance illicit activities is on the rise.[128]

As part of the investigation, the U.S. State Department, one of the agencies that reviewed the study, voiced concern over the port security deficiencies and said that the possibility that an explosive-laden vehicle-borne improvised explosive device (VBIED) could be used against a cruise ship or port facility "should be a matter of great concern to the U.S. government" because it could cause loss of life to Americans, and because of the economic impact on American cruise lines and tourist industries in the United States. This was a sentiment shared by the U.S. Agency for International Development.[129] The U.S. Coast Guard visited selected countries in the Caribbean Basin to inspect the progress of the ISPS Code implementation between October 2006 and June 2007 and found that, although the implementation was not as severely deficient as in the sub-Saharan region of Africa or as far along as in Europe, there appeared to be a wide range of problems, especially in areas such as access control to the ports.

The United States is actively engaged in assisting these Caribbean nations. The U.S. Department of State, through its embassies, coordinates assistance to countries in the Caribbean region and is the lead federal agency in U.S. efforts to fight terrorism, countering the illegal flow of narcotics into the United States, and stopping illegal immigration. The State Department also works with the Organization of American States (OAS) to coordinate and fund projects to improve maritime security in the Caribbean Basin. The U.S. Coast Guard is working with the OAS Inter-American Committee for Counter-Terrorism to facilitate port security capacity-building projects in Latin America, Central America, and the Caribbean. In addition, the Coast Guard's International Port Security Program has been assessing the effectiveness of antiterrorism measures in foreign ports.[130]

The geography of the region presents many obstacles to the control of illegal activities. The Caribbean accounts for about 35 percent of illegal narcotics transported into the United States annually and is a transitional point for drugs coming from South America. Illegal migration from Haiti and the Dominican Republic is a major issue. The Caribbean Basin is also a region of economic significance to the United States. Add to that the importance of the cruise ship industry, and the importance of the links that tie the United States to the region is apparent. The cruise lines can play an important role in helping to mitigate the risks to their operations by working directly with the ports, tourist venues, and government authorities to identify risks. Like all stakeholders, the cruise lines have an enormous vested interest in that outcome of efforts to improve security in the area. If the Caribbean region folds as a cruise ship destination because of terrorist or security concerns, there are few regions left in the world that can fill that vacuum.

CUBAN PORT CALL—A NEW HOST OF PROBLEMS

After the attacks of September 11, the cruise lines altered their itineraries, steering away from the Middle East and the eastern Mediterranean in droves. Although none of the traditional ports of call vacated by the cruise ships in Jordan, Egypt, Turkey, or even Greece were "blacklisted," the cruise lines essentially reacted out of prudence. The cancellations were strictly a response to the perceived threats brought on by the horrific attacks on the United States and the potential for further terrorist acts at the hands of the Islamic terrorists.

Likewise, the U.S. government, through the U.S. State Department Travel Warnings, did not bar Americans from traveling to these regions, although there were strong warnings. Nor has the ISPS Code, enacted in the wake of 9/11, blacklisted any ports available to the cruise lines for their port call needs. Most of the cruise ships have returned to places like Egypt, Turkey, and Greece. The cruise lines, however, are still locked in a constant search for new and viable markets for their expanding fleets. After having had to constantly shift their itineraries in the Middle

East and the Mediterranean because of security concerns during the Gulf and
Iraq Wars, the cruise lines would like to find ports far from this troubled region.

One country that meets that need remains utterly off limits, not for security
reasons but because of a decades-old diplomatic struggle between two stubborn
neighbors. The cruise lines would like nothing more to add Cuba to the burgeoning Caribbean cruise market. Why, then, in the first part of the new century, are
Americans still forbidden to travel to Cuba? To even dream of scheduling port
calls to this country would precipitate a cruise line's downfall, but that is exactly
what is happening. The reason for prohibiting cruise ships from visiting one of
the most desirable ports in the world has been asked of every U.S. president since
John F. Kennedy.

In February 1962, President Kennedy imposed a trade embargo on Cuba because of the Castro regime's ties to the Soviet Union. Pursuant to the president's
directive, the Department of the Treasury's Office of Foreign Assets Control
(OFAC) issued the Cuban Import Regulations. Then, on July 9, 1963, OFAC issued a more comprehensive set of prohibitions, the Cuban Assets Control Regulations, which effectively banned travel by prohibiting any transactions with Cuba.

Remarkably, the travel ban to Cuba was something that JFK's brother, Attorney
General Robert F. Kennedy, recommended against in a December 1963 memo
to then Secretary of State Dean Rusk, written after the president was assassi-
nated, in November 1963. RFK said that the ban on travel to Cuba should be
lifted, stating that it was a violation of American liberties to restrict free travel.[131]
The cruise lines would agree with that statement, not because of civil liberties issues or politics but for their own capitalistic reasons.

By the cruise lines' own statistics, only 14 to 16 percent of the U.S. population
has ever taken a cruise vacation. Despite the security threats evident since September 11 and the fear of possible pirate attacks, the cruise industry continues to
grow. More than 6.8 million U.S. citizens took a cruise vacation in 2001, even taking into account the sharp decline after September 11. This figure accounted for
82 percent of the industry's global passengers. The industry is forecasting even
greater growth in the future; the number of passengers is expected to reach nearly
22 million by 2010.[132]

Bigger ships, a greater diversity of shipboard attractions and amenities, and
lower fares have contributed to the increase in the popularity of cruising over
the past two decades. However, it has been difficult to find new destinations to attract new customers. Toward the end of the 1990s, industry officials hoped that
restrictions on travel to Cuba might be lifted even though President Bill Clinton expanded the trade embargo against that country. Many cruise lines began planning what itineraries would look like with the additions of ports like Havana and
Santiago de Cuba. But if the idea of allowing ships to call in Cuban ports was ever
really being seriously considered, it was quickly dropped after September 11.

While the U.S. trade embargo imposes restrictions on travel to Cuba, under the provisions of that embargo Americans have been allowed to visit Cuba under certain circumstances, such as for humanitarian missions and to visit family members. On any given day, there are as many as 2,000 American tourists in Cuba. They fly into the country from any of five secondary countries: the Bahamas, Jamaica, Canada, Mexico, or the Cayman Islands. Technically, the American travelers are within the spirit of the law by booking travel to Cuba in one of the five countries. All their travel, meals, and tips are paid for in foreign currency because U.S. law prohibits the spending of U.S. currency in Cuba. Cuban authorities do not stamp U.S. passports, so it appears that the traveler never visited Cuba.[133]

While former president George W. Bush further tightened the travel restrictions, there has been growing popular support to lift the travel ban to Cuba. In 2007, Representatives Charlie Rangel (D-NY) and Jeff Flake (R-AZ) authored a bill that does just that. Congressman Rangel, the new chair of the Ways and Means Committee, was the principal sponsor of HR 654, introduced in March 2007. But the bill was effectively stalled in the House until the news that longtime President Fidel Castro would effectively resign his duties as leader of the Cuban state in February 2008.

The bill reads: "The president shall not regulate or prohibit, directly or indirectly, travel to or from Cuba by United States citizens or legal residents, or any of the transactions incident to such traveling." In other words, it makes the travel ban disappear. When it was introduced, more than 100 members of Congress called on then-Secretary of State Condoleezza Rice to review U.S. policy toward Cuba. In their memo to the Secretary of State, they stressed that "current U.S. policy leaves us without influence at this critical moment and that serves neither the U.S. national interest nor average Cubans, the intended beneficiaries of our policy. A complete review of the policy is in order now."[134] President Obama has signaled he is in favor of easing of restrictions, including allowing unlimited visits to family members and transfers of U.S. currency to Cuba. These measures make it appear that Cuba is slowly opening for business. The cruise lines, however, are still holding their breath, and they have every reason to.

A market research company estimated that in the first three years after the lifting of the travel ban more than 750,000 American cruise passengers would visit Havana and that that number would increase to at least 1.8 million passengers by the end of the 10th year, depending on the size and number of the ships calling on the island state. There is also a possibility that high-speed ferry service could be established. But, given the fact that hotel services are not readily available in Cuba, the only logical way to visit would be by cruise ship.[135]

Deploying cruise ships to Cuba would give the cruise lines leverage in attracting new customers and ease the crowding in other Caribbean ports, which during peak travel periods may be visited by up to five large cruise ships at one time.

And the lack of infrastructure in Cuban ports would give the cruise lines an edge; the majority of the new visitors would likely come by cruise ships, a prospect that has excited the cruise lines tremendously. But it is likely that the cruise lines would face new problems and challenges posed by Cuba.

Unless the communist state was abolished altogether, policies aimed at allaying new national security concerns would likely be at the heart of any new relaxed travel regulations. The cruise lines would face new sources of traditional maritime threats, such as stowaways and drug and currency smugglers. Although the island has practically been immune to the threat of terrorism, aircraft and vessel hijackings have been on the increase in Cuba as desperate Cubans seek to escape the country in hopes of reaching the United States. The U.S. State Department warns that U.S. citizens, although they have not necessarily been the targets of the most recent hijacking attempts, might be caught up in violence during an attempted hijacking.[136]

If cruise ships and ferries begin calling on Cuban ports and the communist regime remains in place, the vessels may seem like promising avenues for desperate Cuban refugees trying to stow away. Similarly, the cruise ships may be used by Cubans living abroad to funnel cash or other contraband into Cuba. And the illegal trade is likely to go the other way, as well.

Allowing U.S. tourists to visit Cuba might please the American visitors, and the cruise lines may believe that it would benefit the Cuban people as well, but, in reality, opening Cuba up to tourism would cause greater hardship for the Cuban people as the regime cracked down, determined to limit U.S. influence on their country. Only if Cuba were truly free could the threats to national security be truly mitigated. And it appears that the Cuban government is not wholeheartedly enthusiastic about the idea of having cruise ships visit its shores.

The number of foreign cruise ships visiting Cuba has fallen by 90 percent since 2005, when Fidel Castro remarked that cruise ships leave their trash, empty cans, and papers in exchange for a few miserable pennies. According to Cuban statistics, only about 11,000 cruise passengers visited Cuba in 2007, far less than the 102,000 visitors two years earlier. The giant U.S. cruise line Royal Caribbean had hoped to cash in on the interest in travel to Cuba when it purchased a Spanish company that ran tours to the country through an Italian cruise line. But RCI later canceled those tours. In 2005, Castro told the leaders of other Caribbean states that Cuba did not intend to accept cruise ships and canceled a contract with the Italian company that had operated the island's cruise terminal since 1998 in a joint venture with a government-run company.[137]

So, for the time being, given the fact that Castro and his brother, Raul, appear unlikely to endorse the changes to the existing U.S. travel restrictions that would allow cruise ships to call on the island nation's ports, the prospect of cruise line travel to Cuba remains a distant hope for the cruise lines, much as the hope of reaching America is a dream to so many desperate Cuban citizens. Allowing cruise ships to call on Cuban ports is likely to bring a corresponding increase in maritime threats not accounted for in the current legislation and additional security worries for the cruise lines. In the next chapter, we discuss the many passenger safety issues that the cruise ship industry must deal with before it can take on the prospect of sailing to Cuba.

three

THE CRIME STATISTICS AND STORIES THAT THE CRUISE LINES DON'T WANT YOU TO KNOW

C ompetition for leisure dollars has always been sharp, but, by any standards, the growth in the cruise industry has been phenomenal and continues to grow. The cruise industry has responded to this demand by continuing to add to the number of ships in their fleets and by building larger and more innovative ships with new onboard amenities. New ports of call have been added, coupled with very aggressive pricing aimed at increasing an already high level of consumer confidence. Statistics tell the story. In 1990, 4.5 million passengers took cruises. By 2001, that number had doubled to 8.4 million passengers. In 2006, there were almost 14 million cruise ship passengers. It is estimated that the industry will enjoy another 70 percent increase, to between 17 and 20 million passengers, by 2010.[1] The North American market supplies two-thirds of the global volume, primarily because of the renaissance in cruising destinations in the Caribbean. By the year 2010, the North American market is projected to rise from 6.8 million to 11.9 million; the number of passengers from mainland Europe will grow from 1.3 million to 5.3 million, demonstrating that the cruise industry is a dynamic sector of the global economy.[2]

Statisticians break down cruise travel into six major regions around the world. The most popular region and the staple of the cruise industry is the Caribbean and the Bahamas, which made up 50 percent of all cruise capacity in 2004, a 5 percent increase from 2003. The next largest market is the Mediterranean, with 15 percent market share in 2004, down 6 percent from 2003. Alaskan cruises are the third largest market; they had a 6.7 percent share, an increase of 7 percent over 2003. The Mexican Riviera has become the fourth most popular destination, with 6.6 percent of total capacity in 2004, rising a remarkable 41 percent over its 2003 share, when the west coast of Mexico was ranked sixth. Western and northern Europe saw 5 percent of the cruise ship capacity deployed in their respective waters in 2004, an increase of 20 percent over the 2003 figure. Another 5 percent of the worldwide cruise ship capacity was deployed in the Asia/Pacific region in 2004, a 15 percent decline from 2003.[3]

Other major sailing regions include Hawaii, with almost 2 percent market share in 2004, up 14 percent from 2003. Bermuda remained constant in 2004 with 1.8 percent, and the East Coast of North America enjoyed a substantial increase in 2004, increasing 32 percent from 2003, with a 1.6 percent market share. Finally, with the addition of the *Queen Mary 2* in 2004, the transatlantic market saw a boost of more than 17 percent but still accounted for only 1.3 percent of the worldwide cruise capacity for that year.[4]

Industry statistics were revealing with regard to where cruise ships were going in 2004, especially in relation to world events. While all markets were on an upswing, the rate of growth in the Mediterranean and the Asian/Pacific markets declined by significant margins of 6 percent and 15 percent, respectively. It must be remembered that, in 2004, regional factors such as the Sheraton Hotel attack in Jakarta in August 2003, the Bali hotel bombing in Indonesia in 2002, the SARS scare across the Asian region, and the devastating tsunami that roiled the Indian Ocean in December 2004 were still fresh in the minds of tourists. In the Mediterranean market, the sobering reality of the Iraq war combined with a series of terrorist bombings in Istanbul in 2003 to put a damper on cruise industry growth there. These facts demonstrate potential cruise passengers' unwillingness to book cruises in regions where terrorist violence or similar maritime threats and incidents have occurred. They also demonstrate the cruise industry's ability to counter these phenomena with alternate markets that satisfy the growing market demand.

Statistics are useful for dissecting how market share for the cruise market is divided. They demonstrate that the cruise ship market has been growing steadily to satisfy a growing demand for this form of vacation leisure. Impressive statistics have also been tossed around by the cruise lines as they seek to portray their fleets as model societies at sea. If one were to rely on their figures exclusively, one would conclude that crime aboard these ships is almost negligible and that crew violence is nonexistent. After hard investigative research, and, in most cases, a review of documents from the cruise line's vaults that have been produced under court order, consumer advocacy groups paint an entirely different picture.

WHAT THE CRUISE SHIP CRIME STATISTICS DON'T PROVE

While statistics reveal a good deal about the phenomenal growth in the industry despite the effect of downturns in the economy, regional wars, and pandemic scares, they also reveal a lot about passenger safety. The cruise lines are quick to promote the safety and security of cruising on their ships as their topmost concern. With only one attempted hijacking of a cruise ship and a more recent pirate attack, the cruise lines have boastfully sold their product as safe. The cruise lines were fortunate that only one American was killed in the *Achille Lauro* hijacking; in the *Seabourn Spirit* attack, the cruise ship was able to repel the attackers. Had the pirates boarded the ship and caused harm to the passengers and crew, the economic impact on the cruise industry would have been remarkably different.

Strictly speaking, the historical record shows that there have in fact been few incidents caused by either pirates or terrorists aboard cruise ships. Unfortunately, the statistics also show that the security practices on these behemoths appear insufficient to handle not only the external threats from pirates and terrorists but also the problems that arise from the increasing numbers of passengers who are flocking to these shipboard vacations. Both the cruise lines and the public have a hard time ignoring the headlines they read in the media today.[5] One can hardly avoid coming to the conclusion that these ships are not really as safe as the cruise lines say they are.

The cruise lines boast that cruise ship travel is as safe as if not safer than any land-based vacation. They seem to believe that the inherent risk associated with being on a ship at sea is not as great as the risk one assumes by living in a crowded city. The corporate line is that the per capita number of rapes, assaults, and other criminal acts is lower on ships than on land; cruise line critics argue the contrary. Both critics and the industry embrace statistics to "prove" their side of the argument. One side uses them to prove that crime rates are higher on land than on ships, while the other side uses them the reverse.

In reality, however, both critics and the industry have been misled by the "statistics" and have, figuratively speaking, missed the boat on the issue. They have been ignoring a central question in the debate: how safe are you on a cruise ship? The question is not whether you are safer in a particular city or town than on a cruise ship, but whether you are safe on a cruise ship. When it comes to violent crime, one assault or one rape is one too many, regardless of whether it occurred on land or at sea, particularly if you are the victim.

The existence of *any* crime on cruise ships suggests that there is indeed a problem that must be dealt with. Comparing crime rates on ships and crime rates in a city provides no useful indication of how safe passengers are once on board. According to Michael Crye, president of the International Council of Cruise Lines, a trade association for the cruise industry based in Washington, D.C., taking a cruise is as safe as "your average community in the United States and, I would think, safer than staying at a motel."[6] That comparison in itself can be interpreted differently depending on what you want to prove. If Crye is suggesting that the crime rate on a cruise ship is about the same as the crime rate in Cleveland, Ohio, or in Minneapolis, Minnesota, for example, then crime really is out of control on these ships. Both of these "average" communities in the United States had the highest rates of forcible rape per 100,000 inhabitants in 2005. On the other hand, New York City, perhaps counterintuitively, had one of the lowest rates of forcible rape, just above that for Bakersfield, California.[7] These statistics may be flawed for the same reason that the number of crimes reported on cruise ships is low: they reflect only crime that is known, that is, incidents reported to the police. The point is that the statistics one chooses to use can change the story.

Crye, in congressional testimony following the disappearance of George Allen Smith IV from the *Brilliance of the Seas* in 2005, stated that the violent crime rate in the United States is about 465.5 per 100,000 inhabitants. The Federal Bureau of Investigation (FBI) reports that, on average, only 50 crimes a year against U.S. citizens on cruise ships are both reported and investigated by the FBI. According to the Bureau of Justice, 1 in every 1,000 persons is sexually assaulted on land, whereas on ships there is only 1 alleged sexual assault for every 100,000 passengers.

On the surface, these statistics seem relatively impressive. A careful analysis reveals a deeper problem. The figures are artificially low. The statistics do not include crimes against non-U.S. citizens, which the cruise ships are not required to report to the FBI, and they do not necessarily include crime against crew members committed by other crew members. The statistics also do not reflect crimes against U.S. citizens that go unreported. Unreported crime, of course, is a problem on land, as well; many victims, especially in cases of sexual assault, are unwilling and afraid to report such crimes out of fear of humiliation or embarrassment or because they believe that nothing will be done to bring the guilty to justice and that the crime will go unpunished. They fear that the assault will be disclosed to parents, guardians, husbands, or wives and worry about possible retribution by the alleged perpetrator. It is also nearly impossible to compile statistics on sexual crimes reported by employees of the cruise ships themselves. The FBI records have very little information on this kind of crime.[8] Evidence suggests, however, that crime by crew against other crew members does occur, especially sexual assaults.

As we have seen, one can create statistics to prove just about anything. It is apparent that the cruise lines can use the low occurrence rates for certain types of crime to produce statistics that fit the image of their product that they wish to promote. It would be better, however, to examine the settings in which crime occurs, particularly land-based destinations. If the cruise industry wishes to claim that crime is a "non-event" when debating the safety of their cruise ships, then we should examine patterns of criminal activity and safety concerns at such popular land-based vacation destinations as Disneyland, in Anaheim, California, or Las Vegas, Nevada.

Statistics available as of December 2006, 12 guests and 1 employee have died inside Disneyland since the park's opening, in 1957. A far greater number of guests have been injured. While the California Department of Safety and Health has ruled that some incidents have been Disneyland's fault, the majority of incidents resulted from negligence on the guests' part. Only one criminal act resulted in a death. In 1981, an 18-year-old man from southern California was fatally stabbed with a knife during a fight in the Disneyland amusement park. His family sued the park for $60 million; a jury found the park negligent only in not summoning immediate outside medical help and awarded the family $600,000.[9]

A cruise line is no more able to promise total security and safety on its ships than Disneyland is able to ensure that its guests are provided a reasonable amount of security while in the park. Disneyland has had its share of accidents and resulting injuries and deaths. Like the cruise lines, most injury cases brought against Disneyland are settled in lawsuits and out-of-court settlements, after being fiercely defended by Disney attorneys. However, the big difference is that, unlike with the cruise lines, the vast majority of the incidents reported at Disneyland do not concern criminal activity but are related to park safety.

Las Vegas has some of the largest and most extravagant hotels in the world. These lavish hotels have the same amenities, if on a grander scale, that are found on any cruise ship, but they take fewer security precautions. While security is a major concern in these hotels, most of it is centered on the casinos and gaming activities rather than the theaters, restaurants, bars, pools, and parking areas. Consider that, in the United States at least, hotels do not screen luggage, x-ray personal baggage, or require passengers to walk through metal detectors. Other than a hotel room keycard, guests are not issued any particular access control or identity card. No photo identification is required for entry into the hotel and casino. In fact, the only area in a Las Vegas hotel where someone is likely to be challenged by security is in the casino areas, and then most likely because the person is suspected of being underage.

Obviously, a terrorist cannot hijack a hotel, but that does not preclude the possibility of other terrorist plots. There are certainly other gaps in hotel safety and security that would-be terrorists or criminals could exploit. In late November 2008, Islamic terrorists slipped into Mumbai (formerly Bombay), India, on a merchant vessel from Pakistan. The terrorists then hijacked a fishing vessel, murdered the crew, and used rubber lifeboats to land on the shore, where they began their bloody siege. Among other targets, they attacked several first-class hotels simultaneously, causing nearly 200 deaths.[10] What lessons, if any, can we learn from such experiences, and can they be applied to the cruise ship experience?

Las Vegas hotels have a more difficult problem in securing their environment than do cruise ships. Aside from the massive hotel structures, with their thousands of guest rooms, theaters, restaurants, and meeting rooms, there are oceans of pools and landscaped attractions, not to mention vast acres of parking lots, taxi stands, bus stops, and valet islands. Guests in vehicles can drop off or pick up their passengers only yards from the hotel lobbies. Yet, every day, these venues are able to host large-scale conventions, check in and out thousands of guests, and provide 24-hour entertainment, including restaurants and bars that serve alcohol in abundant quantities, without encroaching on personal privacy. Those security procedures that do exist apply to the bars and casinos areas. Patrons in general face very little risk to their personal safety.

That is not to say that Las Vegas is without its crime. If the type of crime or disappearances that occur routinely to guests on cruise ships were to happen to even a small percentage of visitors in Las Vegas, the city would quickly cease to attract the millions of visitors that it does each year. There is a very good reason why this has not happened despite the city's significant crime problem: Las Vegas has a police force. A well-trained police force is the only way to enforce security in these environments.

Consider that cruise ships, on which people may consume alcohol 24 hours a day, engage in gambling, receive large amounts of cash from cashiers, or hide cash and other personal valuables in hotel rooms (presumably in safes), have no law enforcement personnel on board. On some cruise ships, passengers display an arrogant disrespect for rules and regulations, whereas visitors to Las Vegas hotels understand that they will be obliged to obey the law. They know that the Las Vegas police department has real law enforcement authority and that it will be called to investigate allegations of sexual misconduct or other offenses and that it will arrest trespassers, drunks, or criminals, who will likely end up serving jail time or with a criminal conviction. Unfortunately, the cruise lines hire employees to act as "security" and are very liberal in their approach to the internal policing of their decks. Using Gurkhas or other groups that owe their allegiance to the cruise lines creates partiality and predictable responses to serious security incidents. For example, on the P&O cruise ship *Pacific Sky*, in which Dianne Brimble died in 2002 amid allegations of date rape, there were reports of shocking shipboard conduct, with some passengers running naked through the ship's passageways. Shipboard employees later reported that this behavior is fairly typical and that shipboard security routinely "looks the other way."[11]

Why, then, do the cruise lines continue to be plagued by passengers who disappear under mysterious circumstances? Why are sexual assaults, thefts of personal property, and underage drinking issues on these ships? More important, what happens to the victims of criminal acts on board? The best answer to that question is: it depends. It depends on whom you try to convince that a crime has been committed—an international court of law, a foreign country's criminal justice system, or the cruise lines themselves. It also depends on what risks you are willing to assume when you embark on cruise vacations. The risk that you will be a victim of crime on these ships is slight but not nonexistent. And the risk of personal injury from the ship's environment is also not nonexistent. As Congressman Christopher Shays eloquently put it in his opening remarks to Congress, how many cities or towns have the added burden of protecting their citizens from falling off their city and drowning or must respond to crime without a police force?

THE LAW OF THE SEA: INVESTIGATING CRIMES ON CRUISE SHIPS

The reality is that the safety infractions and crimes committed on cruise ships occur in a lawless environment. The ocean is unregulated, unrestricted, and uninhibited. Without any immediate enforcement on board these ships that is empowered to respond to crime or terrorism, the cruise ships must rely on the only U.S. agency authorized to investigate when something goes wrong, and then only if American passengers are involved. In recent testimony before the Subcommittee on Coast Guard and Maritime Transportation of the House Committee on Transportation and Infrastructure, Salvador Hernandez, FBI Deputy Assistant Director, described the complicated jurisdictional situation that governs the investigation of crimes committed against Americans on cruise ships. According to Hernandez, the FBI's power to investigate crimes committed on cruise ships and to enforce the laws of the United States on the high seas and territorial waters depends on many factors, including such things as the location of the vessel, the nationality of the perpetrator and the victim, the ownership of the vessel, the points of embarkation and debarkation, and the country in which the vessel is flagged. All these elements play a role in determining whether it can enforce the laws of the United States.

Assistant Director Hernandez summarized parts of Section 7 of Title 18 of the U.S. Code: Special Maritime and Territorial Jurisdiction. He testified that the United States can investigate crimes committed on ships under these specific conditions: the ship, regardless of flag, is owned either in whole or in part by a U.S. entity, regardless of the nationality of the victim or the perpetrator; the vessel is within the admiralty and maritime jurisdiction of the United States and out of the jurisdiction of any particular state; an offense by or against a U.S. national was committed outside the jurisdiction of any nation; the crime occurred in U.S. territorial waters, that is, within 12 miles of the coast, regardless of the nationality of the vessel; or the victim or perpetrator is a U.S. national and the infraction occurred during a voyage that departed from or was to arrive in a U.S. port.[12]

These guidelines essentially describe the FBI's investigative jurisdiction for crimes committed on ships close to home, in U.S. territorial waters, and when U.S. cruise lines are involved. When a crime has occurred on the high seas, such as the case of George Allen Smith IV, who disappeared off the *Brilliance of the Seas* in the Aegean Sea, the jurisdictional issues get even more complicated. When incidents occur outside the territorial waters of the United States, Assistant Director Hernandez points out, in addition to the laws of United States, the laws of other sovereign nations and international law will determine the FBI's legal authority to respond or investigate.

Legal attachés, or "Legats," are senior FBI representatives stationed in U.S. embassies around the world. Their ability to conduct investigations overseas varies greatly and must be determined by each Legat on a country-by-country and case-by-case basis. Overseas, the FBI works closely with the Department of State and receives assistance from the Bureau of Diplomatic Security and other investigative agencies at the embassy. In investigating crimes on cruise ships, the FBI focuses its investigative efforts on crimes for which penalties are provided under Title 18 within the authority of the special maritime and territorial jurisdiction of the United States. These specified crimes include assault, murder, attempted murder or manslaughter, kidnapping, sexual abuse, robbery, and theft.

With the exception of investigations resulting from universal offenses such as terrorism and transit of weapons of mass destruction, the FBI is limited in its ability to board a ship. The FBI/Legat cannot simply board a foreign-flagged vessel on the high seas to enforce U.S. laws and it is not in its best interest to do so. Once a Legat has decided to respond to a crime reported on the high seas that involves U.S. citizens or U.S. interests, the Legat must get the consent of the vessel's flag state to board the vessel and conduct the investigation. Virtually all cruise ships that carry American passengers fly foreign flags. Usually, getting permission to access the cruise ship/crime scene is not a problem, but if the ship's flag state or foreign government denies permission to board, there is very little that the FBI can do to conduct the investigation, even though, in most criminal cases, the timeliness of the investigation is of paramount importance in developing a case.

Criminal activity reported on the high seas poses complicated issues for the jurisdictions involved, because it requires international coordination and co-operation as officials board and collect evidence, interview witnesses, and sort out the jurisdictional issues. Ideally, the FBI will attempt to board the vessel at sea to ensure access to witnesses, preserve the crime scene and evidence, and protect life. The on-scene FBI investigator will make a determination on how to best conduct the ship-board investigation based on resources available and on the competency of the host nation to assist or to conduct the investigation.

There is no question of the FBI's competency to conduct criminal investigations; however, its job may be hampered by the host country's law enforcement capabilities and by the skill level of the investigators, as well as by the cruise lines themselves. Time and distance can create problems; there may be a delay in reporting the crime, and it takes time for the cruise lines to organize resources, for the FBI to physically arrive on scene, and for the FBI to assess the jurisdictional issues. Because of these factors, ship crime scenes may be hours if not days old when the authorities arrive.

In most cases, a shipboard incident demands that the cruise ship security department conduct a preliminary investigation. Depending on his level of training, the ship's security officer will conduct interviews with suspects and victims and collect what he perceives to be evidence. Many times, the security department is under pressure from the ship's officers and from the corporate office to return the ship to its normal routine. This may lead the ship's personnel to inadvertently alter, clean, or destroy the crime scene. And who can blame them? It is not in the best interest of the ship to have criminal investigations conducted in the middle of a cruise while paying customers trade gossip in the buffet line, let alone witness ghastly crime scenes filled with blood while the ship waits for the FBI to arrive. Obviously, this is very disturbing to passengers.

Unfortunately, what happens at sea remains at sea, far out of reach of officials and, in most cases, an investigative and legal response. Passengers must be aware of these sobering facts. Sometimes, it seems, things go amiss on a cruise ship for reasons that do not involve passengers' security but that have implications for the safety of both the crew and the passengers. When the cruise line cannot fulfill its promises to the passengers on one of these giant ships, what recourse do the passengers have? Not much if only individuals lodge complaints. But when the passengers stick together, they are a force to be reckoned with.

CRUISE SHIP MUTINY IN THE MAKING

"Mutiny" is an ugly maritime term that, theoretically, should not be part of the cruise line vernacular. A mutiny conjures up images of men in double-breasted frockcoats bearing flintlock muskets and naval cutlasses. "Mutiny," in the military sense of the word, refers to an open rebellion against constituted authority, especially rebellion of sailors against superior officers. The true-life story recounted in *Mutiny on the* [HMS] *Bounty,* with its malevolent Captain Bligh, is a good example. Another example is the fictional story *The Caine Mutiny,* by Herman Wouk, which was made into a movie that earned Humphrey Bogart an Academy Award nomination for his performance as the disturbed Navy captain Queeg. But these were the things of naval lore, not of cruise ships.

There has never been a mutiny, in the strict military sense of the word, on a cruise ship. In 2006, however, something close to one occurred on one of the largest and most luxurious cruise liners to sail on the high seas. However, it was not the crew that rebelled against the officers of the ship; it was the passengers, who turned on the officers and crew aboard Cunard Cruise Line's *Queen Mary 2*. The so-called *QM2* Mutiny played out on the world stage via the Internet, and, while it did not directly threaten the security of the ship, it made for another embarrassing story for the cruise lines, drawing attention as it did to the whims of the companies that operate these behemoths. The question being asked was whether it takes a mutiny to get satisfaction from a cruise line when a ship arbitrarily changes course in order to stay on its schedule. For the passengers of the *Queen Mary 2,* apparently it did.

The *Queen Mary 2* departed routinely enough from Port Everglades, Florida, in January 2006, with 2,500 passengers on the next leg of its 38-day cruise to South America and exotic ports of call. Within hours of setting sail, however, the giant ship experienced propulsion difficulties, the result of the ship having scraped the bottom of the channel during its departure from Port Everglades. The ship was only five miles out to sea when the captain radioed for assistance. With one of its four propulsion pods out of commission, the *QM2* had to be towed back to Fort Lauderdale so that workers could examine the extent of the damage. There, the decision was made to proceed out to sea on three engines but with an altered itinerary, not because of security threats but to keep to the schedule.[13] When news of the altered itinerary reached the passengers, who were by then well out to sea, the passengers embarked on their own form of damage control. Some used the term "kidnapped," while others said they had been held hostage aboard the ship and felt like prisoners. As they viewed their new cruise itinerary, the vacation of a lifetime for the passengers aboard the *QM2* turned into very heated debates and shouting matches with the commodore of the ship over the arbitrary cancellation of three of the port calls in the Caribbean as the ship made a beeline to Rio de Janeiro.[14]

For Cunard Cruise Line, it was difficult to grasp how upset the passengers, who had paid full fare for a Caribbean and South American cruise aboard the luxurious ship, would be upon learning that they would be shuttled to Rio with no stops in between. The arrogance of the cruise line's failure to understand this grievance and the lack of response from the ship's commodore pushed the passengers to organize themselves and to discuss ways of fighting back. As a chief engineer on one of these ships once observed, "It would be very easy to keep these cruise ships running smoothly, all we need to do is get rid of the passengers."[15] As the crew of the *QM2* found out, the passengers were armed for their mutiny with the latest technology—the Internet and cellular phones.

The passengers felt that they had been lied to. The arbitrary decision to head for Rio de Janeiro with no intermediate port calls forced the passengers to take matters into their own hands. E-mail and phone calls soon were spreading the news that the passengers had decided not to get off the ship in Rio until the money they had paid for the cruise was refunded. Internet blogs followed and began to churn out support and, in some cases, criticism of the mutineers. The BBC News Service offered a place for the public to respond to the drama being played out in real time over the Internet. Some bloggers sympathized with the passengers but added that it was their fight and offered hopes that the dispute would be resolved so that the rest of the cruise itinerary would not be affected. One blogger who responded to the BBC after Cunard announced that it would refund 50 percent of the fare put it bluntly: "as father to not one but two passengers on board, I can tell you, that an offer of 50 percent compensation is about as adequate as taping a piece of cardboard to the gaping hole in the *Titanic*. These people have been lied to . . . and what of the 1000 in Rio yet to board?"[16]

The offer to refund half of the *QM2*'s passengers' fare was probably reasonable for Cunard to make under the circumstances. The decision was probably a response to the negative publicity in the media as the dispute played out in real time. But there was more fallout from such concessions. The final blow for Cunard came in an article on the front page of the *Times* of London with the headline "Mutiny on the *Queen Mary 2*."[17] With the prospect of more headlines mocking the drama that was unfolding, Cunard Cruise Line, which is owned by Carnival Corporation, wanted to control further damage, and so it announced that it would offer full refunds, which effectively ended the impasse.

However, the *Queen Mary 2* "mutiny" appeared to have set a precedent for the cruise industry, one that it wishes it could have avoided. A similar incident occurred late in 2007 aboard the Princess cruise ship *Sapphire Princess*, a 2,600-passenger ship on a 16-night voyage, with scheduled stops in Singapore, Shanghai, and other Asian ports. Two late-season typhoons severely disrupted the trip schedule, and Princess Cruises decided to cancel port calls in Vietnam; Okinawa; and Taipei, Taiwan. As the ship approached its final port, near Beijing, a few passengers threatened to barricade themselves in their staterooms unless they received $1,000 in chits and a free cruise.[18]

Passenger resistance collapsed when the captain noted that the police in Beijing would probably not be in the mood for negotiations. Perhaps having learned its lesson from the "*Queen Mary 2* Mutiny," Princess Cruise Lines showed that it, too, could flex its muscle and decided to draw a line in the sand with regard to cruise ship mutinies. But, as cruise ships are built ever larger, some in the maritime industry now question not the passengers' right to mutiny but whether having so many passengers on a single ship is really a good idea in the first place.

WORLD'S LARGEST CRUISE SHIPS

During its short life, the SS *Titanic* was impressive. At more than 46,000 grt (gross registered tons) when fully loaded, it was a giant in its day. It measured 882 feet and carried a total of 3,547 passengers and crew. Along with its sister ships, the *Olympic* and the *Britannic* of the famous White Star Line, it was known for its elegance, speed, and size. The *Olympic,* the first of the three ships, was outfitted with additional lifeboats after the *Titanic* disaster. The ship was involved in two collisions at sea and was scrapped in 1935. The HMHS *Britannic,* completed after the *Titanic,* struck a mine in the Aegean Sea and, despite its improved safety features, sank in a cruel copycat of the *Titanic*'s end four years earlier, although without any loss of life.[19]

Many cruise ships built in the succeeding years surpassed the benchmarks set during the golden age of luxury liners. The *Queen Mary,* the *Queen Elizabeth,* the *Normandie,* and the *Andrea Doria* are some of the more famous liners of that era. The *Queen Mary 2,* launched in 2004, brought back the coveted title "largest cruise ship in the world" to Cunard. Today, each new cruise ship sets a new record. No longer do the prized titles include "fastest liner," which was important in the transatlantic crossing market at the beginning of the 20th century. Even the largest ships, such as the *Freedom of the Seas,* are able to make 21.6 knots with their diesel electric engines. The *Queen Mary 2* can achieve speeds of 30 knots with two gas turbines and four diesel electric engines producing more than 100,300 horsepower.

Today, bragging rights go to the cruise ship company with the greatest gross registered tonnage, the highest number of passenger berths, and the greatest passenger-to-deck ratio. The growth of cruise ships during the past two decades and particularly during the past 10 years has kept pace with the phenomenal growth in the industry. In 1996, Carnival Cruise Lines launched *Destiny,* which, at 101,353 grt, measures 893 feet long and 116 feet wide and carries 2,600 passengers. *Carnival Destiny* was the first passenger ship to exceed the 83,676 tons of the largest transatlantic liner, the *Queen Elizabeth,* launched in 1938.[20]

The title of the world's largest cruise ship changed hands in 1998 when the *Grand Princess* was launched. It outweighed the *Destiny* at 109,000 grt and was slightly longer at 951 feet long. The *Grand Princess* carries 2,600 passengers. The ship held the title for only a short time; in 1999, Royal Caribbean Cruise Line christened the *Voyager of the Seas* class, which leaped to 142,000 grt. It was 75 feet longer than the *Grand Princess* and 10 feet wider and carries 3,114 passengers. Royal Caribbean Cruise Lines later launched four other ships in this class.

The world's largest cruise ships in the *Voyager* class held their title for four years, until Cunard Cruise Line delivered the *Queen Mary 2* early in 2004. Its gross registered tonnage came in at 151,000. The ship was more than 110 feet longer than the *Voyager* class ships. Although greater in size and tonnage, the *Queen Mary 2* actually carries fewer passengers than its competitors. This is because it was designed with passenger-space ratio in mind. The title again changed hands, this time in 2006, with Royal Caribbean's launching of the *Freedom of the Seas* class. *Freedom of the Seas* weighs 158,000 grt and is 1,112 feet long and 126 feet wide. Although 19 feet shorter than the *Queen Mary 2,* it is 7,000 grt heavier and carries more than twice the number of passengers.

How can *Freedom of the Seas* have a larger grt than QM2 when it is shorter and narrower? The answer is the QM2's lack of upper decks at its stern. The QM2 does not have the full height superstructure of the *Freedom of the Seas,* so it has less volume.[21] The *Freedom of the Seas* is really a stretched version of the five 142,000-grt *Voyager of the Seas* class of ships that entered service between 1999 and 2003. It has two sister ships; the *Liberty of the Seas* entered into service in 2007, and the *Independence of the Seas* was delivered in 2008.

All the major cruise lines during the past decade have introduced new ship classes. Not all compete for the title of the "largest cruise ship in the world," but are all giants compared to the *Titanic* or even to the largest of the cruise ships that helped popularize the industry in the 1980s and 1990s. Today's cruise ships offer onboard amenities unheard of 10 years ago. These include themed swimming pools, spas, ice rinks, rock-climbing walls, surfing beaches, large casinos, bars, discos, gymnasiums, basketball courts, scores of themed restaurants, lounges, and outdoor movie screens. There are, of course, the traditional standbys, such as shuffleboard and plenty of deck lounge chairs. Another noticeable trend is the building of suites and mini-suites with balconies. But, as unbelievable as all this sounds, even bigger, more innovative ships are being planned for the very near future.

Royal Caribbean Cruise Line, the second-largest cruise line in the world, planned to outdo even itself. In 2006, it ordered a new ship, dubbed the "Genesis Project." This behemoth cost approximately $1.24 billion, can accommodate up to 6,400 passengers (at full berthing configuration), and registers at 220,000 grt with a length of 1,181 feet. The new ship was delivered to Royal Caribbean Cruise Lines on October 30, 2009 from the from STX shipyard in Turku, Finland. It is the most expensive ship ever built by commercial shipbuilding. Royal Caribbean officially named the two ships in this class the *Oasis of the Seas* and the yet unbuilt *Allure of the Seas.* Ironically, Carnival Cruise Lines, the world's largest cruise line, was beaten to the punch after hesitating over its own design for a similarly sized ship and balking at its price tag.[22] Royal Caribbean Cruise Line is hoping that the trend toward bigger ships and the title "largest cruise ship" will bring in new customers; this is odd, especially since the company already holds that title.

While it is true that many cruise passengers and, more important, potential cruise passengers may be drawn by such enormity, others are not so convinced. Seasoned cruise line passengers already have stated categorically that they are tired of long lines to board and disembark, not to mention the crowded amenities on the ship and the crowds that these ships bring to their respective ports of call. It is not unusual, for example, for ports such as Cozumel in the Caribbean to have 12 cruise ships in port at one time during the peak cruising season. There is something to be said for the cruise experience being diminished as the ships increase in size.[23] Add to this the environmental issues that these ships create, the risks to offshore reefs, and the pollution generated by ships' waste, and the result is that many ports, such as Bermuda, are just saying no to ships of this size. Bermuda's Transport Ministry's plan to expand the island's ports to accommodate the mega-cruise ships provoked a storm of protest from the island's conservationists. One of these groups, the Bermuda National Trust, wrote the transport minister that "The Bermuda National Trust agrees that the cruise ship industry is a vital part of Bermuda's tourism portfolio. We do not agree that the model for the future should be mega-ships, with all their associated difficulties, in each of our major ports."[24]

Today's behemoths, Cunard's *Queen Mary 2* and Royal Caribbean's *Voyager* and *Freedom of the Seas,* although grand in scale, will be dwarfed by even larger cruise ships such as the *Oasis of the Seas.* The design, construction, and onboard amenities obviously require the highest level of imagination, engineering, and market research to pinpoint what will make cruising even more enjoyable in the future. However, some groups have been asking other, equally important questions: has equal thought been given to the effect of these ships on the ports that will serve them? Putting aside the inevitable logistical requirements, is there really a value in placing 5,000 passengers on the doorsteps of a port rather than 3,000, which is currently the norm? And what are the risks of placing that many passengers on a ship, not only because of the threats from maritime terrorism or pirates but the strains on search-and-rescue efforts in the inconceivable event that one of these giant ships might go down because of some calamity at sea?

The giant passenger ship or "mega-ship" is now a growing element in the cruise line industry. With the definition of what constitutes a mega-ship constantly being redefined, the issue of the increasing size of these vessels has also begun to attract the attention of the insurance industry. When one cruise ship can now accommodate 4,000 to 5,000 passengers on a single voyage, some companies have become nervous at the thought of placing so many people in one of these gigantic hulls.[25] There are nervous murmurings from maritime insurers that suggest that "too many eggs in such a huge basket is simply asking for trouble."[26] While the safety of large passenger ships is an issue, one must consider that taking 4,000 to

Rescued passengers from the cruise ship *Sea Diamond* wait in a lifeboat near the Greek island of Santorini on April 5, 2007. The cruise ship struck a charted reef and leaked tons of oil off the resort island at the start of the summer tourist season. The ship eventually sank, and nearly 1,600 passengers from the United States, Canada, and Spain were rescued; however, a French passenger and his daughter drowned. (AP photo)

5,000 souls out to sea on a single ship is no light matter. Even if the companies that operate such ships have good safety records, some people ask whether it is entirely responsible if one considers worst-case scenarios.

To the cruise industry, there is a good economic case for engineering these large passenger ships. It is both a matter of perceived consumer preference and business economics. Operating costs are significantly cut when one ship can carry almost twice as many passengers as smaller ships. Although not every potential passenger is attracted to the increasing size of these ships, clearly the cruise industry is ready to expand into the mega-ship market. They see the potential of the greatly untapped market of cruise passengers, especially in the United States. But does bigger actually mean better with regard to the safety and security of those who sail on these mega-ships? And what of the "cruising experience" we hear the cruise lines speak so much about? While the risks associated with having so many people on a ship with limited spaces are glaringly apparent, there is growing concern in popular ports of call about the logic of this concept. In addition to the risks inherent in depositing such large numbers of tourists on the beach in foreign ports of call, it is questionable why anyone would want to crowd the same beach with 5,000 passengers from just one ship.

As security analysts began to question the vulnerability of cruise ships to terrorism or pirates, they also began to question whether the mega-ships could survive disasters occurring from something on the ship or as a result of damage caused by the sea. In view of the increased ship sizes and passenger loads, concern has focused on whether it is even possible to evacuate very large numbers of passengers from a badly damaged vessel.[27] Recent events have tragically proven that large numbers of passengers can be put at risk if ships are inadequately designed or operated or have been subjected to modifications that may make them less stable in the event of an accident.

THE MOST SERIOUS THREAT AT SEA: CRUISE SHIP FIRES

With notable exceptions, the safety records of modern cruise ships have been relatively good in terms of seaworthiness. Modern cruise ship power plants enable them to accelerate to a speed of 25 knots, which is sufficient to outrun hurricanes and avoid tropical weather threats and even icebergs. The most significant safety threat on board any ship at sea, however, is fire. There are so many potential sources of fire on a ship that it is hardly worth listing them all; suffice it to say that every passenger (and crew member) is a potential source of preventable fires. When fire erupts, panic ensues, and the firefighting ability of the crew is put to the test. There are, strictly speaking, no full-time firefighters aboard a cruise ship; the passengers must depend on the crew for their safety.

On a naval ship, every sailor on board has a firefighting role or is assigned to a repair locker or damage control station. Training is constant and ongoing. Weekly and even daily firefighting drills test the ability of the crew to drop what they are doing and react quickly. Not only must naval crews have the training and ability to extinguish onboard fires quickly, but also they must also be trained to repair damage caused by fire. Contrast this with the situation on a cruise ship. Fewer than a fourth of the entire ship's population on a cruise ship are available to fight a fire. The balance of the ship's population (the passengers) represents a liability in terms of fighting a fire and can even become part of the problem. The passengers must be shepherded to safe areas or evacuation points on the ship. This assumes that the crew members know their assigned firefighting stations and that they will not abandon their posts out of fear, panic, or inadequate damage control or firefighting training.

The greatest threat on a ship is a fire that engulfs the engine room or "main space." The realities of fighting fires on ships can be appreciated only by those who have experienced the real thing. So, how have cruise ships fared?

In 2006, there were several significant fires on board passenger vessels. In March, the *Star Princess*, operated by Princess Cruises and registered in Bermuda,

The *Star Princess* in Montego Bay in 2006, showing extensive damage on the port side after a fire that was started by a smoldering cigarette ignited the flammable material in the balconies. One passenger died as a result of smoke inhalation. (Photo courtesy of the Maritime Accident Investigation Board: www.maib.gov.uk)

grabbed headlines after catching fire while transiting from Grand Cayman Island to Montego Bay, Jamaica. One passenger died when the out-of-control fire spread quickly through the upper passenger deck cabins.[28] The fire was traced to a smoldering cigarette that ignited a balcony railing; because of the highly flammable material used in the railing, the fire spread quickly to other balconies. More than 100 passenger cabins were damaged by the blaze, which was eventually extinguished by the ship's crew. Princess Cruises refunded passenger fares and transportation costs to those passengers stranded in Montego Bay.[29]

By far the most deadly cruise ship fire erupted on the Egyptian-owned, Panamanian-registered ferry *Al Salam Boccaccio 98* while on passage from Duba, Saudi Arabia, to Safaga, Egypt, in 2006. More than 1,000 lives were lost. In May of that year, the Cyprus-registered cruise ship *Calypso* caught fire while crossing the English Channel. Fortunately, there were no deaths or serious injuries. The fires on board the *Al Salam Boccaccio 98* and the *Calypso* were similar in size, but there was a great disparity in deaths and injuries.[30] The ability of the *Calypso* crew to extinguish the fire evidently played a significant role in saving the lives of all aboard.

It is useful to examine recent cruise ship fires to see whether the cruise lines have improved their ability to react to fire and protect both passengers and crew. While there are many incidents, like the *Calypso* fire, in which the crew won praise for how it fought the blaze, one cruise ship fire that occurred in 1996 gives some indication of what it is like to be on a cruise ship when fire breaks out and the crew is not prepared to handle the emergency.

The case of the *Discovery I* fire, in May of that year, is significant because there were several alarming indications of inadequate crew training and of a disorganized ship response once the fire broke out. Most alarming was the fact that the fire could have been avoided because the source of the fire, engine oil, had been spotted at least six hours before the start of the blaze by engine room crew members whose warning was ignored by senior ship officers. Fortunately, no one died as a result of the fire. But the need to evacuate the ship and to transfer more than 700 passengers and crew at sea certainly put lives at risk, on top of the risk to passengers from the fire itself and the panic that it caused.

The *Discovery I*, like many cruise ships not originally commissioned for service to a major cruise line, carried many names and sailed under many registers. In its early life, the *Discovery I* was known as the *Scandinavian Sea*. World Cruises, the ship's owner, began offering daily "booze cruises" or cruises to nowhere, which began and ended in Port Canaveral, Florida. The *Scandinavian Sea* caught fire in 1984, and, although there was no loss of life, the ship was gutted by the blaze, which originated in a crew cabin.

On the evening of March 9, 1984, the ship's plumber discovered a fire in the crew quarters while the ship was at sea, almost 10 miles southeast of Port Canaveral. As soon as the fire was discovered, the vessel quickly returned to Port Canaveral, and the passengers were able to disembark. Shoreside firefighters from various local and federal agencies began combating the fire, but, despite their combined efforts, the fire spread out of control. It was finally extinguished during the afternoon of March 11. No lives were lost, nor were there any serious injuries among the passengers, crew, or shoreside firefighters. The *Scandinavian Sea*, however, valued at $16 million, was subsequently declared a total constructive loss.

Although the cause of the fire on the *Scandinavian Sea* remains unknown, the most likely cause was the intentional or accidental ignition of combustible material in the crew stateroom where the fire was first discovered.[31] The ship's remains were put up for sale and sold "as is." The registered ownership changed hands a number of times until 1985, when the ship was renamed *Venus Venture*. While its rebuilding took place in Valencia, Spain, the ship was sold again in 1986 to Discovery Cruises, which renamed it the *Discovery I* and began offering short cruises from Florida.[32]

On May 8, 1996, the *Discovery I* embarked on a typical three-day Caribbean cruise. The first four and a half hours were like any normal cruise voyage. Passengers sunned themselves and ate from the buffet. Suddenly, at around 12:30 P.M., passengers began to smell smoke. As crew members began running past the buffet lines, passengers heard one of the crew say, "We have a fire."[33] The *Discovery I*'s Greek captain, Georgios Salichos, got on the public-address system and attempted to reassure the passengers about the situation. The passengers, however, found it very hard to understand his instructions because of his thick accent. Every 15 or 20 minutes, the passengers received reassuring updates from the captain indicating that everything was under control. But, as flames shot out of the ship's stack, it was obvious that a fire was raging within the hull. Panic began to set in among the passengers as black smoke began to creep into the interior parts of the ship.

Passengers were confused and later remembered being herded like cattle by crew members. There was no stairwell lighting to show the way to emergency exits, so some resourceful crew members instead lit the way with pen-lights. The rush to the open decks resembled "every man for himself." Fearful young mothers with babies in their arms tried to shield them from the commotion, while other passengers tried to make their own way out onto the lifeboat decks. No one stopped to help the elderly or the young children who began to cry because of the frightening events taking place around them.

Once up on deck, the passengers were little reassured by the sight of the rusted lifeboats. One male passenger remembered looking at an island more than three miles away and thinking if swimming was his only option, he would never make it.[34] Some passengers reported seeing crew trying to pry off fire hydrant heads with heavy tools. When hoses were finally connected, rust-colored water and "black grunge" spewed out.

The passengers described the chaos on the ship as a circus. Crew members were shouting instructions to frightened passengers huddled in the stairwells. The instructions were not understood by the passengers, because the crew members spoke many foreign languages, particularly Spanish. Most if not all of the passengers were Americans, cruising as part of a time-share promotion sponsored by a Fort Lauderdale company. As the chaos reigned around them, the passengers were petrified, and some were frozen, unsure of what to do. One passenger recalled speaking to a crew member before the fire erupted. The crew member had been making fun of the crew's remedial firefighting training and remarked that they were supposed to have a fire drill at least once every month but had not conducted one in more than six months.[35]

All cruise ship crew members are supposed to have firefighting training. But the lack of even basic firefighting knowledge among the crew was evident when, just before this particular cruise, it failed a routine firefighting drill in the presence of U.S. Coast Guard personnel. The fire drill was part of a quarterly inspection designed to test the crew's response to a simulated fire, in this instance one that originated in the ship's purifier room, where engine oil is cleaned and recycled. The firefighting team responded without basic firefighting equipment such as oxygen breathing apparatus and, incredibly, even a fire hose.

The reporting Coast Guard official who observed the drill estimated that if there had been a real fire, "they would have lost six firefighters, three officers and all of the support personnel." Another Coast Guard observer stated that "they were just walking through the drill, playing like it wasn't a real fire."[36] Incredibly, the poor review of the crew's firefighting drill was not enough to keep the ship from sailing. With a stern word of caution to the ship's safety officer from the senior Coast Guard Officer, the ship was cleared for sea.

The cause of the *Discovery I*'s fire, which originated in the engine spaces, was a fuel-line leak that had been reported by engine room personnel to their supervisors hours before it ignited. The crew members, all from Central America, testified before the Coast Guard, which investigated the fire, that at 8:00 A.M., that they observed a minor stream of oil coming from the fuel engine line. Engine room personnel wondered why the ship did not stop for the short amount of time it would have taken to fix the leak. Although the report of the fuel-line leak was received by the chief engineer, the decision was made to put off repairs until the ship made it to Freeport. The engine room crew estimated that the repair to the fuel line could have been completed in minutes if the ship had been stopped.

By noon, however, the small stream of oil had become a major leak that was now being collected in five-gallon buckets. Thick black smoke began to emerge from the engine room. Shortly after this, at approximately 12:30, the engine room's second engineer, fearful that a fire would break out, cleared the space and ordered his assistant out.[37] Within minutes, according to the men who had just vacated the engine space, the oil ignited and caught fire, erupting like a flame thrower.

In conflicting testimony given to the Coast Guard, the chief engineer denied receiving reports of leaking oil from the second or third engineer, to which the Coast Guard Investigator replied, "I don't think you're telling the truth."[38] In any event, as one passenger recalled, the reaction of the ship's crew to the emergency indicated that they clearly did not know what they were doing. The ship's captain testified that he did not sound an alarm or order passengers to lifeboat muster stations during the fire because everyone was already outside (on deck). He assumed that his three announcements about "problems in the engine room" had been understood. He believed that, as he stated in broken English, "because all the passengers come out when I say."[39]

Although the fire on the *Discovery I* had a happy ending, thanks in part to the rescue efforts by the *Freewinds,* a nearby vessel that rendered firefighting assistance, the outcome could have been much worse. Crew members were warned by the cruise line not to talk to the U.S. Coast Guard. Ultimately, three engine room mechanics were terminated as a result of their testimony to the Coast Guard, even though they had months remaining on their contracts. One of the terminated crew members, in defending his decision to go on the record about the fire even though it would inevitably portray the cruise line in an unfavorable light, said afterward, "I could not live with myself if somebody had died on that ship."[40] A spokesman for Discovery Cruise Lines issued a statement afterward downplaying the importance of the bungled May 2 fire drill and praised the crew members for their heroic efforts to save the ship.

Fire on any ship has the potential to cause great loss of life, and it is imperative that fire be controlled before it can threaten the overall safety and integrity of the ship. There is no place to hide on a ship that is on fire out on the high seas. When the cruise ship finally makes its way into a foreign port, the perceived safety shield it offers to its passengers extends to the shore activities that most of the passengers participate in. Yet that is perhaps where the passengers face the greatest risks, risks to which the cruise lines turn a blind eye.

FACING THE RISKS WHEN CRUISE
SHIP PASSENGERS GO ASHORE

When cruise ship passengers go ashore in foreign and domestic ports, they face an unexpected but omnipresent threat—and one poorly understood by both passengers and crew. This threat comprises criminal threats and a multitude of safety-related issues. Unscrupulous merchants prey on unsuspecting tourists and use scams to separate them from their cash.[41] Passengers may become victims in transportation accidents while traveling to and from the ship terminals and while sightseeing. Criminal assaults and robbery occur when passengers stray off the beaten path, and there is even the possibility that cruise ship passengers may be the inadvertent victims or targets of terrorist attacks. While these risks ashore are the same for other foreign tourists who do not arrive by ship, the question remains: what obligation do cruise lines have to protect the safety of their passengers once they leave the ship? It appears both that cruise lines feel little concern for their onshore passengers and that there is little the cruise lines can do once the passengers are off the ship. But, even though cruise ship companies cannot influence crime or terrorism ashore, they still bear a responsibility to make sure all their passengers make it back to the ship safely.

Passengers enjoy the convenience of traveling by cruise ship as a way to visit many countries and to experience different cultures. One drawback in ship travel is that passengers have a limited amount of time to spend in the ports they visit, usually less than one day. This fact alone may actually increase passengers' risks. A typical port call lasts from 7:30 A.M., when the ship ties up alongside the pier or anchors out in the harbor, to 5:30 P.M. or even earlier, when passengers must return to the ship before it sails for the next port of call. This leaves time for one, maybe two planned activities ashore, most likely booked and arranged through the onboard excursion desk. These excursions are usually not provided by the cruise lines or their affiliates. They allow passengers to sample of some of the activities available in a particular port, typically helicopter tours; plane, bus, train, and car sightseeing tours; swimming and snorkeling activities; and visits to local shopping malls, cultural centers, and restaurants.

Cruise ship passengers often do not take seriously issues of sense of safety and security when going ashore. They assume, because of the advertisements of the cruise lines, that the excursions offered have been vetted by the cruise lines and that they are therefore safe. According to the 2006 edition of *Cruise Passenger Rights and Remedies,* by Justice Thomas A. Dickerson, although cruise ships have their share of safety issues, it is usually safer to be on board than on a shore excursion, where the tourist services may offer questionable safety measures. One area of concern is whether the vendor is insured, licensed, and trained. For the passengers, the most important questions are these: has the cruise line evaluated the reliability of the vendor and assumed responsibility for any injuries suffered by its passengers, or has it disclaimed any liability for death or injuries sustained by passengers while participating on a shore excursion, whether or not it was booked through the cruise line?[42]

Justice Dickerson points out that, beyond the ship, there are three zones where accidents usually occur. Accidents may occur when passengers are being transported from ship to shore, on the pier or in areas adjacent or near to it, and in areas away from the ship and pier, such as in town, on local transportation, on a private beach, at a hotel, en route to local sites, at a local site, or at a rented villa. The law to be applied in the event of an accident on shore will depend upon the extent to which a given court wishes to extend the principles of maritime law beyond the confines of the cruise ship. Some courts have taken a conservative position, holding that maritime law ends at the gangplank, while others have interpreted the responsibilities of the maritime law as reaching beyond the cruise ship.[43]

Cruise lines understand the reasons why people go on cruises and book particular itineraries. Although the onboard activities are very appealing, there is no question that shore excursions are big business and are very important to both the ports and the cruise lines. The travel industry publication *Conde Nast Traveler* points out that

almost half of all cruise passengers—some five million a year—participate in shore excursions ranging from simple bus tours in port cities to more adventurous activities such as scuba diving trips and hot-air balloon rides. In general, the safest and most reliable way to sightsee while on a cruise is to purchase shore excursions through the cruise lines. Excursions sold by a cruise line are generally the most convenient to book, and therefore are often more crowded—and more expensive—than those purchased independently. Serious accidents on these trips are for the most part extremely rare and the cruise lines are quick to disclaim any liability for any mishaps that occur. They say that they make every effort to ensure that the businesses they work with are licensed and reputable.[44]

Competition for the cruise lines endorsement is keen among vendors in small ports. It is true that serious accidents are less frequent on tours booked through the ship. These excursions are usually the most popular, and sometimes they are the only excursions available at a particular port of call.

In foreign countries, especially those that cater to the cruise industry, local U.S. embassies are aware of the presence—sometimes on a daily basis—of the large numbers of American passengers that travel on these ships. The embassies have a number of contingency plans for dealing with an extreme security incident or emergency, whether a bus crash, a terrorist attack, or a natural disaster. If significant numbers of U.S. citizens are killed or injured while visiting a particular foreign country, the U.S. embassy may become deeply involved in efforts to conduct an investigation, advising the cruise line on additional threats or risks and assisting with services available to U.S. citizens, such as notifying next of kin in the United States. This is exactly what happened in March 2006, when 12 U.S. tourists from a Celebrity cruise ship, owned by the Royal Caribbean Cruise Line, were killed in a bus crash while on a shore excursion in Chile. In that case, the bus carrying the cruise ship passengers plunged off a 300-foot cliff. A survivor of the crash told the authorities that the bus driver had swerved to avoid an oncoming truck and had gone over the cliff. But a prosecutor in charge of the accident investigation said that the driver might have fallen asleep at the wheel.[45]

While a great number of cruise ships operate in domestic waters or stay relatively close to home, many cruise lines take their fleets into foreign ports of call. The decisions by the cruise lines to cancel or reschedule certain port calls due to changing world events in part reflect guidance from the U.S. government, especially the U.S. Department of State. The U.S. State Department issues travel warnings and travel alerts (formerly "public announcements") for a variety of security reasons, both specific and general. Most U.S. businesses, colleges, and tourist industries consider these the best source of information regarding the U.S. government's position on the safety of Americans overseas. Some groups adhere to them strictly, while others take them with a grain of salt, as sort of "nice to know" pieces of information.

The whole system has gone through many revisions. In August 1991, the General Accounting Office, the investigative arm of Congress, completed a long examination of the advisories and found them wanting. The State Department was heavily criticized for having withheld news of a threat after a Pan Am airliner exploded over Lockerbie, Scotland, in December 1988. The State Department, it was later found, even had several of its own employees aboard the jet when it blew up. Since then, there has been no "double standard" about the release of safety information. Essentially the policy is this: when the State Department and other U.S. government employees are informed of a threat, the public must be told, as well.[46]

Congress also found that there was another problem. When countries were placed on the travel warning list, they essentially remained there forever, since there were no formal procedures for reviewing whether the country still posed a risk and nothing even as simple as an expiration date. This caused considerable grief for travelers and led to economic and political tensions between the United States and the countries involved. Now, the status of all countries on the list is reviewed every six months.[47]

Obviously, no one would consider leaving for a two-week sojourn to Iraq, for example, considering the security concerns. But how about travel to Jordan, Saudi Arabia, Egypt, or Mexico, for that matter? And what if you are not a U.S. citizen but are told that your stop in a particular country has been canceled because of a U.S. State Department warning, even though the country of which you are a citizen has not issued a similar warning? This actually happened after the bomb blasts in Casablanca, Morocco, in 2003, when the British system of warnings was in conflict with that of the U.S. State Department. Princess Cruises, which was once a British company owned by P&O Cruises and for which I worked as the security director at the time, had a policy that stated that, in such instances, it would always defer to the State Department's guidance since it is now wholly a U.S. company. However, these differences in government warnings wreak havoc as companies set cruise itineraries that include countries about which different governments have different opinions regarding the safety of visitors.

Princess's management adhered strictly to U.S. State Department travel advisories. The Princess front office and its marketing and sales departments were in daily contact with my office (i.e., Security) to determine whether the latest world events had made a particular port of call too dangerous to visit. However, not all cruise lines follow these warnings to the letter the way Princess Cruises does. For example, prior to 2005, there was a State Department travel warning concerning Colombia. Since 2000, 32 Americans had been kidnapped in Colombia, including four U.S. citizens in 2004. Despite this, some cruise lines felt that it was safe to bring their ships to the beautiful colonial port city of Cartagena. The State Department warning contained harsh wording advising Americans to stay clear of Cartagena because of its history of drug-related violence.[48] Most cruise lines are now calling on Cartagena because the U.S. State Department later downgraded the travel warning to a travel advisory, essentially downplaying any serious threat to Americans. The State Department still warns Americans about the danger of travel to Colombia but does not advise against all travel by Americans. Although Princess followed the travel advisory during the time in question, its competitors justified the risky port calls by noting that they had advised their passengers not to travel outside the walled city.

In addition to its travel advisories, the U.S. government has set up a "warden system" to advise Americans, including embassy employees and their families and others who have registered with the embassy, of threats, security situations, or issues affecting their safety in a particular country. Warnings disseminated through the warden system can be short term and range from advice to Americans to avoid particular parts of a city on a specified day because of a planned political demonstration to warnings about the potential for violence in the country resulting from a labor strike or government protest of which the U.S. embassy has direct knowledge. Travel warnings, in contrast, are issued when the State Department decides, on the basis of all relevant information, that Americans should avoid all travel to a particular country, particularly to problem areas. Travel warnings can be long term or are temporary and are canceled as soon as the situation improves.

Travel alerts are issued by the State Department to disseminate information about relatively short-term and/or transnational conditions that pose significant risks to the security of American travelers. They are issued any time there is a perceived threat that targets Americans as a group. In the past, travel alerts have been issued to deal with short-term coups, bomb threats to airlines, violence by terrorists, and warnings about anniversary dates of specific terrorist events.

The State Department's Bureau of Consular Affairs also issues "consular sheets" that provide information on U.S. citizen services available through the U.S. consulate or embassy located in that country. Consular information sheets generally do not include advice but provide information in a factual manner so that travelers can make their own decisions concerning travel and safety to a particular country. They are available for every country of the world and include such information as the location of the U.S. embassy or consulate in the subject country, unusual immigration practices, health conditions, minor political disturbances, unusual currency and entry regulations, crime and security information, and drug penalties.[49]

Reading a State Department travel warning may be distressing to anyone considering travel to the country under discussion. Travel consultants who advise their clients on travel to a particular country are quick to point out that the State Department is a government agency and thus is bound to perhaps overstate some threats (by nature of releasing *all* information about a threat, whether pertinent or not). They believe that, although the State Department provides the requisite security information, it is in the business of scaring people. Travel bureaus who have their own vested interest in playing down State Department warnings counter these alleged overstatements by providing recent and detailed information contained in travel bulletins produced by private commercial companies such as Air Security International (ASI) and ijet.com. However, most of the information contained on those commercial Web sites comes directly from the State Department's own travel Web site or from the State Department's Overseas Security Advisory Council (OSAC).

The State Department has made its travel warnings public since 1978. The warnings generally cover everything from civil unrest to health concerns and originate with the U.S. embassy or consulates of a specific country. The Bureau of Consular Affairs—and, occasionally, other federal agencies—has a chance to vet the threat information, usually at a "Country Team" or "Emergency Action Committee" meeting. The final decision to put a country on travel warning status comes from the office of the Assistant Secretary for Consular Affairs under the State Department's Office of American Citizens Services and Crisis Management (ACS), who administers the Consular Information Program. One would expect a country like Iraq to be on the list because, as a war zone, it is considered by the U.S. government to be dangerous to U.S. citizens.[50] The situations in other countries, such as Syria and Nepal, need to be examined more closely to determine whether they pose a threat to U.S. travelers.

The system has been criticized by both U.S. travelers and the individual countries that are put on the warning list. Although it is not a blacklist, some countries view it as such. Many travel experts suspect that politics plays a role in State Department assessments, but the State Department denies this. However, some Middle East tour operators question why, for example, a 2006 attack on the U.S. embassy in Damascus—which was quickly subdued and caused minimal fatalities—was used to justify a long-standing travel warning about Syria when the 2005 bombings of London's public transportation system did not result in a similar warning about the United Kingdom.[51]

After the Bali bombings, in 2005, Asian nations braced for a backlash of empty hotel rooms and beaches. It became apparent that one of the terrorists' main objectives in carrying out the attacks was to cause the kind of economic repercussions that follow governments' travel warnings. Asian countries for which tourism is a major source of foreign revenue accused Western nations of making the situation worse by issuing advisories that scared people away from safe destinations. Immediately after the Bali bombings, the U.S. State Department cautioned citizens against traveling in Southeast Asia, citing the risks of terrorist actions. Asian countries said that the West's perceptions of terrorism were based on partial information after the attack and not on hard intelligence. This causes panic, they say.[52]

Asian leaders meeting at the annual ASEAN conference that year in Cambodia were quick to issue a statement of their own attacking Western travel advisories, which they said only helped achieve the objectives of the terrorists. They declared, "We call on the international community to avoid indiscriminately advising their citizens to refrain from visiting or otherwise dealing with our countries, in the absence of established evidence to substantiate rumors of possible terrorist attacks."[53] As one travel agent in Bangkok pointed out, "You have no travel advisories for Spain, where Basque terrorists stage attacks, but you have them for Laos, Burma, and Thailand, which are among the safest places in the world for tourists."[54]

It would be very bad for business and for the morale of passengers to put such security and safety warnings on the ship's marquee on the gangway. Information in these advisories regarding even the least dangerous countries can appear alarming. Merely by advising that certain tourist businesses in a particular port have safety issues or advisories can cause cruise line bookings and business for shore excursion companies to drop dramatically. In reality and in fairness to the cruise lines, there is very little they can do to stem the high crime rates or terrorist threats in some of the countries that their ships visit. Their perception is that it is not a cruise line's responsibility to fight crime ashore but that this is a problem for governments and local police to deal with. Nor can the cruise lines change or alter the terrorist threat level of a country or region. That is the responsibility of the government, as well. However, If they do not inform ship passengers of known threats in the ports that they visit, they risk being guilty of negligence.

For their part, the cruise lines are off the hook if they abide by the appropriate State Department travel warning system and set the appropriate MARSEC security level on the ship in accordance with the ISPS Code. MARSEC security levels are similar to those designated by the Department of Homeland Security. These measures apply generally to the ship and to the port but do not address the inherent dangers that lie beyond the port. From the cruise lines' point of view, the ship's passengers are incurring the same risk when going ashore that other tourists incur when traveling to the same foreign country. But, because a ship markets a particular port call to a particular country when selling the cruise or offers particular tourist excursion packages to passengers on board, they are not relieved of their obligation to advertise the prevailing crime rates ashore or to inform passengers about potential terrorist threats or the safety records of tourist venues and venders. New legislation, in the form of the 2009 Cruise Vessel Security and Safety Act, may require cruise ships to inform passengers of risks ashore by advising them of current State Department travel information. Unfortunately, there are many cases that illustrate why there is a need for such measures. One example occurred on the day after the worst terrorist attack in U.S. history.

HOLLAND AMERICA AND THE *MS MAASDAM* "FLIGHT-SEEING" TRAGEDY

The tragic events of September 11, 2001, had barely registered on the world's conscience when news of another tragedy began to trickle in to the University of Washington. More than 1,100 fans of the University of Washington's football team had earlier that week boarded Holland America's *MS Maasdam* cruise ship for a weeklong Caribbean cruise billed as the "Husky Legend Tailgate at Sea." The "Husky Legend Tailgate at Sea" is typical of the many special bookings for large groups that the cruise lines cater to. This particular charter was to pull into South Florida at the end of the cruise so that the fans could watch the Huskies take on the University of Miami Hurricanes, at the time the number-one ranked college team in the nation.[55]

The *Maasdam* departed Fort Lauderdale on Sunday. The mood of the cruise was quickly sobered on Tuesday, September 11, when the ship made port in Grand Cayman Island and allowed the passengers to learn details of the attacks on Washington, D.C., and New York City. In Grand Cayman, the itinerary encouraged passengers to enjoy the seven-mile beach, go swimming, enjoy exploring the reefs, or even take a submarine tour. Most passengers stayed on the ship, however, watching the CNN coverage of the terrorist attacks. That evening, a candlelight vigil was held in the ship's theater as a memorial to the victims of the terrorist attacks.[56] Although they did not know it, a more personal tragedy was soon to befall many of those on the cruise.

The ship set sail that evening from Grand Cayman and arrived Wednesday morning, September 12, in Cozumel, just off the Yucatán coast. During the cruise, Holland America had offered passengers on board several shore excursions, including a "flight-seeing" trip from Cozumel to the Mayan ruins at Chichén Itzá. Passengers who asked were told they would be flown aboard an American-made Cessna. "Go ahead," Ron Martin told Barbara Martin, his wife of 34 years, when she called him at home in Washington for reassurance during a port call the day of the terrorist attacks. "Holland America is a good company," he recalls telling her. "They wouldn't put you on an unsafe plane."[57] After a day of touring Mexico's most famous Mayan ruins, 16 Washington residents from the cruise ship settled into the small plane for a short ride in perfect weather to the coast and back to their cruise ship. But the plane, its passengers, and the three crew members never made it.

At 10:20 A.M., the 16 tourists from the *MS Maasdam,* ranging in age from 35 to 75, boarded their sightseeing plane, a twin-prop LET 410 operated by Aero Ferinco, and flew to Kaua, near Chichén Itzá. The airline, based in Cozumel, flies in the Yucatán Peninsula, to Guatemala and Cuba. It specializes in chartered air tours. Its primary customers are American and European tourists interested in touring the Yucatán. The Mexican pilot and his co-pilot, by all reasonable accounts, were experienced with the aircraft and knew the route by heart. The LET 410 aircraft has been popular for years in eastern Europe, and 880 of them are in service worldwide. Most of Aero Ferinco's LET 410s came from the Russian Air Force or from the Russian airline Aeroflot.[58] At 11:00 A.M., the plane landed at the airport in Chichén Itzá, near the Mayan ruins. Aero Ferinco's expedition usually brings tourists from the small landing strip to the ruins, where they can explore on their own. The small group had roughly five hours to take in the vast Mayan ruins before boarding the plane for the 40-minute trip back to Cozumel. The plane left the airport at 4:17 under clear skies and quickly climbed to an altitude of 500 feet.

Five minutes into the flight, the control tower gave the plane permission to make a right turn, and the pilot, after acknowledging the instructions, began to bank to the right when, suddenly, witnesses saw the plane plummet from the sky. It landed in a cornfield near the airport and immediately burst into flames because of the load of unexpended fuel it was carrying.[59] Rescuers to the plane were met by huge flames of fire from the burning fuel. Fearing that another plane had been blown from the sky by terrorists, the local police commander had soldiers from the Mexican Army surround the plane in an effort to cordon it off for security reasons.

Firefighters were hampered in their effort to combat the flames by lack of sufficient hose length and resorted to dousing the flames with buckets of water, handheld fire extinguishers, and dirt shoveled onto the burning mass. It took two hours to extinguish the flames and begin recovery efforts. But there were no survivors. Nineteen persons in all, including the 16 cruise ship passengers, the 2 pilots, and the group's tour guide, were killed. But the death toll could have been higher. The Czechoslovakian-made turboprop is able to carry 19 passengers. The plane left with a couple of empty seats. The University of Washington Husky fans had asked former football coach Don James to go along, but he declined, opting instead for a local day trip.[60]

Whatever happened to the plane was not a result of terrorism. Up to that point, the small charter company Aero Ferinco had apparently never had a crash in its nine-year history. But the flight history of the LET 410 was not so impressive. Several such planes had crashed. One crash had occurred in January 2001 in the West African nation of Sierra Leone, and the year before four people had died when one crashed in Costa Rica. There was one crash in 1999, two in 1998, and one in 1997.[61]

According to accounts given by the Mexican aviation officials, the pilots had not radioed for help before the crash. Other witnesses on the ground saw only one engine operating, which probably accounted for the plane's inability to come out of its sharp right turn before it plummeted to earth. The exact cause of the crash was listed as engine failure. As Holland America began working with the State Department and the U.S. embassy in Mexico to bring the bodies of crash victims home, questions about the plane's safety record were already being asked. And the answers to those questions revealed the indifferent attitude of Holland America, which had apparently preferred to gain a competitive edge over its cruise rivals rather than ensure the safety and lives of its passengers.

Holland America is a cruise line brand owned by Carnival Corporation. Just like other cruise lines, it has a senior safety representative to oversee all aspects of safety for its fleet of ships but not the operations of shore excursions. The crash of the Aero Ferinco LET 410 on September 12, 2001, was an accident, and it was unfortunate that innocent lives were lost. But could the accident and the loss of lives been prevented, and, if so, what was the responsibility of the cruise lines to warn its passengers of the risk they faced? There was no indication that the plane fell from the sky as a result of any terrorist or criminal action. That left only two possibilities: mechanical failure and pilot error. When accidents happen, where does the liability, if any, lie? Holland America prepared itself for the inevitable lawsuit that followed the crash. The company, which is headquartered in Seattle, did not immediately admit any blame or liability in the crash. In its legal responses to the lawsuit, Holland America said it could not be held responsible because passengers had signed a waiver absolving the cruise line of responsibility in the event of an accident and that, because the tour operator and the airline were subcontractors, passengers were responsible for assessing their own risks.[62]

The cruise lines' position is that they are not able to monitor every taxi, bus, train, or piece of snorkeling gear that their passengers may use while in port. But, if complaints about those conveyances or equipment were previously passed on to a cruise line by passengers or if the cruise line was withholding negative information about their safety or security records, it would be absurd to think that that information, when subpoenaed, would not work against them in a lawsuit after an accident. When lives are lost because of an act of negligence, the act takes on criminal implications.

According to documents filed in the lawsuit by relatives of the victims, Holland America knew that the small Mexican airline it used for charter flights had a long and troublesome history of mechanical problems, cancellations, and safety violations in the years before the plane crash that killed the 16 vacationing University of Washington football fans. Some of the cruise line's own employees had urged cancellation of the trouble-plagued excursion to the ancient Mayan ruins years before the ill-fated September 12 flight. Passengers on earlier flights had written letters to Holland America complaining of "white-knuckled" and terrifying experiences aboard the planes used by the charter company, Aero Ferinco, including one flight in which a door fell off while the plane was in the air.[63]

What is disturbing about the crash of the LET 410 is, although perhaps the crash of this plane could not have been avoided, that is not true of the loss of the lives of the cruise ship passengers. These passengers thought they were booking a "flight-seeing" tour that had been vetted by the cruise line because the tour was being sold by the cruise line. Apparently, it had been vetted, but not satisfactorily. According to the court documents, Holland America assured passengers in brochures and in onboard promotions that the tours were "carefully prepared" and "fully insured" and that they used the "best available transportation."[64]

According to a sworn deposition by Holland America's former shore excursion supervisor, even Holland America employees were aware of the safety record of the charter company and had warned the company to cease offering the tour. Apparently, this recommendation to cancel the tours was approved—for exactly one day in 1995 after an internal audit by the company's risk managers singled out the Chichén Itzá tour as being particularly risky because the LET 410s were manufactured in an Eastern-bloc country and because the tour company had almost no insurance.

Holland America's policies at the time required that a tour operator or airline carry a policy of at least $40 million. Court records show that Kirk Lanterman, Holland America's chief executive officer, ordered the tour resumed the next day, even though the risk issues were not resolved. A former shore excursion executive disagreed with the decision to resume the tour before the mechanical problems were resolved. Attorneys for the victims' families say Holland America chose to overlook the airline's problems because the tour to the Chichén Itzá ruins was extremely popular and distinguished the cruise line from its competitors.[65]

Holland America disavowed any knowledge of mechanical problems or safety issues related to the tour company or to the plane, even though documents unsealed by the King County judge showed that Holland America knew "years before the 2001 tragedy" that the Mexican airline that carried Holland America cruise ship passengers to the Mayan ruins had safety problems.[66] In rebuttal, Holland America went to "significant lengths" to keep secret its documents about its own investigation into safety issues related the plane by releasing the following statement: "Holland America Line had no reason to believe that the tour or its operation was unsafe prior to the accident. Furthermore, Holland America Line does not compromise safety, does not knowingly place anyone in harm's way, and most certainly does not allow profits to be more important than the lives of our passengers and employees."[67]

The documents unsealed by the judge demonstrated the opposite. They revealed the following facts: in 1995, as we have noted, Holland America canceled the Mayan ruins air tour for exactly one day because of the operator's inadequate liability insurance and history of mechanical problems, according to sworn statements by a shore excursion supervisor for Holland America; Kirk Lanterman, Holland America's chief executive officer, restarted the tour the next day. The tour was suspended again in 1996 after the incident in which an airplane's door flew off during flight. Nobody was injured. In November 1998, a plane's engine failed while it was on the tarmac, and tour escorts ushered Holland America passengers off the plane. In October 1999, one Holland America passenger described the flight to the Mayan ruins as a "white-knuckled aircraft ride." In June 2001, Holland America passengers had to switch planes after one plane's engine failed.[68] Such incriminating facts were hard for Holland America's lawyers to refute.

Holland America was caught with evidence suggesting that it indeed had known of safety issues with the chartered plane but continued to offer the tour anyway. Contrary to its own public statement, Holland America was aware that the tour it was offering its ships' passengers was at best marginally safe. What is more disturbing is that Holland America was aware that the tour company did not even carry the requisite amount of insurance. Combined with the misleading advertising regarding the type of aircraft, which assured passengers that they would be flown aboard an American-made Cessna and not the Czech-built LET, there was potential for a finding of criminal negligence. Why, then, did the victims' families settle out of court with Holland America? The statement by the attorney representing the victims' families was short and to the point: "Our response was the public had a right to know about the safety issues involving tourism products that Holland America was mass-merchandising to the public."[69]

The sad truth is that loss of a loved one carries a value predetermined by the cruise ship lines. Though the amount of money paid out to the survivors was not disclosed as a condition of the settlement, Holland America's own insurance and risk managers estimated the cruise line's liability in 1995 at $1 million to $3 million per passenger in the event of an accident on an underinsured flight.[70] After such a loss, does the thought of pursuing a criminal negligence case result in any lesser grief? Does a payment of a million dollars purchase peace of mind for such acts? Do those who had the responsibility to prevent such tragedies and who are allowed to walk away after their lawyers are finished sleep with clear consciences at night? Such is the standard operating procedure for the cruise lines. Their deep pockets have successfully shielded them from facing criminal penalties. The only true winners are the lawyers, who for better or worse, have become the cruise ship passengers' only hope for winning redress for the wrongs they have suffered or the losses they have endured.

COSTA CRUISES AND UNDERAGE DRINKING: THE DEATH OF LYNSEY O'BRIEN

While most of the attention about cruise ship safety is centered on passengers and the risks they face from crime and sexual assaults, no international effort has focused on the wellbeing of crew members, who are probably victims of cruise ship violence or accidents on a grand but unknown scale. Regardless of who the victims are, passengers or crew, there is one aspect of cruise ship life that contributes more than any other to criminal acts or safety-related accidents—that is the prevalence of alcohol.

According to the FBI assistant director's own testimony on cruise ship crime before a House committee hearing on transportation and infrastructure, physical assault was the second most frequent crime on the high seas reported to the FBI. The majority of physical assaults took place on cruise ships, rather than on other commercial vessels. Physical assaults took place in myriad locations, including bars and casinos, shared cabins, ship decks, and crew member facilities. These cases usually involved confrontations between adult men. The majority of the physical assaults were connected with domestic disputes and were alcohol related.[71]

In these instances, ship security has limited capability to intervene and restore order to protect both the guests involved in the altercation and the rest of ship's passengers. However, a bigger problem that has not been adequately dealt with by the cruise lines is the excessive use of alcohol as a central part of most ship activities and the misuse and abuse of alcohol by underage passengers and the problems that creates. Simply stated, in the closed environment of a ship, where alcohol is so prevalent, drinking can become a precursor to more serious events such as safety-related accidents, sexual assaults, and even rape.

As inclusive as the price of a cruise ship vacation is, one of the primary amenities that is not included in the fare is the price for beverages, alcoholic or otherwise. While all buffets and restaurants on the ship offer tea, coffee, and concentrated orange juice, the price for sodas and cocktails is an additional charge added to a bar tab. A bar tab can quickly add up, especially over the course of an entire cruise. The cruise environment is essentially cashless. If a passenger is of legal age to purchase alcoholic beverages, all that is needed to order drinks from the multitudes of bar hops and drink servers is the cruise card, which acts like a ship's credit card. This has a sedating effect on the passenger who, not having to present cash, is encouraged to order drinks at frequent intervals. The shock experienced on receiving the ship's final bill at the end of the cruise is enough to sober up passengers who have a hard time comprehending the number of drinks consumed on the cruise and then must pull out a real credit card to pay for them. But the larger issue is not how many drinks were ordered or how much they cost but how easy they are to order and, more important, whether they are served only to those legally of age to order them.

Taking a cruise for the purpose of underage drinking is exactly what many teenagers plan for. Consider what a typical teenager going on a cruise posted on the subject at yahooanswers.com:

> Question: So basically im 20 and am wondering how i will be able to get alcohol on a cruise im taking with some people they are over 21 but im wondering what are some good tips?
>
> Answer: On a lot of ships, if you're at least 18 you can have beer and wine once the ship reaches international waters. But you could always have one of your 21+ friends buy you drinks. Don't make it obvious though, or you could both get in trouble. My cousin and I are 18 and we had a friend buy us drinks in the theater (where it's dark and no one would notice anyway). If you're gonna do it, just be smart about it. Also, a lot of the ports have drinking ages of 18. Check and find out, and then have drinks while on the island.

This answer was chosen as the best by voters on the Web site; however, most answers were similar and suggested ways to get around the age restrictions on drinking on cruise ships.[72]

In the past, cruise ships were havens for juvenile drinkers, especially on spring break and holiday cruises. But with more and more families taking cruise vacations, the cruise lines have tightened up on their alcoholic beverage policy. The truth of the matter is that now, spurred on by such incidents as the disappearance of George Allen Smith IV from a Royal Caribbean cruise ship and the death of Dianne Brimble on a P&O cruise ship in Australia, all cruise lines have strict regulations and policies regarding drinking ages. The age policy of Princess Lines is fairly typical of most cruise lines. Their policy states: "All passengers must be 21 years old to drink alcohol or gamble in the casino; those 18 and under must share a cabin with someone 21 or older." This language is plain and simple and fairly easy to understand. The policies of other cruise lines get confusing from that point with regard to consumption of beer and wine, rules for those between 18 and 20 years old, the need for parent permission, and rules for when the ship is in South American, European, or international waters. Consider the age policies of Royal Caribbean Cruise Line: "All passengers must be 21 years old to drink alcohol, with the exception of Europe and South America cruises if parents cruising with their children sign a waiver allowing their 18 to 20 year olds to consume alcohol.

Passengers must be 18 to gamble in the casino (and 21 on Alaska cruises). If you're under age 21, there must be at least one person in the cabin over 21, unless children are cruising with their parents or guardians and staying in an adjacent cabin or if underage married couples can show proof of marriage certificate." It is apparent from policies such as these that some cruise lines are positioning themselves for every advantage in its serving of alcoholic beverages and gambling activities. Are they endangering any of their passengers with such permissive regulations? Compare Royal Caribbean's policy with that of Disney Cruise Line: "All passengers must be 21 years old to drink alcohol and you must be at least 18 to occupy a cabin without an adult."[73]

Cleverly, several cruise lines are trying to leverage their passengers for revenue opportunities. The bigger issue is whether they enforce the existing rules. Oddly enough, while you can be 18 to gamble and be present in a place where alcohol is served, you cannot order drinks. Teenage gambling is one matter, but placing teens in an environment where they are encouraged to drink, perhaps as a way to influence gambling decisions, is another. This is not a debate over morality. It is a matter of what is and what is not accepted in light of the international environment in which cruise ships operate. For example, if the legal age to gamble in the United States and on Indian reservations is 21, it should be the same on cruise ships? Likewise, most, if not all, states have laws that require that one be 21 to order alcoholic drinks, including beer and wine, which, of course, contain alcohol. The more liberal cruise ships have defined their policies according to what type of alcohol an 18- or 20-year-old can drink, limiting them to beer or wine, which is more than enough to satisfy the drinking requirements of any teenage drinker. This is almost the same as saying you can smoke cigars but not cigarettes because you don't buy cigars by the pack, so you probably smoke fewer of them. The damaging impact on your health is the same. The reason that most states have age restrictions on drinking is not so much to protect teenagers from becoming intoxicated as to protect them (and other motorists) from accidents caused by driving after drinking. The question the cruise lines ships should be asking is whether there is really much difference between giving a teenager a license to drink on a ship, even with parent's permission, if they are limited to just beer and wine and allowing them to drink whatever they want. Parents should not count on the ship's bartender to stop serving drinks to their children after what they consider to be "too much." If bartenders have to make such decisions, it is probably too late. Generally, on a ship, if you get served alcohol, you are probably of legal age. Although the drink servers have an obligation to check IDs if the guest's age is in doubt, many receive a commission or tip for each drink served, so serving drinks is in their best interest, if not in the guest's. Only when behavior crosses certain thresholds do bartenders, and in some case security personnel, get involved. A bigger problem is that, on some cruise ships, an ID check may compound the problem. Consider what happened to a young girl on a Mexican cruise.

Lynsey O'Brien, from Dublin, Ireland, was 15 years old when, accompanied by her parents, she went sailing on Costa Cruise Lines' ship *Magica* in January 2006 in the balmy waters off the coast of Mexico. Lynsey, however, did not return from her cruise vacation, and her body has never been found. The cruise ship environment that encourages drinking, combined with lax enforcement of the cruise line's own alcoholic beverage policy, combined to cut short the life of a young girl, too young to drink legally and not old enough to know the dangers of overindulging in alcohol.

According to a cruise line investigation, the cruise ship company excused itself of complicity by claiming that its personnel had done nothing wrong in serving an excessive number of alcoholic beverages to a 15-year-old girl over a two-hour period. The company said the disappearance was a suicide, but by all indications the young girl, apparently extremely intoxicated, simply fell off the ship.[74] Lynsey, perhaps guided by some of the advice offered on the Web sites or blogs cited previously, presented an identification card to a ship bartender indicating that she was 23 years old. She was served 10 alcoholic drinks over a two-hour period. The bartender went on record as stating that the young girl appeared to be an experienced drinker, despite her young age. He reportedly said, "You could tell straight away that Lynsey drank a lot."[75]

However, her parents, Paul and Sandra O'Brien, maintain their daughter would still be alive today if she had not been served alcohol. They claim she walked to the balcony of her seventh-floor cabin to be sick after consuming the excessive amounts of alcohol. They believe she lost her footing and fell 140 feet into the sea. All the punishment that was handed down to the cruise line was the removal of a bartender from his job on the ship.

In defense of the cruise line, a corporate spokeswoman stated that, although the cruise ship company is not legally required to maintain a minimum drinking age of 21 while at sea, it voluntarily enforces that age limit. The company's watered-down report of the incident concluded: "In violation of this policy, Lynsey O'Brien, along with another guest, ordered, purchased and were served a total of four or five drinks each, which they consumed over approximately a two-hour period. Lynsey is reported to have shown identification to a bartender indicating she was 23 years of age. The bartender stopped serving Lynsey alcohol after being informed she was not 21 years of age. As stated, he was subsequently fired for failing to properly scrutinize her identification."[76]

It is interesting to analyze this tragic situation from the cruise line's perspective. The company is quick to shift blame and says that it has policies that it is not "legally required to maintain." It believes that it is doing the cruise line passenger(s) a favor by "voluntarily" enforcing a drinking age limit of 21 on its ships. Its failure to put in place proper procedures by which its bartenders can verify IDs or make subjective calls on the drinking ability of passengers allows it to keep serving alcohol to passengers clearly inebriated to the point of being a danger to themselves.

Some cruise lines issue cruise cards that have with age restriction embedded in them, but this still does not deal with the obvious problem of underage drinkers who have drinks purchased for them by adults. As Director of Security at Princess Cruises, I proposed a system to deal with the problem of underage drinking on the company's ships. The drinking age policy on Princess Ships was not the issue; how ship personnel could verify whether a passenger was old enough to drink was. I proposed that this problem could be easily solved by issuing a colored wrist band to passengers ages 21 through 26 at the time of embarkation after verification of age via cruise documents, such as a passport or birth certificate, by shore personnel.

Such as policy would take the guesswork out of the process and let the bartenders off the hook, at least for determining the legitimacy of identification. The wrist band would be attached once with a nonbreakable seal, similar to the systems now in use in many discos, clubs, and bars. The wrist band would have the benefit of enabling the ship's security staff or youth security patrols to spot underage drinkers. Princess management, however, did not accept the idea, citing the cost of the wrist bands and the image it would present to the rest of the passengers; more honestly, they did not view underage drinking as presenting as big a problem for Princess as it did for its competitors. Statistics tend to bear that out; however, it is difficult to get around the obvious safety implications of serving alcohol not only to underage drinkers but having it serve as the central theme in most ship activities for patrons of legal drinking age. In the next sections we describe two infamous cases that occurred on two different cruise ships in different regions of the world. Both involved alcohol; one also involved illegal drugs.

ROYAL CARIBBEAN AND THE DISAPPEARANCE OF GEORGE ALLEN SMITH IV

What really happened to George Allen Smith IV, who was lost at sea while enjoying his honeymoon on Royal Caribbean's *Brilliance of the Seas* in the Aegean Sea in July 2005? The answer depends on whose side of the story you want to believe: the widow, the suspects, or the cruise ship and cruise line company? One cruise line executive believes the whole affair to be a "non-incident." After his disappearance, the case received enormous notoriety, just the kind of publicity that the cruise lines seek to avoid. Whether it was a crime, a disappearance, or something in between, it is through publicity that the cruise lines become victims of their own safety and security shortcomings. And, for the victim or surviving family members, there is no universally accepted world court that can investigate and pass judgment on what really happened.

To most people, it appears that the cruise lines must be in some way negligent if a passenger is all of a sudden reported "missing." After all, how does one fall off a cruise ship if the ships are designed so robustly? If the cruise ship's designers and builders were not negligent, then there must be another reason for a disappearance, possibly an accident or a criminal act such as a murder. One other possibility is suicide. In relation to George Allen Smith IV, this seems unlikely. That leaves only the first two possibilities. One thing is certain: the investigation by the ship, the cruise lines, the Turkish authorities, and the FBI have all been inconclusive and demonstrate how complicated a foreign investigation of an alleged cruise ship crime can be. In this instance, the actions of the cruise line and the professionalism of the investigation were called into question. The case drew international attention because of the bizarre circumstances of the disappearance, questions about the thoroughness and professionalism of the Turkish investigation, the response of the cruise ship investigation and charges of an alleged cover-up, the suspicious actions of the suspects, the involvement of cruise ship personnel, the role of the widow in the mystery, and the general lack of certainty about what really happened.

In most cases like that of George Allen Smith IV, the cruise lines attempt to close down all media interest in determining what happened to the lost loved one by making an out-of-court cash settlement. Although the FBI still has an open investigation into the circumstances of the disappearance of George Allen Smith from the *Brilliance of the Seas* and his assumed death, his widow accepted a cash settlement from Royal Caribbean in January 2006, effectively ending any claim on her behalf that the cruise line was negligent or in any way played a part in her husband's disappearance. But what is relevant to this discussion is not so much the "bizarre circumstances" of the honeymoon couple but the actions of the ship personnel, the FBI, and the investigators.

George Allen Smith IV was a handsome, 26-year-old businessman from an upscale Greenwich, Connecticut, home. His stunning new bride, Jennifer Hagel-Smith, was an elementary school teacher. The newlyweds, from the available information, were the ideal couple as they embarked on the Royal Caribbean cruise ship *Brilliance of the Seas* for a honeymoon cruise across the Mediterranean. In July 2005, five days after their storybook wedding, in Newport, Rhode Island, the couple boarded the *Brilliance of the Seas* in Barcelona, Spain, for a 12-day Mediterranean cruise that included port calls in Piraeus, Greece; Rome, Italy; and Kusadasi, Turkey.

Aboard the ship, the couple quickly befriended a group of young men: two Russian nationals and another Russian-speaking man from Brooklyn, New York. Another young man, Josh Akin, from California, who was traveling with his parents, was also seen in the company of the newlywed couple as they engaged in heavy drinking in the ship's disco and casino during the first few nights of the cruise.[77] If George Smith and his wife were not in the ship's disco, they could be found in the casino, usually in the company of the three Russian men and Akin. Some passengers later testified that George Smith spoke of large amounts of cash he had stored in his room safe, and, on one occasion, he returned to his cabin to resupply his wallet to cover his wife's losses at the gaming table. But it was the group's indulgent drinking that many other passengers recalled. Although it was the couple's honeymoon and they were on a cruise ship, the partying did not seem to raise that much concern among the other passengers. However, when things appeared to get a little too cozy between Jennifer Hagel-Smith and the assistant casino manager, some say that things began to fall apart between the couple. On July 4, the ship made port at the Greek isle of Mykonos. Later, the *Brilliance of the Seas* headed across the Aegean Sea en route for the Turkish port of Kusadasi. That evening, events took a turn for the worse for the newlyweds.

In the ship's disco, late in the evening of July 4, Jennifer and the group of men were joined once again by the assistant casino manager. Jealousy or rage, brought on by a constant flow of alcohol, provoked George Smith to allegedly insult his new bride after a heated argument. Jennifer Hagel-Smith was seen to knee George in the groin, making him keel over in pain.[78] A short time later, she left the disco alone. She was seen exiting the ship's elevator on the ninth deck, where her cabin was located. Her whereabouts for the remainder of the night and into the early morning of July 5 remain unknown; she was found unconscious, asleep in the passageway, on the opposite side of ship where her cabin was located.[79]

George Smith was by then extremely intoxicated. At 3:30 A.M., with the disco now closed, the three Russian men and Josh Akin helped George to his cabin. When his bride was not to be found, George changed his shirt, and the five men departed George's cabin at around 3:45 to look for her. After a cursory look in the ship's spa, the group headed back to George's cabin at approximately 4:00 A.M.[80] The different versions of what happened next form the crux of the Mediterranean cruise ship mystery. The three Russian men and Josh, seeing how intoxicated George was, allegedly put him to sleep in his bed in his stateroom and left. The Russian men returned to their own cabin and ordered room service and even took a photo of their feast as it arrived at 4:00 A.M. However, the passenger in the cabin next to George's later stated that, for at least 15 minutes after 4:00 A.M., he heard what appeared to be loud voices arguing and then the balcony furniture being tossed around. After that, the witness said he heard a loud thud on the boat deck canopy below. Many other passengers reported hearing the same loud thud at about the same time.[81] Concerned that something was amiss, the neighbor called security. Security responded and knocked on George Smith's cabin door. There was no answer. Sometime after that, in the early morning, Jennifer Hagel-Smith was found in the corridor and escorted back to her cabin in a wheelchair. She was alone. George Smith was not in their room.

A young passenger on a lower deck below where the Smith's cabin was located looked out of her cabin window the next morning and noticed a large blood stain near a lifeboat canopy. She photographed the suspicious stain and informed ship's security. Because the blood stain was under the upper deck where the Smiths' cabin was located, the ship's staff surmised that someone from that part of the ship might have gone overboard. With everyone accounted for on those decks except the Smiths, they guessed that one of them might be the missing passenger. Jennifer Hagel-Smith was later located that same morning in the ship's spa, wearing the same clothes from the previous evening. She was informed by ship's staff that her husband was "missing."[82]

As the ship made port in Kusadasi, Turkey, that morning, most of the ship's passengers departed for a day tour of the ancient city of Esephus. Turkish authorities, meanwhile, boarded the *Brilliance of the Seas* and began processing the honeymooners' cabin as a crime scene. By 6:00 P.M. that night, the blood stain on the overhanging boat canopy had been cleaned and, according to some passengers, painted over. However, as the initial Turkish investigation on the ship was concluding, both Turkish authorities and the ship's officers questioned Jennifer, Josh Akin, and the three Russian men who were among the last people known to have been seen with George Smith, about what had happened just hours before.[83] The ship also notified the FBI through the U.S. embassy in Ankara. An FBI agent who happened to be vacationing in Turkey near the coastal town of Kusadasi was notified by the U.S. embassy and volunteered to proceed to the ship. This was a dedicated agent who gave up part of his vacation because he realized that it would have taken several days to fly an agent from Washington, D.C., to conduct the investigation on a ship in an international port. Had this incident taken place in another remote region, country, or port, the FBI in all likelihood would have been unable to respond in a timely manner. Ironically, special agents of the Diplomatic Security Service are stationed in every U.S. embassy and U.S. consulate. They have the same criminal investigative training as FBI agents and could have responded to the ship in a matter of hours; unfortunately, they have no jurisdictional authority in these cases. Because the FBI agent was close by, however, he interviewed Jennifer Hagel-Smith in conjunction with cruise ship officials and the Turkish authorities. By order of the ship's captain, Jennifer Hagel-Smith was summarily put ashore and returned home to the United States that evening. What she told the FBI has remained sealed in the FBI's official investigation. However, it was rumored that either blood or a lipstick stain was found on a towel in the Smiths' stateroom.

Jennifer Hagel-Smith is very critical of the way the cruise ship staff and particularly its captain treated her after her husband's disappearance. She later stated that the ship's captain "insisted that I leave the ship in order to undergo a day of interrogation by Turkish officials. The captain lied about where I was going and with whom, but more importantly he appeared satisfied to get me off the ship, expedite the investigation, and keep to his schedule. The captain did not seem very concerned about my husband, and to this day has repeatedly lied about how this tragic news was relayed to us, the way he conducted himself the day George disappeared, and how he prematurely labeled this 'an accident.'"[84]

The so-called suspects were equally critical of the Turkish investigation and their interrogation. It is unknown what the Russian men told the Turkish authorities, but Josh Akin's father accompanied his son to the Turkish police station where he was interviewed. There, he secretly recorded the chaotic interrogation of his son through a hidden video camera. Normally, an American being interrogated by foreign police officers is entitled to have a representative from the U.S. embassy present. But, because Josh Akin had not been formally charged with a crime, he had no such representation. Instead, the Turkish police investigator questioned Josh Akin through an interpreter about what had transpired on the *Brilliance of the Sea* less than 24 hours earlier.

The English interpreter was a Turkish woman who had been summoned on short notice and had her baby infant with her in the room. From the video recorded by Josh Akin's father, it appears that the scene was one of confusion. Over the baby's constant crying, Josh Akin tried to make it clear to the investigator that the assistant casino manager should be interviewed because he was one of the last to see Jennifer Hagel-Smith. But the Turkish authorities wanted a statement from Josh Akin only about when he last saw George Smith, not about Jennifer Hagel-Smith or the assistant casino manager.[85] Akin insisted that both Jennifer and the casino manager were important parts of the story of George's disappearance. At the insistence of his father, however, Josh signed a prepared statement and returned to the ship with his parents.

At the appointed sailing time, the captain of the *Brilliance of the Sea* made a brief and matter-of-fact announcement over the ship's intercom about a "missing passenger." He reassured the other passengers that everything possible was being done by the FBI and the local authorities. With that, the ship drew in its mooring lines and set sail, minus Mr. and Mrs. Smith. Jennifer Hagel-Smith later recalled how she felt that evening: "It seems that an abundance of evidence and many important clues sailed away that evening with the cruise ship as opposed to being uncovered by the FBI. . . . George and I left together newlyweds, in love and so excited about our trip. Now, I was flying home alone, a distraught and confused widow, and all of our lives would never be the same again."[86]

As the U.S. Congress began looking into cruise line security and cases like that of George Smith from the Royal Caribbean ship, an attorney representing Smith's family said on CNN's *Larry King Live*: "We think increasing public awareness as to crimes occurring aboard the ships would help as an increased security presence onboard the ship. . . . Today the cruise line wouldn't answer any questions about the amount of security that they actually have onboard ship or who would constitute actual security officers or qualified security personnel. . . . It leads you to believe, as the Congressman said, if they had a lot of security personnel onboard

Jennifer Hagel-Smith (center) attends a House Government Reform subcommittee hearing in March 2007 on international maritime security involving cruise ships. In July 2005, Jennifer Hagel-Smith and her new husband, George Allen Smith IV, were aboard the Royal Caribbean Line's *Brilliance of the Seas* as it sailed from Greece to Turkey. Smith, a 26-year-old businessman from Greenwich, Connecticut, disappeared after an apparent late night of drinking. No body was ever found, sparking allegations of a cruise line cover-up. (AP photo/Lauren Victoria Burke)

who are qualified they would have wanted to volunteer that information and to have been proud of that."[87]

Obviously, the family of George Allen Smith IV grieved his loss. The FBI still has an ongoing investigation, but, because his widow settled with the cruise line, it is doubtful that there will ever be a prosecution in this case, particularly since no crime has as yet been uncovered. At this point, no charges have been filed against any person. A lawsuit brought by the family of George Allen Smith against Royal Caribbean Cruise Line was dismissed. The family alleged that the cruise line delayed reporting the incident to the FBI, did not preserve the crime scene, and deliberately portrayed the incident as an accident. Lawyers for Royal Caribbean called the lawsuit "frivolous." As the Smiths' attorney concluded on *Larry King Live,* "we believe that the cruise ship industry has deliberately engaged in a systematic pattern or practice of keeping this quiet from the public because it hurts their public image."[88]

As a footnote to the George Allen Smith case, the FBI was also called to investigate an alleged rape that took place on the same ship on the same cruise. Before George Smith's disappearance played out, an 18-year-old woman claimed that the group of Russian men who were persons of interest in the George Smith incident had raped her while the ship was leaving Greece several nights before Smith's disappearance. The Russian men claimed that the sex was consensual. When the ship returned to Naples, the men were escorted off the ship for further questioning.

P&O CRUISES AND THE UNTIMELY
DEATH OF DIANNE BRIMBLE

While the events that occurred in the disappearance of George Allen Smith IV played out in rapid succession and, as Jennifer Hagel-Smith later claimed, important clues literally sailed away the same day, other cruise ship investigations take years to come to the surface. The notoriety that arises from those facts becomes a real issue that the cruise lines must deal with. This was the case in the ongoing investigation of the death of Dianne Brimble, which occurred on Australia's P&O Cruises' *Pacific Sky* in September 2002. At the time, the *Pacific Sky* was owned by Carnival Corporation and managed by Princess Cruises, but it has since been sold.

Dianne Brimble, 42 years old, who had saved for years to go on a cruise, was accompanied by her 12-year-old daughter, her sister, and two family friends on a cruise on the *Pacific Sky.* Within 24 hours of boarding the ship, she was found dead in a room occupied by four men, apparently of a drug overdose mixed with alcohol. The four men in whose cabin Brimble's body was found were part of larger group of eight men with whom Dianne Brimble had been seen dancing in the ship's disco in the early morning of the day she was found dead. Years later, in

2005, DNA evidence found underneath Dianne Brimble's fingernails launched a murder investigation focused on these eight men, all well known to Australian law enforcement for having criminal records, mostly related to drugs. In court, the testimony of witnesses portrayed a bacchanalian night of drinking, drugs, and sex with no restraints, no security oversight, and little regard for the circumstances of Dianne Brimble's final hours. Photos of Brimble having sex with at least two of the men were made known in the investigation; however, the photographs, recovered from the cell phone of one of the persons of interest, were not released because of their graphic content.

When charges of sexual assault are leveled on cruise ships, the usual response of those accused is that the sex was consensual. When the victim is deceased and is unable to testify, as in the case of Dianne Brimble, proof must come from the physical evidence, witness testimony, and the competency of the investigation. This, like all sexual assault cases, may mean dragging the reputation of the victim through the investigative and/or legal process. According to character witnesses, Dianne Brimble was a woman of good moral character. Why, then, her alleged uncharacteristic conduct on the night she died? In the case of Dianne Brimble, there are only two possible answers to that question: her unwilling participation in the use of drugs (and alcohol), which resulted in her being raped, or her agreeing to use drugs and having sex with persons that she had met less than 24 hours before. One of these scenarios ultimately contributed to her death, which has yet to be fully explained.

The circumstances and events of her death were played out in the Australian courts and represented a massive public relations disaster for the management of Carnival Corporation and for the CEO of Princess Cruises, Peter Ratcliffe. Although the events that took place on the *Pacific Sky* occurred in 2002, the fallout from that case and its effect on P&O and Princess management began to materialize only in early 2007, a full five years after the incident. It culminated with a press conference in February of that year in which Peter Ratcliffe announced an undisclosed cash settlement to the husband of Dianne Brimble and made public apologies for Mrs. Brimble's death, outlining also the many security management changes that have taken place at P&O and Princess to prevent another similar tragedy.

In June 2007, Ratcliffe informed Carnival Corporation that he would retire effective March 6, 2008. A Carnival Press release stated that effective immediately, David Dingle was promoted to CEO of Carnival UK with responsibility for the company's British brands—P&O Cruises, Ocean Village, and Cunard Line. He also was appointed chairman of the Carnival PLC Management Committee, with responsibility for P&O Cruises Australia. "It has always been a goal of mine to retire at age 60 and in this case, the effective date is actually my 60th birthday," said

Ratcliffe. "I've had a tremendously rewarding career in this industry and know that I leave the future of my cherished brands in the most capable hands of David [Dingle]," he added.[89] What role, if any, did Dianne Brimble's death play in Peter Ratcliffe's decision to retire as CEO of Princess? Just like Bob Dickinson, the former CEO of Carnival who had referred to the disappearance of George Allen Smith IV as "a non-incident," he may have found that the notoriety from the case did not play well with the company's board of directors.

Fortunately for P&O and Princess Cruises, the settlement effectively ended their culpability in Mrs. Brimble's death, but it did not quell the inquest into her death. The Australians still have an ongoing criminal investigation. This is obviously not what P&O/Princess had hoped for. However, driven by these events, P&O/Princess made some significant changes in its security management, most of which I, as director of security, was involved in.

The outgoing Princess CEO outlined these measures in his press conference in February 2007. They included making one senior officer responsible for all onboard security; creating a new security department headed by the division's chief security officer, who would be based in Los Angeles; appointing a new Sydney-based shoreside management to report to the chief security officer; introducing improved training programs dealing with crime scene preservation, response, and investigation; increasing the number of onboard security personnel from 10 to at least 20; ensuring that security specialists are licensed in either Australia or New Zealand; and implementing more rigorous random drug search procedures.[90] Many of these initiatives already existed in some form or another on P&O ships operating in Australia and were, for the most part, a direct result of the security requirements mandated by the ISPS Code, which went into effect on July 1, 2004.[91]

The larger issue was the so-called schoolies cruises that were so popular with the Australian cruise market and that raised issues the company had long failed to deal with. A year after the death of Dianne Brimble on the *Pacific Sky*, an advertisement for P&O Cruises featured a row of bikini-clad women lounging on deck chairs under the caption "Seamen Wanted." There was, in addition to the "Seamen Wanted" catchphrase, a postcard that featured an image of the *Pacific Sky* and the slogan "More girls. More sun. More fun. There's nothing else a guy needs to know!" P&O later apologized for the ads, calling them "insensitive."[92]

Other changes at Princess and P&O Cruises focused on cultural changes within the company. Management introduced new marketing and advertising protocols that would prevent tasteless and unacceptable advertising; a policy of zero tolerance for excessive behavior that provides that any person involved in such behavior will be taken off the ship, flown home to Australia, and reported to the police where appropriate; a new customer service training program for onboard personnel; the end of "schoolies" cruises; and improvements in the way the company responds to complaints, including a 24-hour hotline so people can contact management.[93]

Another concern at P&O Cruises was the way alcohol is served on its cruise ships. Alcohol is a problem on all cruise ships to varying degrees, but on the *Pacific Sky* and its sister ship, the *Pacific Sun*, the problem was magnified. The "schoolies" cruises were the Australian equivalent of America's spring break; several times each year, cruises were sold as schoolies cruises. The youthful Australian market was no different from its American counterpart, except that the underage drinking, binge drinking, and partying were played out in extremes. In response to these growing concerns, Peter Ratcliffe announced that, in conjunction with the Department of Liquor, Gaming, and Racing in New South Wales, P&O Cruises would ensure that its procedures conformed to best practices in Australia. Also, the company stopped paying commissions on sales to bar staff; stopped passengers from bringing alcohol on board; closed bars in the early morning hours; and strengthened procedures for making sure underage passengers are not served alcohol.[94]

In November 2006, apparently true to its word and among the devastating publicity that followed the Brimble inquest, four rampaging teenagers were kicked off the *Pacific Sun* after a number of serious misbehavior incidents during one of the line's last schoolies cruises. The drunken passengers were caught urinating in corridors and over the ship's side and were involved in other "inappropriate behavior." None of the booted-off students faced criminal charges over the incidents, however. A 17-year-old passenger on a schoolies cruise stated that security staff on board the *Pacific Sun* were watching their every move. "You can't get a drink and they are even watching the older ones to make sure they aren't serving us alcohol," the schoolies cruiser said.[95]

P&O Cruises announced, in October 2006, that it was officially canceling all future schoolies cruises because of trouble on previous voyages. "School leaver and other age-dedicated cruises are not where we see our business developing," P&O said at the time.[96] Although the decision to cancel the schoolies cruises was announced in October 2006, P&O Cruises failed to implement its plan to cancel them until the following cruise season, once again demonstrating that its foremost concern was the company's bottom line, rather than the prevention or avoidance of future criminal conduct on its ships.

Apparently the family of Dianne Brimble was concerned about the plan. A spokesman for the Brimble family, who also represents the International Cruise Ship Victims Association (ICV), said that the company's decision to go ahead with that year's cruises was not good enough. Even Mark Brimble, the widower of Dianne Brimble, said that P&O was not doing enough to ensure passenger safety.

He said, "I think they've done an excellent job in public relations and they're cleaning up their image, but the question is: are they cleaning up their act?"[97]

THE PROBLEM OF CHILDREN ON CRUISE SHIPS

Of all the complaints that cruise ships receive, among the most frequent are complaints related to the supervision of children and adolescents. On almost every cruise blog or cruise review, the issue of children roaming freely on the ship without any apparent parental supervision generates criticism and complaints by passengers who believe that their cruise experience has been diminished or, in some cases, ruined by rowdy juvenile behavior. In fairness to the cruise lines, this is a society-wide problem; the same lack of parental supervision is noted at theme parks, hotels, and schools and in other social settings. But the safety and security problems created by young passengers aboard a ship affect the larger issue of maritime safety. The problem is that most cruise lines cater to families during peak vacation periods such as summer, Christmas, and especially spring break. Families with children are in the majority during these voyages, and children and teenagers can be as numerous as adults. Children and teenagers create special problems on cruise ships that are not designed especially for accommodating and supervising them away from their parents. Children and teenagers are both at risk from the shipboard environment and also from the occasional predator. Disney Cruise Lines has two ships, the *Disney Magic* and the *Disney Wonder*, which normally operate from a base in Miami. As one can imagine, the whole ship is designed around the family, and activities for the children and supervision are on a scale appropriate to the large numbers of children on board. Disney even advertises such attractions as its private island, Castaway Clays, in the Bahamas, where the ships make a port call so that passengers can enjoy the private beach and lagoon. Disney Cruise Lines is planning to launch the *Disney Dream* in 2011. Construction began on the third ship in the Disney Fleet in March 2009 at the Meyer Werft shipyard in Papenburg, Germany. The 128,000-ton vessel will include 1,250 staterooms and will have the capacity to comfortably accommodate 4,000 passengers—along with the over 1,458 crew members.[98]

Some cruise lines have exceptional outdoor attractions, such as surfing, golf, and rock-climbing walls. Royal Caribbean was the first to introduce these features, which are very popular with younger passengers. Use of these attractions, however, is limited normally to the daytime schedule. Some cruise ships have very limited capacity for handling a large influx of young passengers. While Princess ships have "Fun Zones" and dedicated children's swimming pools, outdoors movies, and arcades, management has yet to install rock-climbing walls or similar attractions. The shipboard environments, while child-friendly, are generally geared to an older crowd. That is not to say that, during peak holiday periods, the cruise line is not concerned with the large influx of children, preteens, and teenagers who accompany their parents on popular itineraries.

All cruise ships face the problem of supervision around the pools, spas, and open deck areas. The problem is compounded at night when these attractions are closed and children and teenagers are allowed to roam the ship in search of activities while their parents enjoy the restaurants, lounges, casinos, and theaters. While most ships have theater shows designed for the entire family, kids are not required to attend with their parents and usually prefer to make new friends and explore the ship. The problem of supervision is acute in the case of preteens and teenagers. They are too old for the fun zone supervision and activities and too young to visit the lounges and casinos that come alive at night on a cruise ship. Some ships have special teen discos that come with their own set of problems. While no alcohol is served in these venues, teenagers still find ways to get into trouble.

As with all teenagers, the problem of getting into mischief is compounded when there is nothing for them to do. Most of the trouble comes in the form of noise and boisterous activities in and around the stairwells and open deck areas at night. Complaints to the purser's desk usually come from passengers with cabins near these stairwells. The purser, in turn, asks the security department to check out the source of the disturbance. Usually security's presence solves the noise problem, but it does not solve the problem with the unsupervised kids. They just move on to a new location on the ship.

Passenger complaints that make their way to the cruise reviews and blogs generally criticize the rowdy behavior of children at dinner tables, pools, and buffet areas and the lack of parental control. These behaviors are generally more a reflection on the state of parenting rather than the fault of the cruise lines. Nevertheless, it is the parents who are the paying customers of the cruise lines, and they are very aware of the problems associated with bringing their children along on cruises. Children create liability risks because of the ship environment and because parents, of course, are on vacation as well, and depend in some cases too much on the ship to provide the necessary supervision. Believing that the ship is a self-contained environment, parents allow children to come and go as they please, imposing whatever curfew (if any) they wish. After all, they are on a ship; where can the young people go? The cruise lines and the ships offer varying degrees of supervision and, in some cases, impose their own curfews.

There are many issues to address in trying to solve the problems on holiday cruises where the number of children and teenagers equals or is greater than the number of adult passengers on board. In response to passenger complaints received during and after holiday cruises, Princess decided to add extra shipboard personnel to monitor the kids on board. It introduced the "Youth Security" program now visible on specific Princess ships at varying times of the years. The idea was to add an additional layer of human resources composed of people with experience in dealing with young people to the security already on the ship.

Princess recruited these individuals from the teaching profession, which worked out well from the teachers' perspectives, because they were usually on vacation during the same time of the year that the cruise ships had their largest influx of children. Princess also recruited youth counselors and social workers. Not quite ship employees, they were more like contractors who augmented the staff on popular itineraries, especially in the Caribbean. They were paid a stipend and given room and board. Needless to say, there were more than enough applicants for the program.

The main responsibility of these extra workers was to be visible on decks, at all hours, so that they could be seen by both the adults and the kids. The uniform for the Youth Security contractors was debated at length. Other cruise lines dress their security staff in very nonthreatening attire. On Carnival ships for example, it is hard to tell the security officers from other shipboard staff because they all wear white shirts, blue blazers with a name tag, and grey slacks, giving them the appearance of a theater usher. Princess ships' security officers wear shirts with epaulettes, and the word "security" is prominently displayed.

Because the Youth Security officers had to be visible but look different from the ship's regular security staff, Princess settled on a bright yellow polo shirt with the words "Youth Security" printed largely across the back and on the breast pocket. Officers were allowed to wear khaki shorts and tennis shoes. Other than a radio and flashlight, they carry no law enforcement gear, such as handcuffs. Thus they look more like camp counselors than security officers. Their main task was to keep an eye out for any potential problems associated with kids, while preventing accidents and stopping unsafe activities. They were also a force multiplier, because, although they were not part of the ship security force, they still came under the supervision of the ship security officer, who gave them instructions for keeping an eye on other areas of the ship.

The Youth Security program was generally a success. For the first time, Princess Cruises began receiving compliments and favorable endorsements from passengers who felt that the supervision and safety of all the guests on the cruise was enhanced by these extra set of eyes. Adding an additional layer of security to monitor the activities of one group of passengers may have seemed extreme, but the method of dealing with the problem of unsupervised children on Princess ships pales in comparison to actions taken by other cruise lines, such as Carnival and Royal Caribbean. RCCL, for example, has imposed curfews for children on some of its ships.

The whole purpose of a curfew is to restrict the movement of certain classes of passengers and to limit the times they can be on the weather decks and in the interior of the ship at night. The vast majority of accidents and "disappearances" happen at night. The risk that someone accidentally or purposely will fall off a ship is compounded by nighttime darkness, some weather conditions (especially wind), and the absence of other passengers from the open decks during darkness. Curfews especially designed for children, preteens, and teenagers make sense regardless of the cruise itinerary because children are the passengers most likely to climb railings and engage in risky horseplay around the edges of the ship. Another logical reason for a curfew is to give parents the peace of mind that comes from knowing exactly what time their children are expected to return to their cabin. Cruise ships at night, although brightly lit, have very dark spaces and areas that are not routinely patrolled by security. Sexual assaults have occurred many times late at night, after the bars and discos have closed, when an inebriated adult has crossed paths with a minor wandering the cruise ship alone late at night. Consider the experience of one parent on a recent Carnival cruise, related in a letter written in response to a *Washington Post* article about cruise ship safety:

> I recently went on a Carnival Cruise with my two teenagers who had a great time in the kids club which was supervised until about 0100 am. The clubs were divided by age group and the security at the door had lists of all the kid's names and ages so they made sure that the kids went into the club for their age group and there was no underage drinking. I gave my kids a curfew every night to return to the room. One night my daughter didn't return and so my son and I searched the ship for her for about two hours and couldn't find her. I was frantic!! The ship was quite deserted as most people had gone back to their rooms. I reported this to security and the security guard responded immediately and thankfully found her at the top of the ship. I would like to see the cruise lines have a curfew for kids under 18 to be back in their rooms when the supervised activities end. The cruise ships are like anywhere else, staying out late gets dangerous. It is hard for teenagers to understand this, especially in a vacation environment.[99]

The list of reasons for imposing children's curfews is long and the action justifiable from the standpoint of safety and security, but not from a revenue one. Princess currently opposes the idea. Its reasoning is understandable. It believes that someone paying for the privilege of being on a ship should not be told when and where he or she can be and at what times. Royal Caribbean allows the captains of its ships to impose curfew whenever they consider it necessary to maintain order and peace on the ship. However, doing so may mean admitting that they have lost control of public safety. Unless a curfew is part of the advance cruise plan, the captain will probably never impose one suddenly.

Cruise lines should simply pass a mandate dealing with curfews and get past worrying how adult passengers will react. Once the standard has been universally adopted in the cruise industry, the numbers of both accidents and complaints will decrease dramatically and perhaps a tragedy involving a child or teen will be avoided. The alternative to imposing a curfew is perhaps what Princess decided to do: hiring more staff to watch over the younger passengers. Doing that incurs costs. Unfortunately, cruise lines will continue to maintain the status quo unless there is pressure from outside groups. Despite their appearances, cruise ships, especially at night, are dangerous places. As the ships grow in size and passenger loads increase, the cruise industry will either impose curfews or suffer the (fill-in-the-blank) consequences.

four

PROTECTING PASSENGERS AND CREWS FROM PIRATES, TERRORISTS, AND CRUISE SHIP ACCIDENTS

The position of director of security for a first-class luxury cruise line would seem like a dream job to most people, at least to those who could appreciate the type of security challenges that a cruise ship presents. Unlike buildings or military complexes, cruise ships are constantly moving, crossing seas and oceans and moving from port to port roughly 365 days a year. A cruise ship can carry five times as many passengers as the largest jumbo jet and takes travelers to exotic ports of call. The potential for security incidents both on the ship and in these foreign destinations is enormous; thus, the role of security is particularly crucial. I was aware of a few simple facts about cruise ships before I accepted the job as director of security at Princess Cruises: that their security and safety are significantly disadvantaged by two unpredictable elements, the international environments that these ships operate in and the lawless nature of the sea itself.

I had been employed by the U.S. Department of State for more than 15 years as a Diplomatic Security Service (DSS) Special Agent. The DSS has a broad range of security responsibilities. Part FBI and part Secret Service, the DSS is distinguished from these renowned law enforcement agencies by the fact that, in addition to serving at field offices in the United States as FBI or Secret Service agents do, DSS agents are required to serve overseas for two or three years at a time as the lead security representatives at a U.S. embassy. For my part, I served as a regional security officer at five U.S. embassies and had considerable experience in providing protective and physical security in countries with some of the highest threat levels in the world. I was also a former naval commander with Naval Intelligence. My background was just what Princess Cruises was looking for when it sought a director of security.

The biggest challenge I faced at the outset was conforming the security practices employed by the Princess fleet of cruise ships to the new security standards mandated by the International Ship and Port Security (ISPS) Code scheduled to go into effect in July 2004. The cruise industry implemented the ISPS Code with relative ease because many of the security measures adopted in the Code were already mandated for cruise ships as a result of the *Achille Lauro* hijacking in 1986. In 2004 and prior to the July ISPS Code deadline, Princess Cruises delivered three new cruise ships: the *Caribbean Princess,* the *Diamond Princess,* and the *Sapphire Princess.* In addition to these ships, all other Princess ships received their ISPS certification with the issuance of their International Ship Security Certificate (ISSC). This milestone was something to be proud of. While ships were required to enforce certain new security measures, however, port facilities were also required to be in compliance with their own set of security measures mandated by the ISPS Code. While it is unlikely that any cruise ship today would sail into a port that is not ISPS compliant, smaller cruise ships may visit remote ports that are not in compliance because the ISPS regulations do not require that they be. Some of these "ports" are nothing more than beaches from which small cruise ships anchor out. What is troubling for cruise ship security planners is that even in ISPS-compliant ports, shore security varies from port to port and from country to country.

It is a false assumption that, regardless of the ISPS Code, ship and passenger screening capabilities are up to the same standard around the world. Normally, in U.S. ports, cruise terminals are under contract with cruise lines or are part of a consortium that provides screening services for the cruise ships. After the passenger's belongings have been screened and the passenger has walked through a metal detector in the terminal, the passenger usually need only present a boarding card to gain access to the ship. Overseas, however, where the terrorist threats are more acute, the screening process becomes more critical and security may be more at risk.

Early in 2004, while conducting an unannounced assessment of port security in Barcelona, Spain, I observed a terminal security officer assigned to a screening station for a Princess ship. He was reading a magazine and generally being inattentive as passengers' belongings passed through the x-ray machine he was monitoring. Meanwhile, passengers continued to set their belongings on the conveyor belt and passed through the metal detector to pick up their things on the other side. On September 11, even though the screeners at the U.S. airports were watching their x-ray monitors, the hijackers were able to smuggle simple box cutters aboard the aircraft. This screener was paying no attention at all.

Taking photographs inside the terminal, especially of the security operations, is strictly forbidden. However, the Princess ship's photographer happened to be making his way back to the ship through the screening checkpoint at that very moment I observed the inattentive screener. I spoke to the photographer briefly about an unrelated issue as we continued to watch the screening officer at the security checkpoint. He agreed with us that the guard was being grossly negligent.

When I arrived back in the corporate office after this trip, I was surprised to find a photo, forwarded by e-mail, from the ship's photographer. He apparently had taken a picture somehow of the security guard officer the morning we spoke. The photo showed the guard still holding his magazine, his chair turned away from the x-ray machine. In front of him was a passenger picking up his luggage on the other side of the x-ray machine. I tacked that photo on the wall in my office, hoping to use it on my next trip to Barcelona. Princess management intervened, however, and, while agreeing that the behavior was an egregious example of inattentiveness, suggested I not show the picture to the port officials in Barcelona.

My overseas inspection on that particular trip just kept finding worse and worse things, however. The x-ray problem in Barcelona was similar to a problem in Naples, Italy, my next stop. Next to a truck with Arabic license plates parked 10 feet from the ship's hull, which immediately caught our attention, my security manager pointed out that the metal detector in the terminal was unplugged. It was unplugged not because someone forgot to plug it in but because it did not work. Apparently, the police hoped that no one would notice. Oddly enough, they still made all passengers walk through it. Although these discrepancies meant problems for ship's security, it was almost impossible to raise these concerns to the port police commandant. There seemed to be an attitude in the port that this was the way things are and that we should not be questioning them.

What was distressing about these inspections was that the ports in Naples and Barcelona in particular had all the required ISPS elements in place, at least with regard to passenger screening, well before the July 1, 2004, ISPS deadline for port compliance. Later that year, al-Qaeda successfully bombed several trains in Madrid while I was traversing the Suez Canal on another Princess ship. I could only think back to my security inspection at the port in Barcelona when I heard about the latest al-Qaeda attack and how perhaps we had been lucky in their choice of targets. Physical inspections of the port terminals were very important, and protecting the flanks of the ship was proving to be a daunting physical security challenge. While examining the physical security requirements of the ship, I had to consider not just the waterside approaches to the ship but those on the pier, as well. The National Threat Assessment (NTA) in 2004 concluded that al-Qaeda will most likely use a vehicle-borne improvised explosive device when attacking maritime targets. The NTA suggested that the most likely targets for such an attack are maritime infrastructure, merchant vessels, and warships. The second most likely target is a cruise ship or ferry.[1] It makes sense that if terrorists have a clear avenue to attack the ship with their proven methods of using vehicle-borne improvised explosive devices (VBIEDs), then they may simply try to drive a vehicle straight up and onto the ship and then detonate its payload.

Apart from the gangways where a narrow bridge connects the ship to the pier for passenger access, loading ramps have the capability of accommodating forklifts and small service vehicles used to load supplies and baggage on the ship. The possibility certainly exists that someone might try to exploit this access to the ship. A few drunken Australians proved that. They scaled a perimeter security fence, commandeered a forklift, and drove it up the loading ramp onto the *Queen Elizabeth 2* while the ship was in Fremantle, Australia, in February 2005. Two men and two women managed to gain access to the ship and tried to steal a vase in the ship's grand staircase before their presence on the ship was questioned. This incident irritated me because, a month earlier, I had spent an entire afternoon with the security officer on that ship while it made a rare port call in Long Beach, California. Both of us stood outside on the upper walkway of the port terminal looking down at the ship. I remember raising concerns about the loading ramp doors that were left unguarded. The ramps are used by forklifts loading the ship with supplies. The ship security officer gave me his assurances. In foreign ports, he said, he would ensure that the ramps were guarded. Obviously, in this instance, that did not happen. For me, back at Princess corporate headquarters, the event only highlighted the need to secure vehicle ramps and passenger gangways that could accommodate, at the very least, a small vehicle laden with explosives.

Security equipment is effective only if used. The *Queen Elizabeth 2* was equipped with the new movable vehicle barrier (MVB) that I had persuaded Princess management to purchase for all Princess and Cunard ships. The MVB is a remarkable lightweight, fully transportable vehicle barrier that can be set up in minutes. The devices are manufactured by Miframe Security, an Israeli company that has 40 years' battlefield experience in countering the threat posed by VBIEDs.[2] The MVB is meant to serve as a roadblock preventing direct access to a ship's ramps and is capable of stopping a speeding vehicle dead in its tracks. Suicide vehicle bombs have been used with great effectiveness in all parts of the world, but especially in Israel, Iraq, Afghanistan, and Lebanon. High-risk buildings and structures such as embassies and military facilities are designed with nonmovable vehicle barriers such as bollards, planter boxes, delta barriers, and gates at their access control points, but this tactic does not work for targets that move from location to location, such as ships. The MVB was born out of the Israeli Defense Force experience in Lebanon, where terrorists used a vehicle bomb to attack the U.S. Marine Corps barracks in Beirut in April 1983. In that instance, one explosive-laden truck managed to kill 243 U.S. military service members.[3]

Although the incident on the *QE2* was an embarrassing breach of security, it was not a terrorist attack. If the MVB had been used, it would have at least blocked the forklift's access to the vehicle ramp. The MVB is more of a vehicle "trap" than a barrier, but its bright yellow color clearly gives the impression of a barricade. It is advertised as being able to stop a two-ton vehicle traveling in excess of 55 miles dead in its track. It does this by an ingenious system of claws at its base. The claws actually lift the vehicle up off its wheels, thus transferring the horizontal momentum of the vehicle downward onto its own weight to stop forward progress. I like the device because it is "soldier-proof," meaning that all its parts are interchangeable so that it can be set up and broken down with relative ease. This is important because the eventual operators of the devices are the ship's security force.

Princess management did not necessarily want to depend on the security arrangements or fortifications provided by the ports where its large cruise ships berthed, even for the most secure places, like the port in Piraeus, Greece, during the 2004 Summer Olympics. The MVBs provided a portable access control measure that could be set up wherever there was a risk from vehicles that managed to penetrate the port's defenses. Having considered vehicle approaches and effectively stopped vehicles from driving up into the ships, we turned our attention to the ship's gangways.

Before I assumed my duties as director of security, our fleet security manager had been working on ways to secure passenger access points to the ships. He proposed that Princess install nets over the gangway (walkway ramp) hatches that could be dropped on marauding pirates, terrorists, or anyone else who might be inclined to charge up the gangplank and cause harm to the ship. I was skeptical from the beginning. I doubted any pirates would come running up the gangplank; that is not how they operate. Still, the idea to stop the threat at the gangway was something that the front office was interested in, so we kept investigating.

Not being an engineer myself, I probably had an advantage in approaching this problem. All I knew is what we needed. I envisioned a door made out of reinforced metal or reinforced with Kevlar that had a quick closing mechanism that could roll up and down or swing closed like a gate. The problem was how to fit this into or in front of the ship's gangway vestibule. The vestibule is the place where the gangway ramp is attached to the ship and where passengers and crew access the ship. There are a number of hatches on ships, but only a designated few act as access points for crew and passengers.

I thought such security barriers should be provided by the ports as part of the ISPS security improvements, but, as noted, some countries lack the financial resources to make even modest security improvements. The security manager thought that a better solution was to attach the door to the ship's vestibule. The problem to be solved was how to make the device fit into the ship's vestibule hatch when the hull doors were open. Closing these hatch doors after the gangway is removed prior to sailing takes, on average, several minutes, which is far too long when potential trouble is storming up the gangway. We needed a barrier that we could close at a moment's notice.

The security manager contracted with a local company, Bayless Engineering, to develop a prototype. The resulting product became known as the Doorgate and gave birth to a new company, appropriately called Doorgate Industries of Valencia, California.[4] Princess Cruises agreed to fund the research and development of this product, and, after a prototype was developed and tested successfully, Princess gave the order for the entire fleet to be outfitted with the Doorgate shields. The resulting design was simple and ingenious. It used a high-tension mechanical spring that could close the bulletproof door in less than a second. The problem of securing the door inside the ship's vestibule while the hatch doors were open was also solved by a system of clamps. The door was not an off-the-shelf product; each one had to be constructed to fit each ship's exact measurements. But the final design made the device portable and easy to store, and it could be installed and taken down quickly. The doors were bulletproof and blast resistant. Doorgate Industries has since adapted the idea and the product to other security applications for banks and airports. The capability to close down the gangway in an instant essentially mitigated one of the greatest vulnerabilities faced by cruise ships. To the best of my information, no one has ever needed to activate the Doorgate during an actual emergency.

GUARDING ACCESS TO CRUISE SHIPS

Access to ships in port must be guarded and protected through the most robust and capable means possible. In most cases, where the crew and visitors requiring access to a ship number in only the dozens and not the thousands, the task can be handled with relative ease. However, because of the numbers of the persons that need to be accounted for on cruise ships, the access control measures of the security plan are critical and dramatize how difficult and important this aspect of maritime security is. Although cruise ship access controls are the model for the industry, in my experience, even stringent access controls can be circumvented by criminals or terrorists because of the human element involved in this critical function.

All cruise ships use some form of an automated access control system. While they all track passengers' comings and goings on the ship, few if any new security features have been added over the years to improve these systems. The A-Pass system is an excellent case in point. The Automated Personnel Assisted Security Screening, or A-Pass system, is another innovation pioneered by Princess Cruises and created in 1996 by an entrepreneur in South Florida named Anthony Zagami. As the story goes, Zagami, after taking a cruise in the early 1990s on which passengers were required to show only some form of identification to board the ship, saw both vulnerability and an opportunity to strengthen ship security. Zagami, who had worked for Lockheed Martin in its aerospace division before retiring to South Florida, wanted to develop a product that was cruise specific and that would record real-time data for not only the cruise line itself but also for the government agencies required to have accurate passenger manifests.

With an idea in hand, he decided to come out of retirement to develop SISCO, which stands for Security Identification Systems Corporation, the West Palm Beach, Florida, security company that he has headed since 1996. The A-Pass system satisfied several onboard security and safety requirements and has been the industry standard for more than a decade. The A-Pass had already been installed on vessels that belonged to major cruise lines prior to the terrorist attacks of September 11.[5] Princess P&O was the first to roll out the product on the *Sun Princess* in 1996, way ahead of others in the industry. (Princess P&O was not at that time part of Carnival Corporation.)

The A-Pass idea is simple. At boarding, a high-speed interactive photo ID of each guest is taken and stored in a kiosk at that gangway. The kiosk is connected to the ship's A-Pass computer. When boarding or departing the ship, the passenger must insert his or her boarding card into the specially designed slot located on the kiosk. The computer brings up the stored photo of the person onto the kiosk's monitor, and the attending security officer determines whether the person standing before him or her is the person whose photo is on the screen. Everyone who boards or disembarks the ship, including the ships' officers and crew, is required to observe this practice. The photo is the crucial element of the process. SISCO had to come up with a way for the machine to take photos, align them with the passenger profile, and recall this information when the passenger inserts his or her cruise card on boarding or leaving the ship, all within a fraction of a second. And, unlike a driver's license photo, which may not even resemble the person carrying it because it was taken years earlier, the picture of the passenger is captured at the time of embarkation, so the photo records the person's appearance on the first day of the cruise. The card that is produced acts as the passenger's "Cruise Card" and is the only authorized boarding ID used for onboard access. If the card is lost, a bad guy cannot alter the image of the photo on the card because there is none (at least on Princess ships).

The cruise card is linked to the ship's A-Pass system. In addition to verifying identity when passengers board the ship, the card opens the passenger's cabin door and provides a register of comings and goings internally for the ship's purser. It acts, in essence, as a security register. The A-Pass system keeps all the passengers' information and photos safe on the ship's database rather than storing them on the card. For integrity, Princess wanted to have a human as part of the security process and so decided to have a security officer act as part of the identification process.

The A-Pass has proven to be a vital tool not only to improve security but also to ensure that everyone on board is accounted for before the vessel enters and departs each port. The system, which allows ships' personnel to monitor who gets on and off the ship, also records how many times each person leaves and enters the vessel and can detect if someone is missing from the ship—a problem that has plagued cruise lines over the years. Another function that A-Pass offers is the ability to keep stowaways and fugitives from the law from boarding the vessel. Unauthorized persons who have somehow obtained an A-Pass are not able to board the ship; if they attempt to do so, the photo belonging to the legitimate passenger that has been stored in the kiosk will appear.

The system is also being used by U.S. Customs and Border Protection to conduct name checks on passengers who board the ship. The names are compared against a list similar to TSA's "no- fly" list. Approximately half an hour after the vessel departs, a manifest is sent to Customs agencies to determine if there are any questionable or suspicious individuals on board of whom U.S. officers should be made aware.[6] Although there are some variations to this product (Royal Caribbean, for example, uses a product known as Seapass), most U.S. cruise ships use A-Pass as their fundamental access control system.

Although this does not happen frequently, there have been occasions when passengers returning to a pier where rows of cruise ships are docked have mistakenly tried to board the wrong ship. During the rush to board before the sailing curfew, passengers sometimes mistake gangways and end up being met by the gangway security watch. As passengers pass through a metal detector and have their personal belongings x-rayed, a lot is happening on the gangway, and the security staff, which is sometimes responsible for two gangways, must screen thousands of passengers in a short period of time. The A-Pass system helps keep passengers from boarding the wrong ship.

As good as the system is, however, in its current form, the A-Pass cannot positively identify a person even though the passenger's photo is stored on the cruise card (only visible when inserted into the A-Pass kiosk) and matched with the passenger profile. There is a huge potential vulnerability that can be exploited because some people happen to look like other people on the cruise. If two people look alike, the photo capability alone may not be able to determine who is legitimately supposed to be on board. Someone who resembles a legitimate passenger could conceivably steal, rob, or otherwise obtain that passenger's A-Pass card and board the ship illegally, disguised or in place of the real passenger. The person might be a terrorist or a stowaway, drug smuggler, or other criminal. The photo of the passenger, although captured at the time of boarding, is just a photo. It contains no other biometric information. Additionally, after a day of sightseeing, there may be 2,000 or more people waiting to board the ship. The ship security officer must make split-second decisions about the resemblance between the person's photo and the passenger trying to board.

Because of this vulnerability, it makes good sense to add biometrics to the access control system. Biometrics are those elements of a person's identity that are unique to only him or her. They include among other things, fingerprints, voice tone, and eye patterns. Each one of these biometric qualifiers is used in more sophisticated access control systems throughout the military, the government, and the private sector. Because the A-Pass system was designed initially without a biometric feature, adding that capability after the A-Pass was installed proved to be technically challenging and costly. The obvious choice was to add a fingerprint capability to the A-Pass system. I contacted SISCO to see if it could provide a solution, and company officials were optimistic. They had already begun work for the U.S. government on the "Smart Card" designed to be implemented with the Fast-Trac system at U.S. airports to speed along foreigners' entry into the country. That system uses a unique biometric feature to identify visitors who have submitted to and cleared a background investigation. They are eligible to bypass immigration, instead using kiosks similar to those SISCO developed for the A-Pass system.[7]

For my project, a team was dispatched from SISCO offices in West Palm Beach, Florida, to a Princess cruise ship to conduct trials using designated crew members as test subjects. The crew members submitted their fingerprints for comparison in the test. The results, although encouraging, showed that the device required significant time to make the comparison, and this was found to be unacceptable. The system will ultimately have to have the capability to rapidly correlate biometric information as thousands of passengers attempt to board the ship at once. A delay of less than a minute in retrieving the correct record can conceivably slow the overall boarding process by more than an hour, severely delaying sailing times (not to mention slowing down the already cumbersome boarding process). When a ship's departure is late by even an hour, the ship must then make up that time at sea with a slight increase in speed to make it to the next port on time, increasing fuel costs.

Disney has incorporated the use of biometrics into its access control at the various parks at Disney World, in Orlando, Florida. It is requiring a fingerprint scan in addition to an admission ticket in an attempt to discourage the practice of loaning tickets to nonpaying guests. Disney has invested a lot in an effort to ensure that only paid guests use their multiple-day passes; it is concerned that its one-ticket-one-guest policy be strictly adhered to and therefore has upgraded its entrance kiosks to include a laser scan of each guest's fingerprint.

The inclusion of a biometric feature at the Disney parks has nothing to do with security, however; it reflects instead the need to protect ticket revenues.[8] It may have helped solve the problem of ticket swapping, but it has not made entry into the parks any quicker. At peak hours, when thousands of guests to the Magic Kingdom are trying to enter the park during spring break, the otherwise smooth access flow into the Magic Kingdom, Epcot, and the other Disney parks is disrupted by the fumbling attempts of small children, the elderly, and the uninitiated as they submit to the unaccustomed practice of having a finger scanned and then having this sample compared to the data contained on the admission ticket.

Disney clearly has an advantage over a cruise line in using fingerprint biometrics. Whereas a ship has a single gangway, Disney can open multiple kiosks when the crowd flow demands it. And Disney is not overly concerned about the added length of time or potential delays that such a system creates for entry into its parks. As good as the technology might be today, a cruise ship that uses fingerprint biometrics today would frequently miss its sailing time. And the overriding purpose of biometrics on a cruise ship is to ensure integrity to the access control process, not to prevent unauthorized exchanges of park passes.

The cruise ship lines hope that biometrics are the future of access control on cruise ships. For the moment, though, the A-Pass system still requires a judgment call on the part of the ship security officer, adding a reasonable margin of error that could be exploited. For the cruise lines, biometrics is a not a matter of if; it is a matter of when. Advances in technology will eventually make these systems operate within an accepted rate of speed and lower their costs. In the meantime, unless a serious access control incident allows the wrong person to board the ship, the cruise lines will be content with maintaining the status quo on this issue.

SCREENING CRUISE SHIP PASSENGERS

In his book *Cruise Ship Tourism*, the author Ross Kingston Dowling writes: "Before boarding a ship, passengers undergo extensive background checks by numerous immigration departments and international intelligence agencies such as the Central Intelligence Agency (CIA), the Federal Bureau of Investigation (FBI), and the Australian Security and Intelligence Organization (ASIO)."[9] This statement is incorrect. The cruise lines have no access to these government databases. Cruise ship passengers would feel truly uncomfortable knowing that all their personal and privacy information was being run through government databases in a search for terrorists and wanted criminals.

Dowling is, however, partially correct. As mentioned, the background checks come *after* the ships have sailed, when the ships' manifests are sent to the U.S. Department of Homeland Security (DHS) for checking, and identify only names listed in the DHS's database. The A-Pass system, used as the primary access control tool on cruise ships, is also used by U.S. Customs and Border Protection to screen for terrorists and wanted criminals once the ship has sailed.

The obvious problem with this system is that the criminals or terrorists, assuming there are any, are already on the ship and the ship has left port, precisely the time when it is most vulnerable to hijacking or other terrorist plots. Another problem is that the system assumes that terrorists or other criminals are using their real names and that these names are on the list. While cruise ship passengers are not subject to background checks, airline passengers are subject to a "no-fly" watch list, a list of persons who are considered to be a direct threat to U.S. civil aviation.[10] The list was administered by the FBI until November 2001, when it was transferred to the Federal Aviation Administration (FAA). The Transportation Security Administration (TSA) later assumed administrative responsibility for the list, which was split into "no-fly" and "automatic-selectee" lists. The TSA places persons on these lists as requested by the Department of Homeland Security and other members of the intelligence community. The TSA distributes these watch lists to U.S. air carriers, which, in turn, screen passengers against these watch lists before boarding.

In practice, these watch lists are downloaded into a handful of computer reservation systems used by most U.S. air carriers. As the names of these lists imply, passengers found to be on the "no-fly" list are denied boarding and referred to law enforcement, while those on the "automatic-selectee" list are selected for secondary security screening before being cleared to board.[11] The Intelligence Reform and Terrorism Prevention Act of 2004 (P.L. 108-458) includes a provision that requires the DHS to implement a process for vetting the names of passengers and crew carried on cruise ships against the consolidated terrorist watch list.[12]

This brings up the question of access to ships by passenger and crew members and their belongings. In a recent study on maritime terrorism by the Rand Corporation, researchers assumed that the relative ease of movement on a cruise ship by both passengers and crew would make a cruise ship vulnerable to terrorists seeking to placing explosives to scuttle the ship or to cause numerous human casualties by attacking areas where passengers congregate in large numbers such as restaurants, theaters, or casinos. The study illustrated how C4 or plastic explosives, which are malleable, could be hidden in everyday items brought on board a ship because of the "low level of screening" for passengers and crew.

The study stated that, although more rigorous than before the September 11 attacks, screening requirements for those wishing to board a ship are far less stringent than for passengers using commercial airplanes. Additionally, the study cites other vulnerabilities linked to lax access controls and screening, such as random killings or hostage taking in which terrorists use "pre-deployed assault rifles and pistols from co-opted members of the crew."[13] Such a scenario does not take into account the facts.

As a result of the ISPS requirements for maritime security (MARSEC) screening and the Maritime Transportation Security Act (MTSA) of 2002, which require strict access controls for the port, cruise ship terminals, and piers, it is highly unlikely that a passenger or crew member would be able to smuggle weapons or explosives on board a cruise liner today in the manner described by the Rand Corporation. Our corporate security office was frequently notified when the screeners on the ship found toy gun replicas or air guns in passenger luggage, apparently "overlooked" or forgotten by passengers when they were packing for the cruise. Even bullets and shotgun shells, presumably left over from the passenger's last use of the luggage during a hunting trip, were found with some frequency in suitcases and handbags. Passengers were usually embarrassed that their suitcases contained items that certainly would never have made it through airport screening. Passenger screening is as thorough as TSA screening at airports, and crew screening on cruise ships may be even more stringent. Crew members' belongings are looked at with more scrutiny because of the possibility of smuggling. All crew members' possessions brought on board ship during their contract are screened by gangway x-ray machines, using thermal imagery, and checked for the presence of explosives by bomb-sniffing canines.

Every alarm set-off on a walk-through metal detector must be followed up by a search with handheld metal detectors, just as at TSA screening points at commercial airports. Even at the lowest MARSEC level, the screening requirements are such that the criminals, smugglers, or terrorists would have to guess precisely what they will face: inspection and screening by sniffing canines for explosives, as well as mandated physical searches of stores. Smuggling weapons or explosives aboard a ship would require a giant conspiracy involving bribed officials, port workers, and ship personnel. That stretches the success probability for their operations considerably. I do not assert that screening is not vulnerable to exploitation, however.

Passenger screening is at its weakest when ships anchor out in port and "tender" passengers to and from the ship to the shore by motorboat launches. Sometimes these ports are not designed for large cruise ships and have no terminals available for screening passengers as they return to the ship. Hawaiian ports are typical of this situation. The Big Island of Hawaii and Maui both have anchor-

Cruise ships often anchor out in smaller ports and then "tender" passengers to shore in the ship's motor boats. Cruise ships are most vulnerable to small-boat attacks when they are moored out in a harbor, as happened to the USS *Cole*. Screening procedures in these ports are normally relaxed because of the limited security facilities ashore. (Author's photo)

ages for cruise ships that frequent Kona and Lahina. Anyone who has been to Cabo San Lucas in Mexico has seen the same operation.

Ships sometimes have the choice to screen passengers on the ship or on the pier. Their preference is to have passengers screened in the terminal. In tender ports, the time available for screening passengers returning to the ship via the motorboat launches is very limited. Because of the small platform extended at the waterline where the motorboats tie up, passengers simply have nowhere to stage while waiting to be screened. Thus, the small pier in the port becomes a makeshift screening checkpoint.

At the end of a full day of sightseeing, passengers normally queue in long lines and wait to be screened by security personnel using handheld metal detectors before returning to the ship on the launches. Sometimes, the ship has the capability to erect walk-through metal detectors in certain ports, making the job of screening passengers quicker and more efficient, but the capability for transporting x-ray machines to the pier is limited or nonexistent, so that passenger carry-on bags and packages must be searched by hand. This vulnerability will have to be addressed in the future by the cruise lines, because the requirement is still that every passenger and his or her belongings must be screened before the person can board the ship.[14]

Cruise ships that anchor out in "tender" ports will simply have to allow greater time to accommodate all the passengers who plan to return to the ship—usually all at the same time. As cruise ships get larger, anchoring out will become more commonplace. As many as 5,000 passengers may return to the ship at the same time, requiring the cruise ship to stagger embarkation times or, like the airlines, advise that all passengers plan on arriving back to the ship at least two hours in advance to accommodate security screening. This, unfortunately, may ultimately impact the cruise ship experience for the passengers.

THE RISK FROM CRUISE SHIP STOWAWAYS

Cruise ships are not immune to the problem of stowaways, though it is not as common as on other forms of oceangoing vessels. Stowaways are as much a problem for the port as the ship, but ultimately the ship is held responsible for all souls on board, and that includes stowaways. The port is responsible for controlling access to the port areas, including the piers and terminals. Stowaways who breech port security are essentially criminal trespassers, so ports (which must be encircled by a wall or fence per the ISPS Code) spend a great deal of time and resources both preventing and tracking down unauthorized persons who try to enter (or leave) the port illegally. The presence of stowaways on any ship jeopardizes the safety of the crew, the passengers, and the ship. The stowaway is also taking a great risk when hiding away on a vessel. When stowaways are discovered, ships are put in the difficult position of having to deal with a security, political, and humanitarian problem. There has never been a case of a stowaway who has sneaked aboard any ship and then came out of his hiding place and began a terrorist assault. Most stowaways are only desperate individuals, seeking a way to a better life; they sneak aboard any vessel going their way to escape their situation in life.

Stowing away on a cruise ship or other vessel is dangerous business primarily for the stowaways, who sometimes risk hiding in dangerous spaces to avoid detection. They also risk passing days without food or water. In July 2004, 10 Nigerian and Liberian stowaways were found hidden precariously in a cavity above the propeller shaft on board the *Marble Highway,* a Japanese owned Ro-Ro as the ship docked at Port Elizabeth, South Africa.[15] (A Ro-Ro is a shipping term to describe a type of ship. It stands for "roll-on, roll off," which describes the manner in which cars, trucks, and containers are loaded and off-loaded, as in drive them on and drive them off, as opposed to loading and offloading with a crane.) That they managed to survive the ocean voyage is a miracle and shows the desperation of stowaways and the risks they are willing to take. There have also been documented cases where stowaways were dealt with harshly upon their discovery on a ship;

officials have been known to simply toss them overboard. In November 2003, fishermen in northern Brazil rescued eight African men who had been thrown overboard from the Hong Kong-registered *Tu King* after being discovered stowed away on that Chinese ship. The men, between the ages of 16 and 22, were found swimming about five miles off the coast.[16] This is not the 18th century, but modern merchant ships sometimes deal with stowaways with extreme prejudice, and the problem is rampant throughout the world and growing worse.

Not surprisingly, the ISPS Code put into place in 2004 has not stemmed the flow of stowaways, especially in impoverished regions of the world. Stowaways can be considered a threat anywhere in the world, and no place is considered completely safe from the risk. However, ship owners are aware of regions and countries from stowaways are most likely to have come, including South Africa, Morocco, Tanzania, Algeria, West Africa, eastern Europe, Colombia, and China. The good news for the cruise lines is that relatively few stowaways come from Central and South America and particularly the United States.[17]

There are a number of motives that lead persons to stow away on a ship. Most stowaways are trying to flee an oppressed life in a country or region that offers little economic opportunity or where there is military conflict or instability. But, other stowaways attempt to board ships illegally in order to seek political asylum or simply to immigrate illegally into a country. The asylum seeker, who normally makes his presence known once he is on board, hopes to be granted asylum in a country that is open to such requests. The illegal immigrant who has stowed away tries to remain hidden in hopes of jumping ship close to the final destination. This type of stowaway runs great risks to himself and to the ship and will go to great lengths to protect his hiding place. In many cases, these hidden stowaways have been found months after the ship sailed, their bodies decomposed in crawl spaces around the ship's rudder compartment. In 2005, citing a trend around the world, a U.S. Coast Guard Captain of the Port issued a warning for ship operators to check for stowaways in the rudder compartment of ships where stowaways could gain access to the rudder trunk from the water line when the ship is in ballast.[18] The Coast Guard warned that cruise ships might face fines and detention if stowaways were discovered.

In general, however, with the exception of asylum seekers, all stowaways are treated as illegal immigrants in the country where they are disembarked in accordance with that country's laws and regulations. Normally, stowaways are returned to the country from which they came. However, in certain cases, a country can refuse to land stowaways, citing national security risks. The greatest threat to the ship comes from criminals who may turn violent and who present especially difficult security problems for crew. They have been known to turn on and coerce (blackmail) the ship's master and crew. This is especially true where the crew violates all guiding principles stipulated by the International Maritime Organization (IMO) for dealing with stowaways.

In early January 2006, the 28,000-dwt (dead weight tons) bulker *African Kalahari* departed Mombasa, Kenya, en route for Durban, South Africa. Shortly after the ship was well out to sea, seven stowaways who had secretly gained access to the ship made their presence known to the crew members. Initially, the crew followed the IMO protocol. The stowaways were kept under guarded confinement and given three meals a day, clothes, and opportunity to exercise. However, the crew broke with standard procedures when the stowaways began to tell their stories of hardship back in their country. The crew members were moved and felt sorry for the uninvited guests as they spoke of their hopes for a new life. At the moment the stowaways were discovered illegally on the ship, the ship's master (the captain) had an obligation to notify the ship's owners and flag state in accordance with the IMO regulations. Because the crew felt sorry for the stowaways, however, the captain was persuaded to keep their presence secret.[19]

As the ship was ultimately headed for a port and country that offered less economic opportunity than the country from which they had come, the crew conspired with the stowaways to allow them to "escape" when they made port. When the ship arrived in Durban, South Africa, the stowaways were not declared to the port authorities, and the crew assisted them in sneaking over the side of the ship on rope ladders so that they could swim to shore and attempt to stow away on another ship and head for a better life. However, the conspiracy did not take into account the inability of the stowaways to swim safely to the nearest quay wall or ship. Two of the swimmers drowned, and the remaining five exhausted stowaways were rescued from the water by authorities.

When questioned, the events and circumstances of the tragedy turned 180 degrees when the remaining five stowaways claimed they were thrown off the *African Kalahari* by the ship's crew members. Suddenly, the crew and ship's captain became the accused in a conspiracy to commit murder. The crew members and ship's captain were arrested and imprisoned. A later plea bargain reduced the charge to the equivalent of manslaughter after the crew members, uncertain of their future, made voluntary confessions.[20] They were eventually given suspended prison sentences and heavy fines that were likely passed on to the ship's owners. As a consequence, ships arriving to Durban from Kenya are now carefully inspected, and any stowaways are questioned as to whether they received humane treatment from their hosts.

That any stowaway can sail on a ship from one port to another reveals serious gaps in shore and shipboard security. Their very presence confirms that security, at least on the ship, has failed and that there has been an access control problem.

Controlling the gangway is absolutely one of the most effective measures in stopping would-be stowaways. The whole gangway experience, including the use of the A-Pass, is designed specifically for two purposes: to determine who is and who is not authorized to be on the ship and to gain an accurate head count for Safety of Lives at Sea (SOLAS) purposes.

In January 2002 the IMO amended the 1965 Convention on Facilitation of International Maritime Traffic (FAL Convention) to include standards and recommended practices for dealing with stowaways. This Convention is one of many that formulate standards that the contracting governments agree to and eventually adopt. The new IMO requirements mandate physical security measures to be implemented when calling on ports at risk for stowaways. Similar to ISPS Code measures, the Convention requires ships to search for stowaways; secure hatches, doors, and cargo holds; keep the number of access points to the ships to a minimum; and post extra lookouts. At night, the ship should be adequately illuminated.

The 2002 amendments to the FAL convention also include a standard format for recording stowaway details and require that all stowaway incidents be reported to the secretary general of the International Maritime Organization for statistical purposes. Since implementation of the FAL Convention amendments, there has been some concern over the small number of reports submitted to the IMO by member-states. It is estimated that for every stowaway who is reported, there may be at least one more who has not been reported and repatriated.[21]

The reasons for this are simple enough. The amount of care and nurturing required to care for a stowaway and the documentation, paperwork, and penalties make it tempting to circumvent the IMO reporting requirement.[22] Another aspect of the FAL amendments is the humanitarian issue that requires all stowaways to be treated humanely. Ship captains should balance this requirement against the need to provide for the safety of the ship, as there have been cases where stowaways have jumped overboard for fear of being returned to their country of origin.[23] In general, stowaways are kept in a secure part of the vessel, such as a cabin or store room, where the doors can be locked and any windows secured to reduce the risk of escape.

How safe are cruise ships from the risk of stowaways? Statistically speaking, they are very safe, although not immune. Cruise ships, like all seagoing vessels, have faced their share of stowaways. In July 2000, 10 stowaways from Haiti were discovered on the Carnival Cruise Line ship *Ecstasy,* seeking refuge from that impoverished country.[24] According to Canadian officials, Canada ramped up efforts to inspect cruise ships in 2005 because of the threat of Chinese stowaways after a number of human smuggling rings targeted cruise ships in Canadian ports. The authorities were surprised that smugglers resorted to the high-price option of luxury cruise ships instead of traditional smuggling platforms such as fishing boats and container ships. In late 2005, more than 30 Chinese nationals, using stolen and altered South Korean passports, tried to enter Canada illegally from cruise ships docked in Halifax or St. John's, Newfoundland.[25]

One final thought on the problem of stowaways. There is an obvious question about the threat from terrorists. As we mentioned, no stowaway has attempted to launch a terrorist attack thus far. Using such a method to gain access to a cruise ship or other vessel would stretch the operational planning limits for the terrorist in that it would stake the entire operation, whatever it may be, on gaining access to the ship covertly. What stops a terrorist from accessing the ship by simply buying a ticket? As we have already seen in the case of the *Achille Lauro* hijacking, that is exactly how the most famous of all cruise ship terror attacks was carried out.

THE LRAD: ENFORCING THE CRUISE SHIP RESTRICTION ZONE

The greatest threat to any cruise ship is a water-borne attack by a small boat such as the one that crippled the USS *Cole*. Early in my tenure at Princess Cruises, I focused on finding a deterrent or physical barrier to protect the ship from water-based threats. There was some urgency to this effort, because the *Queen Mary 2*, Cunard Cruise Line's flagship, had been chartered to serve as a floating hotel in the port of Piraeus, Greece, during the 2004 Summer Olympics, and there was talk of terrorist plots against the ship and the Olympics.

I became interested in a company named American Technology Corporation (ATC), in San Diego, and its product, the Long-Range Acoustic Device, or LRAD for short. The LRAD was already in production and being used by the U.S. Marine Corps in Iraq and by the U.S. Navy in the Persian Gulf. After the attack on the USS *Cole*, the Navy realized it needed a method to move its threat recognition capability farther out from its ships as part of its coordinated force protection effort.

While the USS *Cole* was moored in the Yemeni port of Aden to take on fuel, watch-standers on the *Cole* saw a small boat approaching their ship. The *Cole* was ineffective in determining the boat's intentions because there were many similar boats in the harbor and those watching believed that it was part of the refueling party. The small boat, full of explosives, that carried the two suicide jihadists continued toward the ship in a direct and threatening manner.[26] Had the USS *Cole* been able to determine from a greater distance that the boat had no intention of stopping, it would have been able to mount a counterattack and stop the small boat's approach while it was still a safe distance from the ship.

The Long-Range Acoustic Device (LRAD) in use on the *Queen Mary 2* in the port of Piraeus during the 2004 Summer Olympics in Athens, Greece. The LRAD is a hailing-and-warning device used to establish the intent of small boats and other watercraft that violate the restriction zones around cruise ships and naval vessels. The LRAD was on board the *Seabourn Spirit* when it was attacked by pirates off the coast of Somalia in November 2005. (Author's photo)

American Technology's answer to this problem was the LRAD. After the attack on the *Seabourn Spirit* introduced this technology to the world, it was occasionally referred to in the press as a "sonic cannon." The LRAD is really a means to hail and communicate with another vessel or object over great distances through the efficient channeling of sound. A bullhorn can project sound only a few hundred feet and is hard to understand because the farther the sound is projected outward, the more the sound waves are dissipated. The LRAD can concentrate sound into a beam width of 10 to 15 degrees. Much like a focused flashlight that can project light in a narrow beam rather than illuminating a large area like a floodlight, the LRAD directs sound into a very narrow beam and projects it clearly and audibly over long distances, in some cases more than 3,000 yards. The result is that sound is clearly audible to anyone within that beam width and is dissipated outside the beam to the point where it becomes inaudible. When used in a force protection role, the LRAD permits a set of warning instructions to be amplified by the device's built-in microphone or played through a prerecorded message played on an MP3 device.

How does sound provide an advantage? If projected out far enough, it allows the user of the LRAD to determine the intentions of potentially threatening targets at safe distances by directly communicating with them. In Iraq, for example, this technology has meant that a vehicle or truck approaching a roadblock near a police or military checkpoint can be given instructions to stop and to acknowledge instructions without endangering the lives of those in the passenger's vehicle or of the soldiers manning the checkpoint.

The LRAD was a possible answer to Princess's security requirements because it could be deployed with relative ease and because it looked innocuous enough that it would not to raise passengers' suspicion or anxiety by giving them the impression that we were trying to outfit our ships with weaponry. In fact, the LRAD is not a weapon at all but an "acoustical hailing device" that can be used to identify or change threatening behavior. The U.S. Navy has been employing the LRAD in the Persian Gulf, where it has been effectively used by a limited number of ships to determine the intentions of foreign vessels. The Navy ships are capable of issuing a warning in the native languages of the region to threatening boats, advising them to alter their course and speed and to stay clear of the naval ship. The Navy reported great success with the LRAD in the Persian Gulf and has also used it in antipiracy operations in the Indian Ocean.

For the Navy, the LRAD allows it to hail and clarify the intentions of small craft moving toward a ship or crossing into its restricted zone. The small boat can readily be given a set of instructions to stop, turn around, or proceed while still at a safe distance from the Navy ship. If, after the warnings are given, the target continues to move toward the checkpoint or ship in a threatening manner, the rules of engagement become more clearly defined. A warship can then engage the target to stop or impede its progress at significant distances from the ship. It provides a definite standoff capability that allows the military to determine a target's intentions before resorting to lethal force. This provides a boost for the military's force protection capability. A dramatic example of the need for ships to have such a capability occurred in the Suez Canal in March 2008.

Ships transiting the Suez Canal are frequent targets of the local Egyptian merchants and townspeople who inhabit the small villages along its banks. The Egyptians approach the slow-moving vessels in their boats, trying to sell cigarettes and trinkets to the merchant ships passing through, but are advised to stay clear of military vessels transiting the Canal. Many Egyptians in these coastal towns gain their livelihood from this form of commerce. In late March 2008, the U.S. cargo ship *Global Patriot,* under contract with the U.S. Navy as one of its Military Sea-Lift Command ships, was approached by just such a flotilla of small craft bearing merchandise to sell to the ship's crew. Because the *Global Patriot* did not look like a naval vessel, the Egyptian traders assumed it was just another merchant ship making its way through the canal. Ever since the USS *Cole* was attacked, in October 2000, in Yemen, U.S. naval ships have been under stricter rules of engagement. A Navy security team on the *Global Patriot* attempted to hail the small boats, having a native Arabic speaker address them through a bullhorn, and warned them not to continue their approach so close to the ship.

At night, it was possible that the Egyptians could not see the ship clearly or hear the muffled warnings emanating from the ship's bullhorn. Whatever the reasons, one of the small boats continued toward the ship as it made its way through the narrow channel at a slow speed. According to the reports given to the press via the U.S. embassy in Cairo, when the boat ignored the warning, the *Global Patriot* fired warning shots with automatic weapons 20 to 30 feet in front of the little boat's bow. Initial reports from the scene indicated that no casualties occurred on either vessel. Later, however, an Egyptian man was found to have been killed by the gunfire from the *Global Patriot*'s security team.

The U.S. Fifth Fleet issued a statement saying that it regretted the incident and that it has always tried to take adequate steps to identify the intentions of small craft approaching its vessels before using deadly force. Adequate steps probably were taken, but they were ineffective in this instance because the crew of the intended target, the small Egyptian boat, could not hear the warning or, if it did, failed to abide by it. Whatever the reasons, if the *Global Patriot* had used an LRAD to communicate with the boat, the chance of such a tragedy would have been remote; had the ship confirmed that the small boat was indeed a threat, it could have justified the use of warning shots or deadly force.[27]

While the incident involving the *Global Patriot* illustrates the options armed naval vessels have when warnings issued from an LRAD are ignored, cruise ships face a different situation. A cruise ship cannot open fire if a small boat ignores its security warnings. The LRAD, however, has a unique feature that helps determine the target's intention. That is its "tone" capability. The warning tone can be activated once the target has disregarded the LRAD operator's instructions. The tone is a loud, piercing sound that resembles the sound made by a buzzer on an alarm clock but at a higher frequency. The sound is sufficiently intense that it is uncomfortable to stay in its path for any length of time.[28] It not quite the equivalent of raking your fingernails over a chalkboard, but it's the same idea. Obviously, the closer the hearer is to the sound, the more disruptive and uncomfortable it is. Once the sound is activated, if the target nonetheless continues to advance, its intent becomes clear. Because these events occur while the target is at some distance from the ship, the ship has time to take evasive or other defensive actions if the target continues to come closer. Cruise ships equipped with the LRAD have time to notify Coast Guard or law enforcement water patrols and to warn passengers if the crew perceives that there is a threat.

Cruise ships already had imaginary "restricted zones" of up to 500 feet around the vessel in U.S. ports, but they have no way to enforce the boundary. The LRAD is the key to protecting the Princess fleet from the threat of small boats and other watercraft that get too close to the ship without resorting to more costly and drastic security measures such as hiring a private maritime security company. After engaging in some salesmanship with the management of Princess Cruises, including a demonstration of the equipment in the parking lot of the company's headquarters in Valencia, California, I was given permission to allow American Technology to testing the device on the *Queen Mary 2* during a stopover in New York harbor. If the LRAD was successful there, Princess was poised to make the device standard shipboard security equipment throughout its fleet. While moored in New York harbor and with the assistance of the New York Harbor Police, we mounted two LRADs at strategic locations on the stern and the upper weather decks of the ship. The New York Harbor Police patrol boats made approaches to the stern of the ship, and the LRAD was engaged, first with a warning to test its audibility, then with its tone feature engaged. The results of the test were more than impressive enough to convince the New York Harbor Police and our security staff. American Technology Corporation agreed to let Princess Cruises place two LRADs on the *Queen Mary 2* for use in Greece at the 2004 Summer Olympics, where the ship was to act as a floating hotel in the port of Piraeus, welcoming, among other guests, the U.S. men's Olympic basketball team.

THE *QUEEN MARY 2* AND THE 2004 SUMMER OLYMPICS

In the fall of 2003, Princess Cruises was poised to assume the management responsibility for Cunard Cruise Line, which operated the *Queen Mary 2*. At the time, the *Queen Mary 2* was the largest cruise ship in the world and, along with its older sister, the *Queen Elizabeth 2,* was one of the most visible ships in the world. Princess Cruises, along with Cunard and Seaborne Yachts, is owned by the Carnival Corporation. Carnival also owns several other brands of popular cruise lines, such as Holland America and Costa Cruise Lines, as well as its own brand, Carnival Cruises.

Even before its launch, in January 2004, the *Queen Mary 2* had, as I have mentioned, been chartered to serve as a floating hotel for the 2004 Summer Olympics in Athens, Greece. Because Athens did not have enough hotel rooms for the attendees, the port was to be turned into a floating hotel city.[29] It was billed as the largest gathering of cruise ships in the world, presenting a virtual smorgasbord of potential maritime high-value targets.

The *Queen Mary 2* was selected to house the 2004 U.S. Olympic basketball team, along with members of other Olympic organizations and national sport

The *Queen Mary 2* at her berth in the port of Piraeus, Greece, during the 2004 Summer Olympics. Cruise ships were charted as floating hotels because of the lack of hotel rooms in Athens. The U.S. men's basketball team stayed on the ship, as did other national sporting teams. Note the barely visible U.S. Navy's Dunlap barrier, which surrounds the ship to protect it from attack by a small boat. The author wrote the security plan for these cruise ships during their stay in the port of Piraeus. (Author's photo)

teams. In early 2004, however, security concerns arose in connection with the U.S. men's Olympic basketball team; five months before the games were to begin, it was still not certain if the team would even stay on the *Queen Mary 2*. An executive director of the team said that, while the players were not opposed to participating in the Games because of security concerns, the National Basketball Association (NBA) was still greatly concerned for their personal safety.

The men's Olympic basketball team worked diligently to reassure the players that all the appropriate security measures were being taken care of so the that team could concentrate on its game instead of worrying that its members might be victims of international terrorism. While no players cited security concerns as a reason to stay out of the games, global instability and the potential for terrorism certainly weighed on their decisions.[30] As a result, some high-profile players skipped the Olympics altogether.

I was appointed to lead Carnival's security efforts to protect its ships that were scheduled to act as luxury floating hotels. There was genuine concern over the presence of the *QM2* in Piraeus because of the terrorist threats. I was dispatched to Greece on several occasions to evaluate the ongoing security preparations already under way. Science Applications International Corporation (SAIC) had been contracted by the Greek government to provide a $300 million security system for the port.[31]

The system was what is called a C4I system, short for Command, Control, Communications, and Computers. It was designed to link all elements of the security operations in the port and in the various sporting venues in Athens. It was larger than the system SAIC had designed for the 2002 Winter Olympics in Salt Lake City. The maritime portion of the system called for a large control center that linked various cameras and sensors on the sea bottom in and around the port of Piraeus. The overall system, however, was plagued with installation delays, which led the Greek government to hold up final payment of $173 million before the start of the Olympics.[32]

Added to SAIC's difficulties as it worked to complete the installation of the C4I system on time were delays in the construction of the various Olympic venues and terrorist concerns. These issues resulted in lagging ticket sales and made the Olympics something less than the boost the Greek government had hoped for. The estimated $1.5 billion the Greek government spent on security may have seemed like overkill, given that no specific threats were actually received by any intelligence agency before the games started. Shortly before the Olympics began, Interpol issued a statement announcing that none of the law enforcement agencies of its 181 member nations had reported any threats from al-Qaeda or any other terrorist organizations but noting that the potential existed for terrorists to strike at anytime, anywhere, and cautioning the Greek government to remain vigilant.[33]

Gianna Angelopoulos-Daskalaki, the president of the Athens 2004 Organizing Committee (ATHOC), was realistic about the situation and noted that no security measures are foolproof. To compound the security problem in Greece, and as if to emphasize how hard it is to protect an open society, local anarchists had been planting homemade bombs around Athens in the months prior to start of the Olympics. James Ker-Lindsay, director of Civilitas Research, a think tank located in Cyprus, said that anarchist groups like those that had been attacking Athens with small improvised explosive devices had been operating in Greece for many years and rarely injured anyone. Ker-Lindsay suggested that the Olympics were just a great opportunity to scare people.[34]

Although there were no credible threats, there was speculation that, given Greece's proximity to the Middle East, there was an obvious risk of terrorist activity, a risk that fueled fears of a spectacular terrorist event.[35] This possibility sent security preparations into overdrive in all the governments that would be sending teams to the Olympics, including the U.S. government.

The U.S. State Department, the FBI, as well as a host of military and other federal security agencies, planned to be at the Olympics to protect the U.S. athletes. They also were prepared to provide a crisis response for the Greek government should a security emergency develop as happened at the 1972 Summer Olympics in Munich, (West) Germany. Demands for security at the Olympic venues went out from the U.S. and other governments and called for additional protective measures. After diplomatic negotiation, a contingent of FBI agents and special agents of the Bureau of Diplomatic Security (DSS) was allowed to be armed despite the "no-guns-allowed" policy of the Greek government.[36]

The security plan in the port of Piraeus to protect the cruise ships was no less daunting. I believed that the *QM2* needed a physical barrier to protect the sea approaches to the ship. This was especially critical because the only pier large enough to accommodate the giant ship was the first pier, the one nearest the entrance of the harbor. This presented a real threat. A vessel bent on attacking the ship from the sea would not have to be more than 50 yards inside the harbor to be within striking distance of the *QM2*.

I had been in constant liaison with the U.S. embassy in Athens prior to the Games' commencement. I discussed my security concerns about the *Queen Mary 2* with the Regional Security Office in Athens, who had been a colleague of mine in the Diplomatic Security Service. He agreed that the threat to the men's basketball team from the exposed location of the *QM2*'s proposed berth was significant. He suggested that I speak with the naval attaché at the U.S. embassy, who told me that the need to protect the cruise ships in Piraeus had already been discussed at higher levels and originally included plans for a Dunlap "water boom" but that the idea had been dropped because of a lack of funding. The only organization capable of providing such a barrier was the U.S. Navy. Deploying a durable water fence around U.S. aircraft carriers had been standard practice in the Navy for years. Dunlap booms are the same water fences used to protect U.S. aircraft carriers. They are moored to the sea bottom with cable and can be opened and closed only with the assistance of tugs.

The pier where these cruise ships were scheduled to be moored was so close to the seaward entrance to the harbor that even the passing ferries would come close enough for passengers to throw rocks at the ships. Likewise, the C41 sensor system deployed inside the harbor to detect scuba divers and underwater threats would provide little protection against the risks posed by being in such an exposed position. This information, and the important guests who were to be housed on the *Queen Mary 2*, made it crucial that we protect this area of the harbor. I was encouraged to learn from the naval attaché that the threat to the *Queen Mary 2* and the two other cruise ships warranted extra physical protection. The attaché, through his own negotiating skills with the Department of the Navy, finally offered the port of Piraeus a Dunlap boom to help protect the exposed location of the QM2 and other cruise ships.

With the water boom now encircling the QM2 and the two LRADs from American Technology Corporation strategically located on its decks, I arrived in Greece and moved on board the ship to take over the day-to-day supervision of our security operations in the port. I hosted weekly intelligence briefings for the captains of the other cruise ships berthed in the harbor. The briefing was conducted by representatives of the Department of State's Overseas Security Advisory Committee (OSAC) and by agents of the Diplomatic Security Service.

The months of liaison with the Greek Coast Guard and ATHOC paid off substantially in reducing physical security issues during the Games. For example, the Queen Mary 2 not surprisingly attracted enormous attention, and there was always official country delegations coming and going on the ship. This included heads of state who visited the QM2 with their armed bodyguards. Former president George H. W. Bush, an honorary representative to the Greek Olympics, visited the ship with a contingent of Secret Service agents. He enjoyed touring the ship and meeting with some of members of the U.S. basketball team. Later he invited the commodore of the QM2 and other ship officers to visit his chartered yacht, moored in the port of Piraeus, for a reception attended by the press and many world leaders.

I supervised the LRAD operation on the Queen Mary 2 during the Olympics, and they proceeded without a security incident. The Olympics continued for the Queen Mary 2 and for the men's basketball team, but, because the security preparations were so thorough, or perhaps because there were no security-related incidents, my continued presence on ship was no longer considered vital. I was recalled earlier than planned and returned to the Princess corporate office. Because the LRAD had not been used other than to conduct operational tests with the Greek Coast Guard, I believed that the LRAD project was going to be shelved. Much to my surprise, the front office had already weighed in on the device's usefulness and had allotted funding to place an LRAD on every Princess, Cunard, P&O Cruises Australia, and Seabourn ship.

The usefulness of the LRAD was proved in November 2005 when the Seabourn Spirit was attacked by pirates off the coast of Somalia. The decision to take special security measures like those in place at the 2004 Summer Olympics in an effort to protect cruise ships from acts of terrorism was a prudent one, given the environment and the risk of such acts, but, in normal circumstances, improvements to the safety of cruise ships normally come only after some severe catastrophic event that claims innocent lives. It is usually then that the international regulatory bodies or, in most cases, the maritime lawyers step in to protect the seagoing public.

Former President George H.W. Bush and the author aboard his chartered yacht in the port of Piraeus, Greece. President Bush had invited the author and the officers of the *Queen Mary 2* to a reception aboard his yacht during the Olympics where he unofficially represented the United States at the 2004 Olympics. The President visited the U.S. athletes staying aboard the *Queen Mary 2*. (Author's photo)

COLLISIONS, ICEBERGS, AND BOILER EXPLOSIONS

Domestic and international shipping regulations historically have been developed in reaction to a casualty such as a sinking or a fire aboard a ship that involves loss of life. Taking a lesson from the *Titanic* tragedy, the international maritime community was quick to organize itself and call the first Safety of Lives at Sea or SOLAS convention, which led to the passage of many of the passenger safety regulations still in force today. However, keeping up with the technological advances in ship design, safety equipment, and communications in the past 25 years has been very challenging for international maritime regulatory agencies such as the International Maritime Organization (IMO). Especially notable are the growth in the size and tonnage of vessels, the increasing numbers of passengers and crew they carry, the development of new ports and destinations, and the increasing onboard amenities such as those found on the *Voyager of the Seas* and other modern cruise ships. Because current regulations were developed before the trend toward larger ships began, the IMO a decade ago began conducting a comprehensive review of international passenger vessel regulations.[37] William O'Neil, then secretary-general of the IMO, first raised concerns about the very large passenger ships entering service and their particular safety issues. Quite simply, he asked how it would be possible to evacuate and recover upwards of 5,000 people if it proved necessary to abandon one of the new generation of enormous ships.[38] The IMO secretary-general personally took the initiative, raising the issue during the 72nd meeting of the Maritime Safety Committee (MSC) in May 2000.

The MSC agreed to investigate safety-related questions arising from gaps in or obsolete provisions of the existing safety regulations. The review of safety regimes for cruise ships began at the November 2000 meeting of the MSC. The MSC set a baseline requirement that the review of passenger ship safety should focus on five elements: (1) the regulatory framework should emphasize prevention of a casualty; (2) future large passenger ships should be designed for improved survivability so that in the event of a casualty, passengers can stay safely on board as the ship proceeds to port; (3) the regulatory framework should permit alternative designs and arrangements in place of the prescriptive regulations, provided that they achieve an equivalent level of safety; (4) large passenger ships should be crewed and equipped and have in place arrangements to ensure the safety of persons on board and to allow them to survive in the area of operation, taking into account climatic conditions and the availability of search-and-rescue functions; (5) large passenger ships should be crewed and equipped to ensure the health, safety, medical care, and security of persons on board until more specialized assistance is available.[39]

The MSC stressed that prevention is the best way to keep accidents from becoming maritime disasters. It concluded that the best way to avoid having thousands of persons in lifeboats, exposed to the elements and dependent on the response and availability of search-and-rescue units, is to ensure that future passenger ships are robustly designed. This will ensure that, after an incident, both passengers and crew will be able to evacuate to a safe area on board as the ship proceeds to port under its own power. Thus was born the idea for three new concepts in cruise ship design: "safe area," "safe return to port," and "casualty threshold."[40] These concepts, mandated in the new SOLAS regulations, establish the design criteria that new passenger ships will have to meet.

A "safe area" on a ship will have to provide an area free from fire or flooding that protects the passengers from hazards to life or health and contains basic services such as sanitation, water, and food. Safe areas are included in the "safe return to port" concept, which mandates that a cruise ship, even after suffering a casualty such as a fire or flood, have essential ship services such as propulsion, steering, navigational systems, and communications, both internal and external. "Casualty thresholds" are those criteria that determine what systems are available to evacuate the ship if the "return to port" threshold has been exceeded because of the loss of one main vertical zone. Those systems on a ship include internal and external communications, bilge systems (for removal of water used for firefighting), lighting along escape routes, and guidance systems for evacuation.[41]

Finally, the MSC looked at the search-and-rescue capabilities of cruise ships in the event that a cruise ship has to be evacuated. Rescuing large numbers of passengers from the sea is difficult, especially when the ship is in some way distressed. As cruise ships travel into more remote areas seeking new adventure for their passengers, the possibility that large numbers of passengers may be cast adrift in harsh climates in areas where there is not much vessel traffic was something that the committee on cruise ship safety zeroed in on. Some of the recommendations it drafted included provisions requiring advance detailed voyage planning for ships operating in remote areas and guidance on recovery techniques and on surviving in cold water. New performance standards were also incorporated for onboard recovery systems and to ensure that all ships have the capability to rapidly recover people from survival craft (lifeboats) safely and transfer them to the rescue ship.[42]

While these recommendations are comforting, these standards and design concepts will apply mostly to new cruise ship construction, while others measures, such as training requirements, can be readily adopted by shipboard personnel. Passenger ship safety has always been based on a history of cruise ship mishaps. The *Titanic* was perhaps the most famous ship to sink under catastrophic circumstances. Over the years and up to the present time, however, cruise ships have been involved in frequent and similar calamities at sea, some involving loss of life. Their stories should be repeated often to remind us of how fragile these ships are and of the precious cargo they carry.

In their heyday, cruise ships were called ocean liners and were a major form of transportation that shuttled immigrants between Europe and the United States. Even after World War II, ocean liners were the primary means for crossing expansive oceans until the advent of the jetliner effectively ended their reign. But, as the sinking of the *Titanic* proved, they were not immune to the risk that comes with being at sea. Far from the threat of pirates and terrorists who seem intent on inflicting harm to one of these modern marvels, cruise ships, through human error, mechanical failure, or the savageness of the sea itself, have collided with each other, struck submerged reefs, or succumbed to internal emergencies that have put not only passengers' lives but also the lives of the crews at risk. While typically called "accidents," these occurrences over the years make news not only because they are rare but because of questions about whether they could have been prevented. The sinking of the *Andrea Doria*, in 1956, is one such case.

The *Andrea Doria*, named for a 16th-century Genoese admiral, represented newfound pride for Italy, a country that had surrendered to the allies in the Second World War. Of all Italy's ships at the time, the *Andrea Doria* was the largest, the fastest, and supposedly the safest ocean liner. The ship had a gross tonnage of 29,000 grt and a capacity of about 1,200 passengers and 500 crewmembers. Christened in 1951, the ship began routine transits of the Atlantic in 1953. On July 17, 1956, the *Andrea Doria*, with 1,134 passengers aboard, departed Genoa on its 51st crossing from Italy to New York. After stopping at Cannes, on the French Riviera, and at Naples, the ship headed west toward the United States across the Atlantic Ocean.[43]

On July 25, *Andrea Doria* was heading west off the coast of Nantucket, Massachusetts, in an area known not only for dense fog but heavy shipping traffic. The ship was scheduled to arrive in New York the next morning. Earlier that day, the *MS Stockholm*, a small passenger liner belonging to the Swedish American Line, had departed New York heading east toward Gothenburg, Sweden. The ship was cutting through the water at a hefty 18 knots in clear weather. The captain of the *Stockholm* left the bridge and gave control of the ship to the third officer.

The *Andrea Doria*, meanwhile, was now engulfed in heavy fog and reduced its speed from 23 knots to 21 knots, only 2 knots, and sounded its fog horn for six seconds every minute.[44] As the two ships approached each other, one heading west, one heading east, with 17 miles separating them, they were both displaying what navigators call "constant bearing and decreasing range" (CBDR) from each other — they were essentially on a collision course. Their combined speed was 40 knots, and, although they could see each on their surface radars, which were then in use on all ships, there was no radio communication between them.

In the moments just before their impact, the *Stockholm* turned hard to starboard and attempted to reverse its engines to slow the ship. The *Andrea Doria* remained at its speed of almost 22 knots and turned to port in an attempt to avoid the now certain collision, but the maneuver of both ships actually increased the angle at which they eventually would hit. The two ships collided at approximately 11:10 P.M. at almost a 90-degree angle. The *Stockholm*'s sharp bow pierced *Andrea Doria*'s starboard side approximately midway down its length, penetrating three cabin decks to a depth of nearly 40 feet. The ships were joined together for less than a minute and then separated in heavy fog. The *Stockholm* slid down the starboard side of the *Andrea Doria* as it continued forward.

During the short time the ships were joined, remarkably, a 14-year-old passenger from the *Andrea Doria* was thrust onto the deck of the *Stockholm*. Crews for the *Stockholm* found the young teenage girl unhurt during a survey of the damage to their ship. The girl's family members, however, who were asleep in their cabins at the fore end of the *Andrea Doria*, were killed during the initial impact.[45] Of the initial casualties on the *Andrea Doria*, many were immigrant families, who were trapped on the forward lower decks and drowned immediately after the collision because the impact area became submerged. On the *Stockholm*, five crew members were killed outright in the collision.

After colliding, both ships sent immediate SOS messages, and the world instantly became aware of the unfolding tragedy at sea. But, unlike in the *Titanic* disaster, many ships responded quickly to aid in the rescue effort. The SS *Ile de France*, a large eastbound French Line passenger liner that had passed the westbound *Andrea Doria* many hours earlier, turned back to assist in the rescue. Half of the *Andrea Doria's* lifeboats on the port side were unusable because of the severe list to port, which dangled them out over the ocean. Because of the list, the remaining lifeboats were lowered empty to the water. Passengers had to climb down Jacob (rope) ladders to the awaiting lifeboats.[46] After a survey of the *Stockholm* revealed that the ship was not in immediate danger of sinking, the *Stockholm's* captain ordered his lifeboats to rescue the *Andrea Doria's* passengers.

The drama of the *Andrea Doria* played out as journalists snapped photos and recorded every detail of its demise. The ship eventually sank 11 hours after the initial collision with all of the surviving passengers transferred off the ship. In all, 46 persons perished in the disaster. Due to subsequent out-of-court settlements between the two ship companies, official cause and liability in the wreck were never pursued. Although the *Andrea Doria* was thought to be primarily at fault, both ships were traveling at excessive speeds with restricted visibility. The radar on the *Andrea Doria* also was thought to have been set on a scale that displayed the image of the *Stockholm* as if it were at a greater distance from the *Andrea Doria* than it really was.[47]

Today's communication and navigational systems on board modern cruise ships make the possibility of a collision like the one that eventually sank the *Andrea Doria* remote. However, even with the most reliable systems, human error can still sink a cruise ship, as was demonstrated in 2007, when the *Sea Diamond,* a Greek cruise ship operated by Louis Hellenic Cruise Lines, struck a charted reef off the coast of Santorini Island in the Mediterranean. The *Sea Diamond,* built in 1986, was a 22,412 grt cruise ship registered under the Greek flag and was heading to port in Santorini when it struck a well-charted reef. The first concerns immediately focused on navigational errors on the part of the ship's master, but these soon gave way to efforts to evacuate the ship when it became apparent that flooding would soon overtake and sink the ship.

The eventual sinking of the *Sea Diamond* highlighted a number of safety-related issues apart from whether the ship's master was operating the ship in safe water, free from submerged dangers. Although existing SOLAS regulations require passenger vessels to be able to evacuate all on board within 30 minutes, it appeared, according to news reports, to have taken an inordinately long time to evacuate the *Sea Diamond*. It was in sheltered waters, with many other rescue craft immediately at hand, and yet it took over three hours to clear the passengers.[48] The sinking of the Greek cruise ship resulted in the deaths of two French

passengers. Criminal charges were eventually filed against the ship's master for causing a serious pollution incident, and two company representatives from Hellenic
Cruise Lines were charged with failing to take measures to stop the pollution
from the wreck and for failing to provide a plan for removing bunkers (fuel oil)
from the vessel within 48 hours of the incident.[49]

Hellenic Cruises later produced evidence suggesting that faulty nautical charts
were responsible for the accident, but that defense did not appear to hold water. It
did not explain why other ships that apparently had the same charts managed to
avoid the submerged reef. Passengers from the *Sea Diamond* eventually sought
redress through legal action in the U.S. District Court for the South District of
New York against the Hellenic Cruise Lines, seeking punitive damages for alleged
gross negligence.[50]

A little more than a month after the sinking of the *Sea Diamond,* another cruise
ship was forced to evacuate all its passengers and crew following its grounding off
the coast of Alaska. The grounding of the 3,400-grt passenger ship *Empress of the
North* raised concerns about passenger safety in light of the *Sea Diamond* sinking and the sinking, in 2006, of the *Queen of the North,* in Canada, which claimed
two lives. As with the *Sea Diamond,* the grounding of the *Empress of the North*
and the grounding and sinking of the *Queen of the North* were blamed on navigational (human) errors.[51]

When a damaged ship is declared a loss, life-saving efforts to get everyone off
the ship and away from the source of danger is paramount. It is out on the open
ocean that the real struggle for survival begins.

In November 2007, after the sinking of the *Sea Diamond,* the sinking of another passenger ship played out, this time in frigid waters, during an excursion to
Antarctica. The tour operator, G.A.P. Adventures, based in Toronto, offers cruises
to the Antarctic, Greenland, Scotland, and the Amazon. It normally sends a dozen
cruises a year into the Antarctic, all on the small cruise ship *Explorer.* On its final
ill-fated cruise, the *Explorer* hit a submerged object that was thought to be an iceberg. The ship sank after all 154 passengers and crew had been evacuated.[52] Questions quickly were raised in the maritime community about whether the ship,
operating during the southern hemisphere's summer months, was prepared for
navigating in areas known for submerged navigational hazards such as icebergs.

The Collision Regulations (COLREGS) are a set of IMO navigational instructions that help ships avoid hazards at sea; remarkably, even with these regulations,
there is no rule that focuses exclusively on navigation in icebound areas. Some in
the maritime industry offered some logical suggestions after the *Explorer* sinking
and recommended an amendment to the COLREGS that would aid in a vessel's
navigation in areas where ice exists. This would include, at the very least, an increase in the number of lookouts and watchkeepers and a drastic reduction in
speed.[53]

In relation to search-and-rescue efforts in the *Explorer* sinking, questions were also raised about cruises that operate in remote areas like the Antarctic and whether passengers on such cruises can survive in open lifeboats in frigid water. As cold water flooded the *Explorer*'s engine room through a large gash in the ship's underside, the decision to abandon ship was given by the captain. About 1:30 A.M., in the frigid night air, the passengers climbed down ladders on the ship's side into open lifeboats and inflatable craft. Once in the lifeboats, they bobbed for four hours in the rough seas and chilling winds. At daybreak, the survivors were huddled underneath thin foil blankets in 20-degree air and nearly freezing waters.[54] Luckily, the National Geographic ship *Endeavour*, which was in the region, heard the distress call and eventually rescued the survivors of the *Explorer*.

Not all cruise ship emergencies involve sinking, however. There have been other recent mishaps that have injured or killed passenger and crew. Some involved mechanical problems, and others once again demonstrated how vulnerable these ships are to human error. The *Crown Princess*, delivered in 2006, was the newest Princess Cruises Diamond class ship. The 113,000 grt cruise ship was less than a month old when, in July, shortly after leaving Port Canaveral, Florida, en route to New York, it heeled over (tilted) very sharply to starboard. Water poured from swimming pools, and passengers were tossed across the ship's decks, buffets, and staterooms. The listing was described as a 15-degree list by U.S. Coast Guard investigators. However, because the ship's swimming pools were emptied of water by the ship's movement, experts say that a list of 30 to 35 degrees had to have occurred. A 45-degree list is unrecoverable.[55] The toll was serious: 240 people suffered injuries, 94 were sent to hospitals, and 2 were reportedly in critical condition after the incident.

The cruise line spin doctors were quick to blame a steering-gear glitch for the accident, but an ensuing investigation pinned the blame on a junior officer who apparently mistakenly put the rudder over hard, causing the ship to list to starboard. Amid a flurry of press reports generating negative publicity for the cruise line and the prospect of an inquiry by the National Transportation Safety Board (NTSB) into the ship's black box, Princess Cruises finally admitted that "human error" had caused the abrupt listing. In a letter to passengers, the president of Princess Cruises, Alan Buckelow, wrote: "The incident was due to human error and the appropriate personnel changes have been made."[56]

The sharp list that tumbled passengers on the *Crown Princess* was the result of human error, as the company spokesman admitted. In sharp contrast, the Norwegian Cruise Line's *Norwegian Dawn*, in April 2005, was struck by a gigantic "rogue wave" off the eastern seaboard of the United States. The ship was struck by a 70-foot wave that caused superficial damage to the cruise ship and minor injuries to several passengers. The incident later sparked a controversy when it was learned, through an investigation by the National Transportation Safety Board, that the freak wave occurred while the ship was diverted from its original itinerary to permit the filming of a television feature involving Donald Trump. *Norwegian Dawn* passengers threatened to sue Norwegian Cruise Lines, alleging that the cruise line "put their safety at risk."[57]

Far more serious to the issue of cruise ship safety is the legacy of the boiler explosion on the *Norwegian Norway* in May 2003. The explosion in the port of Miami killed eight crew members. The National Transportation Safety Board report into the boiler room explosion initially stated that the probable cause was the deficient boiler operation, maintenance, and inspection practices of Norwegian Cruise Line, which allowed material deterioration and fatigue cracking to weaken the boiler. Inadequate boiler surveys by Bureau Veritas, the international certification agency, also contributed to the accident.

As the NTSB dug deeper, however, it found that boiler troubles aboard the *Norway* were a result of a culture that had paid lip service to such problems for the past three decades. Breakdowns and repairs were commonplace and seemed to have peaked in the late 1990s. Internal memos uncovered by the NTSB indicated that a recommendation for completely replacing the boilers on the *Norway* at a cost $18 million was overturned in favor of retubing the boilers at a cost of $4 million. Another internal memo stressed that the ship was "no longer safe to operate."[58] Norwegian Cruise Lines chose the less costly remedy of retubing the boilers instead of replacing the boilers, which would have guaranteed the overall safety of the ship, crew, and passengers.

With its hands tied by the evidence, Norwegian Cruise Line agreed to plead guilty to negligence in May 2008. U.S. prosecutors said that the plea deal makes the cruise lines liable for at least $500,000 in criminal penalties. The cruise line had to agree to carry out safety inspections of its vessels with an independent safety consultant. While only marginally acknowledging that eight shipboard employees lost their lives due to what amounted to criminal negligence, the cruise line spin doctors issued a watered-down statement saying: "We are hopeful that resolution of the recent *misdemeanor* charge will bring this unfortunate incident to a conclusion" (emphasis added).[59] These examples, taken from the records of the cruise line industry, indicate that the cruise lines' safety record appears to be getting worse, not better. In certain instances, the cruise lines have shown themselves to be negligent, and many of the major accidents can be traced to human error or negligence. Cruise line accidents, however, must be put in prospective. Remembering that cruise ships operate in every region and ocean in the world, 365 days a year, one realizes how infrequently such events happen. But the number of cruise ship accidents that have occurred in rapid succession over the past several years also suggests that perhaps that the rapid growth of the cruise industry has outpaced the cruise lines' capacity to provide robust safety prevention programs and adequate emergency response capabilities. An even more worrisome possibility is that the cruise lines have been ignoring the greater safety issues facing their industry while rearranging their own deck chairs. The tragic boiler explosion on the *Norwegian Norway* is a good example. Either way, the passenger who assumes that all is "ship-shape" below decks must also not assume that the risk that comes with a cruise ship vacation is alleviated by governmental intervention or regulation. As we shall see in the next chapter, in some cases, these have only made the problem worse.

five

THE LIMITATIONS OF U.S. AND INTERNATIONAL MARITIME REGULATORY REGIMES AND MARITIME AGENCIES: PROTECTING CRUISE SHIP PASSENGERS AND CREWS

C ruise lines are acutely aware of the limits on their ability to protect their passengers and crews from a terrorist attack. They also recognize that passengers and crew face a distinct possibility of loss of life in an accident or security incident. For this reason, cruise ships are required to carry insurance coverage for most calamities that can occur on the high seas. After September 11, however, some analysts with an eye on the risk management duties of corporations discussed the possibility that corporate officers and directors might face terrorism-associated liability because of their fiduciary duties or their failure to disclose terrorism risks adequately to their shareholders.[1] The significance of this possibility became especially apparent after the shocking collapse of the Enron Corporation, which ushered in the era of the Sarbanes-Oxley Act of 2002, which imposed requirements for greater transparency and public disclosure on certain public companies, and led to requirements that corporations disclose the financial risks facing their businesses.

An even greater national debate regarding corporate liability emerged after the September 11 attacks. The U.S. government intervened to backstop both the airlines and private-sector insurance mechanisms by assuming terrorist risks under the newly created Terrorism Risk Insurance Act (TRIA) of 2002. After the September 11 attacks, the insurance industry began dropping coverage for terrorism from its policies after it realized how poorly defined terrorism risks were and how large its liability could become.[2] The discussions about insurable risks boiled over into the maritime industry, and a controversy developed over the relationship between the cruise line industry and the maritime insurance clubs and the 2002 Athens Convention protocols. The results of this ongoing debate will have financial implications for the cruise industry and maritime insurance groups as well as for cruise ship passengers should a future maritime disaster occur. As of this writing there is no further progress on the implementation of the Athens Convention protocols. Although the protocol has not come into force because it failed to be ratified by 10 member-states (countries), the compromise has allowed the P&I Clubs and the Hull insurers to carry on with acceptable liability limits.

In diplomatic language, "convention" is another term for "treaty," and, after ratification, a convention has the effect of international law. The Athens Convention protocols were adopted at a diplomatic conference in London in October 2002. The Convention aimed to radically reform the passenger liability regime under the existing Athens Convention as related to the Carriage of Passengers and Their Luggage by Sea. It was supposed to enter into effect after ratification by the member states. Its ratification became stalled, however, because of a debate over issues concerning responsibility for terrorist acts, war risks, and parity in risk assumption between cruise ship companies and other maritime carriers.

Because the largest cruise ships now carry more than 3,500 passengers, cruise lines face a staggering liability risk in the event of a terrorist attack. Other maritime carriers were concerned that the cruise ships' risk was likely to be assumed by all other ship owners as a way to cover the cruise lines' enormous liability potential in the event of a mass casualty such as a terrorist attack on one of these ships. This was possible because of the manner in which the maritime insurance industry is structured; in essence, the loss by one is shared by all.[3] Some members of the maritime community have even suggested that cruise lines should not be insured at all because of the inherent risk in their operations. In the event of a single terrorist attack on one cruise ship, the resulting liability could financially cripple not only the ship owner through individual lawsuits but the maritime insurer, as well.

The maritime insurance industry is referred to as Protection and Indemnity, or "P&I" Clubs. P&I Clubs act as sort of a mutual maritime insurance agency for ship owners, and certain types of insurable maritime assets are covered by financial contributions by all the club members. The present P&I Clubs are the remote descendants of the many small hull insurance clubs that were formed by British ship owners in the 18th century. During the mid-19th century, ship owners faced certain liabilities that traditional underwriters were unable or unwilling to cover. It became more usual for injured crew members and dependents of crew members who had been killed to seek compensation from employers. The huge number of passengers who emigrated to North America and Australia in the second half of the century also raised ship owners' vulnerability to liability claims. Ship owners needed coverage against these risks. As a result, they began to form mutual associations through which they would pool their resources to pay claims against members. Each ship owner paid contributions to the club to cover the extent of his mutual liabilities and, in return, was indemnified for losses not recovered under the standard marine insurances then available.

These mutual clubs were governed by certain rules, the most important being that members would be indemnified only for liabilities already paid for and that members would be thrown out if they ceased to be able to make the required contributions, whether because of bankruptcy or death. These rules continue to govern the current P&I Clubs and are sometimes referred to as the "pay to be paid" rule. These early organizations have developed into the 13 existing mutual insurance associations or P&I Clubs, which together insure the liabilities of some 95 percent of the world's oceangoing tonnage.[4]

The P&I Clubs provide coverage for a ship owner's liabilities but not for the ship itself. That is covered separately by hull underwriters. The risks covered by the P&I Clubs have traditionally included death and personal injury of crew, passengers, and third parties; liabilities in respect of stowaways or persons saved at sea; liabilities arising from collisions, groundings, or damage to fixed and floating objects; liabilities arising from pollution and wreck removal; liabilities arising from towage operations; and liability related to cargo.[5] In short, when calamity strikes, losses are paid out by the Clubs and affect the insurance rates and claims of all members. Because of the way the Athens protocols were designed, however, there is significant concern among other maritime operators that they will be liable for losses incurred by the large cruise line operators. To put it bluntly, the commercial shipping industry believes the cruise industry's risk is much higher than theirs because of the human cargo cruise ships carry and because of the greater potential for loss of life, and commercial carriers do not want to be responsible for paying to insure those risks.

At the core of the Athens protocol of 2002 is the liabilities of the cruise lines with respect to terrorist incidents. The protocols distinguish between terrorist acts and other shipping incidents, such as shipwrecks, collisions, the stranding of the ship, and explosions or fire on ships. Terrorist acts, like acts of war, have traditionally been excluded in the insurance schemes of the P&I Clubs. The Athens Convention, however, has left open the possibility that the cruise lines will be now be liable for damages arising from acts of terrorism.[6] In response, the cruise industry has argued vehemently that it should be exempt from such liability because terrorism has traditionally been considered an act of war. More concerning to the P&I Clubs is that the new 2002 protocols leave open the possibility that the P&I Clubs themselves can be sued by passengers, bypassing the cruise lines. The P&I Clubs and the cruise lines apparently see themselves on the same side of the fence but have differing views of their liability and financial responsibility.

There is little doubt how this debate over liability came about. As was mentioned previously, the idea that an entire ship could be attacked or destroyed with catastrophic loss of life was unthinkable prior to 9/11. However, the destruction and loss of life on that day resulted in the largest insurance loss in history and focused the attention in the insurance world on the risks faced by various forms of transportation. The growing passenger capacity of cruise ships became the focus of the maritime insurance industry. The 9/11 terrorist attacks, according to President Bush, were "acts of war" that propelled the United States and the world into a "war on terrorism."[7] Because there has been no one universally accepted definition of international terrorism, however, this raised the questions as to whether terrorist acts against cruise ships could be categorized by the courts as acts of war, thus excluding them from insurable liability. There was consensus that such acts should be considered terrorism and that they were therefore included in the new coverage scheme put forth in the 2002 Athens Convention. As the international community and the insurance industry wrestled with the possibilities in the context of the new age of terrorism ushered in on 9/11, they were, fortunately, able to study some precedents, drawn from the transportation industry, that grappled with definitions of terrorism and acts of war.

In 1970, a Pan Am 747 en route from New York to Brussels was hijacked by two terrorists who belonged to the Popular Front for the Liberation of Palestine (PFLP). The hijacking was part of a larger terrorist plot in which the PFLP hijacked four airline jets over western Europe. In those days, the terrorist group Black September was as interested in gaining publicity as it was in committing cold-blooded murders; this group would, two years later, kill 11 Israeli athletes and coaches during the 1972 Olympic Games in Munich. The terrorists ordered the Pan Am jet to land in Beirut, Lebanon. There, the plane was loaded with explosives before being flown to Cairo. In Cairo, all 152 passengers were evacuated before the plane was blown up. An insurance suit followed and centered on acts of war and questions of liability. The decision in *Pan American World Airways Inc. v. The Aetna Casualty & Surety Co.* was that terrorist acts were not covered by the war-risks clauses in the relevant aviation insurance policies.

The district court that heard the case ruled that for an event to be classified as a "war," force had to be employed between governments or de facto or quasi-governmental entities and held that the PFLP, which was neither a country nor a government, did not meet this criterion. This finding was affirmed by the Court of Appeals, which held that war is "a course of hostility engaged in by entities that have at least significant attributes of sovereignty" and concluded that the loss of the aircraft was not caused by a warlike act.[8] The significance of the *Pan Am* decision was that it appeared to set a precedent upholding carriers' liability in cases of terrorist acts under the Athens Convention protocols, which worried the cruise industry.

Because war and its effects are potentially so catastrophic and could cripple the private insurance industry and because war's risks are considered "incalculable," it has historically been singled out as a separate category of risk, precisely because it involves acts of "public" rather than "private" violence. It does not appear likely that terrorist acts such as suicide boat attacks can be put in the same category as war-related incidents. Relevant to this debate is that the *Pan Am* decision leaves open the possibility for the U.S. military involvement in Afghanistan and Iraq, for example, might provoke future acts of terrorism. If that were to happen, could such incidents be considered acts of war because we are engaged in a "war on terrorism"? Insurance carriers might invoke the war-acts exclusion, as well as any terrorism exclusion, and deny insurance coverage for any resulting personal injury or property damage losses.[9] Since September 11 and the ensuing "war on terrorism," these possibilities have made it unclear what effects terrorist acts will have on insurable risks and have made it considerably more difficult to assess liability.

The Athens Convention protocols of 2002 have continued to cause great controversy, which has so far prevented their ratification. An examination of the cost of terrorism for the maritime industry and for cruise lines in particular may help explain the level of concern given the implications of these costs for the cruise industry's bottom line. When ratified, the protocols would set cruise lines liabilities of approximately $375,000 per passenger per incident plus an additional $200,000 per passenger in negligence liabilities. The protocol would also allow plaintiffs (victims) to seek redress from both ship owners and their insurers (the P&I Clubs). These passenger limits are significantly higher than anything the cruise industry has indicated it would find acceptable. An additional sticking point is that was that P&I Clubs would not provide proof of insurance for terrorism or war risk, leaving the cruise lines operators with potential uninsured liabilities of close to a billion dollars per ship per incident.[10]

In reality, the figures probably would not represent what a passenger or his or her surviving family members could collect. After litigation, the amounts recovered by each passenger would probably be far lower. But, because cruise ships now carry more than 3,500 passengers, the resulting monetary figure (passenger capacity multiplied by $575,000, the total per-passenger compensation including negligence liability) becomes astronomical and understandably raises significant concern among nonpassenger operators in the maritime industry that, as members of the P&I Clubs, they would have to cover any potential losses by the cruise ships.[11]

A breakthrough to resolve the Athens Convention impasse occurred at the 92nd session of the IMO Legal Committee, held in Paris in October 2006.

A proposal was put forward jointly by the United Kingdom and Norway and by the shipping industry, represented by the International Council of Cruise Lines (ICCL), the Washington, D.C.-based lobbying organization. After four years of complex negotiations, the compromise solution that was agreed to by the Committee took into account the existing exclusions in standard P&I coverage and utilized the insurance capacity in the war risk insurance market. The solution provides for governments to limit the liability of carriers (cruise lines) and, consequently insurers, for terrorism losses to a figure of $500 million overall per ship, instead of the $1 billion as in the previous arrangement. This amount is reserved solely to cover passenger claims. The compromise also requires the P&I Clubs to certify insurance coverage for that amount. The solution recognizes that the certificate of insurance (called a "Blue Card") with respect to terrorism will be separate from and in addition to the Blue Card issued by the carrier's P&I Club for nonwar liabilities.[12]

Michael Crye, the president of the International Council of Cruise Lines (ICCL), representing the cruise lines at the time, said, "Hopefully P&I Clubs could provide certificates of insurance for non-war-risk and non-terrorism cover.... This provides a way forward, allowing ship owner liability to be linked to insurability." He added that the breakthrough was a compromise, not a victory.[13] The debate was really about shifting responsibility for the risk inherent in cruising to the industry. The cruise lines, on one side, attempted to let themselves off the hook by classifying terrorist incidents as acts of war, thus rendering them uninsurable. On the other side were the rest of the ship owners, who, believing such acts to be worst case scenarios, do not want to be held liable for the potentially huge monetary damages under the existing structure of the P&I Clubs.

Although the IMO had the interests of the seagoing public in mind when it proposed revising the Athens Convention in 2002, the opposing sides in the debate never took into account the cruise passengers' stake in the outcome. Winning a reduction in financial liability loss for human life as a result of a terrorist act was obviously seen a victory by the industry. The cruise lines felt somewhat relieved to walk away from the table with at least a set limit to their liability. ICCL considered the breakthrough a compromise but not a victory. Although the solution proposed by the United Kingdom, Norway, and the ICCL represents a well-crafted compromise, the United States has stated that it cannot support a solution that exempts carriers from liability for acts of terrorism without regard to fault. The 2002 Convention has not yet come into force and is unlikely to do so until 2010 at the earliest, and the debate over its ratification may continue for years. There is already talk that the United States is unlikely to adopt the Convention and that consequently passenger claims will not be subject to any kind of limit.[14]

The U.S. Department of State says that ratifying the treaty would amend the terms of the protocols substantively. To exempt carriers from liability for negligent acts inappropriately shifts the consequences of that negligence from the carrier to innocent passengers and governments and should be rejected. Given the far-reaching consequences of any such departure from established treaty-making principles and practices in all areas, the United States cautions against establishing such a precedent and has concerns about whether an instrument could be ratified under these conditions.[15]

Fortunately for the cruise industry, the P&I Clubs, and cruise ship passengers, the Athens Convention protocols have not yet been tested; that is, there have been no large-scale passenger deaths at the hands of the terrorists or/and pirates. This has given the cruise industry a reprieve as the issue of liability continues to be debated.

THE SENATOR FROM NEW YORK INVESTIGATES CRUISE SHIP SECURITY

In 2003, Charles Schumer, the Democratic senator from New York, in conjunction with the New York Police Department and maritime security experts, highlighted the security issues associated with cruise ships docked at busy terminals such as the New York City Passenger Terminal. That facility is the largest U.S. passenger ship terminal outside Florida. Cruise ships and all other maritime carriers were diverted from New York harbor after the terrorist attacks of September 11 and sent to destinations such as Boston. When they returned to New York, the cruise ships brought back one of the largest sources of tourist revenue to the city but also raised concerns about their safety.

Specifically, Senator Schumer addressed questions about New York Passenger Terminal's security that stemmed from the fact that the terminal was operated by a private company, P&O Ports. With the safety and security of nearly one million people at risk, Schumer wrote to Admiral Thomas H. Collins, the commandant of the U.S. Coast Guard, to ascertain the validity of these allegations. Senator Schumer had a long list of concerns for the commandant.

Foremost among the senator's concerns was the risk of a terrorist attack on the terminal from a small boat using the pier or waterside approaches to the docked cruise ships. He noted from his investigation that the busy New York Passenger Ship Terminal was vulnerable to car bombs, that it had a lack of waterside barriers, that the training of security guards was inadequate, that the facility faced threats from unscreened vendors who service the ships, and that unattended luggage left directly under the parking structure next to the pier before being screened was an additional threat.[16] Although the senator was referring to security shortcomings that might make the Port of New York vulnerable to maritime terrorist attacks, he said that these deficiencies could be found, in varying degrees, in any U.S. port and certainly were present in many overseas cruise ship terminals, even after the September 11 attacks.

On the basis of my own assessment of cruise ship terminals, I had to agree with the senator's findings, especially after my inspections of the *Queen Mary 2* in New York harbor and my security surveys in foreign ports in particular. Senator Schumer, through his security resources, had effectively conducted a port vulnerability survey in the days prior to the implementation of the ISPS Code. The ISPS Code had already been ratified by the contracting governments in December 2002 when the senator brought the security shortcomings of the Port of New York to the attention of the U.S. Coast Guard. At the time, compliance with the ISPS Code was still more than a year away from being mandatory in all ports, and the security problems in New York demonstrated the steep hill that still had to be climbed in U.S. ports as they prepared to implement the Code. The shortcoming found by the senator's inspection were alarming, especially in New York in light of the recent terrorist attacks in that city.

Ever since 9/11, vehicles at airports must be parked at least 300 feet from the passenger terminals. For many months after 9/11, while the nation remained at an especially high level of vigilance, curbside dropoffs of passengers in front of terminals were prohibited at most U.S. airports.[17] However, even after 9/11, unscreened vehicles were allowed to park in the 1,000 parking spaces at the New York Passenger Terminal directly above the pier. These spaces are just feet away from the docked cruise ships. It seems reasonable to clear vehicles away from where cruise ships dock, especially because we learned all too well of the destructive capability of truck and car bombs. The U.S. Marine Corps barracks in Beirut, Lebanon, was leveled by one truck bomb in 1983, as was the U.S. embassy in Beirut earlier that year. Car bombs were also used successfully in the attacks on the U.S. embassies in East Africa in 1998.

Overseas, I found unattended vehicles parked even closer to cruise ships than they were in New York. On an inspection of the port of Naples, Italy, for example, I found many issues with the pier security around where one of Princess's largest ships was berthed. A truck with Arabic license plates waiting to be loaded onto a ferry was only feet from the hull of the cruise ship. At my insistence, the port police were able to have the truck moved away from the ship, but it took half the day to accomplish this.

Vehicle bombs have always been one of the terrorist's most reliable methods to destroy buildings. But, especially after 9/11, which demonstrated the terrorist's genius for destroying life and property, the risk posed by a vehicle bomb used against a ship could not be overestimated. After all, why try to smuggle a bomb or terrorists aboard a ship when all you have to do is park a car or truck bomb next to it? Obviously, that way, you do not need to penetrate the ship's security layers, only the port's.

In 2004 the National Threat Assessment (NTA) concluded that al-Qaeda is likely to use a vehicle-borne improvised explosive device (VBIED) when attacking maritime targets. While small boats pose an equal threat, the NTA determined that the most likely method for attacking cruise ships is a VBIED, that is, a truck or car loaded with explosives and parked next to a ship.[18] The reasons are obvious; as stated previously, a terrorist's job is far easier if all he has to do is get a bomb next to a cruise ship while it is in port. The bomb would likely be larger than anything he could load onto a small boat like the one that damaged the USS *Cole.* A car bomb would do a better job of damaging a cruise ship and, if the ship was fully boarded with passengers at the time of the attack, would certainly cause many deaths and injuries. A car bomb would also disrupt port operations and guarantee instant news headlines and coverage.

Keeping all vehicles away from the ships was one of my first priorities when I was arranging security for Princess ships in overseas ports. In some cases, however, especially when cruise ships share piers with vehicle ferries, as they do in Safaga, Egypt, the task is virtually impossible. The risks to cruise ships in these cases come in the form of collateral damage. Ferries are at especially high risk for VBIEDs because of the lax screening employed. Ferries in Safaga, for example, make daily crossings of the Red Sea to Saudi Arabia and Yemen, in the heart of al-Qaeda country. One such ferry, the Panamanian-flagged *Al-Salam Boccaccio 98,* sank off the coast of Safaga in February 2006 from a fire that raged out of control. More than 1,000 lives were lost. Although the tragedy was not caused by an act of terrorism, the vulnerability of these overcrowded and sparsely inspected carriers demonstrates the enormous potential for loss of life should a vehicle or other bomb make its way on board.[19]

In addition to vehicles that are parked too close to the pier, Senator Schumer said that his office was concerned about the lack of water barriers that might be used to protect cruise ships in the water. Interestingly, his investigation was taking place about the same time that our efforts at Princess were focusing on the same problem. I believe that cruise ships should have some form of physical protection that separates them from small boats and other watercraft while they are in port, but it is unlikely that they ever will. Even if ships did have their own water barriers, most ports would not allow them because they restrict navigation. However, it is the inherent responsibility of the port to protect the ship and not the other way around. As long as the barrier does not violate any provision of the ISPS Code or restrict vessel traffic, it seems like a good idea to mark the ship's enforceable boundaries.

A Coast Guard patrol boat escorts a 3,000-passenger cruise ship from the port of Los Angeles. Although maritime security measures like these are standard in the United States, when cruise ships call on foreign ports, additional protection for cruise ships is often nonexistent, leaving ships vulnerable to terrorist attacks. (USCG photo by PA1 Daniel Tremper)

Although the U.S. Coast Guard is tasked with the prevention of terrorist acts in domestic ports and harbors, it does not have the type of resources Senator Schumer was referring to. After 9/11, the U.S. Coast Guard imposed security zones around docked cruise ships and other high-risk vessels, and this imaginary boundary is the only thing that currently protects such ships. The Coast Guard also regularly patrols the approaches to these ships, but, because it has limited resources, it cannot guard every cruise ship in every port.

After 9/11, the chief of naval operations emphasized the need for the expanded use of barrier booms around Navy vessels in U.S. ports to protect them from small boats. I was able to secure support from the U.S. Navy for a temporary water boom to encircle the *Queen Mary 2* while it was berthed in the port of Piraeus, Greece, during the 2004 Summer Olympics. My assessment of the Dunlap barrier used in Piraeus led me to believe that this level of protection would overwhelmingly stop threats from small boats dead in their tracks. Because cruise ships enter and leave port frequently, sometimes on the same day, however, the effort required to rig these water booms around the ships might prevent them from being used in this capacity. Norwegian Cruise Line's *Norwegian Dawn* was one of the first cruise ships home-ported in New York harbor. Senator Schumer said that he did not see any such booms used during the ship's maiden arrival in New York. According to his office, when two or more cruise ships are berthed in New York, a single small boat or jet ski laden with explosives could affect the safety of more than 10,000 people, and Senator Schumer supports the use of barriers and booms in New York to protect cruise boat passengers.

Unfortunately, if the threat level to cruise ships in U.S. ports is not considered to be high, the resources to pay for such protections will not be made available. According to the U.S. Coast Guard, the threat that terrorists might attack U.S. vessels or U.S. citizens on foreign vessels outside U.S. territorial waters in 2004 was considered "significant." However, the overall domestic maritime terrorist threat level for the United States, which is based upon a four-point scale of low, moderate, significant, and high, is presently assessed as "moderate."[20] Thus, the Coast Guard believes that the need for water barriers is significantly greater in overseas ports than in domestic ones.

The Coast Guard decides whether to dedicate resources for this kind of countermeasure according to the threat level it believes is present and the risk to the port or vessel. When the risk becomes unacceptable, then water barriers and patrol boats become plentiful, even in overseas ports. Unfortunately for the cruise lines, if the threat does increase in U.S. ports due to some unthinkable maritime terrorist act, sales may drop off because of consumers' concerns over the security of these ships. Right now, however, cruise ships and other vessels, even in New York, do not warrant that level of protection.

Senator Schumer was correct in believing that the security of cruise ships in at the New York Passenger Terminal is at risk from the baggage-screening process. Under federal regulations developed after 9/11 and codified in the Air Transportation Security Act of November 2001, all luggage at airports must be screened immediately when a passenger is checked in—either in new rooms constructed for this purpose or by baggage screeners adjacent to airline check-in desks. Schumer was told by his source in the port that, while passenger baggage was screened at the New York Terminal, it usually sat for hours under the pier before the terminal operators scanned it. The implication was that the baggage waiting to be screened could contain an explosive device and leave the ship and pier vulnerable to an explosion. Depending on where the explosion took place, there could be hundreds of injuries or deaths among the people on any of the four levels of the pier.[21]

Senator Schumer's investigation of the New York Passenger Terminal found problems that could have existed at any port in the United States prior to the implementation of the ISPS Code. These deficiencies demonstrated just how vulnerable a large and important port such as New York could be. The ISPS Code was seen as remedy for all security concerns related to the world's ports and oceangoing vessels, but, even though it applied to both ships and port facilities, ports were slow to comply with its provisions even when they became mandatory, in July 2004. With the coming of the ISPS Code came new issues and questions about ship and port security and whether the Code has created the security environment promised by its creators.

THE INTERNATIONAL SHIP AND PORT SECURITY CODE

One of the most important developments in maritime security over the past five years, and perhaps over the past several decades, has been the introduction of the International Ship and Port (Facility) Security (ISPS) Code. Along with the Maritime Transportation Security Act (MTSA) in the United States, the ISPS Code provides the cornerstone for today's international maritime security efforts. The September 11 attacks spurred the United States, and the world in general, to rethink its approach to protecting critical infrastructure and to preventing the terrorist threat from using the transportation sector in carrying out further terror attacks. The international community, through the United Nations, was quick to respond to the threat. Through Security Council resolution 1373 (2001), the United Nations called on the international community to increase its efforts to prevent and suppress terrorist acts.

Because the terrorists used the airline industry to carry out their attacks, the first efforts in the United States focused on strengthening that area of vulnerability through the creation of the Aviation Transportation Security Act (ATSA), passed by Congress in 2001. A full year later, the International Maritime Organization (IMO) passed a resolution on maritime security known popularly as the ISPS Code. In the United States, the Maritime Transportation Security Act (MTSA), passed in 2002, complemented the ATSA and implemented certain provisions of the ISPS Code.

The ISPS Code was designed to standardize security methods and measures throughout the maritime industry on land and on ships. A full five years after its appearance in July 2004, however, the ISPS Code has not fully lived up to expectations. It has been criticized for overburdening both ships and port facilities with paperwork and heaping additional security duties onto ship and port workers. Surprisingly, it has also been criticized for not going far enough in protecting ship and shore facilities. One of the biggest concerns has been the creation of a "shore versus ship" security environment.

The cruise industry was very successful in implementing the ISPS Code measures, as was most of the shipping industry. The cruise lines were quick to point out that security has always existed on cruise ships in the form mandated by the ISPS Code. This was not the first time maritime security had been in the international spotlight. The hijacking of the Italian cruise ship *Achille Lauro*, in October 1985, as we have seen, marked one of the first actual terrorist acts recorded in modern maritime history, and it moved the international community to act to prevent another such incident.

After the *Achille Lauro* hijackings, the United Nations asked the International Maritime Organization to look at terrorism and the possible threats to ships, passengers, and crews. In addressing this threat, the IMO's own Security Council—which is devoted to maritime security—was tasked with developing practical technical measures that could be applied to all cruise ships and to issue a Maritime Security Council Circular, modeled on the security standards that were developed for airports and aircraft in the mid-1980s after numerous terrorist hijackings and adopted through the International Civil Aviation Organization (ICAO). The IMO eventually released a circular titled "Measures to Prevent Unlawful Acts against Passengers and Crew On Board Ships" (MSC/Circ. 443a).

The measures applied to passenger ships engaged in international voyages of 24 hours or more and the port facilities that serviced them. The circular, which covered governments, ports, and ships, included, among other things, recommendations for designating ship security officers and the drafting of port and ship security plans based on vulnerability assessments. Many of these measures are now integral parts of the new Safety of Lives at Sea (SOLAS) protocols, issued after the sinking of the *Titanic*, in 1912, and revised in the 1960s, and the ISPS Code. Because of these early forms of regulation, cruise ships had, in essence, a head start when it came to implementing the provisions of the current ISPS Code.[22]

What exactly is the IMO, and how did the ISPS Code become an integral part of the modern maritime security model? The answers to these questions require a brief history of the IMO and a description of how the maritime industry is regulated.

The International Maritime Organization is a specialized body of the United Nations, created by an international conference held in Geneva in 1948. Its aims were to develop and maintain a comprehensive regulatory framework for shipping that encompassed safety, environmental concerns, legal matters, technical cooperation, maritime security, and shipping efficiency. Although established in 1948, the body did not meet formally until 1950 under the name "Inter-Governmental Maritime Consultative Organization," or IMCO. The name was changed in 1982 to the International Maritime Organization, or IMO.

The IMO's main purpose, as stated in its organizing articles, is to "to provide machinery for cooperation among Governments in the field of governmental regulation and practices relating to technical matters of all kinds affecting shipping."[23] This includes setting standards for maritime safety, security, and navigational efficiency and preventing and controlling marine pollution caused by ships. Under its international mandate, the Organization is empowered with the administrative and legal authority to achieve these ends. However, because it is part of the United Nations, the IMO regulates through its conventions and international treaties and has no enforcement authority. That responsibility is left to the contracting governments and controls such as the Coast Guard in the United States.

The first challenges the IMO faced was the revision of one of the most important convention treaties on maritime safety, SOLAS. The 1960 revision to the 1912 SOLAS Convention included new language on the carriage of dangerous goods and revised the system of measuring the tonnage of ships. In the 1960s and 1970s, the IMO turned its attention to preventing environmental pollution brought on by tanker collisions and groundings. The most important measure was the International Convention for the Prevention of Pollution from Ships, adopted in 1973 and modified by the Protocol of 1978. It covers not only accidental and operational oil pollution but also pollution by chemicals, goods in packaged form, sewage, and garbage, as well as air pollution generated by the shipping industry.[24]

In the 1980s, the IMO concentrated on the question of maritime security after the hijacking of the *Achille Lauro*. In the 1990s, it began to involve itself in initiating maritime global search-and-rescue communications for the Global Maritime Distress and Safety System (GMDSS), which became fully operational in 1999. The GMDSS guarantees assistance to ships that are in distress anywhere in the world, even if the ship's crews do not have time to radio for help. A distress message is transmitted automatically from the ship using satellites and ship-board radio systems.

Also in the 1990s, the IMO became involved with the human element in shipping with regard to ship safety and seafarer training. Maritime training standards entered into force in 1997, with the passage of the 1995 amendments to the 1978 International Convention on Standards of Training, Certification, and Watchkeeping for Seafarers.[25] These measures sought to improve the standards for those working on ships and gave the IMO the authority to monitor government compliance with the Convention. In 1998, the International Safety Management (ISM) Code became applicable to passenger ships, oil and chemical tankers, bulk carriers, gas carriers, and high-speed cargo craft of 500 gross tonnage and above. In 2002, the ISM also became applicable to other cargo ships and mobile offshore drilling units.

After the terrifying events of September 11, 2001, the IMO turned its attention once again to maritime security. In November 2001, one month after the attack, it passed a resolution calling for a review of ways to suppress and prevent terrorist acts against ships in port and at sea and ways to generally improve ship security. The resolution aimed at reducing the risks to passengers, crews, maritime facility workers, and vessels from the threat of international terrorism. The IMO acted quickly and amended the SOLAS Convention of 1974 by amending chapter XI and adapting a new chapter, XI-2, which outlines "special measures to enhance maritime security," thereby creating the International Ship and Port Security (ISPS) Code in December 2002.[26] The ISPS Code is part of the SOLAS Convention, so compliance is now mandatory for the 148 contracting governments to SOLAS. Only those countries that are contracting government to SOLAS have a legal obligation to comply with the requirements of the ISPS Code and to submit information to IMO. Fortunately, the signatories include those countries with most of the largest and busiest ports in the world, as well as the major flag registers.

Chapter XI of SOLAS is divided into two parts: chapter XI-1, "Special Measures to Enhance Maritime Safety," and chapter XI-2, "Special Measures to Enhance Maritime Security," which incorporates the new security regulations and requirements for ships and port facilities. These revisions and the new chapters support the ISPS Code under the general assumption that protecting ships and ports is essentially a risk management activity. To effectively deal with a threat, one must first define it. This process of the ISPS Code requires a full assessment of vulnerabilities to determine what security measures are appropriate in each case. Only by evaluating the risks to ships and maritime facilities can governments begin to adjust their security measures to deal with their own vulnerabilities.

The ISPS Code itself is broken down further into two parts. Part A details the mandatory steps that must be implemented; Part B includes additional recommendations. From the outset, there was significant confusion about the meaning of Parts A and B. What were the recommendations meant to provide that the mandatory portion did not specify? Would ships and facilities be required implement both parts, and, more important, would they be penalized if they did not? In the United States, for example, the U.S. Coast Guard indicated that it was going to hold the U.S. maritime industry responsible for both parts.

The confusion, however, basically reflected a misconception about what the two parts were supposed to do. The provisions of Part A were mandatory but depended on the type of ship, its cargoes and/or passengers, its trading pattern, and the characteristics of the port facilities it visited. The guidance given in Part B of the ISPS Code was meant to be taken into account when implementing the SOLAS Chapter XI-2 regulations. In other words, the recommendations were intended to address specific characteristics of a ship or port facility; the Code did not necessarily mean "one size fits all." For the U.S. Coast Guard, at least, compliance with Part A included compliance with the recommendations in Part B.

The ISPS Code entered into force on July 1, 2004, a mere 18 months after its adoption by the international community. The sentiment of the day was that the ISPS Code was not going to be easily implemented, either on land or on ships, because the IMO called for the creation of security infrastructure and resources where, in some cases, especially in the ports, none had existed before. Between the time the ISPS Code was passed by resolution of the IMO, in December 2002, and the time it came into effect, in July 2004, there was concern that the ISPS Code had been forced upon the industry in an unprecedentedly short time and was imperfect.

In reality, however, with the arrival of the entry-into-force date, the near universal compliance with the Code demonstrated that the maritime industry could adopt complex measures within a tight timeframe.[27] Figures on implementation that were regularly made available by IMO to keep the maritime community updated on progress being made indicated that security plans for more than 86 percent of ships and 69 percent of port facilities had been approved by July 1, 2004.[28]

The international community could readily agree on the need to protect the maritime industry from the emerging scourge of transnational terrorist threats, primarily from Islamic extremists, but just how the Code was to be implemented was a subject debated at length in the days leading up to its implementation. A virtual ISPS industry sprang up overnight, with various maritime experts, consulting firms, and "Recognized Security Organizations" (RSOs) willing to assist nations with their ISPS implementation. In reality, such assistance was desperately needed in the many countries that had previously paid lip service to maritime security.

At its core, the ISPS Code is really a political arrangement defined by an international agreement. Previous attempts to solidify security on ships came from guidance issued by the IMO (e.g., MSC/Circ. 443 after the *Achille Lauro* hijacking). However, the ISPS Code differs from these types of guidance in that it is not confined to the shipping industry. It is driven by political impulses that do not respond to the needs of international shipping. Ports are required to control access, screen incoming and outgoing cargo and passengers, and the ships that are end users of the security umbrella that the ports provide. Both the ship owners and the ports face outside pressure based on their particular position within the maritime industry, and these sometimes compete against each other. The ISPS Code has made these arrangements better but not perfect.

At the outset, ports in general had a difficult time implementing the ISPS port requirements, partly because of confusion about its requirements, partly because they lacked the financial resources to improve security infrastructure. The shipping industry, on the other hand, quickly implemented the Code; if it did not, it faced certain shutdown of its ships because they lacked an International Ship

Security Certificate (ISSC), which is required by the security processes contained in the Code. As mentioned previously, the shipping industry had a head start because of the structure put in place after the *Achille Lauro* hijacking. With the all-inclusive provisions of ISPS Code, however, port and ship security were forced to come together at the same time. Ports were always seen as the weaker link in the chain, so, logically, they should have been strengthened first. However, the ports fell behind in their compliance and put extra strain and burdens on the ships, which were pressed to take up the slack in security measures sometimes found at the ports.

Both the ports and the ships were required to complete vulnerability assessments and to create infrastructure where none had existed previously (especially in the ports), but disillusionment soon set in between seafarers and the port with regard to the strict implementation of the ISPS; shipping companies felt that more was demanded of them than of the ports. Ship owners took the position that if security measures worked properly in the ports, then theoretically there would be no unauthorized personnel to threaten their ships in the first place. The ships and ship owners correctly reasoned that, in the final analysis, there is very little they can do to protect a ship against organized criminals or terrorists who breach port defenses.[29]

In the rush to redress the ports' shortcomings in implementing the ISPS Code, the ports sometimes took an extreme position, creating an "us versus them" mentality, as mentioned earlier. On paper, the ISPS Code is the same for all contracting governments; however, because it is a risk-based security process, one size certainly does not fit all. Ports in particular, some of which lacked resources, were given discretion on how to apply the Code in their particular instances. Ships and their crews were supposed to be viewed as the port's partners. However, some ports, either out of a zealous implementation of the security code or a lack of understanding of the process, made the ships virtual prisons.

Ships generally have a limited amount of time in port. During that time, in addition to loading and unloading the ship's cargo or passengers, seafarers and crew members need to go ashore to take care of personal business, seek medical attention, or make a quick phone call. To accomplish this, seafarers are issued an international identification card.[30] The Seafarer's Identity Document Convention (1958) requires governments to issue an identity document to each of their nationals who are seafarers.

This ID acts like a passport and entitles the seafarer to go on land for shore leave in states (countries) that have ratified the Convention; it may also enable the seafarer to pass through a country without a visa to join his ship or for repatriation purposes.[31] Some ports, however, in the rush to catch up with the ships' perceived lead in implementing the ISPS Code, have taken extreme actions against seafarers that have no bearing or measurable effect on the security of the port. In one example, a British chief officer of a tanker was deported from the United States after going down the gangplank to the pier to take a draft reading for his ship. In another example, a Russian officer whose visa was in order but who had not been checked by port officials spent a night in jail before being deported for going ashore to make a call from a public phone booth on the pier that was located only several feet from his ship.[32]

After the ISPS Code came into effect, a study was undertaken to define the differences in perceptions between the ship and the ports regarding implementation of the ISPS Code. The study attempted to determine whether shore and seagoing staffs had the same view of the implementation process. The results of that study found that ship-based personnel did indeed view security differently from their shore counterparts. The study found, for example, that 35 percent of ship-based personnel cited security training as the biggest hurdle to successfully implementing the ISPS Code, whereas barely 18 percent of those on shore found this to be an issue. Conversely, the highest concern among shore personnel was the need for reviewing the new requirements that applied to them; ship personnel did not rate this as a major concern. One concludes from such statistics that the ISPS Code was instituted on the ships in a more orderly manner and with clearer understandings of its goals and objectives than at in port facilities.[33]

Another study suggested that the Security and Safety Management System (SSMS), implemented two years before the ISPS Code, should have been included in the ISPS Code because the two sets of regulations—both products of the IMO—are treated separately and are not fused into the ship's inspection schedule. This study suggested that security and safety aspects of the ship's operation should be checked and monitored simultaneously, not separately, as is currently done, forcing seafarers to treat safety and security as separate functions on the ship.[34]

The ISPS Code has been designed to enhance maritime security on board ships and in the ports, but it has imposed a lot of extra work on already overburdened crews and ship's masters. Extra security watches are piled on safety and fire watches, among other required shipboard duties. Because of the newfound importance accorded security, there is constant pressure on crews to put security issues above other ship functions such as safety or environmental protection.[35] And the estimated cost of implementing the Code has been enormous, for both ships and port facilities.

It was originally estimated that the cost to the shipping industry to implement the ISPS Code was going to be $1.3 billion dollars for the first year alone. Most of that would pay for security management staff and additional security equipment required on the ships. It was estimated that, in the years following the ISPS Code implementation, the shipping industry would pay more $700 million annually to meet requirements. The costs to the ports were harder if not impossible to calculate because of the uncertainty about what the new measures would require in terms additional security personnel requirements, changes to infrastructure, and new equipment and because of the vast differences in labor rates around the world.[36]

The Organization for Economic Cooperation and Development, known as OECD, which did the initial calculations for the costs to the maritime industry of implementing ISPS, concluded that the cost of not doing anything to increase security would be catastrophic. It reported that a large coordinated maritime attack, what might be the equivalent of a "maritime 9/11," would shut down major portions of a country's maritime transport capability, similar to what happened to the aviation industry after the September 11 attacks but on a much grander scale. Governments would scramble to enact countermeasures and additional security requirements. In some cases, entire ports could be closed while lengthy cargo and facility inspections were conducted in both the originating and the receiving ports. The estimated economic cost of such measures in the United States, for example, was estimated to be $58 billion.[37]

The report also contained some good news. The implementation of the new measures, it suggested, would bring benefits not related to antiterrorism measures and improved security. For the shipping industry, these would come in the form of increased efficiency and faster processing times for cargos. The OECD estimated that, through a new electronic manifest handling system for example, U.S. importers might save $22 billion over the next 20 years. The U.S. government would share equally in that savings.[38]

There is a sense that, now that the ISPS Code is in place, the maritime industry and the world can worry less about the threat of maritime terrorism. Nothing could be further from reality. The ISPS Code is applicable to all vessels over 500 gross tons. The Code is designed to deny unauthorized access to ships and to prevent the introduction of weapons onto ships. The Code, however, does not apply to small boats that might be used as weapons against maritime targets. Michael Chertoff, when he was Secretary of Homeland Security, said, in September 2007, three years after the ISPS Code came into force, "We are concerned about four potential security threats with regard to the more than 17 million small boats, ranging from commercial enterprises to passenger ferries to personal watercraft. First, we're concerned about their use to smuggle weapons, including a weapon of mass destruction, into our country. Second, about their use as a water-borne improvised explosive device, a use which was actually deployed in 2000 through al-Qaeda's attack on the USS *Cole*. Third, we want to prevent the use of a small vessel to smuggle dangerous people into our country. And finally, we're concerned about these boats being used as launching pads for an attack on the maritime industry or on critical infrastructure."[39] The ISPS Code does not apply to any of these instances.

Most alarming is that the most recent attacks and plots against ships, including cruise ships, have come from suicide boats laden with explosives or from small boats filled with pirates armed with rockets and machine guns. The ISPS Code does little, if anything, to stop an attack like that on the *MV Limburg*, the French-owned oil tanker that was hit by a suicide boat in the Gulf of Aden. The portions of the ISPS Code that apply to port security certainly did not help the *Limburg* as it sailed from the terminal at Ash Shihr, in Yemen.[40]

Similarly, the ISPS Code did nothing to protect the *Seabourn Spirit* from an attack by pirates in the Red Sea in 2005 or to prevent attacks on other cruise ships off the coast of Somalia; it has done little to prevent piracy in general. Likewise, terrorists have tried attacking ships using standoff weapons like mortar rockets fired from shore positions outside the immediate port area. The attack in August 2005 on the USS *Kearsarge* and the USS *Ashland* in the port of Aqaba, Jordan, is an example.[41] Fortunately, no one was hurt in this attack, and the rockets missed their targets; however, the port provisions of the ISPS Code did not prevent this attack because its provisions do not extend beyond the port.

Other than requiring a ship security officer, the ISPS Code also does not address shipboard security issues like crime investigations and how to structure a seagoing security program. It has been suggested both privately and in public that the maritime industry, and cruise lines in particular, need to enact an "ISPS equivalent" for shipboard security. While the ISPS Code has made seagoing travel safer in terms of external threats, in the same way that the equivalent aviation security measures ushered into after 9/11 have made air transport safer, the Code has made victims of the ports and ships that dutifully rushed to implement the new measures. While ships and ports understood the need for the new measures, they have not always understood their logic. Cruise ship passengers should feel more at ease knowing that the ISPS Code now requires that their baggage be screened and that their personal effects be searched and x-rayed before being allowed on the ship. But, as with the aviation security measures that try to prevent terrorists from slipping through the screening process, the real victims have become the passengers themselves who have been held hostage through more stringent screening measures.

In reality, as with the aviation security measures ushered in after September 11, the ISPS Code has only kept the terrorists one step behind as they try to circumvent the new maritime security measures aimed at preventing the introduction of weapons or other contraband onto ships. Thus far, cruise ships' screening requirements do not require that passengers take off shoes or not bring liquids with them when boarding the ship, as is required of airline passengers in the United States. The ISPS Code certainly helps to prevent attacks on maritime targets in port by pirates or terrorists. Out on the high seas, however, the ships face greater danger. It is essential that the maritime industry be much more innovative in protecting its ships, cargos, and passengers even as it embraces the ISPS Code. It is, after all, a risk-based arrangement. When the need arises, the IMO has shown itself able to revise and update its regulatory conventions. The ISPS in its present form will surely go through revisions and be reshaped to meet tomorrow's threats. From the historical record, however, it is clear that this normally occurs only after a maritime disaster or major terrorist incident. In that sense, the ISPS Code has for the moment bought us a little time.

PROTECTIVE OVERSIGHT OF THE MARITIME DOMAIN

The United States, since September 11, 2001, has been engaged in a "war" against global terrorism. The Obama administration, since taking office, has ordered a name change; now we are engaged in an "overseas contingency operation." Call it what you will, this was not a struggle that the United States sought voluntarily. The terrorists who planned these attacks had to assume that the United States and the rest of the world would respond to their provocations. The attacks on the World Trade Center, in New York, and the Pentagon, in Virginia, and the failed attempt to destroy the Capitol were carried out by exploiting weaknesses in the transportation system that have lingered for years. Varying standards in passenger screening left the air carriers vulnerable.

Swift regulatory action followed the 9/11 attack with the passage of the Air Transportation Security Act in November 2001. To carry out those policies, the federal government went through the largest reorganization since the end of World War II, including the creation of the Department of Homeland Security. The cornerstone of the U.S. plan to protect itself from further attacks on its homeland has been to push the fight as far away from the U.S. borders as possible. And nothing is more crucial in protecting the nation's security than its maritime borders, and nothing, it appears, is more vulnerable to exploitation.

The National Plan to Achieve Maritime Domain Awareness released in October 2005, lays the foundation for an effective understanding of anything associated with the Maritime Domain that could impact the security, safety, economy, or environment of the United States and identifying threats as early and as distant from our shores as possible. According to the plan, the maritime domain comprises all areas and things of, on, under, relating to, adjacent to, or bordering on a sea, ocean, or other navigable waterway, including all maritime-related activities, infrastructure, people, cargo, and vessels and other conveyances.[42] The founding fathers sought to protect this environment by providing for a national defense and the creation of the U.S. Navy. The Navy's initial mission was to protect the new nation's economy by defending the coast and detecting smuggling. More than 200 years later, the economic health of the United States was threatened by the attacks on New York and Washington, D.C.

With ships carrying more than 80 percent of the world's trade, the importance of that mission is as important today as it was in 1789, and the urgency of protecting maritime interests from acts of piracy, terrorism, and smuggling cannot be overstated. This is what "maritime domain awareness" seeks to achieve: the effective understanding of anything associated with the maritime environment that could impact the security, safety, economy, or environment of the United States. While there is conjecture about how much economic damage would be caused by even a brief closure of a U.S. seaport, there is agreement that the closure of any major U.S. port would have a rapidly expanding impact on the U.S. and the world economies, since almost a third of all maritime trade flows into and out of the United States.[43]

Terrorist organizations understand that the maritime domain can be exploited for financial gain, for the movement of equipment and personnel, and for the launching of further attacks. The maritime domain presents a broad spectrum of potential targets that fit the terrorist's operational objectives of achieving mass casualties and inflicting economic harm. This list includes cruise ships, which offer the potential for terrorists to achieve at least their first objective—to inflict casualties and create fear. Ships can be used as weapons and can help terrorists achieve economic disruption by acting as platforms from which to launch attacks on supply chain hubs and population centers. While the greatest threat—the introduction of a nuclear weapon into a U.S. port—might come from within the global supply chain, so too might other threats to the maritime domain, including the smuggling of chemical, biological, radiological, or high-explosive weapons or weapon components or narcotics, currency, stowaways, or other prohibited commodities.[44]

The maritime domain is threatened by a variety of players: terrorists, drug smugglers, as well as illegal immigrants and human traffickers, to name a few. Each source has demonstrated its capability to exploit the maritime domain by committing illegal activities or acts of aggression or by providing sanctuary for criminal or terrorist groups. While the risk of open confrontation on the high seas has been negated with the end of the cold war, nation-states that harbor terrorists and criminals still threaten the world order. Of greatest concern to the maritime environment are those nation-states that are engaged in the unregulated development of weapons of mass destruction (WMD) and in supporting their proliferation to rogue nation-states or terrorist groups. The United States is particularly concerned about this threat, as it believes that the maritime domain would likely be the method of delivery of a WMD into the United States.

Rogue governments may also provide sanctuary for criminals such as pirates and smugglers who exploit the ocean environment. This is certainly proving true in the war torn country of Somalia where pirates find refuge and sanctuary. Because the maritime domain is so vast, there are great opportunities for terrorist organizations to exploit the obvious inability of maritime states to monitor the entire ocean environment. Indeed, the area of pirate activity off the coast of Somalia is a swath of ocean three times the size of Texas. Also of significant concern are the threats from small boats and ships that are not reached by international regulation and the possibility that terrorists might use small commercial or recreational vessels to transport and deliver WMD. Terrorists have demonstrated their capability to use small boats as suicide weapons and have used the oceans as a means of transporting weapons, agents, and resources for carrying out their attacks.[45] It is obvious from these vulnerabilities that the maritime domain, above all else, has the potential to be exploited easily, threatening the security of the world order.

To counter these risks and to ensure that they respond immediately to any threat, all participants must remain aware of the maritime domain. Participants in this effort include foreign governments that pledge their cooperation, the U.S. government, and the private sector. The private sector, which is the principal owner of the maritime transportation system, has the greatest role to play. The private sector must partner with the federal government to share information on threats to the maritime domain. The 21st century presents complex problems of securing the maritime borders of the United States that go beyond just the traditional surveillance of ports, waterways, and oceans.

Some of the relevant issues include the ability of these players to collect, fuse, analyze, display, and disseminate security information and intelligence gathered by operational commanders. Intelligence, more than anything else, allows the private sector to effectively assess and manage risks and threats. This requires methods for efficient communication so that threat information can be rapidly transmitted from intelligence agencies to the private sector in synthesized form. From this intelligence come contingency plans that can be implemented.

This coordinated activity supports the overall goal of protecting the United States from maritime threats by employing an active, layered security defense that combines the resources of both the government and the maritime industry. This strategy allows for a dispersal of defenses far from the borders of the United States and does not emphasize any one element of protection. The logical reason for such a dispersal is that it forces terrorists and criminals to penetrate multiple security layers before they can attack or reach their target.[46] One of the biggest difficulties for the United States or any maritime nation in that effort is the need to accurately track threats as they move through the maritime domain.

Commercial air traffic is tracked across the nation with fair certainty. The Federal Aviation Administration (FAA) controls the movements of aircraft in and around commercial airports. Aviation threats, however, are watched by another agency of the Department of Homeland Security, from which Customs and Border Protection runs the Air and Marine Operations Center (AMOC), located in southern California. AMOC tracks general and commercial aviation over the United States through a variety of sensors and radar placed strategically along the northern and southern borders. It has a sister operation in the Caribbean region, called CAMOC, that almost exclusively watches the Caribbean borders.

AMOC's and CAMOC's primary missions are to interdict suspected air or maritime threats as they cross into U.S. airspace or waterways and to provide a law enforcement response to them. The North American Aerospace Defense Command, commonly called NORAD, is AMOC's equivalent in the Department of Defense; it tracks hostile air threats and provides a military response. While AMOC has some maritime surveillance capabilities, it lacks adequate situational awareness of activities in U.S. coastal waters, waterways, and along tens of thousands of miles of coastline. In addition, the United States does not have a maritime equivalent of NORAD's defensive military capability. Terrorists could exploit this lack of situational awareness to mount a variety of attacks. Terrorists could also employ tactics used by drug smugglers who use noncommercial vessels such as small, fast, private boats with concealed compartments capable of transporting illegal contraband or WMD.

Although the U.S. Coast Guard recognized the critical importance of maritime domain awareness even before the 9/11 attacks, very little progress has been made on increasing situational awareness. The Vessel Traffic Service (VTS) has existed since 1972 and was designed to improve the navigational safety of commercial maritime traffic. There are 10 VTS areas scattered throughout the United States, and these provide limited coverage of the maritime domain. In 1996, Congress required the Coast Guard to improve the VTS, which resulted in the development of the Ports and Waterways Safety System (PAWSS).[47] However, progress has been slow on implementing the system nationwide and may have even contributed to the large *Cosco Busan* oil spill in San Francisco Bay. One of the issues raised by the U.S. Coast Guard's report on the *Cosco Busan* oil spill was that the San Francisco Vessel Traffic System (VTS) operations center does not have the most up-to-date traffic technology. The system used by the San Francisco VTS operations center is the Coast Guard Vessel Traffic System, which was installed in the 1990s. A newer and more advanced vessel traffic management system, the Ports and Waterways Safety System (PAWSS), was only partially installed at the San Francisco VTS operations center due to funding constraints that existed in 2003 and 2004. With PAWSS capability, the VTS watch-standers could have improved their situational awareness of vessel proximity and orientation to the individual bridge columns, which could have helped prevent incidents like the *Cosco Busan* spill from occurring. The Coast Guard was to use base operating funds in fiscal year 2008 to support this upgrade to PAWSS and that deployment of this upgrade was to be completed by March 2009. The Coast Guard was directed to notify the Committees on Appropriations when the San Francisco VTS upgrade is completed.[48]

The Maritime Transportation Safety Act (MTSA) requires large commercial ships and vessels on international voyages to have automatic identification system (AIS) tracking devices that will be monitored by PAWSS. PAWSS-VTS is supposed to automatically collect, process, and disseminate information about the movement and location of ships in ports and on waterways, using a network of radars and onboard ship transponders. However, because PAWSS-VTS is not a national system, it is not designed to provide a complete picture of vessel traffic in the maritime domain the way aviation is tracked over the United States. The system cannot even project the maritime traffic picture in adjacent Canadian and Latin American waters. Instead, it is designed to monitor traffic in and around fewer than half of the 25 busiest U.S. ports.[49]

PAWSS-VTS is also limited in that it is not a border defense surveillance system in the way that AMOC or NORAD's surveillance systems are. It was originally designed for maritime safety and environmental protection missions but was pressed into service to support homeland security responsibilities because of the lack of anything similar in the maritime domain. In this regard, PAWSS-VTS is inadequate to meet emerging security threats; for example, it cannot provide early warning about threats from small boats, even though this is precisely the type of craft that threatens shipping. Further, PAWSS-VTS, because of its limited reach, cannot provide coverage between ports.

The solutions to these issues are both political and costly. The United States can direct additional investments in land-based equipment and other infrastructure required to expand PAWSS-VTS and can require additional marine craft to carry AIS tracking equipment.[50] Movement on the long overdue Automated Identification Systems (AIS) regulations extending AIS carriage requirements to all U.S. navigable water has been bogged down in Washington bureaucracy. The proposed USCG AIS regulations would impact as many as 17,000 vessels including all vessels over 65 feet in length, towing vessels, high-speed vessels carrying more than 12 passengers, dredges, and certain vehicles moving dangerous cargos. The proposed implementation date for those vessels covered by this rulemaking but not currently required to have AIS would be no later than seven months after publication of the final rule, which the Coast Guard hopes will be sometime in 2010.[51] Another remedy might be to rely on the surface and aviation assets of the U.S. armed forces, including the Coast Guard and the Navy, to cover the large remaining gaps. Aside from diverting Department of Defense assets from their traditional seakeeping duties, these options do not appear particularly cost-effective; nor are they flexible enough to address the challenge of providing awareness of threats between ports. And, while the Navy is engaged in supporting the war in Iraq and other missions around the world, it may take a provocative threat to the United States homeland before the government redeploys those assets.

To adequately protect the maritime domain, then, intelligence gathering and information sharing will be of critical importance. Information sharing must be efficiently organized to bring intelligence into focus for those who need to act upon it. The cruise line industry maintains close relationships with the intelligence-gathering agencies of the federal government, primarily through the Cruise Lines International Association (CLIA). CLIA, formed in 1975, is the world's largest cruise association and is dedicated to the promotion and growth of the cruise industry. Its membership is composed of 24 major cruise lines that serve North America. The organization operates pursuant to an agreement filed with the Federal Maritime Commission under the Shipping Act of 1984 and serves as a nongovernmental consultative organization to the International Maritime Organization, an agency of the United Nations. CLIA merged with the International Council of Cruise Lines (ICCL) in 2006 to promote regulatory and policy development in the cruise industry. Prior to its merger with CLIA, the security committee of the ICCL was the primary liaison with the U.S. government security agencies; however, that function now rests with CLIA.[52]

The security committee of CLIA meets bimonthly with U.S. government intelligence agencies, providing a viable avenue for access to federal agencies engaged in maritime security. Representatives from the U.S. Coast Guard, the Department of Transportation, Customs and Border Protection, Office of Naval Intelligence, the Department of Homeland Security, and the FBI, among others, are invited to this forum and have the opportunity to brief cruise line security officials on emerging threats in the maritime domain, both domestic and international. Because small, independent cruise lines are not represented, the effect of this information sharing between the cruise lines and the CLIA Security Council is modest at best. In addition, some federal agencies are chronic absentees, although others, especially the U.S. Coast Guard and Naval Intelligence, are very active participants.

Another problem at these meetings is the national security implications of disseminating intelligence information gathered by the U.S. intelligence agencies to civilians. Although all cruise line security directors are required to have national security clearances adjudicated by DHS, very little of the information imparted at these meetings is at the classified level. The reason for this is simple. The cruise line security representatives who hold these security clearances must be able to discuss threat information obtained from these meetings with cruise line management executives back in their corporate offices. Most, if not all, of these executives are not required to hold security clearances. Security information divulged at these meetings is usually very dated and in some cases may be more than two months old by the time it is briefed to the CLIA Security Council. Cruise line security officials are also not connected to any classified government network system, where the intelligence picture is updated sometimes by the minute. Any classified intelligence must flow through the designated U.S. agency representatives at these meetings.

Normally, threat information is disseminated after the fact rather than representing a serious warning about impending maritime threats. If it is urgent, threat information can be passed by the various intelligence agencies through CLIA and on to the cruise lines, normally through an encrypted phone line. But this method also is rarely used and requires that the briefing take place in the corporate office where the encrypted line is kept. If the cruise line security representative with the clearance is out of the office, is traveling, or is out of the country, the information may have to wait until the representative's return. For this reason, most intelligence information presented at the CLIA security committee meeting is unclassified.

Most of the discussions among the federal agency representatives gathered at the bimonthly CLIA meetings are procedural in nature. Because of the constantly changing security requirements levied on the cruise lines by legislation such as the ISPS Code and MTSA, there is constant debate between the cruise lines and the federal agencies required to enforce them. This takes up precious time that might be spent discussing threats and does not help to increase maritime domain awareness in any great measure. So the cruise lines look for other sources to obtain timely threat information.

One outstanding avenue for obtaining security information that is available to the cruise lines is the U.S. State Department's Overseas Security Advisory Council, or OSAC. OSAC is more effective than the bimonthly CLIA briefings because it does not get bogged down in procedural or regulatory discussions. Rather, it focuses on the direct sharing of threat information at the unclassified level. Information is purposely created in an unclassified format because OSAC serves the overseas U.S. business community. The cruise lines are only one of hundreds of industries that rely on OSAC, and participation is voluntary. Some lines make greater use of its services than others. However, because it serves U.S. business interests overseas, OSAC does not focus exclusively on the maritime environment or on the cruise lines. Also, OSAC is a branch of the U.S. State Department's Bureau of Diplomatic Security, so information involving domestic threats is covered not by OSAC but by the various agencies of the Department of Homeland Security that meet with CLIA.

With the limited exception of CLIA's bimonthly security meetings, the cruise industry is hardly an active participant in creating national strategy for maritime security. Unless it can find more robust avenues for information sharing, it will lag behind the power curve in finding opportunities to increase maritime domain awareness. It seems logical that CLIA would have a vested interest in creating such opportunities, but so far it has not demonstrated this, perhaps because it does not perceive the emerging threats to maritime security as being as significant as other forms of maritime commerce and industries believe them to be.[53]

By agreement, the U.S. Coast Guard (USCG) is the executive agent for vessel and port security. Customs and Border Protection (CBP) is the lead for international cargo security, and the Transportation Security Administration is the principal agent for domestic intermodal security. Because cruise lines are not engaged in the transportation of commodities across the world's oceans, they are not required to participate in ongoing maritime security initiatives such as the Customs Trade Partnership against Terrorism (C-TPAT). C-TPAT is U.S. Customs and Border Protection's ambitions partnership with commercial maritime shipping companies and port facilities. The goal of C-TPAT is to ally the private sector and government to improve the overall global supply chain. Security regulation is mixed with best practices to protect the supply chain against exploitation by terrorists. In exchange for improving the supply chain by taking on direct responsibility for its security, companies are qualified to receive expedited clearance of their cargos.[54] The Container Security Initiative (CSI) is also administered by Customs and Border Protection and attempts to accurately account for cargo shipments bound for the United States by inspecting them at their point of origin overseas.

All maritime infrastructures, including cruise lines, benefit from the voluntary initiatives stipulated in C-TPAT partnerships. For example, the new C-TPAT Importer Security Criteria have standards for fencing, facility lighting, employee background checks, and credential checking for port facilities. This strengthens the security posture in any of the ports where cruise lines share berths. Security, however, is not free. C-TPAT participants incur costs when the organization invests in measures to bolster its security protocols in the shipping industry. Cruise lines piggyback on these security measures but contribute nothing to their implementation. In silence, they welcome the added security to protect the maritime domain but risk relatively little.

Maritime shipping companies, however, risk losing their competitive edge in the marketplace. Stephen E. Flynn, Commander, U.S. Coast Guard (retired), in testimony before a hearing of the U.S. Senate, Permanent Subcommittee on Investigations, Committee on Homeland Security and Governmental Affairs, said that "companies that are sincerely committed to improving their security, have to worry about the likelihood that it has competitors who end up being free riders. In other words, they have to be mindful of potentially putting themselves at a competitive disadvantage by investing in security while others are doing little to nothing but receiving the same benefits."[55] Clearly, it is the maritime shipping companies that bear the brunt of the maritime defense-in-depth strategy. While the current incarnations of C-TPAT and the CSI programs are not without their flaws, increased physical security in and around port facilities is certainly one of their benefits.

There are a number of other maritime security initiatives under way to protect the integrity of supply routes into the United States. Like the cruise lines, all international shippers engaged in maritime transport must also be compliant with the specifications of the ISPS Code and MTSA. Whereas the shipping industry must comply with the ISPS Code and MTSA and can volunteer to participate in C-TPAT and CSI to better position their businesses by cooperating with the U.S. government, there are no national maritime security initiatives that target the cruise industry. Some have suggested that the Sea Marshall program administered by the U.S. Coast Guard is an attempt to partner the cruise lines with the federal government. But the Sea Marshalls represent less a partnership than they do a required preventive measure. Further, the Sea Marshall program does not exclusively target cruise ships. Rather, its emphasis is on high-interest vessels—vessels moving in and out of U.S. ports that are susceptible to being used for transporting WMD or other contraband.

Another program that the cruise lines have voluntarily participated in is the Sea Carrier Initiative. The Sea Carrier Initiative Agreement is a scheme under which carriers and owners of ships calling at U.S. ports agree to apply various security measures to prevent drug smuggling. In the event illegal drugs are found on ships that participate in the program, penalties that would normally be applied as fines may be reduced or mitigated. This agreement is now known as the Carrier Initiative Program (CIP). Customs and Border Protection (CBP) provides antidrug smuggling training to air, sea, and land commercial transport companies. This training is part of the CBP Carrier Initiative and Super Carrier Initiative Programs, under which CBP and the carrier companies cooperate to prevent commercial conveyances from being utilized to smuggle narcotics.

Carrier Initiative training is directed at employees. Those carriers with routes that are at high risk for infiltration by drug smugglers voluntarily sign agreements with CBP to exercise the highest degree of care and diligence in securing their fa-cilities and conveyances against the threat of drug smugglers, while CBP agrees to conduct site surveys and provide appropriate training and recommendations for improving security.[56] The degree of a carrier's compliance with the agreement may become a mitigating factor in the assessment of a penalty if narcotics are found on board a conveyance.

Cruise lines play an important role in the effort to stop drug smuggling. While the war on drugs is an important aspect of national security, CIP does little to protect the security of the cruise ships themselves, but it is in the ships' best interest to cooperate, because it helps them avoid severe monetary penalties if they are found to be carrying drugs. That much they understand. In light of the human cargo that cruise ships carry, it seems obvious that a greater partner-ship between the federal government and the cruise industry aimed at promot-ing the safety of passengers engaged in domestic and international sea travel is warranted.

While the cruise lines are not required to participate in any maritime secu-rity initiatives, they are dependent on the success of these programs. The cruise lines, however, have a different focus from the shipping companies with regard to maritime domain awareness. Unlike the maritime shipping industry, which depends on and is engaged in the protection of the maritime domain as a way to promote a robust economy, cruise lines are, in a sense, relying on the continued safety of the oceans and ports provided by others to grow their industry. In the final analysis, the cruise lines have yet to be asked to contribute more to the pro-tection of the maritime domain and have so far benefited from this convenient relationship. If trouble strikes, though, the cruise lines in all likelihood will owe their economic outcome and safety not to any governmental regulatory partner-ship but to the professionalism and response of the governmental protectors of the maritime domain. What has the cruise industry worried is the ongoing dis-pute over just who that might be.

GUARDIANS OF THE MARITIME DOMAIN

Many people in federal, state, and local law enforcement perceive the FBI as hav-ing the best resources and the most experienced personnel to respond to any ter-rorist threat or criminal act, domestic or overseas. The FBI's reputation as the premier U.S. law enforcement agency is well earned, to be sure, but, at times, the agency has sometimes taken for granted that other federal agencies with which it must work by federal statute have a similar wealth of expertise and unique re-sources. With regard to maritime security, the FBI has had to work with the U.S. Coast Guard in protecting the nation's seaports and maritime domain, and that relationship has not always been smooth sailing. The FBI's record on maritime terrorism thus far has been modest, according to an assessment by the Department of Justice Office of the Inspector General.[57] Its shortcomings dramatically impact the cruise ship industry, which depends on the FBI and other agencies to protect it and the U.S. ports that its ships sail in and out of.

The FBI and the Coast Guard have been partners in protecting the U.S. maritime domain since 1979, when a Memorandum of Agreement signed by the two agencies acknowledged their overlapping roles and the need for cooperation. According to the Memorandum, the FBI was to maintain special weapons and tactic (SWAT) teams and trained hostage negotiators. The Coast Guard was to provide its own resources, such as boats, aircraft, and shore stations staffed with personnel trained to react in a law enforcement capability. This was supposed to eliminate response delays during a terrorist incident and encourage both agencies to work together in preparing contingency plans.[58] Their relationships remained fundamentally unchanged until the events of September 11, 2001, which resulted in the passage of the Maritime Transportation Security Act (MTSA) in 2002. Through this new legislation, the Coast Guard saw its mission in preventing maritime terrorism increase tenfold. The MTSA required the Coast Guard to conduct detailed vulnerability assessments of port facilities and vessels that may be involved in a transportation security incident. The results were to be used to develop a National Maritime Transportation Security Plan for deterring and responding to incidents related to transportation security in U.S. ports.

The MTSA also directed the Coast Guard to create maritime safety and security teams (MSSTs) capable of rapidly responding to maritime terrorism threats in U.S. waters and ports. MSSTs are required to assist with vulnerability assessments of facilities by the maritime stakeholders and to have the ability to conduct high-speed intercepts and to board, search, and seize any harmful article on any vessel or in any port. The MSSTs were required to coordinate their activities with other responding agencies, including the FBI.[59]

In September 2005, the National Strategy for Maritime Security was formulated by an interagency committee in an attempt to more closely align the various federal maritime security missions, including those of the FBI, the Coast Guard, and Customs and Border Protection and the resources of state, local, and private entities. The National Strategy for Maritime Security was supplemented by eight additional plans, including the Maritime Operational Threat Response (MOTR), issued in October 2005. The MOTR describes how the United States intends to respond to terrorist threats in the maritime domain and the roles of the various federal agencies. The MOTR essentially gives the U.S. Coast Guard the responsibility for interdicting maritime threats, while the FBI has responsibility for investigating maritime threats and incidents.

Adding to the confusion over the roles of all these agencies, the Department of Justice's Office of the Inspector General (OIG) report concluded that the MOTR did not resolve potential conflicts between the two agencies in incident command and response. To resolve these conflicts, the OIG examined the FBI's overall maritime threat response by focusing on (1) its initiatives to prevent maritime terrorism, including coordination with the Coast Guard and other agencies; (2) its capability to respond to maritime incidents; and (3) its efforts to assess the maritime terrorism threat.[60] While acknowledging that some progress had been made in all these areas, the OIG's report concluded that serious deficiencies still remain.

Throughout U.S. history, protecting the country from the effects of a national catastrophe or terrorist incident has become a top priority of the U.S. government. Part of that response includes the Federal Bureau of Investigation, which has always assumed the lead role in the investigation of terrorist acts committed against Americans at home and overseas. The U.S. Coast Guard is charged with protecting the nation's waterways and ports. Various other agencies of the Department of Homeland Security, such as Customs and Border Protection, have a significant role in maritime security, helping to keep weapons of mass destruction from entering the United States in containerized cargo. The Federal Emergency Management Agency (FEMA) has the lead role in the emergency response to a national catastrophe. To assess the effectiveness of these agencies, specially designed and coordinated exercises are used to test their capability before they are needed for actual mobilization. Unfortunately, events during the first part of this decade have tested actual U.S. responses to terrorist attacks and to a natural disaster (e.g., Hurricane Katrina). These events have revealed that the federal agencies responsible for our protection are not fully prepared to protect critical infrastructure and to respond with appropriate coordination, resources, and direction.

The events of the attack on the U.S. homeland on September 11 revealed serious gaps in emergency responses in crucial areas such as communications between first responders and coordination of their rescue efforts by federal agencies such as FEMA. FEMA received criticism, before, during, and after Hurricane Katrina, which devastated New Orleans in 2005. The agency's lack of coordination with the Coast Guard and other agencies involved in the rescue efforts demonstrated that key agencies of the Department of Homeland Security lacked adequate resources and that command and control of the rescue effort occurred on an ad hoc basis, with no one command element in place to direct efforts.[61] Any response to terrorist threats or incidents in the maritime domain—at least in territorial waters of the United States—will present similar problems of coordination between the Coast Guard and the FBI and its SWAT team, its Hostage Rescue Team (HRT), and its Hazardous Devices Response Unit (HDRU).

As yet, U.S. ability to react to a maritime terrorist event has not been tested on a scale equal to that of 9/11. Because both the Coast Guard and the FBI have roles to play in responding to a maritime terrorist incident, the question then becomes: what federal agency gets the call to put boots on the deck after a terrorist attack on a seaport, maritime facility, or cruise ship? Both agencies agree that possible terrorist attacks may include the ramming of cruise ships by a boat laden with explosives, a bombing, or a hostage taking and that in general cruise ships present a very attractive targets for terrorists. Both agencies see themselves playing a significant role but differ in their approach to providing a response based on the unique resources of each.

Officials at the FBI and the Coast Guard agree that the Maritime Transportation Security Act of 2002 may have created some overlapping responsibilities between the two agencies and that they have yet to resolve some fundamental questions of the roles each would play in a response to a maritime terrorist attack. This view was validated in a report issued by the U.S. Department of Justice's Office of the Inspector General, released in April 2006, that was critical of both agencies' ability to coordinate an effective response.

The report focused on the structure of each agency's role in maritime terrorist responses and detailed the disagreements between the two agencies during a massive maritime exercise called TOPOFF. This exercise was designed to test the counterterrorist resources of the varied law enforcement agencies that would be involved after a maritime incident, including the FBI and the Coast Guard. Much of the exercise was conducted in and around New London, Connecticut, and simulated the response effort that would follow a chemical weapon explosion near the New London waterfront. Another portion of the exercise called for the FBI and the Coast Guard to respond to a mock hijacking of a 200-foot ferry in Long Island Sound.[62] This was supposedly to test the operational capabilities of the FBI's Hostage Rescue Team, which professes to have the knowledge and equipment necessary to regain control of a ship.

The Coast Guard is the only branch of the military under control of the Department of Homeland Security that has civilian law enforcement duties. The FBI's hostage response teams and the Coast Guard's Maritime Safety and Security Teams (MSSTs), created pursuant to the Maritime Transportation Security Act, enacted after 9/11, were present at the mock terrorist response exercise. The FBI's teams automatically assumed the lead role in the response; according to the FBI, the Coast Guard could not take part in the boarding of the seized ship because the Coast Guard's ability to handle an event in which its boarding teams face an armed enemy is "very limited." The FBI also said that the Coast Guard does not train its people to board moving vessels.[63] Apparently, the FBI has never seen U.S. Sea Marshalls board a freighter or a cruise ship making 8–10 knots through a channel.

A Coast Guard Homeland Security boat establishes a security zone around the passenger vessel *StarShip* while a Coast Guard helicopter hovers overhead with a joint FBI–Coast Guard boarding team aboard. The passenger ship was simulating a vessel carrying hazardous cargo and attempting to enter port with a suspected terrorist aboard during a maritime security exercise called Bay Sentinel 2006. Bay Sentinel was a multi-agency exercise aimed at testing the area's maritime security plan. Cooperation between the FBI and the USCG in such exercises has often been strained over questions of which agency would take the lead role. (Coast Guard photo by PA1 Donnie Brzuska)

The DOJ's inspector general's report concluded that, "in our [Department of Justice's] judgment, unless such differences over roles and authorities are re-solved, the response to a maritime incident could be confused and potentially disastrous."[64] The implication of such a finding by the U.S. government is disturb-ing. The inspector general's report noted that the rivalry between the FBI and the Coast Guard teams was very intense during the training. The inspector general went as far to say that "the FBI repeatedly blocked the Coast Guard's response ef-forts, insisting that they [the FBI] were the lead federal agency." The report noted that, in response, the Coast Guard "changed the scenario to circumvent the FBI's lead federal agency role."[65] Both agencies went on record saying that they were committed to resolving the disagreement; however, an unnamed source at the De-partment of Homeland Security suggested that the DOJ's report had sharpened the debate on maritime security responses and indicated that the report "was writ-ten to bolster the FBI argument that they should remain in charge."[66]

The FBI has an overwhelming responsibility to protect the United States. But it should be remembered that, unlike state and local police or even the U.S. Coast

Guard, which are on the front lines of fighting crime and preventing terrorist attacks, the FBI is an investigative agency with vast jurisdictional authority. Because it has jurisdiction over investigations into all acts and suspected acts of terrorism, the FBI, even with its huge resources, must stretch its manpower to respond to what it perceives to the most serious threats to the security of the United States.

Exercises play an important role in deciding where those resources are used. Maritime exercises are immense undertakings; they require officials not only to devise realistic scenarios that test the command and control elements of all the players but also that all the players be gathered for preplanning lead-ups to the exercise itself. Exercises that are realistic test the responses of key personnel, tactics, weapons, and the communications deployed at the location of the terrorist incident. The maritime communities, including the cruise lines, are invited to participate in these exercises and benefit when they help improve response planning. It is reassuring to know that the FBI and the Coast Guard are both equally concerned about the possibility of maritime attacks and that they are planning to respond to them. These exercises are a great learning tool and bring together the necessary feedback for contingency planning. The cruise line's confidence that it will gain anything useful by participating in these exercises is reduced when the agencies responsible for their protection cannot agree on fundamental questions about chain of command.

Both the appropriate federal agencies and the maritime stakeholders allocate significant assets to events such as these practice exercises. Sometimes, meaningful exercises can be accomplished without the participation of the actual targets involved. But this also limits their effectiveness. Such was the case in the TOPOFF exercise, where a passenger ferry was used to portray a vessel carrying large numbers of passengers, like a cruise ship. The cruise industry is reluctant to offer its ships for exercises, primarily because doing so pulls them out of revenue status. In addition, the industry does not want to be seen participating in such exercises because to do so might send the message to the public that cruise ships, along with passenger ferries and container ships, are potential targets of terrorist attacks.

Assuming that it is true that cruise ships represent potential targets, using a passenger ferry as a proxy for a cruise ship does not make sense when one is planning a response aimed at saving passenger lives. Conducting counterterrorism training on passenger ferries when the real target is a cruise ship may appear to be plausible because they both carry large numbers of passengers, but anything more fails to simulate the operational challenges of rescuing cruise ships. Cruise ships are vastly different from ferries and are designed to carry people in passenger cabins and confined spaces, not in bulk seating compartments like those found on ferries. Other elements of the cruise ship environment, such as theaters, restaurants, and pools, present difficulties for emergency response teams that are not present in a rescue attempt on a ferry. It would be far better to train for emergency responses on cruise ships rather than passenger ferries if at all possible if the goal is to work out best responses for rescuing cruise ships.

The FBI and the Coast Guard have centered their planning efforts around which agency is better able to board a ferry under hostile conditions rather than whether cruise ships represent a likely targets for a terrorist attack. And this division will make it difficult for the security departments of the cruise lines to effectively plan for ships' safety. The problem for the cruise industry is that it may partner with the wrong federal agency, only to find that the contingency plans it devises are worthless in an emergency. When the lives of the seagoing public are hanging in the balance, federal agencies must make unselfish efforts to resolve their differences or risk courting disaster.

In the worst case, however, what happens when, despite efforts by the guardians of the maritime domain, a vessel is damaged or sunk in a strategic channel or harbor by a terrorist attack or maritime accident? Which U.S. agency if any, is called in to get the maritime traffic flowing again and the ports and harbors back open? And what happens if the calls for help after a disaster like the one that devastated New Orleans fall on deaf ears?

SALVAGE CRISIS: WHEN A CRUISE
SHIP BLOCKS A CHANNEL

Most experts agree that sinking a cruise ship by hostile methods would be extremely difficult. Unlike airliners, where even the smallest explosion inside the cabin could seriously damage the integrity of the airplane and cause, at the very least, deaths or injuries from depressurization, cruise ships are built with double-lined hulls and are compartmentalized, with generally excellent watertight integrity. The Rand Corporation undertook a comprehensive study of maritime security and concluded that terrorists would have to have advanced knowledge of structural engineering and of a ship's weak points and also know how to overcome the controls on access before they could place powerful explosives at the ship's structural weak points and thereby sink it.[67] There are, however, a number of other reasons, including collisions caused by human error, that a cruise ship or other type of vessel might sink, leading to hazards to navigation and perhaps catastrophic loss of life.

The Transportation Research Board of the National Academy in 2003 undertook a study to determine the salvage capabilities of the United States in the event of a terrorist or other marine calamity in a U.S. port. It presented two hypothetical scenarios. One concerned a terrorist-caused collision between a cruise ship and a chemical tanker in Houston, Texas. In the scenario, both vessels were sunk, blocking the Houston ship channel; the chemical tanker, loaded with 17,000 tons of mixed but unknown chemicals, exploded, resulting in a huge conflagration and a spill of unknown hazardous chemicals. The passenger ship, which was carrying 2,100 passengers plus crew, suffered fires and flooding and an unknown number of human casualties. The second scenario concerned an incident in New Orleans in which terrorist activity led to the explosion and sinking of a tanker in the Mississippi River, the disabling of the Algiers locks in the Gulf Intracoastal Waterway (GICW), and the destruction of the State Highway 90 bridge across the Mississippi River. The product tanker was sunk across the river, blocking the channel at the Southwest Pass, and access to the Mississippi River was blocked at New Orleans because of the disabled locks and the destruction of the bridge.[68]

The study was formed to assess national salvage response capabilities, with particular attention to the effects of potential terrorist incidents on operations in U.S. ports and waterways. The study found that such incidents, if they cut off access to major waterways in the United States, would cause untold economic repercussions until the channel(s) could be cleared. It also noted that, while the U.S. marine salvage industry has significant capabilities to respond to seaport terrorist incidents, it is uncertain whether that capability is currently adequate to meet a wide range of specific threats and whether it could be sustained over time to meet future threats.

The U.S. Coast Guard has a different view. "Even if the goal of the terrorists were to sink a vessel in a harbor, or to ground it and block a channel, the threat remains overstated," it says.[69] Officials insist that there are few if any locations in the world where small channel width, channel depth, and absence of capable salvage equipment would result in closure of a major waterway for any length of time should a single vessel be sunk. They add that even trained experts, taking limited or no damage control measures, who sink "mothballed" ships to create artificial reefs with high-tech equipment sometimes take days to sink a vessel that is already in poor condition.[70] Despite this, there is compelling evidence that a cruise ship, tanker, or merchant ship, once sunk and blocking a strategic channel, is likely to remain there at least long enough to disrupt commerce in the United States and across the globe. The Coast Guard's optimistic assessment is based on a single ship blocking the channel. The effects would be catastrophic if multiple ships were sunk simultaneously in a specific region in a style that is the trademark of al-Qaeda.

While the Coast Guard, on the basis of an assessment of national salvage capabilities, believes threat of a blocked channel to be slight, that view is not shared in the salvage industry itself. According to Hans van Rooij, salvage director and president of the International Salvage Union, "A salvage crisis is in the offing as ships continue to grow. The international shipping industry has been accused of turning a blind eye to a looming crisis as the size of container vessels and cruise ships outstrip the technical capacity of salvors to handle them."[71] He warned that neither his fellow salvors nor the ship-owning community appears ready to confront the salvage implications of fast-increasing ship sizes.

Perhaps the idea that the terrorists do not as yet have the technical sophistication to sink a vessel using strategically placed explosives is enough to deny the possibility that it could happen. We should remember, however, that, because of the sophistication and planning required to bring down the Twin Towers in New York by commandeering two commercial aircraft, many on September 10, 2001, assumed that such an act was highly improbable, as well. In reality, the sinking of any vessel can be done with minimal planning and few resources, as demonstrated by the relatively unsophisticated attack on the *Superferry 14* in the Philippines in February 2004. That attack, accomplished with just eight kilograms of TNT, showed how much human life can be lost and how much damage can be caused by even small amounts of explosives. The *Superferry 14* bomber placed the explosives, hidden in a television cardboard box, not for their effect on structural stability, as the bomber allegedly admitted later under interrogation, but for their effect on the passengers— to engender panic, death, and destruction. The ship eventually caught fire, foundered, and partially sank in Manila Bay, with a loss of more than 100 lives.

While maritime experts assume that the level of skill needed by the terrorist to sink vessels such as cruise ship in a specific location would be extremely difficult to achieve, it would be naïve to deny the possibility that terrorists might nonetheless try to do it. Sinking a cruise ship would serve the terrorists' aims of inflicting mass casualties, instilling fear, and inflicting incalculable economic losses, especially if the ship was sunk in a strategic location. The idea that a cruise ship or any vessel, once sunk in a channel, could be raised quickly, thereby minimizing the economic disruption and the impact on shipping, is also overly optimistic. To refute the Coast Guard's optimism, one need only point to what occurred when only one ship was sunk at the entrance to one of the nation's most important waterways.

The Southwest Pass is the only deep-water entrance to the Port of New Orleans and the Mississippi Delta. On February 21, 2004, after colliding with the cargo ship *ZIM Mexico III* in fog, the *MV Lee III*, a small supply ship, sank, closing the Southwest Pass for the first time in 50 years. Three crew members on the *Lee III* were killed in the collision, and the closure of the entrance to the channel stranded more than 100 ships waiting to enter the port or heading for other Gulf of Mexico ports.

The disaster and the four-day closure of the port caused enormous economic losses for the local and national economy, estimated to be upwards of $30 million a day. The collision sparked a debate on admiralty law that prevents vessels that lose commerce because of an accident in which they are not involved from seeking compensation for their lost revenue. The ruling, established in the 1927 Supreme Court ruling *Robins Drydock & Repair v. Flint,* held that vessels not physically damaged in a collision could not recover economic losses.

In other words, the stranded vessels that were unable to engage in maritime commerce because of the collision could not file insurance claims against the insurer of the *Lee III* because they had not been physically damaged by that ship. This included cruise ships, which were estimated to have lost between $1 and $3 million a day. Although Royal Caribbean carries business interruption insurance, for example, it was forced to refund full fares to the 2,018 passengers on board the *Grandeur of the Seas,* which was headed for a Caribbean itinerary when the channel became blocked.[72] During the four days that it took to recover the sunken vessel, the river was closed, and the cruise and container ships, longshoremen, and oil refineries waited impatiently, losing revenue each day.

The situation could have been much worse. The salvage of the *Lee III* was accelerated by the fact that Bisso Marine Company, which recovered the wreck, was headquartered in New Orleans and maintained its large barge-mounted cranes there. Bisso Marine was able to clear the *Lee III* from the channel with the help of two derrick barges, a dive support vessel, and eight divers. The cost of the recovery was not released by the salvage company, but operations of that size typically cost $20,000 a day; the cost was paid by the Port of New Orleans and passed on to the *Lee III* owners. The incident highlighted the need for a national salvage capability and policy. The quick salvage of the *Lee III* was possible only because the salvage company with the resources to do the job was located within the port of New Orleans. It probably would have taken days for the necessary equipment to reach New Orleans from other ports or harbors if Bisso Marine had not possessed the necessary cranes and barges.

The impact of the closure of a strategic waterway was significant, and many observers believe incorrectly that the federal government will come to the rescue in future incidents. Calling on the federal government for help would not clear the channel any quicker because the government would have handed the job over to a commercial salvage company. If a terrorist attack or other event were to sink a vessel in a strategic port or channel, even if the Army Corps of Engineers were called in to clear the wreck, it would most likely contract out the job to a company like Bisso Marine. Most of the larger salvage crews, however, are not waiting around for an incident to occur. Their equipment is leased out via private contracts around the world. Europe, unlike the United States, subsidizes its indigenous salvage industry.[73] Without additional funding, the U.S. salvage industry cannot assume the role of responder to national maritime terrorist attacks.

As devastating as the September 11 attacks were, an attack on the maritime infrastructure of the United States, including the obstruction of a harbor channel

Bisso Marine, a salvage company out of New Orleans, uses salvage cranes to lift the hull of *Lee III* out of the channel in the Southwest Pass of the Mississippi River, near New Orleans, on February 23, 2004. The wreckage of the *Lee III*, which had collided with another ship in fog, killing three people, closed entrances to the port of New Orleans and cost the maritime economy of the Gulf Coast more than $120 million. Salvage capabilities such as these would be hard to come by in U.S. ports in the event of the simultaneous sinking of ships. (USCG photo by PA2 Kyle Niemi)

or the simultaneous blockage of the entrances to several militarily and economically strategic ports, would have dire consequences for the national economy. As was demonstrated on a small scale by the blockage of the Port of New Orleans after the sinking of the *Lee III,* such an event would have an impact that would reach beyond the cruise industry as the affected ports scrambled to find the necessary salvage equipment to clear the blockage. The *Lee III* was salvaged in a relatively short period of time because the needed local resources were available in the Port of New Orleans; this is not always the case. An example is the inadequate response to the stranding of the *MV New Carissa* on the Oregon coast in 1999. In that incident, the ship eventually broke apart and polluted a stretch of the Oregon coast near Coos Bay after it was determined that the only two salvage vessels on the Pacific coast capable of performing the rescue were unavailable.

The threat to maritime commerce is not limited to attacks by terrorists. Random violent hurricanes such as Hurricanes Katrina and Rita in 2005 illustrate the need for a national salvage response strategy. These hurricanes demonstrated that agencies of the Department of Homeland Security such as the Coast Guard and FEMA and the Army Corps of Engineers, part of the Department of Defense, had no prestaged salvage resources. During the recovery efforts that followed these storms, the maritime salvage efforts of the Coast Guard, the Army Corps of Engineers, and the Navy were literally made up on an ad hoc basis, with command elements lacking a consistent command structure.[74]

The reason that the United States lacks the necessary resources for salvage of its maritime resources in times of a national emergency is simple. There have been too few maritime accidents or disasters like Hurricane Katrina to make salvage a worthy marine industry. Training crews and investing capital in ships are losing investments for companies dedicated solely to salvage; there is simply not enough salvage work to justify them. But the lack of maritime salvage work is hardly justification for placing the national economy at risk.

The lack of a coordinated national policy and the paucity of salvage resources have left the U.S. maritime industry at risk of an ever-increasing dependence on foreign-flagged vessels to fill the gaps in a national salvage effort. The recovery of the Egypt Air passenger jet that crashed in 1999 off the coast of Rhode Island (under mysterious circumstances) relied on foreign salvage vessels. The U.S. Navy used foreign-flagged heavy-lift ships to salvage the USS *Cole* in Yemen in 2000. And, in 2001, the recovery of the *Ehime Maru* after it was struck and sunk by a U.S. submarine off the coast of Oahu, Hawaii, used foreign salvage equipment.[75] These examples demonstrate that, should the unthinkable happen, the U.S. economy would suffer unimaginable consequences as maritime commerce was recued; in addition, countless lives would be in jeopardy during the time it took the salvage companies to reach them. The cruise lines, if not directly involved, would be forced to sit and wait like everyone else until the sea lanes were once again opened.

The possibility that a cruise ship might be sunk in a strategic channel by pirates seems remote. Pirates would much rather keep a vessel afloat, for obvious reasons. But when the threats come from suicidal terrorists bent on the destruction of cruise ships and all who sail on them, the risks are significant. As we shall see in the next chapter, those threats to sink cruise ships come not only from other ships on the water but from anything that flies in the air or swims under the sea.

six

CLEAR AND PRESENT DANGERS FOR CRUISE SHIPS AND FUTURE REMEDIES

D espite predictions of worst-case scenarios and isolated incidents of maritime terrorism, maritime attacks are still rare. They constitute only 2 percent of all international terrorist incidents committed over the past three decades.[1] The ocean is a very big place, however, and an examination of current trends and plausible scenarios suggests that there is an alarming potential for attacks directed against commercial shipping and especially cruise ships. As one leading maritime journal notes, "aircraft, trains and buses have already been attacked, so perhaps it is only a matter of time before a passenger ship becomes a target."[2] Although there are many plausible attack scenarios involving cruise ships, the larger question is this: if you are a terrorist, why attack a cruise ship? If your goal is to kill Americans and Westerners, such an attack certainly provides ample opportunity to achieve that goal, but it could also be a double-edged sword.

Most if not all commercial cruise lines are foreign flagged, meaning that they are registered in countries other than the United States. Sometimes referred to as "flags of convenience," foreign flags are sought by ship owners because the countries where the ships are registered provide favorable tax advantages. Bermuda, the Bahamas, Gibraltar, Liberia, and Panama are some of the most common flags of convenience and are some of the flags flown by the ships owned by Carnival Corporation, a U.S. corporation that owns and operates Carnival Cruise Lines, Princess Cruises, and Cunard Lines, among others. While the corporate personnel are almost exclusively American, most of the crew members who work on the ships, including the security staff, are foreign nationals.

Like the terror attack on the British Consulate in Istanbul in November 2003 or the East African bombings of two U.S. embassies in 1998, which killed mostly innocent Muslims, a terror attack on a cruise ship would undoubtedly kill, in addition to Western nationals, a large number of crew members who are nationals of developing countries.[3] While a terrorist attack on a cruise ship would probably be seen as a symbolic attack on the United States or the West, it could do more harm than good especially if it was perceived to have killed innocent Muslims. But, given that such collateral damage has apparently not been a concern for al-Qaeda as it chose targets in Turkey, East Africa, and Iraq, it is shortsighted to believe that the organization would not attack cruise ships because its crew included non-Westerners.

Although they are high on al-Qaeda's target list, cruise ships remarkably have not been attacked since the ill-fated attempt by the PFLP to hijack the *Achille Lauro* in 1985. Ferries, merchant vessels, and warships, in contrast, have been attacked with deadly frequency. These facts may represent a shift in the terrorists' planning as they attack softer targets and inflict mass casualties with minimal planning and resources. Passenger ferries, for example, present fewer security obstacles than cruise ships, and, because some ferries transport vehicles as well as people, their risk is doubled because vehicles and trucks are not routinely searched before boarding. The attacks on the passenger ferry *City of Porus* and the bombing of *Superferry 14* in the Philippines, as well as attacks on river cruise boats on the Nile River in the mid-1990s, are prime examples. These terrorist operations were carried out with unsophisticated weapons and tactics but still resulted in large numbers of casualties and deaths. A greater threat to passenger vessels appears to be random attacks on smaller vessels plying more exotic waters.

One such incident occurred in early August 2009 in South America along the Amazon River. The *MV Aqua* is a small cruise vessel with accommodations comparable to those of a five-star hotel. The ship belongs to a company called Aqua Expeditions and offers cruises up the Ucayali River in the Peruvian Amazon to the Pacaya-Samiria National Reserve. The reserve is considered the jewel of Peru's northern Amazon jungle and is home to more than 80 lakes, as well as spectacular wildlife. In an attack similar to one that had occurred just nine days earlier, nine armed bandits boarded the vessel from a small speedboat early in the morning and overcame the two police officers guarding the ship. They rousted the cruise vessel's passengers out of their beds and forced them to hand over their valuables at gunpoint. They then bound the hands and feet of the 20 passengers, who included Britons, Americans, Australians, and Spaniards, and fled the ship at a time of poor visibility. Police later recovered some of the valuables taken from the robbery in a shootout with the bandits as they fled to their jungle hideout.[4]

Cruise ships still remain the prize for the terrorists, however. Abdul al-Rahim al-Nashiri, who planned the attack on the USS *Cole,* had also planned to attack cruise ships. Today's terrorists have two primary goals in attacking cruise ships: to inflict mass human casualties and to generate economic losses. Islamic terror groups such as al-Qaeda would see in an attack on a cruise ship the potential to cause significant loss of life, thereby satisfying one of their main goals. Even though the crew members come from many different countries, cruise ships represent to Islamic extremists the very elements of Western society and culture that they despise, such as drinking alcohol, dancing, mingling of unmarried men and women, gambling, and permissive sex.[5]

Although cruise ships and passenger ferries account for less than 4 percent of all commercial vessels, because of the human cargo they carry, they obviously present the greatest potential for loss of life on the high seas if attacked. Attacks on other forms of shipping would result in far fewer human casualties but have a significant impact on infrastructure and commerce. The attack on the French-owned *MV Limburg* is a case in point. In October 2002, the ship was attacked by an al-Qaeda suicide boat that exploded against its hull off the coast of Yemen. The attack occurred near the spot where, where two years previous, the deadly attack on the USS *Cole* had occurred. The explosion and resulting conflagration caused the death of only one crew member on the *Limburg,* as well as that of the suicide bomber.

At the time of the attack, the *Limburg* was carrying 397,000 barrels of oil from Iran to Malaysia. The ship was in the Gulf of Aden to pick up another load of oil. When the dinghy packed with explosives exploded against the Limburg's port side, the ship caught fire, and 90,000 barrels of oil leaked into the Gulf. In the month after the attack, a panic throughout the oil tanker industry caused a rise of more than 300 percent in insurance rates for Yemeni shippers and dramatically reduced shipping to Yemen by 50 percent.[6] In an ironic twist, although owners of oil tankers faced significant economic consequences and spikes in insurance rates after the attack, it effectively backfired on the terrorists; Yemen, considered to be at the heart of al-Qaeda country, suffered the most severe economic consequences.

Unlike the USS *Cole,* which was stationary in the port of Aden, Yemen, when it was attacked, both the *Limburg* and the *Seabourn Spirit* were moving when they were attacked, a much more difficult operation. The terrorists or pirates have to consider both the problems associated with surveillance of a seagoing target out on the open ocean and sea conditions, which can change dramatically from those originally planned.[7] Additionally, although terrorist groups such as al-Qaeda have been meticulous in their planning and have shown an ability to adapt to the technical challenges presented by their chosen target, they certainly need special maritime skills in diving, navigation, coastal piloting, and ship handling, to conduct operations on vessels. Also, attacks on the open ocean are less likely to be instantly covered by the media, reducing the publicity that terrorists so desperately crave.[8]

Despite these difficulties, however, attacks on cruise ships, especially while at sea, have unquestionable benefits for terrorists or pirates. The greatest advantage for both groups is that, once out to sea, the ship is far beyond the protective umbrellas of the ports, coast guards, or navies. Once attacked, cruise ships offer the possibility of additional human casualties and collateral deaths because of the time lapse before rescue ships arrive.

Media attention may even be more dramatic if an attack takes place on the high seas and give a boost to the so-called CNN effect. The media were willing to place their reporters on the frontlines of the war in Iraq or at ground zero on September 11; it does not seem unrealistic to believe that they would be equally able to get news cameras to the farthest reaches of the oceans, especially to cover a sea disaster (as they did in the *Maersk Alabama* hostage rescue in April 2009). And the target-rich environment of the cruise ship might be irresistible for furthering the goals of the pirates and terrorists. For terrorists, ships offer a concentrated group of victims; for the pirates, they offer affluent passengers to rob or kidnap for ransom.

An even greater potential for cruise ship attacks comes from outside the known terrorist actors. The discussion thus far has focused on threats from al-Qaeda and its leader, Osama bin Laden, who gave approval to Abdul al-Rahim al-Nashiri to attack the *Cole* and the *Limburg*. What threats do rogue actors purporting to represent al-Qaeda present? International terrorist efforts such as the ones that are fueling al-Qaeda may also give rise to efforts by localized cells to attack targets of opportunity; this appears to be what happened in the London subway bombings in July 2003. There was also a planned attack on Israeli cruise ships in Turkey by Loa'i Mohammad Haj Bakr al-Saqa, also known as Lu'ai Sakra, who was purportedly acting on his own accord, without formal instructions from al-Qaeda. Such rogue terrorists who plan their own operations are force multipliers for the worldwide jihad and present serious threats to all security planners.

A case in point is the discovery of a New Jersey cell of al-Qaeda sympathizers who planned to attack Fort Dix in early May 2007. In a case similar to the Ft. Hood massacre in early November 2009 in which a lone Islamist zealot killed 13 service members, a group of al-Qaeda sympathizers planned to murder large numbers of military personnel with automatic weapons on Fort Dix. In a press briefing, the U.S. Attorney in the case said that, had the men managed to carry out their plan, "it could have been a disaster. These people were ready for martyrdom; once they got on to that base and started to shoot, everyone was in danger." An FBI special agent in charge of the FBI's Philadelphia office who investigated the case said at the time, "Today we dodged a bullet; these homegrown terrorists can prove to be as dangerous as any known group."[9] Like the attack on the *Achille Lauro*, which was planned by a rogue faction of the PLO thought to be loyal to Yasser Arafat, the next terrorist attack on a cruise ship, if and when it comes, may not be orchestrated by Osama bin Laden or his planners but instead may be carried out by home-grown sympathetic cell groups that decide that a cruise ship not only represents a viable target but is vulnerable to attack.

There are additional potential threats to the cruise ship industry, not from out-side but from within the maritime industry. Often overlooked in the discussion of maritime security is the vulnerability of infrastructure to acts by employees in the ports or on ships who have an intimate knowledge of operations and facilities and who can easily access transportation and port facilities. Those with access to se-cure areas could employ a wide range of terrorist tactics, such as deliberate sabotage or the use of improvised explosive devices. Foreign commercial vessels, including cruise ships, may be particularly vulnerable to such exploitation. Many commer-cial ships fly flags of convenience, making the nationality of the owner difficult to identify.

Terrorists could potentially infiltrate the shipping industry by posing as mari-ners filling a variety of jobs. The Philippines, which is home to a number of Islamic terrorist groups, accounts for approximately 20 percent of the world's seafarers, almost 250,000 of them. Indonesia has more than 75,000 seafarers and faces a similar terrorist problem from Islamic fundamentalists.[10] This is not to suggest that Philippine or Indonesian seafarers are terrorists; it only suggests that mem-bers of Islamic extremist groups could infiltrate maritime industry and orga-nize themselves in sleeper cells to await further direction from their terrorist leaders.

To estimate the economic damage that could result from a terrorist or pirate at-tack on cruise ships, one need only look at the terror attacks of September 11. The drop in airline ticket sales after September 11 was devastating and precipi-tated the bankruptcy of many of the major air carriers. The cruise lines also suffered after the tragedy, but, because their industry was not directly attacked, the effects were not as acute. A successful attack on a cruise ship, one that resulted in the cap-ture or sinking of the ship or the murder of innocent passengers, would lead most if not all cruise lines to suffer economic damage; some might cease to operate for an indefinite period of time. A few small cruise lines might even go out of business. There would also be a residual impact on dependent businesses and tourism, both domestically and abroad. But a more significant result of 9/11 was the fact that the cruise lines woke up to the inherent risk they faced. Because of new security measures that were put in place after the hijacking of the *Achille Lauro* incident, the thought of an entire cruise ship being attacked, seized, or held for ransom had seemed remote at best. After September 11, 2001, however, the idea that an entire ship could be destroyed in a single act of terrorist destruction raised new concerns about the economic risks facing the entire cruise industry.

THE ECONOMIC IMPACT OF TERRORISM ON THE CRUISE SHIP INDUSTRY

"When people are using duct tape, they aren't buying vacations," said Micky Arison, chief executive officer of Carnival Corporation, in mid-2003.[11] A spokesman for the company expressed concerns that the war in Afghanistan and fears of terrorism were still depressing the demand for sea vacations, with a high proportion of bookings occurring only a month or less before sailing. In addition, the war in Iraq had further economic implications for the industry. These sentiments were expressed at a press conference in which Carnival Corporation said that, despite such fears, its quarterly earnings had fallen less sharply than Wall Street had expected. While attacks on cruise ships would open up new venues for terrorism and call into question international efforts to prevent such incidents from occurring in the maritime domain, such acts against cruise ships would not cripple the world's economy in the way that attacks on other forms of commercial shipping might. Attacks on oil shipping, in particular, would likely have far greater and longer-lasting impacts on Western economies. Although terrorists have attacked cruise ships (*Achille Lauro*), passenger ferries (*Superferry 14*), and commercial shipping (*MV Limburg*), they thus far have concentrated the bulk of their targeting and attacks on U.S. military ships and platforms. But attacks on cruise ships still seem to serve the terrorists' goals of inflicting great loss of life and creating economic chaos.

Al-Qaeda's "prince of the seas," Abdul al-Rahim al-Nashiri, the architect of the USS *Cole* and the *MV Limburg* bombings, was captured in Yemen in November 2002 while he was en route to Southeast Asia. Al-Nashiri was found with a 180-page dossier listing maritime targets of opportunity, including diagrams and sailing times of cruise ships. The interrogation of al-Nashiri yielded substantial information on al-Qaeda's operational planning for attacks on supertankers.

As demonstrated by the *Limburg* attack, al-Qaeda was particularly interested in commercial shipping's vulnerability to suicide attacks and the economic impact of such operations. In an October 2002 broadcast, Ayman al-Zawahiri warned that al-Qaeda "would target the nodes of your [the West's] economy."[12] Commenting on the attack on the *MV Limburg,* al-Qaeda stated, on October 13, 2002, "If a boat that did not cost $1,000 managed to devastate an oil tanker of that magnitude, imagine the extent of the danger that threatens the West's commercial lifeline, which is petroleum."[13]

Fears of attacks on cruise vessels sent chills down the cruise industry's spine. Immediately after the September 11 attacks, leisure companies and cruise lines

Abdul al-Rahim al-Nashiri was al-Qaeda's chief of maritime operations and planned the attack, in October 2000, on the USS *Cole,* which killed 17 U.S. sailors. He was captured in Yemen in 2002. At the time of his arrest, he had a dossier containing sailing times of cruise ships from Western ports. Al-Nashiri was allegedly water-boarded, which has led the Obama administration to delay pressing charges against him. (FBI photo)

faced weak demand. Nine days after the terrorist attacks on New York and Washington, Micky Arison told investors that as many as half a dozen "relatively weak players" might not survive the free fall in cruise line bookings and cruise stock prices.[14] Renaissance Cruises became the industry's first casualty of the terrorist attacks. Industry analysts said the company's shutdown, on September 25, 2001, was a result of long-term financial problems that were aggravated by a sharp decline in cruise bookings after the attacks. Renaissance operated 10 ships and had a 4 percent share of the cruise market. An analyst at Bear Stearns, the giant New York financial investment firm that itself collapsed in March 2008 and was bought by JPMorgan Chase, said that the attacks had a "devastating impact on demand, with bookings dropping 5 to 50 percent depending on the cruise ship and its location."[15]

Attacks on a cruise ships, either by terrorists or by pirates, would impact primarily the industry's ability to promote itself as safe and would affect consumer confidence for months or even years. This would especially hurt the industry's ability to increase its revenue base, given that only a small percentage of the U.S. population has ever taken a cruise vacation. The cruise industry would potentially lose the confidence of the untapped cruise market, which would come to view cruise vacations as dangerous and risky, and a significant percentage of the U.S. population that had already cruised and upon which the cruise lines depend as repeat customers.

Fears of terrorism have been on the minds of cruise industry executives since the *Achille Lauro* hijacking. While no cruise ships were attacked or threatened directly on September 11, 2001, there was a trickle-down effect on many industries and economies that the cruise lines support. The cruise industry and the tourist markets it caters to suffered not from loss of actual life but loss of economic life. Scarcely noticed in the tragic events of September 11 was the devastating blow it dealt to several Latin American and Caribbean economies that are only now, years later, recovering. Another large-scale terrorist attack, especially in the

maritime domain, could mean an immediate cessation of trade activity with the
United States while countries wrestled with new security measures in addition
to those already required by C-TPAT and CSI. While a large-scale maritime terrorist attack would have a devastating impact on the U.S. economy, it would deal
an even greater blow to some of the smaller export-based economies of the region. The currency left by visiting cruise ships accounts for 70 to 80 percent of
some Caribbean countries' foreign exchange earnings.[16]

Egypt's tourism suffered dramatically in 1997 after terrorists targeted foreign
visitors to the Temple of Hatshepsut in Luxor. Egypt's tourism industry was effectively sent into turmoil. In the year after the attack, tourism dropped by almost
50 percent. Tourism is Egypt's second largest foreign exchange earner, and Egypt
accounts for 50 percent of all tourist arrivals to Africa and the Middle East. The
cruise lines cater heavily to the popularity of Egyptian ports of calls on their
Mediterranean itineraries; if they were to pull out of this market, Egypt would
immediately feel the economic effects.[17] Other countries in addition to Egypt are
vulnerable to the effects of terrorism on their economies because tourism is a significant part of their gross national product. Jamaica, in the Caribbean, which has
a large tourism-based economy, is another example; like Egypt, its ports are popular with the cruise lines. Conversely, countries such as Japan, which have diverse
economies and are not as dependent on tourism, would likely emerge from a local
terrorist incident with little economic impact.

While localized terrorist incidents might impact regional economy that is dependent on cruise ship tourism, the significance of a single maritime 9/11 cannot be overstated in terms of its effect on all of the world's economies. As terrible
as the effects of 9/11 were on the aviation industry, they did not cause world economies to collapse. This was true because the world's economies do not depend on
the aviation industry or air freight shippers; most goods are transported by sea
as containerized cargo. The truth is that attacks on any element of the maritime
industry, whether it be cargo, container, oil, passenger ferry, or cruise line, would
severely impact the whole industry by increasing insurance rates, disrupting or
potentially close vital sea lanes, and instilling fear and lack of confidence in the
security of maritime commerce. If supply lines between the United States and its
trading partners were to be disrupted or cut, especially those that carry oil, the life's
blood of the U.S. economy would literally cease to flow.

A look at what happened during the most recent closure of the port of Los
Angeles and other West Coast ports may give some indication of the likely effects of an attack on a port, perhaps one using WMDs. In October 2002, all 29
ports along the West Coast of the United States were shut down as the result of
a labor dispute between longshoreman unions and management. The lockdown
of the ports lasted only two weeks but delayed more than 200 ships transporting

more than 300,000 containers from Asian ports to the United States. The direct cost to the U.S. economy of the cargo disruptions alone were estimated at $467 million; the disruption created a backlog of shipments from prominent Asian exporters such as Hong Kong, Singapore, and Malaysia.[18]

While the cruise lines were only marginally affected by the strike, a similar incident involving the closure of ports while officials searched ships and containers for possible WMD or a closure resulting from a blocked harbor entrance because of a terrorist incident would be catastrophic for the United States and its shipping partners for months and possibly years. The cruise lines would suffer from loss of access to embarkation ports and cancellations of bookings due to fears associated with ocean travel.

If the maritime domain were threatened, discretionary spending on cruise vacations would be severely affected and cruise ship markets would shrink as potentially dangerous regions were removed from itineraries. The cruise industry would either have to raise prices for cruise vacations to make up lost revenue or severely discount them to fill their ships. The effects of the recent oil crisis in 2007–2008 also played into the economics of all the transportation industries. When the price of oil surged, cruise ship companies added a separate charge for fuel. Such pricing schemes were a clever attempt by the cruise industry to disguise the higher costs of fuel by adding a surcharge to passenger tickets. It is almost as if the industry wanted passengers to believe that the cost of fuel was not originally included in the price of their tickets. Cruise ship passengers were asked to overlook up to $70 in additional fuel charges.[19]

The increased fees passed on cruise ship passengers do not stop there. Separate charges for security are also being itemized on the cruise passenger's tickets. Like the airlines, which were required to improve their security after 9/11 and added a security tax onto the cost of a ticket, the cruise lines have conveniently passed the cost of implementing their security programs on to the passengers through a separate security charge. Unlike fuel charges, which can be linked to the rising cost of oil, passengers are unclear what a security surcharge actually covers. Perhaps if cruise ship passengers really understood the threats that the cruise lines now must try to protect themselves against, they would be less inclined to complain about the small increase in ticket prices.

AL-QAEDA'S PHANTOM NAVY

Immediately after September 11, 2001, there were constant reports about phantom ships in the command of terrorists, aptly named "al-Qaeda's Navy." The possibility that Osama bin Laden had at his disposal his own personal naval force was enough to send shivers through the entire maritime industry. Al-Qaeda had already shown its capability to strike at maritime targets, and there were more than enough threats being circulated that included plots to attack the *Queen Mary 2* and other cruise ships. But did such a force really exist, and what threat, if any, did the terror navy pose to the maritime community? If the intelligence reports are correct, the maritime industry has much to worry about.

Depending on the intelligence reports, al-Qaeda has between 15 and 50 ships, possibly more, maybe fewer. According to the reports, they range in size and shape from oceangoing vessels to nondescript coastal freighters. A few facts regarding the maritime assets of al-Qaeda are known. As early as 1994, al-Qaeda had purchased a ship; in that year, one of its members, Wahid El-Hage, who was sentenced to life imprisonment on terrorism conspiracy charges in 2001 for his role in the bombing of the U.S. embassies in Nairobi, Kenya, and Dar es Salaam, Tanzania, had bought a small freighter, the *Jennifer.* That ship sank off the coast of Oman in 2000. It was also reported that al-Qaeda had used one of its freighters to deliver the explosives used in the East African embassy bombings in 1998.[20]

It is easy to see how frustrated the intelligence community is over the prospect of tracking ships belonging to a deadly terrorist organization. The U.S. intelligence community has the capability to track suspect ships by satellite and via surveillance platforms such as submarines and reconnaissance planes. It also relies on allied nations to supply information on ships that call on overseas ports. But keeping track of suspect ships is very difficult because ships can be easily repainted, renamed, and reregistered by fictitious corporate owners with news flag states.

The situation is complicated by the extensive use of "flags of convenience" by maritime shipping companies. Western companies register their ships in countries with lenient maritime regulations and oversight to avoid the stringent safety and environmental standards imposed by the U.S. and western European countries. The giants in the flags-of-convenience business are Panama and Liberia, with some 4,680 and 1,432 ships, respectively, reported on their registers.[21]

The job of the intelligence watchdogs is almost overwhelming. They must sift through the ownership and ownerships, both legitimate and suspect, of more than 120,000 of the world's merchant vessels. As one government official said about keeping track of the possible threat from questionable ownership, "This industry is a shadowy underworld. . . . After 9/11, we suddenly learned how little we understood about commercial shipping. You can't swing a dead cat in the shipping business without hitting somebody with phony papers."[22]

Once the suspect ships are found, a decision by allied navies to board and search the vessels usually leads to more frustration. Take the case of the freighter *Baltic Sky,* seized off the coast of Greece by Greek Special Forces in June 2003. While the ship's manifest said the ship was carrying fertilizer, when the ship was searched it was found to be carrying 750 tons of TNT and 8,000 detonators. The ship's crew of seven, mostly from Ukraine, said the ship's owners had given them instructions to deliver the cargo to Sudan. While the explosives had been loaded in Tunisia and were destined for the Sudan, presumably for mining operations, the ship had taken a circuitous route around the Mediterranean, through the Aegean Sea, and into the Black Sea before returning to the Ionian Sea off the Greek coast, where the Greek Navy caught up with the ship.

The Greek investigation revealed that the mining company was fictitious and consisted of a postal box in Sudan's capital, Khartoum. The Greeks impounded the ship pending the identification of the ship's owners.[23] Had the ship exploded under the Bosphorus Bridge while sailing the Bosphorus Straits at the entrance to the Black Sea, the implications could have been disastrous, because such an act could have blocked the busiest shipping channel in the world. The Bosphorus handles 30 percent more ship traffic than the Straits of Malacca. It would have taken up to a year to clear the blockage, and would have caused hundreds of billions of dollars in economic damage.[24]

Just as frustrating are the times when the intelligence leads to a dead end or when the terrorists appear to be one step ahead of their pursuers. In December 2001, acting on an intelligence tip that the ship was carrying "terrorist material," British antiterrorist officers intercepted and boarded the *Nisha,* an Indian-owned bulk carrier, in the English Channel. The vessel was carrying raw sugar to a refinery on the River Thames, near London's Canary Wharf financial and residential district. Three days of searching found nothing suspicious, and the *Nisha* was allowed to dock and unload at the Thames terminal in early January.[25]

Similarly, in October 2003, acting on an intelligence tip from the United States, New Zealand customs officers boarded the *Athena,* a Greek-owned cargo ship in the port of Christchurch, in the south island of New Zealand. The freighter normally carries fertilizer and cement between New Zealand and Asia. The ship was due to leave for South Korea when customs officials gave it an unusually thorough inspection, including checks on the identities of all crew and a full search of the vessel. Everything seemed to be in order. The interest in the *Athena* did not end there, however. When the ship arrived in the port of Kunsan in South Korea, it was checked again by Korean authorities, who said they searched for weapons and forged passports but found nothing unusual on board.[26] Clearly, if the *Athena* was a terrorist ship, either it had been engaged in legitimate trade at the time of the search or it had been tipped off, or both.

Because terrorist ships, if they do exist, do not look like navy vessels or sit at anchor waiting for the next terrorist operation, the problem for antiterrorist planners becomes trying to defeat an enemy who uses such ships for what appears to be legitimate business most of the time and for terrorist plots when it suits them. It has now been speculated that the mother ships that are launching dhows that then attack ships off the coast of Somalia are flying Panamanian flags, making it more difficult to establish their connection to piracy.[27] These ships can be used to support terrorist operations or piracy, as the case may be, in any number of ways, ranging from transporting ammunition and explosives to themselves serving as weapons. The implications for shipping and for cruise ships are obvious. These terror and pirate ships are literally hiding in plain sight.

A far worse scenario for security planners is the possibility that a terrorist ship engaged in legitimate shipping might transport a weapon of mass destruction to an unsuspecting port. This has remained the West's greatest fear, and it has shifted most if not all maritime security resources away from alleged plots to sink cruise ships. To date, such plots involving WMD are mere speculation, but aggressive steps to prevent such an occurrence are currently being taken in the United States by the Department of Homeland Security Customs and Border Protection. In the wake of such terrorist hysteria, efforts to detect "al-Qaeda's Navy" may be made even more difficult. So far, the intelligence agencies and maritime watchdogs have focused on merchant shipping and on efforts to keep terrorists from introducing WMDs into a Western port. A much greater risk, one that the cruise lines were warned of after 9/11, is the immediate threats posed by small boats and watercraft, which have already been used by al-Qaeda against ships, with deadly results.

CRUISE SHIPS AND THE SMALL-BOAT THREAT

Shortly after September 11, 2001, the Coast Guard began to require that security zones be enforced around cruise ships. The size of the required zones varies by port but generally is set at between 100 yards and 500 yards in most U.S. ports. The security zone travels with the cruise ships as they make their way in and out of harbors. The problem for cruise ships has always been to keep small boats and watercraft from straying too close to the ship when it is in port. Generally, boaters are unaware of the regulations and of the punishments for willful violations of the limits, which include fines of up to $250,000 and/or 10 years in prison. Further, a person who uses a dangerous weapon or engages in conduct that threatens the safety of any maritime officer engaged in enforcing this regulation can be charged with a felony and can be imprisoned for up to 12 years.[28] These are serious penalties and should not be taken lightly by recreational boaters who may be intent on getting a closer look at cruise ships. What the restriction was really meant to prevent, however, is another attack like the one on the USS Cole.

The threat from small boats has not decreased, and it appears that the U.S. Coast Guard is still very concerned. Admiral Thad Allen, Commandant of the

Coast Guard, said that, despite public opposition to increased registration and tracking of vessels used primarily for recreation, "we need to be moving in that direction." Speaking in reference to the November 2008 terror attacks on Mumbai, which were launched from the sea by terrorists in small boats and which killed 166 persons, Admiral Allen acknowledged (in August 2009) that there were no "credible threats" of an attack against the United States launched by a small boat, but he also said "it should not take an event" to prompt a debate on the need for more restrictive measures.[29] Indeed, an examination of the historical record reveals that the biggest maritime threat to cruise ships does come from attacks by small boats. The Rand Corporation undertook an extensive study of maritime risks to all types of vessels from various methods of attack. For cruise ships, the threats studied included shots fired at the cruise ship with standoff weapons like artillery, rockets, or small arms; damage from mines; and attacks by small boats filled with high explosives. Although the study doubted whether a small-boat attack could actually sink a cruise ship, it concluded that an external ramming attack by a small boat could cause extensive damage to the ship.[30]

Small-boat attacks have already been used successfully against the USS *Cole* and the *MV Limburg* and was the tactic chosen for the destruction of Israeli cruise ships by an al-Qaeda–linked militant, Lu'ai Sakra, before the plot was discovered. It should be noted that the failed attempt to sink the USS *The Sullivans* by al-Qaeda prior to the *Cole* attack also involved the use of a small boat laden with explosives. Because cruise ships often anchor out in foreign ports for up to 24 hours, they are especially vulnerable to waterborne attacks.

During these prolonged stops, a cruise ship is most exposed to a collision assault from either a fast-moving, explosive-laden suicide craft or from a more sizable boat that is deliberately smashed into the cruise ship's side. Terrorists seek to exploit predictability. Practically all cruise ships sail on precise schedules, and preplanned itineraries of cruise ships are available on the Internet or through travel agents.[31] Although other forms of public transportation, such as airlines and railways, operate on regular schedules, the certainty of cruise ships' schedules, which ensure that the target will be there when the attack is scheduled to occur, removes one operational concern for the terrorists, pirates, or drug smugglers.

Although security zones are set up around cruise ships in domestic ports, no such agreements prevail in foreign ports. Most small boats in any port normally stay clear of naval vessels. The attack on the USS *Cole* was the primary motivation behind the development of the LRAD by American Technology Corporation, which, as we have discussed, is used by the U.S. Navy to help it evaluate the intentions of small craft while they are at a safe distance from naval vessels in port. This must be done before a decision can be made whether to neutralize the target with deadly force according to the ship's rules of engagement.

The terrorists who used a suicide boat to attack the *Cole* prevailed because, by the time the hostile intent of the small boat was clear, it was already past the point of defensive action on the part of the ship. Hamas has also used this method of attack against the Israeli Navy on several occasions. In November 2000, a month after the USS *Cole* attack, a Hamas suicide bomber using a fishing boat attempted to sink an Israeli patrol craft sailing off the Gaza Strip. Alert crew members on the Israeli boat detected the threat and sank the boat before the Hamas operative could detonate his boat against the ship.[32]

The threat posed by small boats being used as weapons is a complex issue. The thousands of small craft that operate up and down the coasts of the United States as well as on inland waterways and lakes make it impossible to determine which if any boats pose a threat. Small-boat threats may involve any form of watercraft and method of weapon delivery. Vessels may range from large commercial merchant freighters, private yachts, recreational motor boats, and speed boats to rowboats, jet skis, and even small submersible submarines. Boats can be filled with high explosives and have a crew or a lone suicide pilot. They can be set on autopilot or remotely detonated. What is most alarming is that any one of these water conveyances could conceivably deliver WMDs of varying size and complexity.[33] However, nuclear WMDs might be better suited for attacks against maritime infrastructure rather than against a cruise ship or similar high-value target. But it is certainly not out of the realm of possibility that terrorists might use small boats to attack naval vessels, especially nuclear-powered ones.

Compounding the problem of defending against small boats is the fact that law enforcement along the waterfront has limited capacity to neutralize any threat in time to stop an attack once a plot has been discovered. Even if stopping a small boat is necessary, doing so may involve the use of deadly force, which may be a negative factor for law enforcement personnel, who may not have adequate time to discern the real nature of the threat and who may hesitate to fire if they are uncertain about the approaching boat's intentions. Rules of engagement across local, state, and federal agencies are not consistent on this matter.[34]

Even the LRAD and other nonlethal technological devices, while effective in helping officially determine a small boat's potential for causing harm to a ship, are not offensive weapons capable of taking out a surface target. Attacks by small boats can occur at some distance from land, as evidenced by the *Limburg* suicide attack, which took place 12 miles off the coast of Yemen and while the ship was under way. But, as mentioned previously, terrorists like predictability. High-value ships like cruise ships, which carry thousands of passengers, and tankers, which carry hazardous materials, are much more vulnerable when entering or leaving restricted navigable waters along the U.S. coastline, in port areas, or along domestic waterways than they are on the open seas. During these periods, a large ship typically has a pilot on board, is moving at a low speed, and is following a tight and predictable course.

After 9/11, the world organized its response to maritime terrorism through the adoption of the International Ship and Port Security (ISPS) Code. The ISPS regulations have only marginally aided in protecting cruise ships against threats from small boats. Cruise ships, like all other vessels over 500 grt, are required to conduct vulnerability assessments, draft ship security plans, and hire company and ship security officers. While these measures may raise awareness of the threat, they simply do not provide any viable defense. Additionally, the ISPS Code requires that ships weighing more than 500 tons provide 96 hours notice to the U.S. Coast Guard before entering U.S. waters. This requirement does not apply to small-boats and other watercraft.[35]

Carrying out a small-boat attack, fortunately, is not as easy as it sounds. In the failed attack on the USS *The Sullivans* in Yemen, al-Qaeda operatives found that they failed to calculate what effect the weight of the boat once it was laden with explosives would have on their ability to maneuver it to the target. The terrorists did not have the necessary maritime skills in this first attempt to strike at a U.S. warship. They had not even conducted a rehearsal, which resulted in their original craft sinking, along with its load of high explosives, on its way to the target. However, their ability to learn from these mistakes enabled them to successfully bomb the USS *Cole* a year later. At a minimum, maritime attacks using small boats require recruiting, training, and planning; surveillance and intelligence collection; operational security; logistical support; rehearsals; information operations; and execution planning, as well as maritime skill and knowledge of such things as tides, currents, piloting, and navigation.[36]

Considering that the small-boat scenario seems to be, for the time being, the most likely method of attack against cruise ships, it seems logical that the need for protecting the water perimeters of cruise ships would be paramount in cruise line security strategy. However, my experience with the LRAD program, which has been so successful for Princess Cruises, convinced me that most other cruise lines feel there is little need to invest in such protective measures. Most security directors are hesitant to suggest to their cruise lines that the price tag of these devices represents a reasonable investment in view of the threat. I find this response incredible, but my faith and belief in the LRAD were established by the high praise given it by the U.S. Navy's Fifth Fleet commanders.

In the hostile waters of the Persian Gulf, the LRAD has been used in a force protection role, enabling the Navy to determine the intentions of small craft around Fifth Fleet warships while the small craft were at safe distances from the ships. The deadly attack on the USS *Cole* and the USS *Firebolt (PC10)* proved the importance of having this capability. The LRAD is also being used effectively by the U.S. Navy in antipiracy operations by Task Force 51 in the Indian Ocean. The Navy is quickly realizing the necessity of establishing contact with potential surface threats to avoid possibly injuring or killing innocent boaters. This was demonstrated in the case of the U.S. cargo ship *Global Patriot*; if an LRAD had been available when it was traversing the Suez Canal, it is possible that the loss of life that occurred would have been prevented (see chapter 4). Despite this, many cruise lines have been unreceptive to outfitting their own ships with the LRAD because of the relative high cost.[37] But that cost has come down in recent years since; a cruise ship can now outfit itself with ample LRAD equipment for less than the cost of one lifeboat. Still, officials have remained reluctant to purchase the LRAD—but that is about to change with the mandatory requirements of the Cruise Vessel Security and Safety Act of 2009, which will require acoustic and hailing devices mandatory on all cruise ships in U.S. waters.

Another aspect of water security is that ports and cruise line have made little progress in providing a physical water barrier around cruise ships. I was successful in making a case for the encirclement of the *Queen Mary 2* with a Dunlap barrier (described in chapter 4) while in the port of Piraeus, Greece, during the 2004 Summer Olympics. In domestic ports, the U.S. aircraft carriers are always protected in this fashion. In San Diego harbor, for example, the carriers share the harbor with the cruise ship terminal. Dunlap barriers prevent any vessels from getting inside the aircraft carriers' security zone. Likewise, a naval patrol vessel guards the narrow entrance to the artificial security harbor. Obviously, cruise ships differ from aircraft carriers in just about every way, especially in their propulsion systems. Today, the fleet of U.S. naval aircraft carriers is exclusively nuclear. These ships demand a higher level of physical protection while in port. What terrorist group, given the opportunity and a choice of targets, would not choose to attack an unprotected cruise ship pier rather than a heavily protected aircraft carrier?

While the need for a water barrier to protect high-risk vessels while they are in special situations, as was the *Queen Mary 2* while it was anchored in the port of Piraeus, Greece, during the 2004 Summer Olympics, seems obvious, the practicality of placing a permanent barrier around cruise ships is something the cruise lines are not required to implement at any of the three levels of maritime security imposed by the ISPS Code. Princess Cruises came close to developing a cruise ship–deployed water barrier but soon discovered that the prototype available was rendered impractical by the unacceptable storage requirements on the ships, which included accommodation for scores of containers, and by the extensive time required to deploy it once the cruise ship was in port.

Countering the threat from small-boat attacks is very complicated, but the best approach may be not to depend on any one method but to employ a layered defense that begins with situational awareness of the maritime domain. Cruise ships sailing into domestic ports and especially overseas must understand the threats and be willing to accept risks they cannot mitigate. They must focus on those efforts that have the greatest potential for protecting the ship. Maritime domain awareness demands that current and timely intelligence be processed, synthesized, and disseminated to ships operating in high-threat areas. From that awareness comes the proactive efforts on the part of the ships to use all available resources such as lookouts, radar, and LRAD technology if available to identify threats as soon and as far from the ship as possible. When possible, the cruise line can co-opt the service of the port's coast guard or similar maritime law enforcement presence. While this is one of the best defenses against small-boat threats, it cannot be counted upon in foreign ports.

Another preventive measure to mitigate the risk of an attack by a small boat is to have on board armed Sea Marshalls. The Sea Marshall program directed by the U.S. Coast Guard is usually focused on ships entering the port rather than on those that are departing. Marshalls normally are placed on "high-interest vessels," or HIVs. This category sometimes includes cruise ships. Sea Marshalls provide a comfort factor for the cruise ships but are not there primarily to protect the ship from external threats. While that is a secondary mission, their focus once aboard is to maintain vigilance over the harbor pilot, conduct searches of the ship for contraband, and verify and review maritime documentation and crew lists. Their greatest benefit in fending off small-boat threats is that, because they are heavily armed, they can help turn away surface craft intent on attacking the ship. But if the ship does not have a method like the LRAD to enable it to verify the intent of a small boat, that intent will probably become evident too late to avoid the attack.

Fortunately, the Coast Guard also provides armed escorts by patrol craft for ships as they enter and leave selected ports, allowing the Sea Marshalls to conduct their business internally on the ship. This level of external security against small boats and other surface threats is normally provided only at large commercial ports with a large Coast Guard presence. Given the multitude of missions that the Coast Guard conducts on a daily basis, cruise ship escorts may not always be given priority. If the Coast Guard cannot provide patrol boats or Sea Marshalls, the cruise lines are limited in their options. Cruise ships in some ports, particularly in Miami and Port Everglades, are required to place a picket boat in the water and patrol around the ship. This measure has limited effects because the crews on these boats have no law enforcement authority and are almost exclusively foreign nationals. Their value lies primarily in deterrence.

Vigilance by the cruise ships is ultimately the best defense regardless of the maritime security or threat level because it is an al-Qaeda trademark to come out of nowhere. Any effort to protect ships have to mesh seamlessly with the normal functions of the cruise ship while in port or at anchor. There are a number of other activities taking place near the ship when in port, and scores of vessels and

A Sea Marshall from Station Miami Beach watches over the harbor pilot as he brings the inbound cruise ship *Voyager of the Seas* through the port of Miami shortly after the attacks of September 11, 2001. Armed law enforcement officers accompany the harbor pilot aboard incoming cruise ships from sea as part of the nation's heightened security measures but are not part of the ship's security crew. (USCG photo by Telfair Brown Sr.)

small craft, including bunkering vessels, water taxis, and motor launches ferrying passengers to and from the ship, make routine approaches to the ship to render essential services while the ship is anchored in the harbor. The possibility that a rogue motor launch might be turned against the ship must be considered.

Unlike other forms of commercial vessels, which can devote many of their resources to the threats from small boats, cruise ships are intended for the purpose of providing a vacation experience. Their very presence in harbors and ports naturally attracts great attention from watercraft. The LRAD give ship officials a unique capability to discern the existence of any threat while the ship is in port and should be used robustly. Minus this tool, the cruise ship captain and crew should never lose appreciation of the threat posed by an attack by a small boat. These attacks, with their deadly precision, can occur in any location in the world. Ships must be aware of the possibility of not only an attack from the surface of the water but also of an attack launched from under the sea.

UNDER THE SEA: DANGER LURKS FOR CRUISE SHIPS

Al-Qaeda has shown interest in, if not the capability for, launching attacks throughout the entire maritime domain; this includes attacks on the surface, from the air, and from below the water. George Tenet, during his tenure as director of the Central Intelligence Agency, told the U.S. Senate Committee on Intelligence in February 2003 that al-Qaeda was developing new methods of striking and that these included the use of "underwater methods to attack maritime targets."[38] A few months earlier, the FBI had become concerned that terrorist scuba divers might try to place explosives on vessels. Intelligence suggested that al-Qaeda and some affiliated terror groups, like the Abu Sayyaf Group in the Philippines, were developing an underwater diving capability or at least had shown that they were intent on learning this skill much as they had prepared for the terrorist attacks of September 11.

These views were shared with the Department of Homeland Security (DHS), which warned that international terrorist groups might be planning to strike from under the water. Officials were worried that explosives could be attached to the hulls of ships by terrorist divers. The DHS issued a bulletin to the maritime community stating that it believed that such an attack might occur in U.S. ports. DHS also indicated that, over the previous two years, there had been suspicious activity involving surveillance of port facilities, naval bases, and cruise ship piers.

This intelligence was coupled with reports of suspicious individuals making inquires about underwater propulsion diving vehicles at dive shops and diving schools. While there was no specific information to indicate that a swimmer attack was actually in the making, the Department said that "such targeting would be consistent with al-Qaeda's objectives."[39] Clearly, the threat from the sea is something that concerns the federal government very much.

How do ships protect themselves against threats that they cannot see and that at any moment, without warning, might cause destruction? The cruise lines were particularly aware of these threats. Not all threats, however, came from terrorists. In July 2004, days after the new ISPS Code went into effect worldwide, a distressing report about the *Queen Mary 2* was received at Cunard Cruise Lines. The report detailed how several swimmers who, apparently noticing the *QM2*'s bulbous bow (the bow of the ship under the water that resembles a submarine's nose), thought it would be a good idea to swim up to the ship from their small boat, climb on the bulbous bow, and have their picture taken. Two boys and their father climbed the bulbous bow of the 151,400 grt cruise ship when it was at anchor at Geirangerfjord, on the west coast of Norway. As dangerous as this stunt was for the trespassers, who could have been sucked underneath the ship by intake valves, it is even more distressing that the *QM2* did not even know that they were there. Another ship passing by in the harbor called the ship on the bridge-to-bridge radiophone and reported that there were people hanging out on the bow of the ship.[40]

At Princess Cruises, the risk posed by swimmers who come close to the ship and threaten its security was taken very seriously. The ongoing efforts to hire divers to examine the underneath of cruise ship hulls in various Princess ports is among the most proactive measures taken by the line to protect its ships in port. The problem is that divers are not always available in every port, and contracting for such investigations are driven by threat information, rather than undertaken as a matter of procedure. Underwater inspections are random, and that is enough to keep the terrorists guessing.

Professional divers with military experience say that mounting a successful underwater attack against a ship or offshore installation would be more difficult than attacking with an explosive-laden boat. Even so, that terrorist swimmer should not be given unfettered access to the ship without understanding the possibility that some underwater force field, sonar, or similar measure may neutralize his efforts. But, even if a swimmer, even suicide ones, were to make it to the ship, mounting an attack would not be that easy. Underwater strikes require specialized equipment, training, and explosive charges. Even for professionals, they can be complicated by adverse currents, tides, and poor underwater visibility, not to mention deafening engine noise. Experts say that a relatively untrained swimmer strapped with heavy explosives and battling stress and fear would have a very difficult time.[41]

That is not to say that al-Qaeda has not looked into the requirements for underwater attacks. Al-Nashiri, al-Qaeda's former maritime operative, had four major elements to his strategy for attacking Western maritime interests. One of them was to train underwater demolition teams to attack ships.[42] This tactic focused primarily on Navy ships. One of al-Qaeda's chief operators in Southeast Asia, Omar al-Faruq, was captured in Indonesia in late 2002. Al-Faruq was turned over to the United States and told interrogators that he was planning scuba attacks on U.S. naval vessels calling on Indonesian ports. Plots to use divers trained by al-Qaeda to attack the U.S. Navy in the Strait of Gibraltar were also uncovered.[43]

More alarming was an incident that occurred in the Philippines and that involved Abu Sayyaf Group, which has links to al-Qaeda. The terror group kidnapped a maintenance engineer in east Malaysia in 2000 and held him until June 2003. When he was released, he told authorities that the terrorists knew he was a diving instructor and wanted to learn how to dive. Similarly, in another part of Malaysia, information was developed that suggested that a group of ethnic Malaysians wanted to learn about diving, but not about the effects of decompression, indicating possibly that they were not interested in resurfacing.[44]

According to a report in Lebanon's *Daily Star* newspaper, al-Qaeda terrorists have a naval manual on how to attack vessels using limpet mines and underwater scooters for suicide attacks.[45] This information, if true, has enormous implications for cruise ships. Further proof of the existence of this maritime manual is found in the use of "suicide underwater scooters" as one of the tactics that were to be employed by Loa'i Mohammad Haj Bakr al-Saqa, in a failed attack on an Israeli cruise ships near Antalya, Turkey (see chapter 2). Lu'ai Sakra had already purchased a diver's submersible sea scooter and was planning to use it in his attack.[46]

If the threat from underwater swimmers is difficult to confront, an even greater risk to ships comes from the omnipresent threat from mines laid by hostile countries or terrorists. Even the threat of underwater mines could stop maritime commerce in its tracks.

From an historical perspective, mines have been more effective than any other method or weapon used to attack shipping. The U.S. Navy indicates that there are more than a quarter-million mines in the inventories of more than 50 navies. More than 30 counties produce mines, and 20 of these export them to the rest of the world. The estimated number of maritime mines does not include devices that can be easily and cheaply fabricated. During the Persian Gulf War, in 1991, Iraqi floating mines of this type were used in abundance and littered the Persian Gulf.[47]

Generally speaking, mines are easy to acquire or build and are relatively inexpensive, costing from just a few dollars to $25,000 or more for the most advanced weapons. To put this in perspective, in 1987, during the so-called Tanker Wars, the U.S. warship USS *Samuel B. Roberts* struck a Soviet-designed contact mine in the Persian Gulf. The ship almost sank, with potentially great loss of life, but was kept afloat by the courageous damage control efforts of the crew. Repairing the damage caused by a $1,500 weapon cost the United States more than $96 million.

A few years later, in 1991, in the same general area where the strike on the *Roberts* took place, the helicopter assault ship USS *Tripoli* encountered an Iraqi contact mine, which blew a hole 23 feet by 25 feet in its starboard side. Four hours later, the Aegis guided-missile cruiser USS *Princeton* was almost broken in half by an Italian-made Manta bottom mine in approximately 65 feet of water. The *Princeton* had to be taken out of service, and the total cost to repair that ship came to more than $110 million, all from a single mine costing about $15,000.[48]

What was true then about mines still has relevance today, as Admiral C. A. H. Trost, then Chief of Naval Operations, noted in July 1989, at the height of the Persian Gulf mine strikes: "Very little sophistication is required to manufacture and deploy mines. Any nation with either money to buy mines on the open market, or the capability to forge metal and make explosives, can become an active participant in mine warfare. Minefields can be seeded by anything that flies or floats. And again, crude but effective mines are cheap, easy to stockpile, and easily concealed in holds of ships and fishing boats."[49]

Normally, floating and contact mines can be deployed from aircraft, submarines, and surface vessels. Limpet mines are designed to be placed directly on targets by combat swimmers or, in the future, by unmanned undersea vehicles. Mines placed surreptitiously in channels or harbors can be used to create a spectacular incident if they explode against a crammed passenger ferry or cruise ship. Additionally, even if no ships are sunk or damaged by a mine, the threat of a mined channel or harbor is enough to shut down an entire port, with catastrophic consequences for the nation's flow of commerce until the mines are cleared.[50] Despite the threat that harbors could be mined surreptitiously, security budgets devoted to the security of ships and ports appear to be relatively low. This is all the more alarming if one considers the scope of the economic damage that could be done by terrorist covertly mining a strategic port. The damage to the nation's infrastructure would be incalculable.[51]

If the threat from combat swimmers, limpet mines, and maritime minefields were not enough, a new threat to shipping has emerged as an offshoot of the war on drugs that may find a new role in terrorist operations—the use of underwater vessels. In September 2000, a submarine that was smuggling drugs was discovered in Bogotá, Colombia, that was capable of carrying 150 to 200 tons of cargo plus 12 crew members. In August 2006, another submarine, possibly abandoned after an abortive test run, was found drifting off Spain. The discovery demonstrated that underwater technology of this type is a growing problem and these vessels are apparently easy to construct. A small manned submarine or semi-submersible can be assembled with only basic materials and skills. Since 2005, Colombia has captured 11 homemade submarines constructed of fiberglass.[52]

Late in 2006, the U.S. Coast Guard, conducting joint maneuvers off the coast of Costa Rica, intercepted a 50-foot submarine heading north at 7 knots and filled with millions of dollars' worth of cocaine. The Coast Guard was alerted to the vessel when lookouts spotted three plastic pipes skimming across the surface of the water. Though simple in design, the submarine functioned remarkably well for a vessel made solely of wood and fiberglass. The ship used an air-breathing gasoline engine (hence the intake pipes) to cruise six feet beneath the surface and used a basic pump device to control the depth. The Coast Guard captured the vessel more than 100 miles into the Pacific and several hundred miles from Colombia, where it had originated—proof of how stable and seaworthy it was even with several tons of cargo.[53]

A famous cruise ship was approached by one of these homemade submarines, but for reasons that were not sinister. In August 2007, the *Queen Mary 2* had a frightening encounter with an unknown underwater craft one morning when a strange shape was spotted in the water in New York harbor next to the ship, which had just moored at Pier 41. When authorities arrived to investigate, they found a crude round submersible vessel made out of plywood, coated with fiberglass, and topped off with portholes and a hatch bought from a marine salvage company. Pumps in the bottom allowed the man inside to add or remove water as necessary for ballast.

A New York City Police Department harbor vessel maintains security between the *Queen Mary 2* and a replica of a Revolutionary War submarine in the water off Red Hook in Brooklyn, New York, August 3, 2007. Police arrested three men involved with the vessel; however, they said that the incident was unrelated to terrorism. Homemade semisubmersible submarines now in use by the drug cartels have dangerous implications for cruise ship security; they could be adapted by terrorists and used in an attack. (AP photo/U.S. Coast Guard, Petty Officer 3rd Class Christopher Taylor)

Inside, the vessel's captain and sole occupant was intent on getting close to the ship, not to attack it but to take a photo. The man apparently was an artist whose various other art projects had previously landed him in trouble with New York police. This project was a rough replica of what is believed to have been America's first submarine, an oak sphere called "the Turtle." It was said to have seen action in New York harbor during the Revolutionary War. New York authorities were quick to downplay the stunt and indicated that the *QM2* was never in danger. The Coast Guard issued the artist a citation for violating the ship's 100-yard security zone. The police then issued two more, for unsafe boating.[54]

This incident near the *Queen Mary 2* turned out to be harmless. But, the possibility that terrorists might use similar crude technology to attack cruise ships or other high-value ships is frightening. Cruise lines should be alert to the possibility of underwater threats but have thus far employed very few countermeasures. Emerging technology may help make detection and deterrence easier. Underwater inspections by trained divers are necessary even if expensive and time-consuming. Because underwater threats are so great, cruise lines might consider employing underwater security divers either to travel on their ships or to form part of the corporate security team.

Good intelligence will make the difference between stopping an underwater terrorist operation in the making and becoming the victim of such an attack. Although it is speculative at best to think that terrorists could lay a great number of mines in U.S. harbors, even the threat of mines is enough to shut down the sea lanes. More alarming is the reality that the shipping industry should not necessarily depend on a federal response to such underwater threats. The Coast Guard plays a crucial role as local federal maritime security coordinators but has no countermine or minesweeping capabilities. That job belongs to the Navy. The Navy has the expertise and equipment to do the job but is currently occupied with military operations of its own.[55] If the threat from mines were to materialize, the real question is whether the Navy's forces could respond quickly enough to neutralize the threat before ships start disappearing under the water.

THE VULNERABILITY OF CRUISE SHIPS TO AERIAL ATTACKS

Before joining Princess Cruises, I served as a regional security officer with the Department of State at the U.S. embassy in Moscow and had a top-level assignment— planning for the security of the new U.S. chancery building. The old U.S. embassy had been razed to the ground and rebuilt in 2000 to counter the hostile intelligence efforts of the Russian intelligence services. In planning defenses for the new embassy, I listened to many experts who had interesting things to say about not only the intelligence threat posed by the Russian Intelligence Services but also about physical threats to the embassy from international and domestic terror groups.

Several Moscow apartment buildings near the U.S. embassy had been bombed in the previous months by Chechen rebels. I remember speaking to one security expert as we stood atop the new U.S. embassy building; he detailed the threat from paragliders that could fly from the towering Russian apartment buildings overlooking the U.S. embassy compound and land where we were standing. Russian paragliders attacking the U.S. embassy? To me, such outlandish terrorist plots did not exist outside the realm of a John le Carré novel. This discussion was less than one year before the events of September 11, 2001.

Presenting the 9/11 Commission Report to the American people, Commission chairman Thomas Kean summarized its findings succinctly in the following manner: "the attacks," he said, "resulted from, above all, a failure of imagination."[56] I agree with this assessment and subscribe to the possibility of the impossible happening. Planning for the defense of cruise ships, one has to think like the terrorists.

I believe that it is just a matter of time before the terrorists, beaten on all fronts, their leadership captured or in retreat, return to tactics that have worked so well for them in the past and that can be readily applied to the maritime environment. Specifically, I believe that they will likely resort to suicidal aerial attacks for their next attack on shipping. Al-Qaeda used this method very successfully against the West to bring down its tallest buildings. Could it not achieve the maritime equivalent with fewer resources on the open ocean, free from any countermeasures or defenses? Planning such an attack on a cruise ship eliminates several problems that the 9/11 hijackers had to prepare for—boarding passes issued to men using false identities, security screening lines that the terrorists must circumvent while trying to smuggle onboard weapons or explosives, and concerns that the plot will be detected onboard by some unknown security measure.

Air attacks have been a preferred tactic for the terrorists before and after the attacks on New York and Washington in 2001. But consider the fact that, even after September 11, our national air defenses in 2002 failed to detect a 15-year-old suicidal al-Qaeda sympathizer who piloted his Cessna 172 over McDill Air Force Base and then crashed it into the Bank of America building in Tampa, Florida. The plane made no attempt to evade radar tracking even though air traffic control received a warning of a potential threat at the time of the plane's takeoff. The time required to access the threat and select a course of action was enough to allow the plane to fly over a U.S. Air Force base and then crash into a public building.[57] If the pilot had selected a more sensitive target or loaded his plane with explosives or a chemical, biological, or radiological element, the results would have been far more serious than the damage caused by an ill-attempted "attack" by a homegrown terrorist.

Unmanned aerial vehicles or "UAV" technology has developed significantly in the past five years; a relatively small UAV can now potentially deliver payloads of from 2 to 20 kilograms across regional distances and can even fly from one continent to another. These UAVs are relatively inexpensive and require little ground support and infrastructure, making them ideal for terrorist applications. UAVs, equipped with altimeters and satellite navigational systems, could be launched across national borders or at sea.[58]

The challenges of defending against UAVs and general aviation threats involve intercepting civil aviation and UAVs over nation-size areas, discriminating between innocent aircraft and those that present a threat, and negating any such threat before the UAV can strike their targets. According to one Customs and Border Protection Intelligence Officer, the threat that terrorists will use civil aviation for an attack is real and is extremely difficult to defend against using current air, radar, and surveillance resources. Countermeasures to defeat such threats are few. The best defenses are to increase those measures already available to civil aviation (e.g., securing airfields, requiring positive identification of aircraft, screening passengers, installing cockpit intrusion protection, and arming pilots). An adequate response may also include keeping ground-fighter aircraft on alert near likely targets.[59]

But the risks of attacks that rely on civil aviation and the difficulty of stopping an attack once the plane is in the air are significant, as demonstrated by the wayward attack on the Bank of America Building in Tampa. If a 15-year-old pilot with limited flight experience can crash into a building, how much harder can it be to target and hit a ship? Most likely, the training needed by suicidal pilots would not reach the level of sophistication needed to fly a modern jetliner, and, depending on the plot, the need to hijack an aircraft would be eliminated. A small plane would simply be loaded with explosives or other payload and take off, possibly from a remote or foreign airfield.

Responses to the September 11 aerial attacks centered primarily on commercial aviation, rather than private aviation. According to testimony by Dennis M. Gormley before the Senate Subcommittee on International Security, Proliferation, and Federal Services on June 11, 2002, small aircraft converted for terrorist purposes could not begin to approach the fuel-carrying capacity of a jumbo jet (60 tons of fuel), but the mere fact that gasoline, mixed with air, releases 15 times as much energy as an equal weight of TNT makes the threat significant.[60] This means that even a relatively small aircraft can do significant damage to a civilian industrial target.

The easiest and most reliable aerial weapon is a plane piloted by someone bent on crashing it into a designated target. UAV technology offers other avenues for the terrorists but requires a greater level of skill. Converting a small airplane or transforming an airplane "kit" into an autonomous weapon—one carrying attack platform—may sound easy on paper, but it is not necessarily easy to accomplish, and technology is helping to bridge the gap. The flight management systems and associated system support needed for successful UAV applications that allow for the transformation of manned aircraft into autonomous UAVs are being sold today by commercial companies. Kit-built airplanes do not require a hardstand to take off but require only a space much shorter than the length of a football field.[61]

Added to the threat posed by manned aerial attacks and UAVs is the threat now posed by cruise missiles, acquired through the black market by terrorists. These missiles can be launched from sea. According to some National Intelligence Estimates, the possibility that a converted container ship could be used as a launch platform for these missiles is something that has the United States worried. Even a large, bulky cruise missile like the Chinese Silkworm could fit easily into a standard 12-meter shipping container equipped with a small internal erector for launching.[62]

There have been no terrorist attacks using UAVs thus far. However, in July 2006, Hezbollah, the Iranian-backed terrorist group based in Lebanon, launched an attack on an Israeli patrol boat using what was first reported to be a drone. The missile struck the Israeli corvette *Ahi Hanit* off the coast of Lebanon, killing four sailors and severely damaging the sophisticated ship. A similar attack narrowly missed another Sa'ar 5 corvette ship but hit a Egyptian-flagged merchant ship, sinking it. On July 31, there were reports of similar firings, though no ships were hit.

What made this attack so significant was that it marked the first time a terrorist organization had attacked a seagoing target with this type of technology. Neither Jerusalem nor Washington had any idea that Hezbollah had such a missile in its arsenal. The Israeli ship had not even activated its missile defense system because intelligence assessments had not identified a threat from such a radar-guided cruise missile.[63] The significance of these unprecedented sea attacks was overshadowed by the daily barrage of Katyusha rockets on the northern border of Israel. But navies around the world woke up to the reality that Hezbollah now possesses a capability never before imagined.

The terrorists, who are adept at adapting to new technology, have already frustrated efforts to track them through use of the Internet and cellular phones. They would be just as adept in using readily available public services, including global positioning systems (GPS) to their advantage.[64] UAVs are an example of an unmanned aerial vehicle; a variety of aircraft exists that are guided by means other than a pilot on board; that is, the aircraft performs its flight functions automatically, using onboard systems or relying on remote control. Aircraft that are guided remotely using communication channels are referred to as remotely piloted aerial vehicles (RPAVs). Cruise missiles are usually referred in international agreements such as the Missile Technology Control Regime (MTCR) in another subcategory of UAVs because they are generally used only once. The MTCR prohibits export of UAVs capable of delivering a payload of more than 500 kilograms (1,102 pounds) and able to fly distances greater than 300 kilometers (186 statute miles).[65]

Unmanned aerial vehicles are cost-effective for terrorist applications because they carry no pilot, have the potential to attack targets that are difficult to reach (e.g., maritime targets), and are capable of inflicting a significant number of deaths, especially if a chemical or biological weapon is used. Additionally, the UAV allows for covertness in acquisition, preparation, launch site, and the possibility of achieving long range and acceptable accuracy with relatively inexpensive and available technology.

The few countermeasures available to defend against low-flying UAVs and the likelihood that an attack will have a strong psychological effect, terrorizing the general public, make this tactic and weapon a good choice to use against maritime targets.[66] George Tenet, former director of the CIA, stated, in his testimony before the Senate Select Committee on Intelligence in February 2004, that "many countries remain interested in developing or acquiring cruise missiles, and aerial vehicles are of growing concern."[67]

Converting airplanes into UAVs is a technically challenging task but is certainly not beyond the capability of terrorists who have expertise in bomb making or who have mastered the flight controls of a 767. Amateur model-airplane builders have built a model airplane that has crossed the Atlantic, demonstrating how easy this technology is to acquire and master. In 2003, a TAM-5 aircraft model weighing 5 kilograms (11 pounds) started in Canada and flew in an automatic mode, landing 39 hours later in Ireland, 3000 kilometers (1,864 miles) away.[68] However, the technology curve is not limited to model airplanes. The possibility that terrorists could construct their own cruise missiles was alarmingly demonstrated by a New Zealand engineer; his project—to design a small cruise missile powered by a pulsejet engine—was a provocative demonstration of just how feasible the job might be. The cruise missile plans were advertised on the Internet. According to the engineer, whose name is Bruce Simpson, Iran had contacted him and offered to invest in the production of such weapons. Simpson was forced to stop his experiment by the New Zealand government, which allegedly had been pressured by the United States. Simpson told the BBC after shutting down his operation that he had proved that "by using off-the-shelf technology in a suburban garage, a terrorist can create a weapon for which there is no effective defense."[69]

This is not to say that Simpson's prototype was actually viable or that parts from commercial sources could be integrated into a reliable system. What Simpson had produced was a "proof-of-concept" cruise missile design capable of incorporating only several kilograms of a potential payload, not effective enough to be used as an explosive weapon but certainly capable of carrying WMD, which would explain Iran's interest. According to most experts on the subject, UAVs are most effective for terrorists' purposes if used with WMD, especially a biological or chemical weapon.

Aerosol is easily dispersed from a UAV over a wide area. An article in the *National Academy of Sciences* in 2003 indicated that an attack using very small amounts of anthrax would have a devastating effect on the population. According to the study, if 900 grams (32 ounces) of anthrax were dropped from a height of 100 meters upwind from a large U.S. city, 1.5 million people would become infected. This might eventually lead to more than 120,000 deaths.[70] Consider the contamination and effect that would ensue if anthrax were sprayed over a cruise ship. It's quite possible that the cruise ship, once it realized that it had been subjected to some type of WMD attack and notified the nearest port of its predicament, would be denied permission to make port to seek emergency care for fear of contamination. But the use of a biological attacks to inflict casualties on a cruise ship would not have the explosive impact that the terrorists desire. A biological (or chemical) attack would not produce images of burning ships with plumes of black smoke that attest to the attack's devastating nature. The nature of a biological attack, in contrast, is difficult to assess quickly, and therefore such an attack would probably not be terrorists' top choice in going after a maritime target.

Terrorists look to create the type of mass fear and destruction that draw media attention—the reaction that a small explosive device mixed with burning gasoline and air could create. Such a spectacular explosion would meet their need for sensationalism quite nicely. Cruise ships, already high on the terrorists list of potential terrorist targets, could provide the kind of isolated and daring choice of target that would create its own media shock value.[71] From a technical standpoint, terrorists would have only the problem of aiming the UAV or suicide plane at the ship near a coastline or on the open ocean. And that is exactly what the terrorists have already been planning.

Captured maritime al-Qaeda terrorist Abdul al-Rahim al-Nashiri, mastermind of the USS *Cole* attack, had planned to crash a kamikaze aircraft into the bridge (the control deck of a ship) of a naval vessel in port Rashid in the United Arab Emirates. After his success in the Gulf of Aden against the *Cole*, al-Nashiri became chief of operations for al-Qaeda on the Arabian peninsula, consulting with bin Laden on the formulation of new maritime attack plots. Al-Nashiri based his operational planning on four pillars: (1) using a zodiak speedboat packed with explosive to ram warships or other ships; (2) using medium-size boats as bombs to be blown up near ships or ports; (3) using airplanes to crash into boats; and (4) using underwater demolition teams to destroy ships with mines and explosives.[72]

Clearly, al-Nashiri had a blueprint for further maritime attacks and was working his way down his list of attack methods. The first two tactics had been used successfully against the USS *Cole* and the *MV Limburg*. Had he not been captured in 2002, it is possible that attack teams under al-Nashiri's direction would have launched assaults against maritime targets under his direction using one of the other four pillars, including perhaps suicidal aircraft strikes.

When al-Nashiri was captured, he was alleged to have had a 180-page dossier of potential targets that included cruise ships leaving from Western ports. One of the potential targets included was the *Queen Mary 2*, during its maiden voyage. The list indicated that, at least for maritime targets, al-Qaeda had shifted from going after hardened targets such as naval vessels to high-value civilian "soft targets," such as cruise ships.[73]

Ironically, at the same time the threat to the *Queen Mary 2* was reported, a deadly plot by two Islamic suicide pilots was thwarted by Saudi intelligence agents. The plot highlighted the terrorists' preference for aerial attacks. The suicide pilots were in the process of loading small attack planes with explosives when

A U.S. Coast Guard officer stands guard as the *Queen Mary 2* makes its way past the Statue of Liberty in New York harbor on its maiden voyage, April 22, 2004. An alleged terrorist plot fueled speculation that the *QM2* was the target of Abdul al-Rahim al-Nashiri, al-Qaeda's "prince of the sea." (USCG photo by PA1 Tom Sperduto)

they were captured. They had intended to crash the planes into a Boeing 777 jet as it was about to take off on Saudi Arabia's King Khalid International Airport, in Riyadh.[74] The plane was loaded with 380 passengers and crew. There were no casualties, as the attack was foiled just before it was to be launched. But, as this example illustrates, al-Qaeda has had a fascination with small airplanes that goes beyond their potential use against maritime targets.

Small plane attacks had been considered by the 9/11 terrorists before they shifted to jetliners. According to an article in the *Toronto Post* in June 2002, Mohamed Atta, al-Qaeda leader of the attack on the twin towers of the World Trade Center, as well as the attack on the Pentagon, told a Department of Agriculture official that he wanted to obtain a $650,000 loan to start a crop-dusting business in Florida. In the loan application, Atta stated that he intended to purchase a six-seat, twin-engine crop duster from which he was planning to remove the seats so that he could load a large chemical tank, leaving room only for the pilot. Clearly, Atta had a suicide use in mind for the stripped-down crop duster before the operation was changed to the plot to attack the Twin Towers by hijacking commercial aircraft.[75]

At the same time this plot was being hatched, plans were already on the al-Qaeda drawing board that included using unmanned airplanes filled with plastic explosives to kill G-8 members at the 2001 summit in Genoa, Italy. In another plot, a British national being held at Guantanamo Bay confessed to being part of an al-Qaeda plot to attack the House of Commons with an unmanned airplane loaded with anthrax.[76] Clearly, the terrorists see the potential for private light aircraft to be used in attacks against high-value targets.

In early 2003, U.S. intelligence agencies became aware of a plot by al-Qaeda to attack the U.S. consulate in Karachi, Pakistan, with aircraft, not jetliners like those used in the September 11 attacks but small commercial aircraft capable of carrying enough explosives (plus fuel) to create damage on a limited but deadly scale. Al-Qaeda was apparently in the late stages of planning for the attack on the consulate as a way to retaliate for Pakistan's commitment to the war on terrorism. The plot was uncovered after the arrest in Karachi of Walid bin Attash and five other men accused of belonging to al-Qaeda. About 300 pounds of explosives and a cache of weapons were seized.[77] Walid bin Attash was a suspected recruiter and a former bodyguard for al-Qaeda leader Osama bin Laden. In addition to allegedly helping prepare al-Qaeda defenses around the Afghan stronghold of Tora Bora, he was also suspected of helping to recruit at least two of the 9/11 hijackers and one of the suicide bombers involved in the USS *Cole* attack. He also belonged to a cell that had planned the bombings in Riyadh, Saudi Arabia, in 2003, that killed 40 people.[78]

The U.S. consulate in Pakistan is no stranger to terrorist attacks. Suicide air plots against the U.S. consulate seemed to be the next logical attack method. It is possible that the Pakistani al-Qaeda contingent was becoming frustrated in its attempts to attack the consulate with conventional car bombs and indiscriminate attacks. In June 2002, a Suzuki pickup packed with explosives was rammed into the outer wall of the U.S. consulate in Karachi. Twelve people were killed and 51 injured, all Pakistanis. The consulate erected cement barricades around the building for extra security. In February 2003, at least two Pakistani policemen protecting the consulate were killed when a gunman opened fire on them.[79] An investigation by ABC News revealed that the Karachi plot may have been connected with a plot by al-Qaeda to hijack a plane at London's Heathrow Airport in 2003 and smash it into a London skyscraper.

The London attack was one of three foiled al-Qaeda hijack plots that may have included targets in the United States, Australia, and Italy. The report noted that nine terrorist plots unearthed since the September 11 attacks have involved the use of hijacked or explosive-laden aircraft, indicating that al-Qaeda has an ongoing commitment to what has worked well for it in the past. A Department of Homeland Security advisory stated: "Such a plot, along with one uncovered last year in which al-Qaeda planned to fly a small plane into a United States warship in the Persian Gulf, demonstrated a 'fixation' on using aircraft in attacks."[80]

Additionally, in view of the ingenuity required to hijack the planes and to conceal bombs and stun guns, although not the stuff of James Bond, it seems that the al-Qaeda planners have already taken into account the need to circumvent new aviation security screening methods.[81]

The Department of Homeland Security was very concerned about the overseas aviation plots and raised the national threat level to orange, the second highest in the five-color alert schema put in place after 9/11, in 2003 because of this and other threat information. Although it could not confirm aviation threats against the United States, its advisory said that al-Qaeda could try to use small planes because they are easily available and require less pilot skill than large jets. The advisory noted that security procedures are less rigorous for small aircraft and with such planes there is no need to control a large group of innocent passengers. These planes, it noted, could be rented with nothing more than a credit card. The warning stated that the DHS had received "reliable information" indicating that al-Qaeda operatives might use experienced, non-Arab pilots to rent three or four light aircraft under the guise of wanting to take flying lessons.[82] Apparently, U.S. intelligence agencies had specific information about terrorist plots that called for the use of small planes.

It is easy to understand how al-Qaeda might be fixated on this tactic. The precedent for aerial suicide attacks had already been established with deadly success by the Japanese kamikaze attacks on U.S. naval warships in the Pacific. During the battle for Okinawa, where this new form of warfare was first used, U.S. ships suffered catastrophic losses inflicted by wave after wave of Japanese suicide dive bombers, flown by young pilots, most of whom were not trained how to land an aircraft but were instructed to aim and crash their explosive-laden aircraft into the U.S. fleet. Today's jihadists may well be tomorrow's kamikazes. Most alarming is that their mission would meet no challenge from the intended victims. During the war in the Pacific, anti-aircraft fire from ships' guns was able to knock out of the sky scores of would-be suicide kamikaze before they could complete their missions.[83] Despite the defensive actions, the suicide attacks caused enormous damage. The jihadists have an advantage in that no one will be shooting at them.

My mission at Princess Cruises, as I understood it, was to put in place defenses against pirates and terrorists who might try to storm up the gangplanks wielding machine guns or climb up the sides of the ship using grappling hooks. That they might fall out of the sky was not considered. That remained in the realm of improbability to most security experts. After several cruises on Princess ships and after discussing the threat of aircraft with the ships' captains, I came to learn that although there are international prohibitions against buzzing ships, planes have always flown over cruise ships, sometimes at close range. One flew over the

Star Princess in the Red Sea while I was on board; the incident caused significant concern because of our proximity to Egypt and Saudi Arabia.

Cruise ships are built with double-bottomed hulls and structurally watertight integrity, but they are not battleships, and certainly they have no armor plating on their decks. Any hole in a cruise ship's hull caused by an explosion would cause considerable damage but probably not enough to sink the ship. However, the greatest threat to any ship, cruise ship or otherwise, is fire. Considering that a small plane attack would probably be the equivalent of a flying gas can filled with high explosives, the resulting destruction to any ship is not hard to imagine. And, just as the World Trade Center buildings were brought down not by the crash of the jets but by the fire that resulted, an aerial attack on a cruise ship would wreak the greatest damage through the fire that follows the initial crash, as devastating as that would be. I am not now suggesting that cruise ships be under the cover of a Combat Air Patrol, but that may become a necessity if maritime terrorism takes its cue from terrorist groups such as Hezbollah, which has already employed cruise missiles against maritime targets. If and when that happens, the cruise industry must have in place a plan for reacting quickly to protect the seagoing public.

MEASURING SUCCESS IN CRUISE SHIP SAFETY

Initially, given the absence of terrorism or piracy, it was difficult to justify the large expenditure of capital for the LRAD, moveable security barriers, quick-closing bulletproof hatches, and new baggage-screening equipment on Princess ships. Although cruise ships were considered desirable terrorist targets, no act of terrorism had been directed against one since the *Achille Lauro* hijacking, and, until the attack on the *Seabourn Spirit,* no pirates attacks on the high seas had been attempted. So, while Princess Cruises made the decision to invest in upgrading its security program, other cruise lines have managed to get by with only the standardization brought about by the ISPS Code and the Maritime Transportation Security Act (MTSA) requirements.

This is not to suggest that the other cruise lines have not planned and implemented their own innovative security initiatives. However, these changes certainly have not been as robust as those mentioned in this discussion, especially with regard to meeting the threat presented by piracy and terrorism. At the very least, maritime threats to cruise ships have remained constant; in the worst case, the risks have increased as the world's economy has begun to shrink and as the international jihad continues unchecked in all regions of the world. The risk to cruise ships from stowaways and criminals has also not subsided. This suggests that even Princess Cruises should not rest on its laurels.

The internal security issues facing the cruise ships are increasing, and there has been growing media and congressional scrutiny of cases involving passengers who mysteriously disappear or who are physically or sexually assaulted. The external threats, however, although they have not been less prevalent, get lost in the discussion of "cruise line security." The discussion does not focus on the possibility of a major catastrophe waiting to happen. As harsh as it may sound, the cruise lines will probably survive the regrettable loss of another passenger gone missing under mysterious circumstances. But what risk are they willing to tolerate with regard to a maritime 9/11? Does even the slightest increase in security budgets fade in importance when measured against the loss of a single human life at sea?

Absent any external security incidents such as a terrorist attack that would grab immediate international headlines, what performance measures can we apply to gauge the effectiveness of maritime security on cruise ships? The attack on the cruise ship *Seabourn Spirit* is a good place to start. It demonstrated how effective a piece of technology—the LRAD—could enable the crew to defend itself against a boarding attempt by heavily armed pirates. It accomplished this feat without transforming the cruise ship into a "man-o-war," thus spoiling the cruise experience. Most of the passengers did not even know that the ship carried such a device. From a business standpoint, such a security measure would be deemed "successful."

What worked for the *Seabourn Spirit*, however, may not work for another cruise ship. What matters is that, in this particular instance, one act of piracy directed against a cruise ship was prevented from becoming an international catastrophe that quite possibly could have claimed innocent lives and threatened the economic survival of the cruise industry. While applauding the actions of the crew and careful to reference the security precautions onboard these cruise ships, the cruise lines were eager to move on. Dwelling on this success was seen as damaging to the business model that they sought to protect.

While the hijacking of the *Achille Lauro* might seem to offer a useful subject of analysis for those charged with improving cruise line security, the hijacking is not useful as a performance measure. While terrorism is still terrorism, the security available on cruise ships in the days of the *Achille Lauro* does not resemble the security model used on cruise ships today. Security models need to be evaluated against the known threats and against what is plausible. Lack of imagination, as we have learned, is a precursor to failure. Almost everyone in the intelligence community in the 1990s knew that al-Qaeda was a threat to the United States, but no one believed that some of its members could hijack four jet aircraft and fly three of them into buildings simultaneously. Given what is known about terrorist intent and capability in the maritime domain, would the cruise lines' current security measures be effective against a *Cole* or *Limburg* attack? Against an underwater attack or even an aerial attack?

The sobering answer is that no single measure or technology would be effective against these types of attack scenarios or any others discussed. No one measure such as the LRAD, Doorgate, or A-Pass should be considered as the premier defense. A realistic security approach is to evaluate specific threats and to avoid regions where terrorists or pirates might try to attack. Because cruise ships are not warships capable of mounting an armed response to hostile threats, the only solution is to use a mix of layered defenses, good intelligence, and information sharing. In the final analysis, information sharing and good intelligence are the most important part of preventing the next terrorist attack on a cruise ship.[84] The cruise lines will have to have the ability to connect the dots as they process the intelligence and threat information they receive and apply it to a robust risk management program.

The best measure by which to judge whether efforts to protect cruise ships should continue is to simply ask this: have the threats gone away? Although some analysts would answer in the affirmative, including some in the cruise industry itself, the answer is obviously that the threat has not in the least diminished. Piracy has increased, and attacks on cruise ships are now on the menu. Therefore, contingency planning must continue to keep pace with the emerging threats and changing tactics. Some would argue that, because of the capture of al-Qaeda's maritime terror strategist, Abdul al-Rahim al-Nashiri, who planned the successful attack on the USS *Cole*, and of Loa'i Mohammad Haj Bakr al-Saqa, the al-Qaeda operative arrested in Turkey after a failed attack on an Israeli cruise ships, the crisis is over.[85] As demonstrated by the attacks in 2001, the threat against the World Trade Center in New York did not disappear after the first unsuccessful bombing attempt in 1993. The enemy came back with a new tactic after conducting its due diligence.

For the terrorists, the struggle is ongoing and will continue as long as there is a will to fight. Apparently, even the strong response of the United States in Iraq and Afghanistan has not lessened their resolve. When there is no terrorist activity, it is fair to assume that terrorists are evaluating the layers of security and defenses around their next targets, whether a cruise ship or something else. More alarming for cruise ships is the fact that the terrorists have already successfully attacked airplanes, buildings, naval ships, merchant ships, passenger ferries, military vehicles, military bases, hotels, trains, buses, and subways. As these targets have been hardened, al-Qaeda and their imitators will surely look for softer targets. Although never off the terrorists target lists, cruise ships may have been moved up to the top by default.

Some will argue that it is the government's or the international community's responsibility to confront and defeat these threats and not the cruise lines'. Such reliance on government is too risky and far too optimistic. The U.S. government, unfortunately, has not shown any particular effectiveness in organizing itself to respond to a maritime crisis, especially one involving the cruise lines. Its focus for the foreseeable future will be on preventing a maritime catastrophe such as the smuggling of WMDs into a port to be detonated or a nightmare scenario involving an explosion of liquid natural gas (LNG) tankers in a large metropolitan port. To that end, the government's resources are spread very thin, and maritime patrols cannot be everywhere at once to protect every ship. High-risk vessels will continue to receive the most attention from maritime security organizations such as the Coast Guard.

Ports have also begun to improve their infrastructure through the application of technology. Most of these upgrades have come through the federal government, which has made available port grant money to upgrade critical port infrastructures. But not all ports benefit from this security umbrella, and certainly it does not stretch outside the United States to foreign ports, where most cruise ships call on a regular basis. The federal government's aim is to protect the U.S. homeland, which leaves Americans traveling to foreign ports vulnerable. Terrorists therefore might simply ask, Why attack a cruise ship in Florida when it will eventually sail up to the terrorist's or pirate's front door in the Middle East, Latin America, or Asia? This certainly proved true in the case of the USS *Cole.*

Although organizations such as the IMO have heaped safety and security regulations upon the maritime industry to help solve some of these problems, they lack any enforcement capability to enforce the implementation of these measures. Those nations and other entities that choose to comply will do so, and those that cannot afford the costs of such measures, especially the ports, will not. Standardization of the security process through the ISPS Code was a necessary step in the evolution of maritime security. But, thus far, the ISPS Code has not stopped piracy, which in many regions has actually increased dramatically. The ISPS Code has also not reduced the level of smuggling activity or the number of stowaways to any measurable degree, especially on merchant ships.

A number of well- or ill-intentioned groups devote themselves to cruise ship victims and their plights. Some have hidden agendas, while others are a voice for change. However, judging only from reports made public through the media, the ISPS Code does not seem to have significantly decreased or diminished the threat to passengers from internal shipboard security incidents. To remedy that, the maritime industry and the cruise lines in particular must embrace an ISPS Code for internal ship security. This is something that the cruise lines will obviously oppose.

To date, there is no international standard for shipboard security force. The ISPS Code specifies only that a maritime company have a company security officer and a shipboard security officer. The use of Gurkhas for shipboard security may impress the casual observer, but they are not required by any international standard, nor are they empowered with any law enforcement authority, international or otherwise. At the end of the day, all impressive titles aside, they are employees of the cruise lines and owe their allegiance to them.

Given the size of today's cruise ships, the number of passengers that they now can carry, and what they potentially represent, is not now the time to shed the old security models and outdated risk mentality and instead devote the resources to protect the seagoing public? If cruise lines hope to see a return on their capital investments in their burgeoning fleets and to tap into the large percentage of the U.S. public who have never been on a cruise but would like to, security will have to be visible, robust, and capable of mitigating not only the old threats but also the new ones. Unfortunately, the cruise lines may not act until a serious incident has occurred, and by then it may be too late. It is difficult to estimate the number of years it will take to rebuild consumer confidence after a successful attack.

Although the public returned to air travel soon after 9/11, it was more out of necessity than by choice. The public has a choice whether to vacation on the sea and is more likely to vote with its feet than its pocketbook if it perceives its safety to be at risk. One thing to keep in mind is that security is only one facet of the cruise industry. It is not the overriding element that drives the direction of the business. Running a cruise line is an extremely complex process, especially because of the environment in which these companies operate. Their primary assets are constantly changing locations and must be fueled and resupplied all over the world on schedule or the buffet tables will be empty and the cocktail lounges will run dry. These elements, after all, are what people take cruises for, not to stand in security lines. Whether security can be made seamless will depend on how well the cruise lines, governments, and the international community organize themselves and bridge the gaps in maritime security.

THE CRUISE VESSEL SECURITY AND SAFETY ACT OF 2009

The U.S. Congress has been looking into the security and safety of the cruise industry for quite some time. From the very beginning, it was clear that one of the biggest problems facing the victims of cruise ship crime and their families was that cruise lines did not take the legal responsibility for investigating crimes on a cruise. It also became apparent that the cruise lines did not take legal responsibility for the shore excursions they sold to cruise passengers. It was not until the events of September 11 and a number of high-profile cases involving the disappearances of cruise ship passengers and sexual assaults that Congress moved closer to approving legislation to protect American lives at sea.

The partial passage (the bill was passed in the House of Representatives on November 17, 2009 and is awaiting Senate approval) of the Cruise Vessel Security and Safety Act of 2009 had many influences, but, in particular, it is the story of one man's personal loss and his campaign to make the cruise industry more transparent to its customer base. Kendall (Ken) Carver was a successful businessman and father before a personal tragedy propelled him to become the voice for cruise victims worldwide. The loss of his daughter Miriam Carver from a Royal Caribbean Cruise ship in 2004 led him into an unimaginable nightmare during which he uncovered a pattern of lies, cover-ups, and corporate dishonesty. Carver hired personal investigators and lawyers to try to uncover what had happened to his daughter. Sometime during the cruise, the 40-year-old Miriam Carver went missing. The ship's steward responsible for making up the young woman's cabin reported this strange circumstance to his supervisor, who told the steward not to worry about it. In the interim, the ship's officers did nothing. At the end of the cruise, the crew, with full corporate knowledge, dutifully packed up her belongings from her stateroom and gave them to charity and then failed to report her missing to either the authorities or family members until five weeks later.

In an attempt to further expand his efforts to bring attention to his daughter's disappearance and countless others like it, Ken Carver formed the nonprofit International Cruise Victims Organization (ICV), which he still leads today. In addition to the first congressional hearing (the Subcommittee on National Security, Emerging Threats and International Relations), held in 2005, members of the ICV, including Ken Carver, participated in three additional hearings, in March 2006, March 2007, and September 2007. They also testified in the U.S. Senate in June 2008. After these hearings, Ken Carver was able to meet with Senator John Kerry (D-MA). Miriam Carver had been a resident of Cambridge, Massachusetts, and Ken Carver was able to tell the senator of his loss and how the cruise line had stymied his efforts to uncover the truth about his daughter's disappearance. Senator Kerry listened intently and was concerned over the lack of oversight in this industry that had been uncovered during the Senate hearings. This led him to introduce the Cruise Vessel Security and Safety Act of 2008. The bill was sponsored in the House by Congresswoman Doris Matsui (D-CA) under H.R. 6408. With the coming national election in November, however, the bill never made it out of committee.

The bill gained momentum in early 2009 when members of the ICV made another trip to Washington, D.C., to meet with congressional members. The bill still had considerable support from its original sponsors, Senator John Kerry and, in the House, Congresswoman Doris Matsui. The bill was re-introduced in the Senate in March 2009, and, after the Cruise Line International Association (CLIA) agreed to a number of compromises, it passed unanimously with the group's endorsement. The bill subsequently passed in the House by a near unanimous vote in November 2009. The bill is expected to easily pass in the Senate in early 2010 and be signed into law by President Obama.

Many have asked why the Cruise Vessel Security and Safety Act was necessary in light of other steps taken to increase security in the maritime industry, such as the MTSA, passed by Congress in 2002, and the ISPS Code agreed to by the IMO in 2002 and implemented in 2004. The answer is quite simple. Those laws and regulations were enacted in direct response to the perceived threat of terrorism to all oceangoing vessels, not just cruise ships, after the events of September 11. While the ISPS Code requires certain stringent security measures and practices on all vessels meeting the Code's requirements, there is very little in the MTSA and ISPS Code that calls for crime prevention or an investigative response on cruise ships or any other vessel. Both measures are designed to prevent external threats such as terrorism from causing harm to ships, but they have been criticized for not preventing internal security incidents, such as sexual assaults or other criminal acts.

The Cruise Vessel Security and Safety Bill of 2009 was structured after a 10-point plan offered by ICV in an agreement with CLIA in July 2007. That plan required background checks for crew members and officers, the presence of an international police force not affiliated with the cruise lines on each cruise ship, training of ship security personnel in crime scene investigation, increased railing height, the placing of additional surveillance cameras on ships and 24/7 monitoring, the wearing of ID bracelets on ships (mandatory for minor children), improvements to prevent people from accidentally falling overboard, improvements to medical care including the use of rape kits, increased cruise line accountability for onshore excursions, and increased overall cruise lines accountability under maritime law. Some but not all of these provisions made it into the bill's final draft.

Included in the legislation are measures to improve ship safety and protect vessel security zones (to thwart pirate attacks). The legislation originally called for cruise ships operating in U.S. waters to install guard rails 54 inches in height. This requirement was one of the provisions that the Cruise Line International Association (CLIA) and the Senate sponsor of the bill, Senator John Kerry, compromised on; their agreement excluded any requirement to raise the height of ship's railings, which eventually cleared the way for CLIA's endorsement and the bill's passage. Other measures in this section of the bill require that entry doors to each passenger stateroom and crew cabin have peep holes, security latches, and time-sensitive key technology. Ship owners are required to implement fire safety codes and install technology to detect when a passenger falls overboard. The legislation enhances the cruise ship's communication and warning capability to enforce the Coast Guard security zones of up to 500 yards while in U.S. ports. This last measure is a reference to LRAD technology, about which the ICV had consulted me; it was not in the original legislation in 2008. At the time of the bill's passage in the Senate Committee on Science, Commerce, and Transportation, in March 2009, piracy along the eastern shores of Somalia and the approaches to the Red Sea was an international problem of immense proportions (it still is). LRAD technology or, more appropriately, acoustic hailing-and-warning devices, had already been installed on all Princess, Cunard, P&O Australia, and Seabourn Yachts. The technology's use had been demonstrated in November 2005 in the successful defense of the *Seabourn Spirit* against Somalia pirates. Congress was convinced of the utility of this technology in protecting ships from the threat of terrorism and piracy; most of the other physical security measures called for in the bill were already standard on most cruise ships.

The next section of the bill provides transparency in reporting cruise ship crime. In its original form, the legislation would have established a reporting structure based on the current voluntary agreement in place among the cruise industry, the FBI, and the Coast Guard. Additionally, each ship would have been required to maintain a log book to record all deaths, missing individuals, alleged crimes, and complaints by passengers or crew member related to theft, sexual harassment, and assault. The log books would have been available electronically to the FBI and the Coast Guard, as well as to any law enforcement officer upon request. Statistical information would have been posted on a public Web site maintained by the Coast Guard. During its negotiations with Senator Kerry, CLIA objected to the "all deaths" provisions," which would have forced the cruise lines to report deaths not related to crime, such as those caused by heart attacks or strokes. Because of the varying standards of cruise ship medical personnel, the bill improves medical and crime scene response by requiring each ship to provide antiretroviral medications and medications used to prevent sexually transmitted diseases after a sexual assault and to have equipment and materials used to perform a medical examination to determine if a victim has been raped. Originally the bill called for a medical practitioner licensed by a U.S. entity to be on board every cruise ship subject to the bill to perform the necessary examinations and to administer treatment; however, CLIA was able to get this provision dropped. Private medical information will be protected, and written authorization will be required for its release. Additionally, all passengers will be given free, immediate, and confidential access to a National Sexual Assault Hotline and the FBI.

The legislation also will improve the training of shipboard security personnel by establishing a program designed by the Coast Guard and the FBI and certified by the administrator of the Maritime Administration to train appropriate crew members in crime scene investigation. Each ship will be required to have one crew member who has been trained and certified under such a program. An attempt to have the U.S. Coast Guard serve as an agent to enforce safety and environmental standards related to waste treatment and disposal and act as public safety officers by securing and collecting evidence of alleged crimes was not included in the final version of the bill. More controversial was the exclusion of the provision to expand the Death on the High Seas Act (DOHSA), which would have greatly increased cruise ship passengers' families' legal rights to bring suit against the cruise lines for deaths occurring on a cruise ship outside the 12-mile territorial limit, as is permitted for relatives of victims of commercial aviation accidents over the oceans. The Death on the High Seas Act was originally passed in 1920 to make it easier for widows of seamen to recover damages for lost future earnings when a seaman's death occurs in international waters. The airline industry has used the law to limit damage awards when a plane crashes more than three miles from the U.S. coast, though a U.S. District Court recently applied a 12-mile limit in the case of TWA Flight 800 (which exploded in the air while off Long Island, New York, in 1996). This section of the act was amended in 2000 to provide for recovery of damages for loss of care, comfort, and companionship by families of victims of aviation accidents occurring at sea. Under the current law, family members are barred from collecting damages if they did not rely on the deceased for income; if they did so rely, they may receive compensation only for economic losses. The International Cruise Victims Organization originally attempted to align DOHSA with the provisions provided for victims of airline accidents occurring outside the 12-mile limit instead of accepting the current limit of three nautical miles set for victims of maritime accidents. In the negotiations between CLIA and Senator Kerry that cleared the way for the bill's passage in the Senate and later in the House, CLIA objected to any provision that would amend the current DOHSA legislation. ICV believes that a person's legal rights should not depend upon whether one perishes in a plane or a boat, and it intends to seek support in Congress to address this deficiency in future legislation.

CLIA's endorsement of the legislation was perhaps its acknowledgement that the time has come for its members to do more to police themselves and to take responsibility for what occurs on their ships. The Cruise Vessel Security and Safety Act of 2009 is unprecedented in that, for the first time, it holds the cruise industry in the United States accountable to the U.S. government for criminal activity. This is something that, for the most part, the cruise lines have tried to avoid as they try to protect the image of their product.

Other governmental measures to protect cruise ships, including efforts to include Sea Marshalls on ships comparable to those who currently are present on flights over the United States have thus far failed at the national level, although a similar measure came very close to passing in the California legislature in 2008 under a program called "Sea Ranger." ICV intends to continue to press for an independent professional law enforcement presence on all cruise ships to guarantee the impartiality of hired security crews on cruise ships and to provide a professional law enforcement response in emergencies. These measures, especially the passage of the Cruise Vessel Security and Safety Act of 2009, while long overdue, help bridge the gaps in cruise ship security only for the moment. Such efforts need to continue to build public awareness; groups like the ICV, with public support, will help to improve the cruise ship experience for all concerned.

BRIDGING THE GAPS IN CRUISE SHIP SECURITY

This book has examined the external and inherent threats facing the security of the cruise lines in port, at sea, and on the ships themselves. Depending on one's point of view, the threats are overwhelming and hopeless or calculable and manageable. I tend to be cautiously optimistic that, in the end, cruise lines will do whatever is necessary to be competitive in the effort to meet the growing public demand for cruise ship vacations. That will include strengthening their security programs, both internally, to protect passengers against sexual predators or other criminal activity, and externally, to protect them from the threat of piracy or terrorism. Changing the security paradigm for cruise lines requires changing the way we think about the threats and applying new methods and technologies to meet those challenges head on. Some but not all cruise lines still believe that cruise ships are at great risk of being overwhelmed by a band of terrorists, as was the *Achille Lauro*. This is the primary threat against which cruise lines are still preparing themselves. While such a threat still exists, the greater threat now comes from pirates, rather than terrorists, and they have entirely different motives. Likewise, today's terrorists are more inclined to try to destroy a cruise ship outright and to kill as many persons on board as possible. Creating mass death and destruction is their one and only goal. Therefore, security specialists must think "outside the box" and in essence try to think like a terrorist to determine how such a person might go about effecting the destruction of a cruise ship, rather than focusing on how to add more layers of security at the gangway to make it more difficult for passengers to board with all their belongings.

Today's threats come from all directions and domains—surface, subsurface, air, space, and even cyberspace. Security for any industry, organization, or government is therefore a risk management process. Risk management is the heart and soul of the International Ship and Port Security (ISPS) Code that was imposed on the maritime community after 9/11. Management must determine which risks it will assume and which risks it will attempt to mitigate through the application of countermeasures.

What form those countermeasures (if any) may take is limited only by imagination and budget. There is a positive side to this, if it makes any difference to the maritime industry. Security improvements, whether mandated by the ISPS Code or undertaken through the initiative of the ship owners, should theoretically produce cost savings in the long run. Many of these security measures have distinct benefits, including reduced delays, faster processing times, fewer losses due to theft, and decreased insurance costs, among others.[86] These savings can be significant and serve to counterbalance the investment and increase in security costs.

In attempting to protect the cruise ships sailing under the Princess flag, I presented many new technologies, programs, and methodologies that have taken the protection of these ships to new levels of security, levels not required by regulation but put in place by choice. These measures illustrate what is possible if management is really willing to confront the threats. All elements of the security program examined in this book either are visible on Princess and other cruise ships or, in the case of the LRAD, have been tested under fire. That is not to suggest that these are the only defenses protecting cruise ships. To be sure, there are other measures, hidden from view, that protect cruise ships on even a grander scale. The seagoing public never sees these measures, nor should it. They complete the risk management process by closing security gaps. While they are not universally applied in all cases and in all situations, the fact that the visible deterrents on these ships are so robust should give the terrorists a moment of pause. A countermeasure is no less effective simply because it is visible. Terrorists, pirates, drug smugglers, and stowaways still must plan on overcoming the visible deterrents before they can move on to the ones they think exist. Just as we are all aware of security requirements as we board aircraft or ships, terrorists and criminals intent on doing harm to either the ship or the airplane must assess the hidden defenses to determine if there are vulnerabilities they can exploit to carry out their plots.

Cruise ships, like other forms of maritime conveyances, have inherent risk, and when the risk level exceeds what the cruise lines feels is acceptable, a risk management decision is required. In cases where cruise ships visit ports that have inherent crime risk, the company can choose to mitigate the risk by employing extra guards, increasing security checks, or warning passengers to be vigilant. All of these measures are bad for the image of the cruise lines, however. An easier solution may be to simply bypass dangerous ports or regions in favor of less vulnerable ports of call. Doing this makes the cruise lines appear to be concerned about the safety of its clientele without their having to reveal in any great detail the security reasons behind changes to their itineraries. This is a good business practice and far outweighs the risks to passengers by continuing to frequent popular ports where the crime situation is out of control. Carnival Cruise Lines showed how easily this can be done when, in 2002, it cancelled calls to the Caribbean port of St. Croix. Carnival did not simply make an impetuous decision but tried to give the St. Croix government warning that it was concerned about the increasing level of violent crime. When the St. Croix government ignored its request to improve security, Carnival simply stopped calling there.[87] Where the threats come from piracy, cruise ships can bypass swaths of ocean known for pirate activity and transit less hostile waters until the situation comes under control, perhaps after efforts by the international community.

The threats facing the cruise lines are great; they include everything from underage drinking by shipboard guests to bombings by terrorists. Each threat requires a response; none can be ignored. As I said in the beginning of this book, to ignore the facts does not make them go away. Eventually they will manifest themselves in one form or another. But, because every threat cannot be mitigated and because the company security officer cannot be everyplace at once, the company must look for force multipliers (anything that provides an edge) and ways to shore up weak defenses.

The appearance of tight security is enough to suggest to the terrorist that a target's defenses are too hardened and that a "softer" target must therefore be sought. Security, after all, strives to maintain the status quo, and a lack of activity is the most effective yardstick by which to measure success. That means that the criminals, pirates, stowaways, or drug smugglers have moved on for greener pastures. When the cruise line's assets remain intact while there are increases in criminal activity in other forms of transportation or industries, then the fair assumption is that, although a ship may have been the criminals', pirates', or terrorists' first choice, they have decided against an attack because of the ship's real or perceived defenses.

Applying countermeasures to vulnerabilities for which the company does not want to assume risk is part of the risk management process. Countermeasures may include any technology, procedure, or operational planning that neutralizes a threat. Some threats can be neutralized by applying good operations security (OPSEC) measures to protect critical parts of the operation and to protect essential elements of information. OPSEC is crucial to military planning, and al-Qaeda understands this. It should be a subtle part of the cruise line's security strategy. A starting point may be an effort by cruise lines to examine their essential elements of information as contained on their internet Web sites or in travel brochures or visible on their ships.

Cruise lines, however, are not about covertness, or secrecy, or hiding what they are doing. Their message is one of fun, entertainment, and adventure. They sail on predictable schedules with regular stops at predictable ports of call. It would be nearly impossible to change all of these operating parameters; thus, cruise lines need to look to other measures to mitigate these vulnerabilities. This will require an even greater commitment from the cruise lines, and technology will certainly play a significant part in helping them bridge security gaps.

Some of the technologies I have helped place on cruise ships led their inventors to win U.S. patents. One of the most vulnerable areas on the ship is its open gangway door. When this vulnerability could not be mitigated by anything available on the market, even though there were initial setbacks, a solution was found that used a common-sense approach and a little American ingenuity. Thus was the Doorgate born out of a need mixed with some ingenuity. In some cases, existing technology, like the LRAD, was taken from the military to provide a defense for cruise ships. Later, the device was found effective against boarders, as well.

The increase to security did not come without a price tag, but there is no price one can put on a human life when there are viable ways to prevent acts of crime, terrorism, or piracy. The world unfortunately has changed for the worse with regard to these threats. The cruise line industry now faces a flood of new security requirements, which have hurt their bottom lines. It is a fundamental assumption of the risk management process that you cannot mitigate every threat, however, and the cruise lines are no exception to this. They would like to guarantee the safety and security of their passengers and crew, but they know they cannot do this.

The surprise and shock of September 11 and the terrorist events that followed have resulted in a flood of new security technologies and services. Security is a growth industry, and we have really only scratched the surface of what is possible to protect the maritime domain. New threats will require new technologies and new ways of approaching problems. But security requirements cannot be imposed on the cruise lines or airlines for security's sake. Policy and standards must meet on some middle ground between the public's need to be safe on aircraft and ships and its ability to enjoy what is left of these forms of transportation.

Security must make sense and not reflect knee-jerk solutions, unless absolutely necessary. The prohibition of liquids in carryon luggage on aircraft is a perfect example. When the threat posed by the so-called shoe bomber exposed the danger of allowing liquids on board aircraft, the government quickly stepped in and prevented liquids, mouthwash, toothpaste, soda cans, and lattes from passing beyond the Transportation Security Administration (TSA) screening points. This is in contrast to what the Greek government did. A year before TSA instituted its prohibition on liquids, I traveled to Greece ahead of the *Queen Mary 2*'s arrival for the 2004 Summer Olympics and was impressed by the security screeners at the Athens Airport, who required passengers to drink from bottles of water, coffee, or soda that they intended to bring on the plane. That seemed like a fairly easy way to determine whether the container actually contained gasoline or some other flammable liquid. Given that there is no viable technology that quickly and reliably tests the liquids that passengers pack in their carry-on baggage, however, the sensible solution is simply to prohibit them.

This leads us to the final question: what next? What will be the next piece of the carry-on ensemble that presents a threat to airplanes or cruise ships? Perhaps new threats will emerge from cellular phones or from laptop computers. When this happens, how will the airlines and cruise lines react? Will these items be prohibited, as well? Are we facing a time when the passenger cabin will be a sterile environment and we lose what little dignity we have left when traveling on these technological marvels? Will technology lead by example through the initiative of the private sector or will it simply be regulated by governments and international organizations, which is the current preference? Will those engaged in commerce in the maritime domain take the problem in hand, or will they continue to rely on risk management until sooner or later they are forced by an unimaginable catastrophe to confront the issue? In considering the answer to these and other security questions, I like to remember back to when I served as an Officer of the Deck on one on the largest warships in the U.S. Navy. There was one piece of advice, written into the Captain's Night Orders, that I was required to read and sign every night before assuming the watch. It said simply: "The price of safety at sea is eternal vigilance."

So what, then, is my position on cruising today? Considering the foregoing discussion, would I take a cruise today? I cruised a few times before assuming the role as lead security executive for a major cruise line. I spent years at sea on a ship in the U.S. Navy. Compared to those seagoing days, taking a cruise vacation is a like a dream. However, as a security director, I became involved in the complex security planning that is necessary to make these cruise vacations appear seamless to vacationers. I became aware of the fine line between protecting passengers and imposing onerous security requirements that these vessels must walk and the real potential for danger that exists both on the ship and off.

There is a part of the human soul that is nurtured by being on a cruise ship out on the open ocean. Taking a cruise ship vacation is a great way to experience the peace found only at sea. Even so, I have never lost my awareness of the risk that comes along with cruise ship vacations. If I were to take my family on a cruise, I would apply some simple risk management principles and realize that no vacation, especially a cruise, is risk-free. I would understand that traveling on a cruise ship is not without inherent risks, not the least of which is that one is on a ship on the high seas along with enough people to populate a small town with good and bad elements. Prospective passengers need to trust the cruise ship to provide them with a safe environment in which to enjoy their cruise; passengers really do not want to worry about their security while on vacation.

Cruise ships should never suggest that theirs is a risk-free environment. The passenger must not assume that the boundaries of the ship provide absolute protection and must understand that the protections that do exist do not extend to shore activities. When the international community, governments, flag states, ports, cruise lines, and cruise ships operate in unison to protect the seagoing public, then all the passenger will really need to take along on a cruise vacation is a healthy dose of common sense.

As the director of security at Princess, I was required to travel frequently on Princess ships to conduct port security preparations and provide additional security support on certain itineraries. Knowing what goes on behind the scenes on these ships, I appreciated the planning and hard work of all the dedicated security and other professionals, who, despite all appearances, have very difficult jobs. Most if not all persons employed by the cruise lines are hardworking people who are just trying to make a living the best way they know how.

From the employees who work exceedingly long hours in the ship's galleys, restaurants, laundries, and engine rooms or standing watch on the bridge, to the corporate executives who do the cruise line's advance planning, cruise ship employees operate as a team. Unlike hotels, cruise ships are constantly on the move, stretching the supply chain to the limits. I have always been impressed by how ships are able to keep to tight sailing schedules as they cross oceans, making port day after day and taking on stores and passengers, all the while providing their guests with first class accommodations and services.

That said, remembering what a cruise ship is all about is the best way to understand its strengths and weaknesses. Unlike an airplane, which takes you to a vacation, being on a cruise ship is the vacation, and the ships deliver; that much is true. And, as the song goes, it's the journey, not the destination, that counts.

NOTES

FOREWORD

1. Rep. Doris Matsui Continues Fight to Make Cruise Vacations Safe for American Families. March 17, 2009, http://www.matsui.house.gov/index.php?option=com_content&task=view&id=1569&Itemid=98.

2. Kerry Demands Cruise Ship Safety for Passengers. June 19, 2008, http://kerry.senate.gov/cfm/record.cfm?id=299426.

CHAPTER 1

1. Sam Howe Verhovek, "2 Disasters Lead a Cruise Ship into 2 Nights of Vigils and Prayer," *New York Times,* September 15, 2001, http://query.nytimes.com/gst/fullpage.html?res=9C07EFD61E38 F936A2575AC0A9679C8B63.

2. "Cruise Ship Damaged, Flooded by 70-Foot Wave During Storm," WashingtonPost.com, April 18, 2005, http://www.washingtonpost.com/wp-dyn/articles/A61873-2005Apr18.html.

3. Gina Pace, "Chile Bus Crash: Was Driver Dozing?" CBS News.com, March 23, 2006, http://www.cbsnews.com/stories/2006/03/22/world/main1431963.shtml.

4. "Fire Breaks Out Aboard Cruise Ship; One Dead," CNN.com, March 23, 2006, http://www.cnn.com/2006/US/03/23/ship.fire/index.html.

5. "Heeling Accident on M/V Crown Princess Atlantic Ocean off Port Canaveral, Florida, July 18, 2006," National Transportation Safety Board Accident Report, 08/01, http://www.ntsb.gov/publictn/2008/MAR0801.pdf.

6. Laura Bly, "Cruise Ship's Sinking Puts Safety in Focus," USAToday.com, April 13, 2007, http://www.usatoday.com/travel/news/2007-04-12-cruise-ship-safety_N.htm.

7. "Cruise Ship Goes Down off Antarctica," Associated Press.com, November 24, 2007, http://www.msnbc.msn.com/id/21935099/.

8. "Missing Honeymoon Groom, George Smith's Family Calls for CEO of Carnival to Resign," Sacred Monkeys, March 17, 2006, http://missingexploited.com/2006/03/16/missing-honeymoon-groom-george-smiths-family-calls-for-ceo-of-carnival-cruise-to-resign/. Carnival president Bob Dickinson blamed the media for making the public believe there is an increase in crime on board cruise ships. He called Smith's disappearance a "non-issue" that was hyped by cable news. "It's a non-event," he said. "It's more entertainment than anything else. The facts of the case, the story of a husband and wife, the bride and groom. It's just so absolutely bizarre."

9. Ibid.

10. "Florida Caribbean Cruise Association, Cruise Industry Overview," 2005, http://www. f-cca.com/downloads/overview-2005.pdf. "Of the total US population that is 25 years or older, with household earnings of $40,000+, 34% has ever taken a cruise, 17% has cruised in the past three years. Of all cruisers, 51% took their last cruise within the last three years. Cruisers spend approximately $1,632 per person, for their cruise and onboard expenses. It is estimated that 16% of the total US population has cruised ever and 7 to 8% have done so within the last three years. Cruisers average age is 50 with a household income of $99,000. 65% are college graduates and 24% are post-graduates. 83% are married, 58% work full-time, and 93% are white/Caucasian." See also William J. Holstein, "Casting Off the Myths of Cruises," *New York Times,* http://travel.nytimes. com/2007/0721/business/21interview.html.

11. Ibid.

12. "Congress Directs Cruise Line International Association to Work with International Cruise Victims (ICV) to Improve Safety and Assist Victims," press release, April 30, 2007, http:// internationalcruisevictims.activeboard.com/index.spark?aBID=102842&p=3&topicID=114940 29. "Congressman Christopher Shays (R-CT) says in an e-mail, I am working on a bipartisan legislative proposal to improve disclosure on crimes on cruise ships in order to increase the transparency of the industry. Passengers have the right to know the safety records of the vessels they board."

13. "Shays, Souder Hold Hearing on Cruise Line," U.S. House of Representatives, Subcommittee on National Security, Emerging Threats, and International Relations, December 13, 2005, http://www.house.gov/shays/news/2005/december/deccruise.htm.

14. In July 2007 a meeting was initiated by the ICV and the FBI, held at FBI headquarters, to review the concerns of March 2006 between the FBI, U.S. Coast Guard, and CLIA and to discuss whether or not the FBI had the authority to enter into an agreement that was generated by CLIA, which represents foreign-owned corporations, without having this agreement reviewed and authorized by the Attorney General. The FBI essentially worked out details to support CLIA's own "Zero Tolerance Policy for Crimes Committed Onboard Ships" issued in 1999. ICV questioned the timing of the agreement, issued immediately before the announced Congressional hearings in March 2007 even though negotiations on the agreement had been ongoing for approximately seven months previous. A key element was a standardized reporting mechanism for reporting shipboard crimes. Deputy Assistant Director Salvador Hernandez (of the FBI) stated that he did not see any benefit to having cruise victims or their families participate in the discussions, http:// www.internationalcruisevictims.org/files/Total-testimoney1a-1-with_titles.pd.

15. Testimony of Kendall Carver, President and CEO of the International Cruise Victims Association (ICV), before the House Subcommittee on Coast Guard and Maritime Transportation, September 19, 2006.

16. Jake Tapper and Mathew Jaffe, "Scandal on the High Seas? Congress Holds Hearings on Cruise Ship Safety amid Assault Allegations," ABC News, September 19, 2007, http://abcnews. go.com/US/Story ?id=3627042&page=1.

17. Ibid.

18. Ibid.

19. Brian Michael Jenkins, James O. Ellis III, et al., "Terrorism: What's Coming: The Mutating Threat," Memorial Institute for the Prevention of Terrorism (MIPT), 2007, p. 7. http://www.ter rorisminfo.mipt.org/pdf/Terrorism-Whats-Coming-The-Mutating-Threat.pdf.

The Memorial Institute for the Prevention of Terrorism (MIPT) is a nonprofit, nationally recognized think tank creating state-of-the-art knowledge bases and sharing information on terrorism. For more on MIPT, please visit www.mipt.org.

CHAPTER 2

1. "Editorial: What Security," *Lloyd's List,* May 2, 2003, p. 7. "The International Ship and Port Security Code may be up for implementation, and at least one element in the 'axis of evil' has been

disposed of. But, according to data from the ICC International Maritime Bureau, this new focus on security has failed to register with those who like to attack shipping for a living. The first three months of the year have seen 103 attacks on ships, up from 87 in 2002. The usual suspects head the list, with southeast Asian waters, the wild coast of Somalia and lawless offshore Nigeria remaining as dangerous as ever."

2. "Vigilance is a ship's best defense against invaders," *Lloyd's List,* October 13, 2005 (No. 59018), p. 6.

3. International Chamber of Commerce, Commercial Crime Services, "Piracy Doubles in First Six Months of 2009," July 15, 2009, http://www.icc-ccs.org/index.php?option=com_content& view=article&id=362:piracy-doubles-in-first-six-months-of-2009&catid=60:news&Itemid=51.

4. Allen Cowell, "Pirates Attack Maersk Alabama Again," *New York Times,* November 18, 2009, http://www.nytimes.com/2009/11/19/world/africa/19pirates.html.

5. International Chamber of Commerce, Commercial Crime Services, "Piracy Doubles in First Six Months of 2009."

6. "Keep Away from Somalia," *Tradewinds* 16, no. 45 (November 11, 2005), p. 42. "The 300-passenger luxury cruise ship Seabourn Spirit ignored warnings about traveling too close to the Somali coast before it was attacked and fired on by bazooka-wielding pirates. Security experts now believe avoiding the area altogether may be the only way to escape pirates operating in the region." See also "Seabourn Heroes Get Queen's Honors," *Cruise Critic,* June 23, 2007, http://www.cruise critic.com/news/news.cfm?ID=2071. "In a lawsuit filed against Seabourn Yachts, Michael Groves, the Ship Security Officer on the Spirit, stated that the ship, en route from Egypt to Kenya, was in 'blatant violation' of instructions by government entities, including the U.K.'s Department for Transport) to stay at least 170 miles off the coast of Somalia because of the threat of piracy attacks."

7. Mary Braid and Simon Calder, "Pirates Fire at Luxury Liner Seabourn Spirit—Terrified British Passengers Cower as Rocket-Propelled Grenades and Bullets Hit £20,000-a-Trip Ship," *The Independent* (UK), November 6, 2005, http://www.independent.co.uk/news/world/africa/pirates-fire-at-luxury-liner-514175.html.

8. Ibid.

9. Colin Fernandez, "The Sailor's Hosepipe That Sent These Pirates Packing," *The Daily Mail,* May 17, 2007, http://www.dailymail.co.uk/pages/live/articles/news/news.html?in_article_id=455343&in_page_id=1770.

10. Ibid.

11. See photo of RPG lodged in *Seabourn Spirit*'s hull on page 23.

12. Personal correspondence dated February 2006, received from anonymous source at American Technology Corporation, quoting from the report of the commanding officer of the USS *Gonzales* on the attack on the *Seabourn Spirit.*

13. Interview by author with anonymous former Princess Cruise employee, October 18, 2007, Riverside, California.

14. "Seabourn Heroes Get Queen's Honors," *Cruise Critic,* June 23, 2007, http://www.cruise critic.com/news/news.cfm?ID=2071.

15. Interview by author of LRAD sales personnel at the ASIS Security Product Exhibition, September 23–24, 2007; see also www.atcsd.com.

16. "Cruise Ships Vulnerable to Attacks," Associated Press, November 9, 2005, http://www.military.com/NewsContent/0,13319,80133,00.html.

17. Ibid.

18. "Accused Somali Pirate to Be Tried as Adult," Associated Press, April 21, 2009, http://www.msnbc.msn.com/id/30313755/.

19. Oliver Smith, "Pirates Attack Cruise Ship Off Somali Coast," Telegraph.co.uk., December 1, 2008, http://www.telegraph.co.uk/travel/cruises/3538744/Pirates-attack-cruise-ship-off-Somali-coast.html.

20. "Kiwi Slams Security in Pirate Attack," TVNZ, May 3, 2009, http://tvnz.co.nz/national-news/kiwi-slams-security-in-pirate-attack-2698696.

21. John Hooper, "Cruise Ship Fends Off Pirate Attack with Gunfire," *The Guardian*, April 26, 2009, www.guardian.co.uk/world/2009/apr/26/italian-cruise-ship-pirates.

22. Ibid.

23. Unfortunately, just as some of the pirate headlines quieted down, the cruise lines faced another crises with an outbreak of the H1N1 virus (swine flu) in Mexico, which forced the cruise lines to cancel multiple port calls in Mexico in April 2009.

24. John McLaughlin, "Vago Calls for Debate over Arming Cruiseships," *Lloyd's List*, April 27, 2009, abstract found online at http://www.eturbonews.com/8999/vago-calls-debate-over-arming-cruise-ships.

25. "Maersk Alabama Captain Testifies on Arming Crews against Pirates," Marinelog.com, May 2009, http://www.marinelog.com/DOCS/NEWSMMIX/2009may00040.html.

26. Ibid.

27. Ibid.

28. "Did the USSR Give Birth to Somali Pirates?" *Fairplay Shipping News*, May 20, 2009, http://blog.usni.org/?p=2872.

29. Debra Klein, "Practical Traveler: After Attack, Cruise Ships Rethink Security," *New York Times*, December 4, 2005, http://travel2.nytimes.com/2005/12/04/travel/04prac.html?_r=1&oref=slogin.

30. This fact was confirmed by the special ordnance team of the USS *Gonzalez*, which responded to the ship the following day and found the warhead's spent rocket motor lodged in the hull.

31. "Seabourn Siege Called 'Act of Terrorism,'" *Tradewinds* 16, no. 45 (November 11, 2005), p. 42. "Diplomatic sources characterize the attack on the cruise ship Seabourn Spirit off Somalia over the weekend as a terrorist incident. UK officers union Numast says two different sources have pointed to it being a terrorist attack, with one having 'pretty solid evidence' to support the claim. Diplomatic sources in the region have told the union that fundamentalist militia have infiltrated into Somalia from the Middle East and have established a base near a village called Meca, with the capability to track ship movements and monitor communications between vessels."

32. Giles Tremlett, "Somali Pirates Guided by London Intelligence Team, Report Says," Guardian.co.uk., May 11, 2009, http://www.guardian.co.uk/world/2009/may/11/somali-pirates-london-intelligence.

33. "Al Qaeda Urges Somalis to Attack Ships," CBSNews.com, April 16, 2009, http://www.cbsnews.com/blogs/2009/04/16/world/worldwatch/entry4949488.shtml.

34. Ibid.

35. "Gulf of Aden Pirates Foiled by Joint Naval Forces," *Lloyd's List*, December 17, 2004 (No. 58811), p. 3.

36. "Navy Ships Urged to Get Involved as Somali Attacks Continue," *Crime International* 23, no. 6 (November 2005), p. 2.

37. "Italian Ship Escapes Pirates Off Somalia," *Lloyd's List*, July 25, 2005 (No. 58961), p. 12. See also "Italy Throws Down the Gauntlet to Indian Ocean Pirates as Warship Is Dispatched," *Lloyd's List*, August 1, 2005 (No. 58966), p. 1.

38. "Somali Pirates Free UN Aid Ship," *Lloyd's List*, October 4, 2005 (No. 59011), p. 3. See also "Pirates Make Raid Using Food-Aid Ship," *Tradewinds* 16, no. 39 (September 30, 2005), p. 46, and "Somali Aid Cargo Intact," *Lloyd's List*, August 22, 2005 (No. 58981), p. 3.

39. Sugunta West, "Piracy Revenues Financing Warlords in Somali Insurgency—Terrorism Focus," Jamestown Foundation 4, no. 42 (December 9, 2007), http://www.jamestown.org/single/?no_cache=1&tx_ttnews%5Btt_news%5D=4618.

40. Ibid.

41. Ibid.

42. Ibid.

43. Kristoffer A. Garin, " Troubled Waters," Concierge.com, January 2006, http://www.concierge.com/cntraveler/articles/10156.

44. Simon Elegant and Kuala Sepetang, "Dire Straits," *Time*, November 29, 2004, http://www.time.com/time/magazine/article/0,9171,832306,00.html.

45. "Piracy Attacks on Chemical Tankers Bring Fears of Terrorism Dry Runs," *Lloyd's List*, March 31, 2003, p. 7. "Attacks on three chemical tankers in the Malacca Strait by pirates armed with automatic weapons in the last month have raised fears of maritime terrorism in South East Asia. While the attacks—in which two chemical tankers, the Suhailaand the Oriental Salvia, were fired upon with automatic weapons, and another, the Dewi Madrim, hijacked for an hour—have been classed as piracy attacks they have raised security concerns."

46. Michael Richardson, "A Time Bomb for Global Trade," Institute of Southeast Asian Studies Publications, 2004 pg 7, http://www.southchinasea.org/docs/Richardson,%20Time%20Bomb%20for%20Global%20Trade-ISEAS.pdf,

47. Catherine Zara Raymond, "Maritime Terrorism in Southeast Asia—Potential Scenarios," *Terrorism Monitor* 4, no. 7 (April 6, 2006).

48. Ibid.

49. Nazery Khalid, "Cruising for Bruising?—An Assessment of the Perceived Security Threat against Passenger Vessels along the Straits of Malacca," paper presented at the SEA-PAX Asia Conference at Hong Kong Convention & Exhibition Center, Wanchai, Hong Kong, February 28–March 1, 2006.

50. Raymond, "Maritime Terrorism in Southeast Asia—Potential Scenarios."

51. Khalid, "Cruising for Bruising?"

52. Ibid.

53. Simon Elegant, "The Return of Abu Sayyaf," *Time*, August 23, 2004, http://www.time.com/time/magazine/article/0,9171,501040830-686107,00.html.

54. Ibid.

55. Akiva J. Lorenz, "The Threat of Maritime Terrorism to Israel," September 24, 2007, www.maritimeterrorism.com, p.3; http://www.maritimeterrorism.com/wp-content/uploads/2008/01/the-threat-of-maritime-terrorism-to-israel1.pdf.

56. Ibid., p. 7. See also "PLO Figure George Habash Dies at 81; Founded Faction Known for Hijackings," *Washington Post*, January 27, 2008, http://www.Washingtonpost.com/wp-dyn/content/article/2008/01/26/AR2008012602355.html.

57. "Islamic Terrorism Timeline," Prophet of Doom, October 24, 2006, http://www.prophetofdoom.net/Islamic_Terrorism_Timeline_1973.Islam.

58. "The Yom Kippur War of 1973," http://www.historylearningsite.co.uk/yom_kippur_war_of_1973.htm.

59. Lorenz, "The Threat of Maritime Terrorism to Israel," p. 8.

60. Ibid., p. 9.

61. Ibid.

62. Ibid., p. 10.

63. "Bodies of Coastal Road Massacre Perpetrators to Be Handed Over," Israel Matzav, July 2, 2008, http://israelmatzav.blogspot.com/2008/07/bodies-of-coastal-road-massacre.html. "Israel has agreed to turn over to Hezbollah in exchange for the bodies of kidnapped IDF soldiers Ehud Goldwasser and Eldad Regev, the bodies of the perpetrators of one of the worst terror attacks in Israel's history: The Coastal Road Attack. The bodies of two Palestinians who hijacked an Israeli bus in Tel Aviv in 1978 will be handed over in the prisoner swap with Hezbollah, the Fatah-affiliated Dalal Al-Mughrabi Brigades announced on Tuesday. Dalal Al-Mughrabi was killed in the ensuing battle with Israeli troops on March 11, 1978, and Yehyah Muhammad Skaf died later in an Israeli jail. The Brigades said in a statement that the bodies had been kept in a mortuary for the past 30 years."

64. "Incitement to Violence against Israel by the Leadership of the Palestinian Authority," Israel Ministry of Foreign Affairs, November 27, 1996, http://www.mfa.gov.il/MFA/Archive/Peace+Process/1996/INCITEMENT%20TO%20VIOLENCE%20AGAINST%20ISRAEL%20BY%20LEADERSHI.

65. Lorenz, "The Threat of Maritime Terrorism to Israel," p. 11.

66. Ibid., p. 14.

67. James O. Ellis III, ed., "Terrorism: What's Coming: The Mutating Threat," Memorial Institute for the Prevention of Terrorism, 2007, p. 41, http://www.terrorisminfo.mipt.org/pdf/Terrorism-Whats-Coming-The-Mutating-Threat.pdf. "The 'new terrorism' has displayed other distinctive characteristics as well. Suicide bombings have become the emblematic form of terrorist attack. The modern suicide bombing, 'an operational method in which the very act of the attack is dependent upon the death of the perpetrator,' is a tactic first used in Lebanon in 1982–83, then adopted by a long list of terrorist organizations in other parts of the world. Mass murder is the other key attribute of Religious Wave terrorism. The religiously-driven terrorists of the current era are distinguished from their more secular predecessors in their desire to kill large numbers of people on an indiscriminate basis; the 9/11 attacks and later operations carried out by Al Qaeda-linked groups in Bali, Casablanca, Madrid, London and other locales exemplify the point."

68. Jeffrey D. Simon, "The Implications of the Achille Lauro Hijacking for the Maritime Community," Rand/P-7250, August 1986, p. 1, http://www.rand.org/pubs/papers/2008/P7250.pdf.

69. "The Achille Lauro Incident," The Eighties Club, undated, http://eightiesclub.tripod.com/id301.htm.

70. Ibid.

71. "Willem Ruys- Achille Lauro," undated, http://www.simplonpc.co.uk/WillemRuysPCs.html; "Chandris pulled out after the much-publicized hijacking in October 1985 affected passenger numbers. Lauro struggled on until 1987, when it was bought by the Swiss-based Mediterranean Shipping Company, who rebranded the company as StarLauro Cruises. This venerable ship served with them until November 1994, when she caught fire on a Genoa-South Africa cruise. The ship was abandoned, and sank two days later."

72. Sean K. Anderson and Peter N. Spagnolo, "Case Study: The Achille Lauro Hijacking," undated, http://www.isu.edu/~andesean/AchilleLauroCaseStudy.htm.

73. Simon, "The Implications of the Achille Lauro Hijacking for the Maritime Community," p. 8.

74. Anderson and Spagnolo, "Case Study: The Achille Lauro Hijacking," citing John Tagliabue, "Italians Identify 16 in Hijacking of Ship," New York Times, November 20, 1985, p. A3.

75. Simon, "The Implications of the Achille Lauro Hijacking for the Maritime Community," p. 9.

76. "A Hijack on the High Seas, Part One," BBC online, May 7, 2002, http://www.bbc.co.uk/dna/h2g2/A730900/.

77. Anderson and Spagnolo, "Case Study: The Achille Lauro Hijacking."

78. Ibid.

79. Ibid.

80. BBC, "A Hijack on the High Seas, Part Two," http://www.bbc.co.uk/dna/h2g2/alabaster/A731701.

81. Anderson and Spagnolo, "Case Study: The Achille Lauro Hijacking."

82. Ibid.

83. The Eighties Club, "The Achille Lauro Incident."

84. Definition of the CNN effect, http://www.answers.com/topic/cnn-effect-1.

85. Simon, "The Implications of the Achille Lauro Hijacking for the Maritime Community," p. 10.

86. "Israeli Cruise Attack Plot Exposed: Turks Charge Suspected Al Qaeda Militant for Terror Plan," CBS News, August 11, 2005, http://www.cbsnews.com/stories/2005/08/11/terror/main771152.shtml.

87. Michael K. Bohn, The Achille Lauro Hijacking: Lessons in the Politics and Prejudice of Terrorism (Dulles, VA: Brassey's INC, 2004), pp. 148–152.

88. Simon, "The Implications of the Achille Lauro Hijacking for the Maritime Community," p. 3.

89. Ammonium nitrate-fuel oil (ANFO) blasting agents represent the largest industrial explosive manufactured (in terms of quantity) in the United States. This product is used primarily in mining and quarrying operations. The components are generally mixed at or near the point of use for safety reasons. The mixed product is relatively safe and easily handled and can be poured into drill holes in the mass or object to be blasted. http://www.globalsecurity.org/military/systems/munitions/explosives-anfo.htm.

90. Lorenz, "The Threat of Maritime Terrorism to Israel," pp. 23–24.

91. Lorenz, "The Threat of Maritime Terrorism to Israel," http://www.maritimeterrorism.com/wp-content/uploads/2008/01/the-threat-of-maritime-terrorism-to-israel1.pdf.

92. "Terrorist Alert Diverts More Israeli Cruiseships Away from Turkey," *Lloyd's List,* August 9, 2005 (No. 58972), p. 1.

93. Dominik Cziesche, Juergen Dahlkamp, et al., "Aladdin of the Black Forest," Spiegel Online, August 15, 2005, http://www.spiegel.de/international/spiegel/0,1518,371214,00.html.

94. Ibid.

95. In 2007, former CIA director George Tenet wrote in his book *At the Center of the Storm* (New York: HarpersCollins, 2007) that "a source we were jointly running with a Middle Eastern country went to see his foreign handler and basically told him something big was about to go down" (p. 160). This is very likely a reference to Sakra, since no one else comes close to matching the description of telling a Middle Eastern government about the 9/11 attacks one day in advance, not to mention working as an informant for the CIA at the same time. Tenet's revelation strongly supports the notion that Sakra in fact accepted the CIA's offers in 2000 to work for them and that he had been working with the CIA and other intelligence agencies at least through 9/11.

96. Karl Vick, "A Bomb-Builder, 'Out of the Shadows'—Syrian Linked to Al Qaeda Plots Describes Plan to Attack Cruise Ship in Turkey," *Washington Post,* February 20, 2006, http://www.washingtonpost.com/wp-dyn/content/article/2006/02/19/AR2006021901336_pf.html.

97. Ibid.

98. Lorenz, "The Threat of Maritime Terrorism to Israel," pp. 23–24.

99. Vick, "A Bomb-Builder, 'Out of the Shadows.' "

100. Ibid.

101. "Terror Suspect: 'I Was Going to Attack Israeli Ships,'" *USA Today,* August 11, 2005, http://www.usatoday.com/news/world/2005-08-11-turkey-terror_x.htm.

102. "Cruise Ship in Terrorists' Sights Despite Turkey Arrests," *Lloyd's List,* August 16, 2005 (No. 58977), p. 1.

103. Richard Miniter, "Losing Bin Laden," (Washington, DC: Regnery, 2003), p. 219.

104. Al-Qaeda eventually tried three more times to attack the U.S. Embassy in Sana'a. The most recent deadly attack took place September 17, 2008, when 16 people were killed, including six terrorists, four civilians, and six Yemeni soldiers guarding the embassy in a rocket and suicide car bomb attack at the gates of the U.S. Embassy. Among the dead civilians was an 18-year-old American girl who was standing in the visa line with her parents. The weapons used were similar to the cache of ammunition and explosives found in the al-Qaeda safe house in the summer of 2002. "Yemen Attack Brings Fears of More Terror," MSNBC, September 17, 2008, http://www.msnbc.msn.com/id/26751142/.

105. Akiva J. Lorenz, "Al-Qaeda's Maritime Threat," Maritime Terrorism Research Center, April 15, 2007, pp. 9–10, http://www.maritimeterrorism.com/wp-content/uploads/2008/01/al-qaedas-maritime-threat1.pdf.

106. Miniter, "Losing Bin Laden," pp. 217–218.

107. Lorenz, "Al-Qaeda's Maritime Threat," pp. 22–23.

108. "USS Cole Attack 'Plotter' Charged," BBC, June 30, 2008, http://news.bbc.co.uk/2/hi/americas/7482385.stm.

109. Commanding Officer's Report-USS Firebolt, Subj: Actions of the USS Thunderbolt Crew on USS Firebolt during the 24 April 2004 Attacks on Iraqi Oil Platforms in the Northern

Arabian Gulf, 16 July 2004, SER 045, Declassified by CNO (NO902) OPNAVINST 5513.16 Series, DATE: 14 Nov 2005, http://www.history.navy.mil/shiphist/f/pc-10/2004.pdf.

110. "Jordanian Claims Suicide Attacks on Iraqi Terminal-Statement Issued in al-Zarqawi's name," MSNBC, April 26, 2004, http://www.msnbc.msn.com/id/4829643/.

111. "Countering Maritime Terror, U.S. Thwarts Attacks, Builds Up Foreign Navies: Resistance Encountered in Critical Malacca Straits Region Foreign Crews to Be Investigated for Terror," June 17, 2004, JINSA Jewish Institute for National Security Affairs, http://www.jinsa.org/articles/articles.html/function/view/categoryid/1701/documentid/2567/history/3,2360,655,1701,2567.

112. Lorenz, "The Threat of Maritime Terrorism to Israel," p. 23.

113. Department of Homeland Security, Customs and Border Protection, *Frontline*, Spring 2008, p. 20.

114. Hilary Howard and Nick Kaye, "The Cruise Issue; Where Cruisers Are Headed," *New York Times*, February 17, 2008, http://query.nytimes.com/gst/fullpage.html?res=9F07E3D91F39F934A25751C0A96E9C8B63.

115. Elizabeth White, "FARC Hostages Return to America," Associated Press, July 3, 2008, http://www.nysun.com/national/farc-hostages-return-to-america/81248/. "Three American hostages rescued from leftist guerrillas at Colombia were back in America today, more than five years after their plane went down in rebel-held jungle. The American military contractors—Marc Gonsalves, Thomas Howes and Keith Stansell—had been held by the Revolutionary Armed Forces of Colombia since their drug-surveillance plane went down in the jungle in February 2003. Nowhere in the world have American hostages currently in captivity been held longer, according to the American Embassy at Bogota."

116. Frank Hyland, "Terrorism Focus, Peru's Shining Path Gaining Ground?" Jamestown Foundation 4, no. 28, September 11, 2007, http://www.jamestown.org/terrorism/news/article.php?articleid=2373637.

117. Arlene B. Tickner, "Latin America and the Caribbean: Domestic and Transnational Insecurity, Coping with Crisis," International Peace Academy, February 2007, http://www.ipacademy.org/media/pdf/publications/cwc_working_paper_latin_america_at3.pdf.

118. Ibid.

119. Chris Zambelis, "Radical Islam in Latin America," *Terrorism Monitor* 3, no. 23 (December 2, 2005), http://www.jamestown.org/terrorism/news/article.php?articleid=2369844.

120. Tickner, "Latin America and the Caribbean: Domestic and Transnational Insecurity, Coping with Crisis."

121. Toby Westerman, "Terrorists Active in U.S. 'Backyard': Latin America Hotbed for Both al-Qaida, Hezbollah," WorldNetDaily.com, May 7, 2002, http://www.wnd.com/news/article.asp?ARTICLE_ID=27521.

122. Mugniyah was killed in a car bomb in Damascus, Syria. Hezbollah claims that it was an Israeli assassination plot. Israel, which had always maintained that Mugniyah was responsible for the Buenos Aires bombings, denied responsibility for his death in Syria. Mughniyeh was reputed to have led a group that hijacked a TWA plane to Beirut in 1985. A U.S. Navy diver was killed in the incident. He has also been implicated in bloody terror attacks in Lebanon against the U.S. Embassy and the Marine barracks in 1983, in which 241 Marines were killed. By Edward Yeranian, "Top Hezbollah Commander Killed in Damascus Car Bombing," Voice of America, Beirut, February 13, 2008, http://www.voanews.com/english/archive/2008-02/2008-02-13-voa7.cfm?CFID=212628242&CFTOKEN=32042063.

123. Pablo Gato and Robert Windrem, "Hezbollah Builds a Western Base from Inside South America's Tri-border Area, Iran-linked Militia Targets U.S.," Telemundo and MSNBC, May 9, 2007, http://www.msnbc.msn.com/id/17874369/.

124. Ibid.

125. Chris Zambelis, "Radical Islam in Latin America," *Terrorism Monitor* 3, no. 23 (December 2, 2005) http://www.jamestown.org/terrorism/news/article.php?articleid=2369844.

126. Joseph Farah, "Al-Qaida South of the Border; Rumsfeld: Human Smuggling Rings Tied to bin Laden's Terrorist Network," WorldNetDaily.com, February 16, 2004, http://www.world netdaily.com/news/article.asp?ARTICLE_ID=37133.

127. Chris Zambelis, "Jamaat al-Muslimeen on Trial in Trinidad and Tobago," *Terrorism Monitor* 4, no. 5, March 9, 2006, http://jamestown.org/terrorism/news/article.php?articleid=2369924. See also Mark P. Sullivan, "Latin America Terrorism Issues," Congressional Research Service, January 8, 2008, Order Code RS21049.

128. "Port Security in the Caribbean Basin Presented to the Cognizant Committees as Required by the SAFE Port Act of 2006 April 13, 2007," Government Accounting Office Publication GAO-07-804R, pp. 14–16.

129. Ibid., p. 6.

130. Ibid., p. 22.

131. "Robert F. Kennedy Urged Lifting the Travel Ban to Cuba in '63," National Security Archive, June 29, 2005, http://www.gwu.edu/~nsarchiv/NSAEBB/NSAEBB158/index.htm.

132. "Cruise Lines Industry and Cruisers," Oceana.org, http://www.oceana.org/uploads/ !Cruise_Line_Industry&Cruisers.pdf.

133. Peter Greenberg, "Preparing for a Cuban Vacation after Castro," June 4, 2007, http://www.msnbc.msn.com/id/19034753/.

134. "104 Members of Congress Call for Review of U.S.-Cuba Policy," Washington Office on Latin America, www.wola.org, February 20, 2008, http://www.wola.org/index.php?option= com_content&task=viewp&id=646&Itemid=8).

135. Edwin McDowell, "New York Times Travel Advisory—Correspondent's Report: Cuba, So Close, Remains Distant for Cruise Lines," http://query.nytimes.com/gst/fullpage.html?res= 9C03E6D6153BF934A15752C0A9649C8B63.

136. U.S. State Department Travel Web site, http://travel.state.gov/travel/cis_pa_tw/cis/ cis_1097.html#safety.

137. Andrea Rodriquez, "Cuba Cruise Visitors Plunge 90 percent," Associated Press, January 23, 2008, http://news.moneycentral.msn.com/ticker/article.aspx?Feed=AP&Date=20080 123&ID=8083867&Symbol=RCL.

CHAPTER 3

1. Tony Peisley, "Global Changes in the Cruise Industry 2003–2010," *Avid Cruiser*, [undated], http://www.avidcruiser.com/news/newsdetail1.php?NID=1659.

2. Michael Crye, International Council of Cruise Lines, testimony before the House Subcommittee on Commerce, Trade, and Consumer Protection, October 17, 2001, http://republi cans.energycommerce. house.gov/107/hearings/10172001Hearing402/Crye676.htm.

3. "Spring 04 Market and Brand Growth," *Cruise Industry News*, April 2004, http:// www.cruiseindustrynews.com/Articles/Articles/Spring_04%3A2004_%3A_Market_and_ Brand_Growth/.

4. Ibid.

5. "Deep Blue Mysteries—Mysterious Disappearances on the Deep Blue Ocean Go Unsolved—Last month George Smith and Jennifer Hagel were enjoying a wedding cruise in the Mediterranean. The weather was great, the ports of call wonderful, and like the travel brochure-life aboard ship consisted of dancing, drinking, and gambling with their fellow passengers. But on July 5th, something went terribly wrong. The new bride may now be a new widow" (MSNBC August, 2005); "Dozens Injured When Cruise Ship Tips—Miami, Florida—A cruise ship listed sharply off Port Canaveral, Florida, injuring at least 93 passengers, 16 of them seriously, according to the Cape Canaveral Fire Department" (CNN—July 2006); "Scandal on the High Seas?— Congress Holds Hearing on Cruise Ship Safety Amid Assault Allegations: It's estimated that more than 10 million Americans go on cruises every year. Now, after complaints of onboard assaults,

thefts and even mysterious disappearances, Congress investigated today how safe these vacations are" (ABC News —September 2007).

6. Christopher Elliott, "Mystery at Sea: Who Polices the Ships?" *New York Times,* February 26, 2006, http://travel.nytimes.com/2006/02/26/travel/26crime.html.

7. "Crime Rates for Selected Large Cities, 2005—Offenses Known to the Police per 100,000 Inhabitants," May 15, 2008, http://www.infoplease.com/ipa/A0004902.html.

8. Elliott, "Mystery at Sea: Who Polices the Ships?"

9. "Incidents at Disney Parks," http://en.wikipedia.org/wiki/Incidents_at_Disney_parks. See also Anastasia Toufexis, "No Mousing Around," *Time,* March 11, 1985, http://www.time.com/time/magazine/article/0,9171,962597,00.html.

10. "The Mayhem in Mumbai—Making Sense of India's Terrorist Attacks," *Newsweek,* November 26, 2008, http://www.newsweek.com/id/171006.

11. "Cruise Death Case: 'Naked Behavior Not Unusual,' " *Lloyd's List,* June 27, 2006 (No. 59195), p. 3.

12. Testimony of Salvador Hernandez, Deputy Assistant Director, Federal Bureau of Investigation, Statement before the House Committee on Transportation and Infrastructure, Subcommittee on Coast Guard and Maritime Transportation, March 27, 2007, http://www.fbi.gov/congress/congress07/hernandez032707.htm.

13. "QM2 Limps into Port with Pod Damage," *Lloyd's List,* January 19, 2006 (No. 59085), p. 1.

14. "QM2 Passengers Make Mutiny Threat—Passengers on the luxury Queen Mary 2 cruise ship are threatening to mutiny after the ship set sail from Florida with a damaged propeller," BBC, January 22, 2006, http://news.bbc.co.uk/1/hi/world/americas/4637240.stm.

15. "Customers are right, right?" *Fairplay* 356, no. 6364 (February 2, 2006), p. 2.

16. BBC, "QM2 Passengers Make Mutiny Threat."

17. Will Pavia, "Mutiny on the Queen Mary 2," *London Times,* January 24, 2006, http://www.commondreams.org/headlines06/0124-10.htm.

18. Joe Sharkey, "Growing Rebellion on the High Seas," *New York Times,* December 16, 2007, http://www.nytimes.com/2007/12/16/business/16bug.html?ex=1357275600&en=865f8fa43d4cdd81&ei=5088&partner=rssnyt&emc=rss.

19. "Titanic Sister Ships," http://www.starway.org/Titanic/Sister_Ships.html.

20. "20th Century Ships," http://www.ayrshirescotland.com/ships/ships/001introduction.html.

21. Ibid.

22. "Royal Caribbean Cruise Lines Orders the World's Largest Cruise Ship," msnbc.com, February 6, 2006, http://www.msnbc.msn.com/id/11199685/.

23. Ibid.

24. "Bermuda 'Mega-Cruiseships' Plan Causes Storm," *Lloyd's List,* August 4, 2005 (No. 58969), p. 10.

25. "Editorial: Precious eggs," *Lloyd's List,* March 11, 2004 (No. 58614), p. 7.

26. "Ibid.; see also "Editorial: Thinking the Unthinkable," *Lloyd's List,* March 12, 2007 (No. 59375), p. 7.

27. "Putting Evacuation in Perspective," *Fairplay Solutions,* no. 118 (July 2006), pp. 28–29.

28. "One Dead, 11 Injured in Cruise Ship Fire," *USA Today,* March 23, 2006, http://www.usatoday.com/news/nation/2006-03-23-cruise-ship-fire_x.htm.

29. "Cigarette Eyed as Cruise Fire Cause," MSNBC, March 24, 2006, http://www.msnbc.msn.com/id/11975460/.

30. "Safety Recommendations Awaited from Three Ship Fire Investigations," *Lloyd's List,* May 11, 2006 (No. 59163), p. 7. See also "Lookout: Cruise Fire Shows How Safety Should Be Organized," *Fairplay* 357, no.6378 (May 11, 2006), pp. 1–2.

31. Defense Technical Information Center, Accession Number ADA173287, December 28, 1985, http://stinet.dtic.mil.

32. From Discovery Cruises, http://www.simplonpc.co.uk/DiscoveryCruises.html.

33. Jim Morris, "As Cruise Industry Grows, So Do Concerns about Passenger Safety," *Houston Chronicle,* September 28, 1996, http://www.chron.com/content/interactive/special/maritime/96/09/29/cruise29.html.

34. Ibid.

35. Ibid.

36. Ibid.

37. Ibid.

38. Ibid.

39. Ibid.

40. Ibid.

41. Money scams come in many different forms. One instance that I investigated while at Princess Cruises involved a passenger from a Princess ship who reported that he attempted to give a merchant in a Caribbean port a $100 bill for a gift that cost $50. The merchant gave him a counterfeit $50 bill in return. When the passenger protested being given a counterfeit note, the merchant called the police, who were conveniently standing outside. The merchant claimed that the cruise ship passenger was trying to pass counterfeit money. Fearing being arrested in this Caribbean country, the passenger was required to pay a $100 fine on the spot to the two police officers before being allowed to leave.

42. Justice Thomas A. Dickerson, "The Cruise Passenger's Rights & Remedies: 2006," September 17, 2006, prepared for publication in the *Travel & Tourism Law International Revue,* http://www.Classactionlitigation.com/librarycruisepassengersrightsremedies2006.html.

43. Ibid.

44. Krista Carothers, "Cruise Control," *Conde Nast Traveler,* July 2006, http://www.concierge.com/cntraveler/articles/10361? &pageNumber=5&articleId=10361&pageNumber=5.

45. Robert D. McFadden, "Bus Plunge That Killed 12 in Chile Echoes in New York Area," *New York Times,* March 24, 2006, http://travel.nytimes.com/2006/03/24/nyregion/24bus.html.

46. Betsy Wade, "Practical Traveler—State Department Simplifies Its Overseas Advisories," *New York Times,* January 23, 1993, http://query.nytimes.com/gst/fullpage.html?res=9F0CE2D8123AF937A15752C0A965958260.

47. Ibid.

48. Jayne Clark, "Cartagena: Colombia's Magical City Rebounds," *USA Today,* October 11, 2007, http://www.usatoday.com/travel/destinations/2007-10-11-cartagena-main_N.htm.

49. From "Country-Specific Information," www.travel.state.gov.

50. Darell Hartman, "State Department Travel Warnings Explained—*Travel & Leisure* Magazine explains why State Department travel warnings should inform, but not necessarily govern, your next trip," *Travel & Leisure,* January 2008, http://www.travelandleisure.com/articles/state-department-travel-warnings-explained/page/1.

51. Ibid.

52. "Asian Countries Unhappy with Travel Warnings!" no date, http://www.chinaadviser.com/us_state_department.html.

53. Ibid.

54. Ibid.

55. Sam Howe Verhovek, "2 Disasters Lead a Cruise Ship into 2 Nights of Vigils and Prayer," *New York Times,* September 15, 2001, http://www.nytimes.com/2001/09/15/us/2-disasters-lead-a-cruise-ship-into-2-nights-of-vigils-and-prayer.html.

56. Ibid.

57. Christine Clarridge, "Cruise Line Warned before Fatal Trip," *Seattle Times,* March 5, 2005, http://www.nwcn.com/statenews/washington,/stories/NW_030105WAB_SEATTLEONLY_hollandsettleLJ.f6129cc6.html.

58. Scott Sunde, Ruth Schubert, et al., "UW Mourns 'Terrible, Sad Loss,'" *Seattle Post-Intelligencer,* September 14, 2001, http://seattlepi.nwsource.com/local/38979_crash14.shtml.

59. Ibid.

60. Ibid.

61. Ibid.

62. Clarridge, "Cruise Line Warned before Fatal Trip."

63. Ibid.

64. Ibid.

65. Ibid.

66. Ibid.

67. Kathy George, "Cruise Line Tried to Seal Records over 2001 Air Crash, but Families of Victims fought Holland America," *Seattle Post-Intelligencer,* March 2, 2005, http://www.seattlepi.com/local/214193_crashcase02.html.

68. Ibid.

69. Ibid.

70. Ibid.

71. Salvador Hernandez, Deputy Assistant Director Federal Bureau of Investigation, Statement before the House Committee on Transportation and Infrastructure, Subcommittee on Coast Guard and Maritime Transportation, March 27, 2007, http://www.fbi.gov/congress/congress07/hernandez032707.htm.

72. From http://answers.yahoo.com/question/index?qid=20061207180734AAn2GgS.

73. Heidi Sarna, "Can I Sea Some ID? The ABCs of Cruise Line Age Policies," *Frommer's,* November 8, 2006, http://www.frommers.com/ID%3F+The+ABCs+of+Cruise+Line+Age+Policies.

74. Independent National News, "Cruise Ship Company: Don't Blame Us for Teenager's Death," *Independent,* April 26, 2006, http://www.independent.ie/national-news/cruise-ship-company-dont-blame-us-for-tragic-teens-death-103947.html .

75. Ibid.

76. Ibid.

77. "Wife's Whereabouts Detailed in Cruise Probe—Cruise line: Woman was not in assigned cabin when her husband vanished," MSNBC, January 5, 2006, http://www.msnbc.msn.com/id/10724353/.

78. "Mr. and Mrs. Smith," *Friction Powered,* February 23, 2006, http://frictionpowered.wordpress.com/2006/02/23/mr-and-mrs-smith/.

79. Ibid.

80. MSNBC, "Wife's Whereabouts Detailed in Cruise Probe."

81. Ibid.

82. *Friction Powered,* "Mr. and Mrs. Smith."

83. Dennis Murphy, "Few Clues in Honeymoon Cruise Disappearance," *Dateline,* December 13, 2005, http://www.msnbc.msn.com/id/9356611/page/4/.

84. Jennifer Hagel-Smith, "Royal Caribbean Honeymoon Tragedy," International Cruise Victims, undated, http://www.internationalcruisevictims.org/LatestMemberStories/George_Allen_Smith_IV_Spouse_Story.html.

85. Murphy, "Few Clues in Honeymoon Cruise Disappearance."

86. Hagel-Smith, "Royal Caribbean Honeymoon Tragedy," International Cruise Victims.

87. *Larry King Live,* Interview with family of George Smith, CNN, aired December 13, 2005, http://transcripts.cnn.com/TRANSCRIPTS/0512/13/lkl.01.html.

88. Ibid.

89. Peter Ratcliffe, Carnival Corporation press release, June 21, 2007, http://google.brand.edgar-online.com/EFX_dll/EDGARpro.dll?FetchFilingHTML1?SessionID=N25uW5Eo2m1AQy0&ID=5259863.

90. Ibid.

91. While I was the chief security officer appointed to head security for all Princess, P&O Cruises Australia, and, later, Cunard Cruise Lines, the "changes" ordered by the Princess CEO were actually part of the ISPS reformation already under way in 2004. P&O Australia prior to this had a shoreside manager who had taken on security as a collateral duty. I helped recruit a P&O Cruises U.K. manager to assume security duties full time in Australia. The Brimble case was never officially discussed in 2005 as a reason for the transfer of this manager from London to Sydney; the reason was the realization that things were indeed out of control on the two P&O Cruises Australia ships.

92. Jano Gibson, "Apology Over Cruise Ship's Crude Ad," *Sydney Morning Herald,* June 14, 2006, http://www.smh.com.au/news/national/apology-over-cruise-ships-crude-ad/2006/06/14/1149964582254.html.

93. "Carnival Cruise Lines Does Public Relations Damage Control in Wake of Brimble Settlement," Carnival Corporation press release, February 22, 2007, http://www.cruisebruise.com/carnival_press_release_feb_22_2007.htm.

94. Ibid.

95. Kate Sikora, "Rampage on Schoolies Cruise," *Daily Telegraph,* November 29, 2006, http://www.news.com.au/dailytelegraph/story/0,22049,20837559-5001021,00.html.

96. Ibid.

97. "Cruise Company Drops Schoolies Trips," ABC News, October 10, 2006, http://www.abc.net.au/news/newsitems/200610/s1759333.htm.

98. Disney Cruise Line, "Disney Dreams," http://disneycruise.disney.go.com/ships-activities/ships/dream/.

99. Gary Lee, "Are Cruise Ships Safe?" *Washington Post,* October 4, 2007, http://blog.washingtonpost.com/travellog/2007/10/are_cruise_ships_safe.html.

CHAPTER 4

1. U.S. Department of Justice, Office of the Inspector General, Audit Division, "The Federal Bureau of Investigation to Protect the Nation's Seaports," Audit Report 06-26, March 2006, p. 52.

2. Interview by author with Miframe Security Corp. sales representative at the Las Vegas Convention Center, ASIS Security Product Exhibition, September 23–24, 2007; see also www.miframsecurity.com.

3. Ibid.

4. Interview by author with Doorgate sales representative at the Las Vegas Convention Center, ASIS Security Product Exhibition, September 23–24, 2007; see also Doorgate Industries Web site, www.doorgate.com.

5. "Card-Carrying Members Only," *Marinelink,* February 13, 2002, http://www.marinelink.com/Story/Card-Carrying+Members+Only-7416.html.

6. Ibid.

7. Ibid.

8. As of 2009, Disney does not require fingerprint samples to enter Disneyland in California.

9. Ross Kingston, *Cruise Ship Tourism* (Cambridge, MA: CAB International, 2006), p. 429.

10. Even though the 9/11 hijackers entered the United States legally, they exploited loopholes in the immigration system. Many were under suspicion by the FBI. Prior to 9/11, the airline industry relied on the Computer Assisted Passenger Prescreening System, often called CAPPS, administered by the FBI and the FAA, which sought to screen the checked bags of selected passengers who had been preselected because of certain intelligence or law enforcement information. Under CAPPS, most of the 9/11 hijackers were selected for prescreening of their checked luggage on September 11 but not for additional screening of their hand baggage.

11. Bart Elias, William Krouse, et al., "Homeland Security: Air Passenger Prescreening and Counterterrorism," Congressional Research Service (CRS) Report for Congress, March 4, 2005, http://www.fas.org/sgp/crs/homesec/RL32802.pdf.

12. See also C. William Michaels, *No Greater Threat: America after September 11 and the Rise of a National Security State* (New York, Algora Publishing, 2005).

13. Michael Greenberg et al., *Maritime Terrorism: Risk and Liability* (Santa Monica, CA: Rand Corporation, Center for Terrorism Risk Management Policy, 2006), p. 76, http://www.rand.org/pubs/monographs/2006/RAND_MG520.pdf.

14. To illustrate how inadequate hand searches of carry-on belongings are, three days after 9/11, I had to fly from Beirut, Lebanon, to Los Angeles through Frankfurt, Germany, on Lufthansa. The chaos in the airport was apparent from the outset, and all passengers went through a hand search of their belongings prior to boarding at their gate. I submitted my one carry-on to this search, and it appeared to me that the bag was given a thorough going-over. I was amazed when I arrived in Los Angeles and unpacked my bag to find a large Swiss Army pocket knife in one of the bag's compartments.

15. "Opinion: ISPS Fails to Halt Stowaways Plight," *Tradewinds* 15, no. 31 (July 30, 2004), p. 2.

16. "Stowaways on Chinese ship Thrown Overboard," *Lloyd's List*, November 17, 2003 (No. 58535), p. 1.

17. "Stowaways, an Increasing Problem," *Signals* Special no. 6 (March 2001), http://www.nepia.com/risk/publications/newsletters/specials/pdf/special6.pdf.

18. "Warning Over Rudder Stowaways," *Tradewinds* 16, no. 2 (January 14, 2005), p. 39.

19. Michael Heads, "The Importance of Not Befriending Stowaways," 2006, http://www.swedishclub.com/tm_loss_prevention/Stowaways%20links/Stowaways%20from%20Letter%20 1-2006.pdf.

20. "Durban Deaths Open Can of Worms," *Fairplay* 356, no. 6362 (January 19, 2006), p. 9.

21. Pernilla Ljunggren, "Stowaways," The Swedish Club Letter, http://www.swedishclub.com/tm_loss_prevention/Stowaways%20links/Stowaways%20-%20Binding%20regulations_TSCL%202-2003%20.pdf.

22. "The Perils of Stowaways—Part Solutions to a Growing Problem," *Fairplay*, November 16, 2000, pp. 44–45.

23. "Comment: Can Charity Survive Security Requirements?" *Lloyd's Ship Manager*, July–August 2004, p. 2.

24. "Stowaways Seek 'Ecstasy' Trip," *Fairplay* (July 27, 2000), p. 8.

25. "Cruise Option for Discerning Stowaways," *Fairplay* 355, no. 6356 (December 1, 2005), p. 12.

26. Richard Minitar, *Losing bin Laden* (Washington, DC: Regnery, 2003), pp. 217–218.

27. "U.S. Ship Fires on Boat in Suez Canal," *CNN Reports*, March 25, 2008, http://www.cnn.com/2008/WORLD/africa/03/25/us.suez.ap/index.html.

28. Interview by author with American Technology Corporation sales representatives at the Las Vegas Convention Center, ASIS Security Product Exhibition, September 23–24, 2007; see also American Technology Corporation Web site, www.atcsd.com.

29. Brock N. Meeks, "Record Expense, Security Plans Set for Olympics Summer Games Will Make Greece 'Security Superpower,' Official Says," MSNBC, July 30, 2004, http://www.msnbc.msn.com/id/5490540/.

30. Liz Robbins, "OLYMPICS: Security at Summer Games in Athens Is Topic A, B and C for U.S. Basketball," *New York Times*, April 29, 2004, http://query.nytimes.com gst/fullpage.html?res=9C01E6D7163 DF93AA15757C0A9629C8B63.

31. Carol Migdalovitz, *Greece: Threat of Terrorism and Security at the Olympics*, Congressional Research Service (CRS) Report for Congress, p. 5, http://fas.org/irp/crs/RS21833.pdf.

32. Meeks, "Record Expense, Security Plans Set for Olympics Summer Games."

33. Brian Murphy, "Interpol Chief No Known Threats for Athens Olympics," *USA Today*, June 29, 2004, http://www.usatoday.com/sports/olympics/athens/news/2004-06-29-interpol-threat_x.htm.

34. "Olympics: How Safe?" *Business Week*, June 28, 2004, http://www.businessweek.com/ agazine/content/04_26/b3889056_mz011.htm.

35. Migdalovitz, *Greece: Threat of Terrorism and Security at the Olympics*, pp. 3–4.

36. Miron Varouhakis, "Armed Guards to Protect American Athletes before Olympics," *USA Today*, July 9, 2004, http://www.usatoday.com/sports/olympics/athens/news/2004-07-09-us-security_x.htm.

37. "IMO Passenger Ship Safety Initiative," *Proceedings of the Marine Safety and Security Council* (Fall 2007), pp. 55–57.

38. "Editorial: A Recurring Concern," *Lloyd's List*, November 4, 2005 (No. 59034), p. 5.

39. Jack Westwood Booth, "The IMO Passenger Ship Safety Initiative," November 1, 2007, www.imo.org.

40. Ibid.

41. Ibid.

42. Ibid.

43. "Secrets of the Dead: The Sinking of the Andrea Doria," PBS, http://www.pbs.org/wnet/ secrets/case_andreadoria/.

44. Ibid.

45. From "Andréa Doria," http://en.wikipedia.org/wiki/SS_Andrea_Doria.

46. Ibid.

47. "Secrets of the Dead," PBS.

48. "Letter: Passenger Safety Attitude Is a Disaster in the Making," *Lloyd's List*, April 11, 2007 (No. 59395), p. 3.

49. "Warrants Issued over Sea Diamond Sinking as Passengers File Lawsuit," *Lloyd's List*, June 18, 2007 (No. 59441), p. 9.

50. "U.S. Passenger sue Louis Hellenic over Sea Diamond 'Negligence,'" *Lloyd's List*, August 29, 2007 (No. 59492), p. 3.

51. "Fresh Concerns after Cruise Ship Grounding," *Tradewinds* 18, no. 20 (May 18, 2007), p. 55.

52. "Lady Luck Lent a Hand in Efficient Evacuation," *Lloyd's List*, November 26, 2007 (No. 59,555), p. 3.

53. "Icy Waste," *Fairplay* 361, no. 6458 (November 29, 2007), pp. 1–2.

54. "Icy Rescue as Seas Claim a Cruise Ship," *New York Times*, November 24, 2007, http://www.nytimes.com/2007/11/24/world/americas/24ship.html.

55. "Heeling Accident on M/V Crown Princess Atlantic Ocean off Port Canaveral, Florida, July 18, 2006," National Transportation Safety Board Accident Report, August 2001, http://www.ntsb.gov/publictn/2008/MAR0801.pdf.

56. "Crew Caused Cruise List," *Tradewinds* 17, no. 30 (July 28, 2006), p. 35.

57. "US Safety Board Looks into NCL TV Debacle," *Lloyd's List*, April 22, 2005 (No. 58897), p. 12.

58. "Decades of Boiler Woes End in Norway Deaths," *Fairplay* 354, no. 6333 (June 23, 2005), p. 13.

59. "Norwegian Cruise Line to Plead Guilty to Negligence," *South Florida Business Journal*, May 5, 2008, http://triangle.bizjournals.com/triangle/othercities/southflorida/stories/2008/ 05/05/daily10.html.

CHAPTER 5

1. Michael D. Greenberg, Peter Chalk, et al., "Maritime Terrorism: Risk and Liability," The Rand Corporation, Center for Terrorism Risk Management Policy, Santa Monica, CA 2006, p. 50 http://www.rand.org/pubs/monographs/2006/RAND_MG520.pd.

2. Ibid., p. 70.

3. Jonathan Hare, "Athens Convention 2002 and Terrorism—Skuld Defense Services: Reports from the Latest IMO Legal Committee Meeting," Skuld.com, October 26, 2006, http://www.skuld.com/templates/newspage.aspx?id=1214.

4. Robert C. Seward, Tindall Riley (Britannia) Ltd. "The Role of Protection and Indemnity (P&I) Clubs," 2002, http://www.intertanko.com/pubupload/protection%20%20indemnity%20HK%202002.pdf.

5. Ibid.

6. Ibid.

7. Paul Myburgh, "Categorizing Horror: Marine Insurance Coverage and Terrorism," 2002, http://www.maritimelaw.org.nz/myburgh/Horror.pdf.

8. Ibid.

9. Ibid.

10. "Cruise Terror Liability Breakthrough," http://rubendotmaritime.blogspot.com/2006/10/cruise-terror-liability-breakthrough.html.

11. Jonathan Hare, "Passenger Cover, the Athens Convention and Terrorism," Legal Notes—Beacon, April 2007, http://www.skuld.com/upload/News%20and%20Publications/Publications/Beacon/Beacon%202007 %20189/Beacon%20189%20p%2022-23.pdf.

12. "The 92nd Session of the IMO Legal Committee Implementation of the 2002 Athens Protocol—Terrorism," IGP&I News, 2006, http://www.igpandi.org/downloadables/news/news/LEG%2092%20-%20Athens+terrorism.pdf.

13. "Cruise Terror Liability Breakthrough," May 19, 2008, http://rubendotmaritime.blogspot.com/2006/10/cruise-terror-liability-breakthrough.html.

14. Hare, "Passenger Cover, the Athens Convention and Terrorism."

15. "36. U.S. Statements on Athens Convention," http://www.state.gov/s/l/2006/98262.htm.

16. Office of Senator Charles Schumer, press release, November 9, 2003, http://www.senate.gov/~schumer/SchumerWebsite/pressroom/press_releases/PR02158.html.

17. Alexander T. Wells and Seth B. Young, "Airport Planning and Management," (New York: McGraw-Hill Professional, 2003), p. 237.

18. U.S. Department of Justice, Office of the Inspector General, Audit Division, "The Federal Bureau of Investigation to Protect the Nation's Seaports," Audit Report 06-26, March 2006, p. 52.

19. "1,000 Feared Lost on Doomed Egypt Ferry," The Daily Star, February 5, 2006, http://www.thedailystar.net/2006/02/05/d60205011814.htm.

20. "2004 Worldwide Maritime Threat Assessment," U.S. Coast Guard Publication CG-MTT-069-05, August 1, 2005.

21. Office of Senator Charles Schumer, press release.

22. Chris Trelawny, "Maritime Security and the Cruise Industry," Business Briefing: Global Cruise, 2004, http://www.touchbriefings .com/pdf/858/trelawny.pdf.

23. See "What Is the IMO?" http://www.imo.org.

24. Ibid.

25. Ibid.

26. See "What Is the ISPS Code?" www.IMO.org.

27. Claudia Burmester, "International Ship and Port Facility Security: (ISPS) Code—Perceptions and Reality of Shore Based and Sea-going Staff," Southampton Institute of Higher Education, United Kingdom, undated, http://www.iamu-edu.org/generalassembly/aga6/s2-burmester.php.

28. "Focus on Maritime Security," World Maritime Day 2004, Background Paper, International Maritime Organization, 2004, http://www.imo.org/includes/blastData Only.asp/data_id%3D9886/Englishbackground.pdf.

29. Burmester, "International Ship and Port Facility Security."

30. Alsnosy BALBAA, "Protecting Seafarers' Rights—The Need to Review the Implementation of the ISPS code," College of Maritime Transport and Technology Arab Academy for Science,

Technology and Maritime Transport, Nautical Department, Alexandria, Egypt, undated, http://www.iamu-edu.org/generalassembly/aga6/pdf/s2-balbaa.pdf.

31. Ibid.

32. Ibid.

33. Burmester, "International Ship and Port Facility Security."

34. Vladimir A. Loginovsky, Alexander P. Gorobtsov, et al., "The ISPS Code as a Component of Onboard Resources in Bayesian Analysis," Admiral Makarov State Maritime Academy, Navigation Department, St. Petersburg, the Russian Federation, undated, http://www.iamu-edu.org/generalassembly/aga6/s2-loginovsky.php.

35. Ibid.

36. Hartmut Hesse and Nicolaos L. Charalambous, "New Security Measures for the International Shipping Community," *Journal of Maritime Affairs* 3, no. 2 (2004, October), pp. 123–138.

37. Ibid.

38. "Security in Maritime Transport: Risk Factors and Economic Impact," Organization for Economic Cooperation and Development, July 2003, http://www.oecd.org/document/30/0,33 43,en_2649_34389_4390494_1_1_1_1,00.html.

39. Secretary Michael Chertoff, U.S. Department Of Homeland Security, testimony before the House Committee on Homeland Security, Washington, DC, September 5, 2007, http://www.dhs.gov/xnews/testimony/testimony_1189114519132.shtm.

40. Anuj Chopra, "ISPS Code: Is the World Safer Today?" *Marine Log,* March 1, 2005, http://www.allbusiness.com/transportation-equipment-manufacturing/ship-boat-building/392083-1.html.

41. Headquarters, U.S. Central Command, News Release Number 05-08-20, August 19, 2005, http://www.globalsecurity.org/military/library/news/2005/08/mil-050819-centcom01.htm.

42. Department of Homeland Security, National Plan to Achieve Maritime Domain Awareness for the National Strategy for Maritime Security, October 2005, p. 1, http://www.dhs.gov/xlibrary/assets/HSPD_MDAPlan.pdf.

43. Department of Homeland Security, Maritime Commerce Security Plan for the National Strategy for Maritime Security, October 2005, pp. 3–4, http://www.dhs.gov/xlibrary/assets/HSPD_MCSPlan.pdf.

44. Department of Homeland Security, National Strategy for Maritime Security, September 2005, pp. 3–5, http://www.dhs.gov/xlibrary/assets/HSPD13_MaritimeSecurityStrategy.pdf.

45. National Plan to Achieve Maritime Awareness for the National Strategy for Maritime Security, p. 5.

46. National Strategy for Maritime Security, pp. 20–22.

47. James Jay Carafano and Alane Kochems, "Making the Sea Safe: A National Agenda for Maritime Security and Counterterrorism," Heritage Foundation, Special Report SR-03, February 17, 2005, p. 12.

48. House Report 110-862—Department of Homeland Security Appropriations Bill, 2009, http://thomas.loc.gov/cgi-bin/cpquery/?&sid=cp110rrE1E&refer=&r_n=hr862.110&db_id=110&item=&sel=TOC_254594&.

49. Carafano and Kochems, "Making the Sea Safe: A National Agenda for Maritime Security and Counterterrorism."

50. Ibid.

51. Alan M. Weigel, "Coast Guard Proposes Expanded Automatic Identification Systems Requirements," Martindale.com, March 29, 2009, http://www.martindale.com/admiralty-maritime-law/article_Blank-Rome-LLP_656038.htm.

52. See "About CLIA," www.cruising.org.

53. Princess Cruise management was given an opportunity in 2004 to be an active participant along with a government agency in identifying suspicious port activity relating to terrorism. Although company officials were sympathetic to the needs of the program, they judged that their

role in the effort was not in the best interests of the company and could lead to a public relations nightmare.

54. Maritime Commerce Security Plan for the National Strategy for Maritime Security, p. 11.

55. Stephen E. Flynn, Commander, U.S. Coast Guard (ret.), Jeane J. Kirkpatrick Senior Fellow in National Security Studies, Council on Foreign Relations, testimony before the Senate Permanent Subcommittee on Investigations, Committee on Homeland Security and Governmental Affairs, May 26, 2005.

56. "Carrier Initiative Program," http://www.cbp .gov/xp/cgov/border_security/interna tional_operations/partnerships/cip.xml.

57. U.S. Department of Justice, Office of the Inspector General, Audit Division, "The Federal Bureau of Investigation to Protect the Nation's Seaports," p. 6.

58. Ibid.

59. Ibid., pp. 7–8.

60. Ibid., p. 8.

61. "The Need for a New National Maritime Salvage Policy in View of the Terrorist Threat and Hurricane Lessons Learned," undated, www.trb.org/MarineBoard/Spring07/Salvage.pdf.

62. "FBI, Coast Guard Clashed during Terrorism Drill," Marinelink.com, April 5, 2006, http://www.marinelink.com/Story/Report:+FBI,+Coast+Guard+Clashed+During+Terrorism+Drill-202657.html.

63. Ibid.

64. Ibid.

65. Eric Lipton, "Report Sees Confusion Likely in a Sea Attack by Terrorists," New York Times, April 4, 2006, http://www.nytimes.com/2006/04/04/us/nationalspecial3/04ports.html?r=1&oref=slogin.

66. Ibid.

67. Greenberg, Chalk, et al., "Maritime Terrorism: Risk and Liability," p. 77.

68. "Marine Salvage Capabilities Responding to Terrorist Attacks in U.S. Ports—Actions to Improve Readiness," Committee for Marine Salvage Response Capability: A Workshop, The National Academies, 2004, http://www.nap.edu/catalog.php?record_id=11044.

69. Excerpt from "U.S. Coast Guard Response—Rand Report: Maritime Terrorism: Risk and Liability," unclassified USCG report, December 2006.

70. Ibid.

71. "Salvage Crisis In the Offing as Ships Continue to Grow Says ISU Chief," Lloyd's List, January 23, 2006 (No. 59087), p. 1.

72. "Businesses in Wake of MV Lee III's Sinking Get No Financial Redress," New Orleans City Business, March 1 2004, http://findarticles.com/p/articles/mi_qn4200/is_20040301/ai_n10174651.

73. "Hazardous Sea—Maritime Sector Vulnerable to Devastating Terrorist Attacks," JINSA Online, April, 10, 2004, http://www.jinsa.org/articles/articles.html/function/view/categoryid/1701/documentid/2426/history/3,2360,655,1701,2426.

74. Richard Hooper, "The Need for a New National Maritime Salvage Policy in View of the Terrorist Threat and Hurricane Lessons Learned," www.trb.org/MarineBoard/Spring07/Salvage.pdf.

75. Ibid.

CHAPTER 6

1. "How Real Is the Threat from Maritime Terrorism?" PINR Power and Interest News Report, December 12, 2005, http://pinr.com/report.

2. "Safety at Sea Investigates," Safety at Sea 41, no. 461 (July 2007), p. 24.

3. Michael D. Greenberg, Peter Chalk, et al., "Maritime Terrorism: Risk and Liability," The Rand Corporation, 2006, pp. 83–84, http://www.rand.org/pubs/monographs/2006/RAND_MG520.pdf.

4. "Gunmen Storm Aqua Expeditions Tourist Cruise Ship in Peru in Dawn Robbery," Tele graph.co.uk, August 6, 2009, http://www.telegraph.co.uk/travel/travelnews/5982789/Gunmen-storm-Aqua-Expeditions-tourist-cruise-ship-in-Peru-in-dawn-robbery.html.

5. Ibid., p. 70.

6. Paul W. Parffomack and John Fritelli, "Maritime Security: Potential Terrorist Attacks and Protection Priorities," Congressional Research Service, January 9, 2007. See also http://en.wikipedia.org/wiki/Bombing_of_the_Limburg.

7. Parffomack and Fritelli, "Maritime Security."

8. James Pelkofski, "Before the Storm: al Qaeda's Coming Maritime Campaign," *Proceedings—U.S. Naval Institute* 132, no.12 (December 2005): 20–24.

9. "6 Arrested in Plot to Kill Soldiers at Fort Dix," *Star Ledger* (N.J.), May 6, 2007, http://blog.nj.com/ledgerupdates/2007/05/6_arrested_in_plot_to_kill_sol.html.

10. James Carafano and Alane Kochems, "Making the Sea Safe: A National Agenda for Maritime Security and Counterterrorism," The Heritage Foundation, Special Report SR-03, February 17, 2005, p. 16.

11. "Carnival Shares Rise on Earnings Report," *New York Times,* March 23, 2003 http://query.nytimes.com,/gst/fullpage.html?res=9907E1DC1F31F931A15750C0A9659C8B63.

12. Zachary Abuza, "Terrorism Monitor: Terrorism in Southeast Asia: Keeping Al-Qaeda at Bay," *The Jamestown Foundation* 2, no. 9 (May 6, 2004), http://www.jamestown.org/single/?no_cache=1&tx_ttnews%5Btt_news%5D=396.

13. Ibid.

14. Edwin McDowell, "Fall/Winter Cruises: Ships Go Trolling for Passengers," *New York Times,* October 21, 2001, http://query.nytimes .com/gst/fullpage.html? res=940CE6D7103CF937A25753C1A9679C8B63 &sec=&spon=&pagewanted=all.

15. "Cruise Operator out of Business," *New York Times,* September 26, 2001, http://query.nytimes.com/gst/fullpage.html?res=9E04E2DE133AF935A1575AC0A9679C8B63.

16. Martin Edwin Andersen, "Latin American Seaports Forced to Confront Global Terrorism," December 7, 2005, http://www.offnews.info/verArticulo.php? contenidoID=1671.

17. "Economics of Terrorism," http://www.sonic.net/~schuelke/TerrorismVsTourism.html.

18. Martin C. Libicki, Peter Chalk, et al., "Exploring Terrorist Targeting Preferences," The Rand Corporation, 2007, p. 84, http://www.rand.org/pubs/monographs/2007/RAND_MG483.pdf.

19. Anita Dunham-Potter, "Pier Pressure: Cruise Lines Boost Ticket Costs" MSNBC, November 16, 2007, http://www.msnbc.msn.com/id/21755394/.

20. John Mintz, "Al-Qaeda Fleet Takes Terrorist Threat to Sea," *Washington Post,* January 1, 2003, http://www.washingtonpost.com/ac2/wp-dyn/A56442-2002Dec30?language=printer.

21. Colin Robinson, "Al Qaeda's 'Navy'—How Much of a Threat?" Center for Defense Information, August 20, 2003, http://www.cdi.org/friendlyversion/printversion.cfm?documentID=1644.

22. Mintz, "Al-Qaeda Fleet Takes Terrorist Threat to Sea."

23. John Jorsett, "The Mysterious al Qaeda Navy," *Free Republic,* May 19, 2004, http://www.freerepublic.com/focus/f-news/1138797/posts.

24. Ibid.

25. Martin Bright, Paul Harris, et al., "The Armada of Terror," *The Observer,* December 23, 2001, http://www.guardian.co.uk/world/2001/dec/23/september11.terrorism1.

26. Michael Richardson, "A Time Bomb for Global Trade: Maritime-Related Terrorism in an Age of Weapons of Mass Destruction," Institute of East Asian Studies, February 25, 2004, http://www.southchinasea.org/docs/Richardson,%20Time%20Bomb%20for%20Global%20Trade-ISEAS.pdf.

27. Arnaud de Borchgrave, "Somali Pirates: Al Qaeda's Navy?" Atlantic Council, August 11, 2009, http://www.acus.org/new_atlanticist/somali-pirates-al-qaedas-navy.

28. U.S. Coast Guard Homeport, Port of Miami, Title 33 of the U.S. Code Section 1232, http://www.uscg.mil/d7/units/SecMiami/pdf/MIAMISecurityZoneFlyer.pdf.

29. Andrew Beatty, "Small Boats Threaten Maritime Security: U.S. Coast Guard," Agence France Presse, August 6, 2009, http://www.google.com/hostednews/afp/article/ALeqM5jAg Rq-8DPaPrTaz03xtw9I-yyIOQ.

30. Greenberg, "Maritime Terrorism: Risk and Liability," pp. 73–78.

31. Ibid., p. 77.

32. James Jay Carafano, "Small Boats, Big Worries: Thwarting Terrorist Attacks from the Sea," The Heritage Foundation, June 11, 2007, p. 3, http://www.heritage.org/Research/Homeland Defense/bg2041.cfm.

33. Ibid., p. 2.

34. Ibid., p. 4.

35. Ibid., p. 5.

36. Ibid., p. 2.

37. At the time of the *Seabourn Spirit* attack by pirates in the Red Sea in November 2005, Princess Cruises and its three subsidiary lines (Cunard, P&O Cruises Australia, and Seabourn Yachts) were the only ships outfitted with LRADs. Even after the attack, no cruise lines were interested in the product despite its obvious potential for protecting the ship in these hostile circumstances. After the attack, I contacted American Technology Corporation and was surprised to learn that no other cruise lines were knocking down the company's door. This demonstrated to me that, even when a security model had been tested under fire, the cruise lines preferred to stick with their outdated security paradigms, believing that an attack will never happen to one of their ships. The LRAD proved that new security technology can be found to counter emerging threats and can co-exist with the relaxed cruise ship environment without raising passengers' anxiety. All it takes is a commitment to bear the initial costs. I respected Princess Cruises CEO Peter Ratcliffe at the time for believing that protecting cruise ships from surface threats was one aspect of the business on which you could not cut corners.

38. Stefano Ambrogi, "Iraq War Could Spur Al-Qaeda Sea Attacks in Gulf," Reuters, February 21, 2003, http://intellnet.org/news/2003/02/21/17092-1.html.

39. Charles R. Smith, "Al-Qaeda Plans Scuba Diver, One Man Submarine Attack," Cyber Diver News Network, August 26, 2003, http://www.cdnn.info/industry/i030826/i030826.html.

40. "QM2 Security Is Child's Play", Maritime Institute of Malaysia (MIMA) Newsflash, July, 2004, http://www.mima.gov.my/mima/htmls/mimarc/news/newsflash_files/news-cut/july04.htm#qm2.

41. Sebastian Rotella, "Fears Persist of Al-Qaeda Terrorist Link to Dive Center," *Los Angeles Times,* July 31, 2003, http://www.latimes.com/la-fg-scuba31 jul31000428, 0,6784229.story.

42. Christopher Dickey, "High-Seas Terrorism," *Newsweek,* January 27, 2003, http://www.accessmylibrary.com/coms2/summary_0286-22216221_ITM.

43. Michael Richardson, "A Time-Bomb for Global Trade," Institute of Southeast Asian Studies Publications, 2004, p. 18, http://www.southchinasea.org/docs/Richardson,%20Time%20Bomb%20for%20Global%20Trade-ISEAS.pdf.

44. Ibid., p. 19.

45. Eric Watkins, "Terrorism Monitor: Facing the Terrorist Threat in the Malacca Strait," *The Jamestown Foundation* 2, no. 9 (May 6, 2004), http://www.jamestown.org/single/?no_cache= 1&tx_ttnews[tt_news]=26473.

46. Ruşen Çakır, "Terrorism Focus: Turkey in Denial of al-Qaeda Threat," *The Jamestown Foundation* 5, no. 2 (January 15, 2008), http://www.jamestown.org/single/?no_cache=1&tx_ttnews[tt_news]=4652.

47. Scott C. Truver, "Underwater: Mines, Improvised Explosives: A Threat to Global Commerce?" *National Defense,* April 1, 2007, http://goliath.ecnext.com/coms2/gi_0199-6442341/Underwater-mines-improvided-explosives-a.html.

48. Ibid.

49. Ibid.

50. Ibid.

51. "Executive Overview: Jane's Underwater Security Systems and Technology," *Janes,* January 22, 2008, http://www.janes.com/news/transport/juwt/juwt080122_1_n.shtml.

52. Ibid.

53. "DIY Cocaine Smuggling Submarine," Vestal Design, November 26, 2006, http://www.vestaldesign.com/blog/2006/11/diy-cocaine-smugglin.-submarine.html.

54. Randy Kennedy, "An Artist and His Sub Surrender in Brooklyn," *New York Times,* August 4, 2007, http://www.nytimes.com/2007/08/04/arts/design/04voya.html?_r=2&oref=slogin&oref=slogin.

55. Truver, "Underwater: Mines, Improvised Explosives: A Threat to Global Commerce?"

56. Joseph Straw, "The New Need to Know," *Security Management Magazine,* September 2007, p. 93.

57. R. C. Evans, "Challenges, Solution Profiles, and Key Technology Needs," The Mitre Corporation, http://www.mitre.org/work/tech_papers/tech_papers_04/04_1108/04_1108.pdf.

58. Ibid.

59. Interview by the author of anonymous Customs and Border Protection intelligence officer, Riverside, California, March 23, 2008.

60. Testimony by Dennis M. Gormley before the Subcommittee on International Security, Proliferation, and Federal Services, U.S. Senate, June 11, 2002, http://hsgac.senate.gov/061102gormley.pdf.

61. Ibid.

62. Ibid.

63. Matt Hilburn, "Hezbollah's Missile Surprise," Military.com, September 28, 2006, http://www.military.com/forums/0,15240,115199,00.html.

64. Eugene Miasnikov, "Threat of Terrorism Using Unmanned Aerial Vehicles: Technical Aspects," Center for Arms Control, Energy and Environmental Studies, Moscow Institute of Physics and Technology, 2005, p. 5, http://www.armscontrol.ru/uav/UAV-report.pdf.

65. Ibid., p. 10.

66. Ibid., p. 4.

67. Ibid., p. 5.

68. Ibid., p. 13.

69. Dennis M. Gormley, "On Not Confusing the Unfamiliar with the Improbable—Low Technology Means of Delivering Weapons of Mass Destruction," The Weapons of Mass Destruction Commission (WMDC), October 24, 2004, pp. 10–11, http://www.wmdcommission.org/files/No25.pdf.

70. Ibid., p. 7.

71. Greenberg and Chalk, "Maritime Terrorism: Risk and Liability."

72. Akiva J. Lorenz, "Al Qaeda's Maritime Threat," p. 22, http://www.cicte.oas.org/Database_/50637-Al%20Qaeda's%20MaritimeThreat.pdf.

73. "Al-Qaeda Targeting Ocean Liners," Fox News, December 28, 2003, foxnews.com/story/0,2933,106814,00html.

74. Ibid.

75. Mark Steyn, "Mohammed Atta and His Federal Loan Officer," *National Post* (Toronto), June 10, 2002, http://www.freerepublic.com/focus/news/698145/posts.

76. Testimony of Dennis M. Gormley, Senior Fellow, Monterey Institute Center for Nonproliferation Studies, before the Subcommittee on National Security, Emerging Threats, and International Affairs, U.S. House of Representatives Committee on Government Reform, March 9, 2004, http://cns.miis.edu/research/congress/testim/testgorm.htm.

77. "US Alert on Karachi Consulate", BBC News, May 2, 2003, http://news.bbc.co.uk/1/hi/world/americas/2997315.stm.

78. "Profile: Key US terror Suspects," BBC News, February 11, 2008, http://news.bbc.co.uk/2/hi/americas/5322694.stm.

79. "US alert on Karachi Consulate," BBC News, May 2, 2003, http://news.bbc.co.uk/1/hi/world/americas/2997315.stm.

80. "Aftereffects: Al-Qaeda; U.S. Reports Plot to Fly a Plane into U.S. Consulate in Pakistan," *New York Times,* May 3, 2003, http://query.nytimes.com/gst/fullpage.html?res=9C02EFD7143CF930A35756C0A9659C8B63.

81. "Heathrow 'Attack' Foiled," June 6, 2006, http://www.news24.com/News24/World/News/0,,2-10-1462_1955477,00.html.

82. *New York Times,* "Aftereffects: Al-Qaeda."

83. See http://www.historylearningsite.co.uk/kamikazes_and_world_war_two.htm: "The probability of a kamikaze actually getting through to a target was limited due to the vast gun power the American Navy had at its disposal. At Okinawa in 1945, out of 193 kamikaze attacks, 169 planes were destroyed. But the results of the successful attacks at Okinawa were staggering. The kamikazes did a great deal of damage—21 ships sunk and 66 damaged. However, this damage would have been much greater if more planes had got through to their targets."

84. Straw, "The New Need to Know," p. 94.

85. Çakır, "Terrorism Focus: Turkey in Denial of al-Qaeda Threat."

86. Carafano and Kochems, "Making the Sea Safe: A National Agenda for Maritime Security and Counterterrorism," p. 7.

87. Edwin McDowell, "Travel Advisory: Two Cruise Lines Cancel St. Croix Calls," *New York Times,* July 28, 2002, http://query.nytimes.com/gst/fullpage.html?res=9A05E0DB163BF93BA15754C0A9649C8B63.

INDEX

About the Author

COMMANDER MARK GAOUETTE (USNR-Ret.) is a security consultant to the Department of Homeland Security. As director of security for Princess Cruises and Cunard Cruise Lines, he oversaw the implementation of the International Ship and Port Security Code and Maritime Transportation Security Act regulations in 22 cruise ships at 250 ports worldwide. He also pioneered the deployment of Long-Range Acoustic Devices (LRADs) on cruise ships to repel pirates. Commander Gaouette served as a naval intelligence officer with the Naval Criminal Investigative Service (NCIS) as a force protection officer during Operation Enduring Freedom, and as a regional security officer (RSO) with the Bureau of Diplomatic Security, U.S. Department of State, assigned to high-threat U.S. embassies in Eastern Europe, the Middle East, and Latin America.